本著作得到河南理工大学2018年度国家社科予
生态后现代主义视阈下安乐哲著作（Roger T. Ames）的中国文化形

U0500549

FROM WESTERN LITERARY CRITICISM TO TRANSLATION TEXTS:

ANALYSIS ON ENGLISH TRANSLATION VERSIONS OF CHINESE CLASSICS BY AMES & HALL

西方文论与译本的再创造解读

——以安乐哲的中国典籍英译本为个案

李芳芳 李明心 著

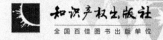

知识产权出版社

全国百佳图书出版单位

图书在版编目（CIP）数据

西方文论与译本的再创造解读：以安乐哲的中国典籍英译本为个案 = FROM WESTERN LITERARY CRITICISM TO TRANSLATION TEXTS: ANALYSIS ON ENGLISH TRANSLATION VERSIONS OF CHINESE CLASSICS BY AMES & HALL：英文 / 李芳芳，李明心著 . -- 北京：知识产权出版社，2019.1（2019.8 重印）
ISBN 978-7-5130-5983-1

Ⅰ.①西… Ⅱ.①李… ②李… Ⅲ.①儒家 – 著作 – 英语 – 翻译 – 研究 Ⅳ.① B222 ② H315.9

中国版本图书馆 CIP 数据核字 (2018) 第 274821 号

责任编辑：许　波　张冠玉　　　　　　　　责任印制：孙婷婷

西方文论与译本的再创造解读：以安乐哲的中国典籍英译本为个案

XIFANG WENLUN YU YIBEN DE ZAICHUANGZAO JIEDU: YI ANLEZHE DE ZHONGGUO DIANJI YINGYIBEN WEI GEAN

李芳芳　李明心　著

出版发行：知识产权出版社 有限责任公司	网　址：http：//www.ipph.cn
电　话：010–82004826	http：//www.laichushu.com
社　址：北京市海淀区气象路 50 号院	邮　编：100081
责编电话：010–82000860 转 8699	责编邮箱：zhangguanyu@cnipr.com
发行电话：010–82000860 转 8101	发行传真：010–82000893
印　刷：北京九州迅驰传媒文化有限公司	经　销：各大网上书店、新华书店及相关专业书店
开　本：720mm×1000mm　1/16	印　张：20.5
版　次：2019 年 1 月第 1 版	印　次：2019 年 8 月第 2 次印刷
字　数：450 千字	定　价：78.00 元

ISBN 978-7-5130-5983-1

出版权专有　侵权必究
如有印装质量问题，本社负责调换。

Preface

From Western Literary Criticism to Translation Texts-analysis originates in my work as a postgraduate student since the end of 2010s. Hence after anything about the relationship between literary criticism and translation came up with me along with my learning days. All the elements are subsumed in what is effectively a history of literary criticism from ancient Greece to the present. My project is to trace the origins of the situation in which every comparative literature researcher and teacher work today, should find the translation text will show a new look to the reader and ask for more interpretations. With the explicit aim of locating alternatives, the book aims at bringing new perspective and ideas for comparative literature study, in particular, for translation text-analysis.

The historical narratives presented here span centuries and national literature, but even though based on detailed research, they are necessarily selective in articulating key moments when academic research so inevitably associated with culture and times. I welcome a diverse audience for the book, including researchers on literature, writers and translation theorists and critics as well as reviewers of literature, publishers. Most of all, I wish to speak to translators and readers of translations, both professional and nonprofessional, focusing their attention on the ways that literary criticism are written, the contribution that various schools of literary criticism made to their ages and the meaning from which cases we choose — American sinologist Roger T. Ames's translation version on Chinese cultural classics are displayed in light of different literary criticism.

Translation is a rewriting of an original text. All rewriting, whatever their intention, reflects a certain ideology and a poetics as such manipulate literature to function in a given situation in a given way. In a sense, translation is a recreation process. Rewriting in its positive aspect can help in the evolution of world literature and intercultural communication, therefore, the study of the recreation processes of literature as exemplified by translation can move us towards a great cognition of the world in which we live.

Li Fangfang

Henan Polytechnic University

前　言

　　《西方文论与译本再创造解读》这本书的创作是我与同事李芳芳多年的学习积累。本人主要研究跨文化与翻译方向，李芳芳老师以外国文学方向为主，从我们当年读研时学习西方文论课程，就萌发了将文学理论与译本结合起来研究的想法。

　　时光荏苒，有关文学批评与翻译相关性的构思日渐成形。文学理论的研究都被纳入从古希腊到后现代主义时期的文学批评史中。本书旨在追寻研究比较文学与翻译的根源，寻求翻译文本带给读者的多重阐释，更希望为比较文学研究，尤其是翻译文本的分析提供新的视角和思路。

　　西方文论的历史叙事展现了跨越时空的文本，使文本与文化和时代有了必然的关联，文本成为被历史节点选择的重要篇章。我欢迎各类读者都来评读本书，包括文论家、作家、翻译理论家与评论家，以及文学评论家和出版商。重要的是，我诚挚地希望翻译家和译本读者，无论是专业人士还是非专业人士，请他们对文学批评的写作方式予以关注，各种文学批评流派对其时代做出的贡献使不同的文论流派异彩纷呈，也赋予我们所选择的文本案例 —— 美国汉学家安乐哲的译本具有时代意义。本书将从不同的文学批评视角来诠释安乐哲的中国文化经典译本。

　　本书从西方文论的发展到重点介绍后现代主义时期的文论流派，以及文论对翻译理论生成的影响。每一章在主要理论内容介绍后添加了运用该理论对安乐哲英译本的分析案例。便于对理论的理解，也加深读者对安乐哲汉学英译本的认知。除第八章女权主义未给出文本分析（考虑到女权主义理论与安乐哲英译中国文化典籍文本边界较远），其他后现代主义的主义流派均有文本分析。

　　翻译是对原文的改写。所有的改写，无论其意图如何，都反映了特定的思想意识形态和对文学进行操控的诗学理论，从而使翻译活动在特定的情境中以一定的方式运作。从某种意义上说，翻译就是一个再创作的过程。积极的改写有助于促进世界文学的发展和文化交流。因此，以译本为例研究文学的再创作过程也能够促使对我们生活的世界有深入的认知。

李明心

2018 年 10 月于河南理工大学

ACKNOWLEDGEMENTS

A project with this sort of intention and scope will inevitably come to rely on the help of many people in different fields of literary and translation expertise. Over the past several years of teaching, discussion and criticism, they make me realize "unity is strength, solidarity means victory."

I am grateful to American sinologist Roger. T. Ames who provides me with the detailed information and first-hand data. Many thanks should go to my dear supervisor Professor Fei Xiaoping, Professor R.M.W. Rajapakshe and Mrs.Wickramsinghe. Without their help, this book would not be completed. I also extend my sincere thanks to the staff of University of Kelaniya, School of English Studies, the staff of Social Science Department, the library and other departments whom to be concerned of Henan Polytechnic University. There are many authors and researchers who did a lot of previous research, and they all deserve my heartful thanks. Especial gratitude goes to my co-author Ms. Li Fangfang, who did a special job of helping me in checking documents and searching for literature information.

We are grateful to editors, who supported my work and made it possible for publication.

Li Mingxin

Henan Polytechnic University

October 2018

CONTENTS

PART I LITERATURE AND LITERARY CRITICISM

CHAPTER I   THE DEFINITION OF CRITICISM, THEORY AND LITERATURE

Having assigned his literature class Flannery O'Connor's short story "A Good Man Is Hard to Find" and knowing O'Connor's canon and her long list of curious protagonists, Professor George Blackwell could not anticipate whether his students would greet him with silence, bewilderment, or frustration when asked to discuss this work. His curiosity would soon be satisfied, for as he stood before the class, he asked a seemingly simple, direct question: "What do you believe O'Connor is trying to tell us in this story? In other words, how do you, as readers, interpret this text?"

Although some students suddenly found the covers of their anthologies fascinating, others shot up their hands. Given a nod from Professor Blackwell, Alice was the first to respond. "I believe O'Connor is trying to tell us the state of the family in rural Georgia during the 1950s. Just look, for example, at how the children, June Star and John Wesley, behave. They don't respect their grandmother. In fact, they mock her."

"But she deserves to be mocked," interrupted Peter. "Her life is one big act. She wants to act like a lady — o wear white cotton gloves and carry a purse — but she really cares only for herself. She is selfish, self-centered, and arrogant."

"That may be," responded Karen, "but I think the real message of O'Connor's story is not about family or one particular character, but about a philosophy of life. O'Connor uses the

Misfit to articulate her personal view of life. When the Misfit says Jesus has thrown 'everything off balance,' O'Connor is really asking each of her readers to choose their own way of life or to follow the teachings of Jesus. In effect, O'Connor is saying we all have a choice: to live for ourselves or to live for and through others."

"I don't think we should bring Christianity or any other philosophy or religion into the story," said George. "Through analyzing O'Connor's individual words — words like tall, dark, and deep — and noting how often she repeats them and in what context, we can deduce that O'Connor's text, not O'Connor herself or her view of life, is melancholy, a bit dark itself. But to equate O'Connor's personal philosophy about life with the meaning of this particular story is somewhat silly."

"But we can't forget that O'Connor is a woman," said Betty. "And an educated on at that! Her story has little to do about an academic or pie-in-the-sky, meaningless philosophical discussion, but a lot to do about being a woman. Being raised in the South, O'Connor would know and would have experienced prejudice because she is a woman. And as we all know, Southern males' opinion of women is that they are to be barefoot, pregnant and in the kitchen. Seemingly, they are to be as nondescript as Bailey's wife is in this story. Unlike all the other characters, we don't even know this woman's name. How much more nondescript could O'Connor be? O'Connor's message, then, is simple. Women are oppressed and suppressed. If they open their mouths, if they have an opinion, and if they voice that opinion, they will end up like the grandmother, with a bullet in their heads."

"I don't think that's her point at all," said Barb. "I do agree that she is writing from personal experience about the South, but her main point is about prejudice itself — prejudice against African Americans. Through the voice of the grandmother we see the Southern lady's opinion of African Americans: They are inferior to whites, uneducated, poor, and basically ignorant. O'Connor's main point is that we are all equal."

"Yes, I agree," said Mike. "But if we look at this story in the context of all the other stories we have read this semester, I see a theme we have discussed countless times before: appearance versus reality. This is O'Connor's main point. The grandmother acts like a lady — someone who cares greatly about others — but inwardly she cares only for herself. She's a hypocrite."

"I disagree. In fact, I disagree with everybody," announced Daniel. "I like the grandmother. She reminds me of my grandmother. O'Connor's grandmother is a bit self-centered, but whose old grandmother isn't? Like my grandma, O'Connor's grandmother likes to be around her grandchildren, to read and to play with them. She's funny, and she has spunk. And she even likes cats."

"But, Dr. Blackwell, can we ever know what Flannery O'Connor really thinks about this story?" asked Jessica. "After all, she's dead, and she didn't write an essay titled "What 'A Good Man is Hard to Find' Really Means." And since she never tells us its meaning, can't the story have more than one meaning?"

Professor Blackwell instantly realized that Jessica's query — Can a story have multiple meanings? — is a pivotal question not only for English professors and their students but also for anyone who reads any text.

1.1   A TEXT HAVE MORE THAN ONE INTERPRETATION

A quick glance at the discussion of O'Connor's "A Good Man Is Hard to Find" in Professor Blackwell's classroom reveals that not all readers interpret texts in the same way. In fact, all of the eight students who voiced their understandings of the story gave fundamentally different interpretations. Was only one of these eight interpretations correct and the remaining seven simply wrong? If so, how does one arrive at the correct interpretation? Put another way, if there is only one correct interpretation of a text, what are the principles of hermeneutics for readers must use to discover this interpretation?

On the other hand, if a work can have multiple interpretations, are all such interpretations valid? Can and should each interpretation be considered a satisfactory and legitimate analysis of the text under discussion? In other words, can a text mean anything a reader declares it to mean, or are there guiding principles for interpreting a text that must be followed if a reader is to arrive at a valid and legitimate interpretation?

Or need a reader be thinking of any of these particulars when reading a text? Can't one simply enjoy a novel, for example, without considering its interpretation? Need one be able to state the work's theme, discuss its structure, or analyze its tone in order to enjoy the act of reading the novel itself?

These and similar questions are the domain of literary criticism: the act of studying, analyzing, interpreting, evaluating and enjoying a work of art. At first glance, the study of literary criticism appears daunting and formidable. Jargon such as hermeneutics, Aristotelian poetics, deconstruction, and a host of other intimidating terms confront the would-be literary critic. But the actual process or act of literary criticism is not as ominous as it may first appear.

1.2　BECOMING A LITERARY CRITIC

When the students in Professor Blackwell's class were discussing O'Connor's short story *A Good Man is Hard to Find*, each of them was directly responding to the instructor's initial question: What do you believe O'Connor is trying to tell us in and through this story? Although not all responses were radically different, each student viewed the story from a unique perspective. For example, some students expressed their likings of the grandmother, but others thought she was a selfish, arrogant woman. Still others believed O'Connor's was voicing a variety of philosophical, social, and cultural concerns, such as the place of women and African Americans in southern society, or adherence to the teachings of Jesus Christ as the basis for one's view of life, or the structure of the family in rural Georgia in the 1950s. All had an opinion about and therefore an interpretation of O'Connor's story.

When Dr. Blackwell's students stated their personal interpretations of O'Connor's story, they had already become practicing literary critics. All of them had already interacted with the story, thinking about their likes and dislikes of the various characters; their impressions of the setting, plot, and structure; and their overall assessments of the story itself, whether that assessment was a full-fledged interpretation that seeks to explain every facet of the text or simply bewilderment as to the story's overall meaning.

None of the students, however, had had formal training in literary criticism. None knew the somewhat complicated language of literary theory. And none were acquainted with any of the formal schools of literary criticism.

What each student had done was to read the story. The reading process itself produced within the students an array of responses, taking the form of questions, statements, opinions, and feelings evoked by the text. These responses coupled with the text itself are the concerns of formal literary criticism.

Although these students may need to master the terminology, the many philosophical approaches, and the diverse methodologies of formal literary criticism to become trained literary critics, they automatically became literary critics as they read and thought about O'Connor's text. They needed no formal training in literary theory. By mastering the concepts of formal literary criticism, these students, like all readers, can become critical readers who are better able to understand and articulate their own reactions and those of others to any text.

1.3   THE DEFINITION OF LITERARY CRITICISM

Matthew Arnold, a nineteenth-century literary critic, describes literary criticism as "A disinterested endeavor to learn and propagate the best that is known and thought in the world."[①] Implication in this definition is that literary criticism is a disciplined activity that attempts to describe, study, analyze, justify, interpret and evaluate a work of art. By necessity, Arnold would argue, this discipline attempts to formulate aesthetic and methodological-principles on which the critic can evaluate a text.

When we consider its function and its relationship to texts, literary criticism is not usually considered a discipline in and of itself, for it must be related to something else — that is, a work of art. Without the work of art, the activity of criticism cannot exist. And it is through this discerning activity that we can knowingly explore the questions that help define our humanity, evaluate our actions, or simply increase our appreciation and enjoyment of both a literary work and our fellow human beings.

When analyzing a text, literary critics ask basic questions concerning the philosophical, psychological, functional, and descriptive nature of the text itself. Since the time of the Greek philosophers Plato and Aristotle, the answers to these questions have been debated. By asking questions of O'Connor's or any other text and by contemplating answers, we too can participate in this debate. Whether we question whether the motives of O'Connor's character the grandmother in wanting to take her cat on the family's vacation or whether the Misfit is the primary reason the grandmother experiences her epiphany, we are participating in an ongoing discussion of the value and enjoyment of O'Connor's short story while simultaneously engaging in literary criticism and functioning as practical literary critics.

Traditionally, literary critics involve themselves in either theoretical or practical criticism. Theoretical criticism formulates the theories, principles, and tenets of the nature and value of art. By citing general aesthetic and moral principles of art, theoretical criticism provides the necessary framework for practical criticism. Practical criticism (also known as applied criticism)

---

① LAKSHMI S. Matthew Arnold as a Literary Critic[EB/OL]. (2008-06-09) [2018-08-10] http://www.literature-study-online. com/essays/arnold.html.

applies the theories and tenets of theoretical criticism to a particular work. Using the theories and principles of theoretical criticism, the practical critic defines the standards of taste and explains, evaluates, or justifies a particular piece of literature. A further distinction is made between the practical critic who posits that there is only one theory or set of principles a critic may use when evaluating a literary work — the absolutist critic — and the relativistic critic, one who uses various and even contradictory theories in critiquing a piece of literature. The basis for either kind of critic, or any form of criticism, is literary theory. Without theory, practical criticism could not exist.

1.4   THE DEFINITION OF LITERARY THEORY

When reading O'Connor's "A Good Man is Hard to Find," we necessarily interact with the text, asking many specific, text-related questions and often-times rather personal ones as well. For example, such questions as these may concern us, the readers:

· What kind of person is the grandmother? Is she like my grandmother or any grandmother I know?

· What is the function or role of June Star? John Wesley? Bailey? The mother?

· Why was the grandmother taking Pitty Sing, the cat, on the family vacation?

· What is the significance of the restaurant scene at The Tower?

· Right before she is shot, what does the grandmother recognize about the Misfit?

· What is the significance of this recognition?

Such questions immediately involve us in practical criticism. What we tend to forget during the reading of O'Connor's short story or any other text, however, is that we have read other literary works. Our response to any text, then — or the principles of practical criticism we apply to it — is largely a conditioned or socially constructed one; that is, how we arrive at meaning in fiction is in part determined by our past experiences. Consciously or unconsciously, we have developed a mindset or framework concerning our expectations when reading a novel, short story, poem, or any other type of literature. In addition, what we choose to value or uphold as good or bad, moral or immoral, or beautiful or ugly within a given text actually depends on this ever-evolving framework. When we can clearly articulate our mental framework when reading a text and explain how this mindset directly influences our values and aesthetic judgments about the text, we are well on our way to developing a coherent, unified literary theory — the assumptions (conscious or unconscious) that under gird one's understanding and interpretation of language, the construction of meaning, art, culture, aesthetics, and ideological positions.

Because anyone who responds to a text is already a practicing literary critic and because practical criticism is rooted in the reader's preconditioned mindset concerning his or her expectations when actually reading a text, every reader espouses some kind of literary theory. Each reader's theory may be conscious or unconscious, whole or partial, informed or ill informed, eclectic or unified. An incomplete, unconscious, and therefore unclear literary theory leads to illogical, unsound, and haphazard interpretations. On the other hand, a well-defined, logical, and clearly articulated theory enables readers to develop a method by which to establish principles that enable them to justify, order, and clarify their own appraisals of a text in a consistent manner.

A well-articulated literary theory assumes that an innocent reading of a text or a sheer emotional or spontaneous reaction to a work cannot exist, for theory questions the assumptions, beliefs, and feelings of readers, asking why they respond to a text in a certain way. According to a consistent literary theory, a simple emotional or intuitive response to a text does not explain the underlying factors that caused such a reaction. What elicits that response, or how the reader constructs meaning through or with the text, is what matters.

Making Meaning from Text

How we as readers construct meaning through or with a text depends on the mental framework each of us has developed concerning the nature of reality. This framework or worldview consists of the assumptions or presuppositions that we all hold (either consciously or unconsciously) concerning the basic makeup of our world. For example, we all struggle to find answers to such questions as these:

· What is the basis of morality or ethics?

· What is the meaning of human history?

· Is there an overarching purpose for humanity's existence?

· What is beauty, truth, or goodness?

· Is there an ultimate reality?

Interestingly, our answers to these and other questions do not remain static, for as we interact with other people, our environment, and our own inner selves, we are continually shaping and developing our personal philosophies, rejecting former ideas and opinions and replacing them with newly discovered ones. But it is our dynamic answers — including our doubts and fears about these answers — that largely determine our responses to a literary text.

Upon such a conceptual framework rests literary theory. Whether that framework is well reasoned or simply a matter of habit and past teachings, readers respond to works of art via their world view. From this philosophical core of beliefs spring their evaluations of the goodness, worthiness, and value of art itself. Using their worldviews either consciously or unconsciously as a yardstick by which to measure and value their experiences, readers respond to individual works of literature, ordering and valuing each separate or collective experience in each text based on the system of beliefs housed in their worldviews.

1.5   THE READING PROCESS AND LITERARY THEORY

The relationship between literary theory and a reader's personal worldview is best illustrated in the act of reading itself. When reading, we are constantly interacting with the text. According to Louise M. Rosenblatt's text *The Reader, the Text, the Poem* (1978), during the act or event of reading,

> A reader brings to the text his or her past experience and present personality. Under the magnetism of the ordered symbols of the text, the reader marshals his or her resources and crystallizes out from the stuff of memory, thought, and feeling a new order, a new experience, which he/she sees as the poem. This becomes part of the ongoing stream of the reader's life experience, to be reflected on from any angle important to him or her as a human being.

Accordingly, Rosenblatt declares that the relationship between the reader and the text is not linear, but trans-actional; that is, it is a process or event that takes place at a particular time and place in which the text and the reader condition each other. The reader and the text transact, creating meaning, for meaning does not exist solely within the reader's mind or within the text, Rosenblatt maintains, but in the transaction between them. To arrive at an interpretation of a text, readers bring their own "temperament and fund of past transactions to the text and live through a process of handling new situations, new attitudes, new personalities and new conflicts in value. They can reject, revise, or assimilate into the resource with which they engage their world." Through this trans-actional experience, readers consciously and unconsciously amend their worldview.

Because no literary theory can account for all the various factors included in everyone's conceptual framework, and because we, as readers, all have different literary experiences, there can exist no meta-theory — one overarching literary theory that encompasses all possible interpretations of a text suggested by its readers. And there can be no one correct literary theory, for in and of itself, each literary theory asks valid questions about the text, and no one theory is capable of exhausting all legitimate questions to be asked about any text.

The valid questions asked by the various literary theories often differ widely. Espousing separate critical orientations, each theory focuses primarily on one element of the interpretative process, although in practice different theories may address several areas of concern in interpreting a text. For example, one theory stresses the work itself, believing that the text alone contains all the necessary information to arrive at an interpretation. This theory isolates the text from its historical or sociological setting and concentrates on the literary forms found in the text, such as figures of speech, word choice, and style. Another theory attempts to place a text in its historical, political, sociological, religious, and economic setting. By placing the text in historical perspective, this theory asserts that its adherents can arrive at an interpretation that both the text's author and its original audience would support. Still another theory directs its chief concern toward the text's audience. It asks how the readers' emotions and personal backgrounds affect a text's interpretation. Whether the primary focus of concern is psychological, linguistic, mythical, historical, or from any other critical orientation, each literary theory establishes its own methodology whereby readers can apply this theory to an actual text.

Although each reader's theory and methodology for arriving at a text's interpretation differ, sooner or later groups of readers and critics declare allegiance to a similar core of beliefs and band together, thereby founding different schools of criticism. For example, critics who believe that social and historical concerns must be highlighted in a text are known as Marxist critics, whereas reader-response critics concentrate on the readers' personal reactions to the text. Because new points of view concerning literary works are continually evolving, new schools of criticism and therefore new literary theories will continue to develop. One of the most recent schools to emerge in the 1980s and 1990s, New Historicism or Cultural Poetics, declares that a text must be analyzed through historical research that assumes that history and fiction are inseparable. The members of this school, known as New Historians, hope to shift the boundaries between history and literature and thereby produce criticism that accurately reflects what they believe to be the proper relationship between the text and its historical context. Still other newly evolving schools of criticism such as post-colonialism, gender studies, and African-American studies continue to emerge and challenge previous ways of thinking and critiquing texts.

Because the various schools of criticism (and the theories on which they are based) ask different questions about the same work of literature, these theoretical schools provide an array of seemingly endless options from which readers can choose to broaden their understanding not only of the text but also of their society, their culture, and their own humanity. By embracing literary theory, we can thus learn not only about literature but also about tolerance for other people's beliefs, By rejecting or ignoring theory, we are in danger of canonizing ourselves as literary saints who possess divine knowledge and can therefore supply the one and only correct interpretation for a work of literature. To oppose, disregard, or ignore literary theory is also to be against questioning our own concepts of self, society and culture and how texts help us define and continually redefine these concepts. By embracing literary theory and literary criticism (its practical application), we can participate in that seemingly endless historical conversation and debate concerning the nature of humanity and its concerns as expressed in literature itself.

What is Literature

Because literary criticism presupposes that there exists a work of literature to be interpreted, we could assume that formulating a definition of literature would be simple. But it is not. For centuries, writers, literary historians, and others have debated about but failed to agree on a definition for this term. Some assume that literature is simply anything that is written thereby declaring a city telephone book, a cook book, and a road atlas to be literary works along with *David Copperfield* and the *Adventures of Huckleberry Finn*. Derived from the Latin "littera", meaning "letter," the root meaning of literature refers primarily to the written word and seems to support this broad definition. However, such a definition eliminates the important oral traditions on which much of our literature is based, including Homer's Iliad and Odyssey, the English epic Beowulf, and many Native American legends.

To solve this problem, others choose to define **literature** as an art, thereby leaving open the question of its being written or oral. This further narrows its meaning, equating literature to works of the imagination or creative writing. To emphasize the imaginative qualities of literature, some critics choose to use the German word for literature. Wortkunst, instead of its English equivalent, automatically implies that the imaginative and creative aspects of literature are essential components of the word **literature** itself. By this definition, written works such as a telephone or cook book can no longer be considered literature, being replaced or superseded by poetry, drama, fiction, and other imaginative writing.

Although such a narrowing and an equating of the definition of literature to art seemingly simplifies what can and cannot be deemed a literary work, such is not the case. That the J. Crew and Victoria's Secrets clothes catalogs are imaginative (and colorful) writing is unquestioned, but should they be considered works of literature? Or should Madonna's book Sex or the lyrics of the rap song "Cop Killer" be called literary works? Is Madonna's text or the rap song an imaginative or creative work? If so, can or should either be considered a work of literature? Defining and narrowing the definition of literature as being a work of art does not immediately provide consensus or a consistent rule concerning whether a work should be called a work of literature.

Whether one accepts the broad or narrow definition, many argue that a text must have certain peculiar qualities before it can be dubbed literature. For example, the artist's creation or secondary world often mirrors the author's primary world, the world in which the creator lives, moves and breathes. Because reality or the primary world is highly structured, so must be the secondary world. To achieve this structure, the artist must create plot, character, tone, symbols, conflict, and a host of other elements or parts of the artistic story, with all of these elements working in a dynamic relationship to produce a literary work. Some would argue that it is the creation of these elements — how they are used and in what context — that determines whether a piece of writing is literature.

Still other critics add the test-of-time criterion to their essential components of literature. If a work such as Dante's *Divine Comedy* withstands the passage of time and is still being read centuries after its creation, it is deemed valuable and worthy to be called literature. This criterion also denotes literature's functional or cultural value: If people value a written work, for whatever reason, they often declare it to be literature whether or not it contains the prescribed elements of a text.

What this work may contain is a peculiar aesthetic quality — that is some element of beauty — that distinguishes it as literature from other forms of writing. Aesthetics, the branch of philosophy that deals with the concept of the beautiful, strives to determine the criteria for beauty in a work of art. Theorists such as Plato and Aristotle declare that the source of beauty is inherent within the art object itself; other critics, such as David Hume, say that beauty is in the eye of the beholder. And some twentieth-century theorists argue that one's perception of beauty in a text rests on the dynamic relationship between the object and the perceiver at a given moment in time. Wherever the criteria for judging beauty of a work of art finally resides most critics agree that a work of literature does have an appealing, aesthetic quality.

While distinguishing literature from other forms of writings, this appealing aesthetic quality directly contributes to literature's chief purpose: The telling of a story. Although it may simultaneously communicate facts, literature's primary aim is to tell a story. The subject of this story is particularly human, describing and detailing a variety of human experiences, not stating facts or bits and pieces of information, For example, literature does not define the word courage, but shows us a courageous character acting courageously. By so doing, literature concertizes an array of human values, emotions, actions, and ideas in story form. And it is this concretization that allows us to experience vicariously the stories of a host of characters. Through these characters we observe people in action, making decisions, struggling to maintain their humanity in often inhumane circumstances, and embodying for us a variety of values and human characteristics that we may embrace, discard, enjoy, or detest.

1.6 LITERARY THEORY AND LITERATURE TRANSLATION THEORY

Is literature simply a story that contains certain aesthetic and literary qualities that all somehow pleasingly culminate in a work of art? If so, can texts be considered artifacts that can be analyzed, dissected, and studied to discover their essential nature or meanings? Or does a literary work have ontological status: That is, does it exist in and of itself, perhaps in a special neo-Platonic realm, or must it have an audience, a reader, before it becomes literature? And can we define the word **text**? Is it simply print on a page? If pictures are included, do they automatically become part of the text? And who determines when print becomes a work of art? The reader? The author? Or Both?

The answers to these and similar questions have been long debated, and the various responses make up the corpus of literary theory. Providing the academic arena in which those interested in literary theory (literary theorists) can posit philosophical assumptions concerning the nature of the reading process, the epistemological nature of learning, the nature of reality itself, and a host of related concerns, literary theory offers a variety of methodologies that enable readers to interpret a text from different and often conflicting points of view. Such theorizing empowers readers to examine their personal worldviews, to articulate their individual assumptions concerning the nature of reality, and to understand how these assumptions directly affect their interpretation not only of a work of art and but also of the definition of literature itself.

Although any definition of literature is debatable, most would agree that an examination of a text's total artistic situation would help us decide what constitutes literature. This total picture of the work involves such elements as the work itself (an examination of the fictionality or secondary world created within the story), the artist, the universe or world the work supposedly represents, and the audience or readers. Although readers and critics will emphasize one, two, or even three of these elements while emphasizing the others, such a consideration of a text's artistic situation immediately broadens the definition of literature from the concept that it is simply a written work that contains certain qualities to a definition that must include the dynamic relationship of the actual text and the readers. Perhaps, then, the literary competence of the readers themselves helps determine whether a work should be considered literature. If this is so, then a literary work may be more functional than ontological, its existence and therefore its value being determined by its readers and not the work itself.

Overall, the definition of literature depends on the particular kind of literary theory or school of criticism that the reader or critic espouses. For formalists, for example, the text and text alone contains certain qualities that make a particular piece of writing literature. But for reader-response critics, the interaction and psychological relationships between the text and the reader help determine whether a document should be deemed literary.

When literary works go beyond time and space, and passed down by generations, the interpretation will display the various meaning, especially when it translated by different target language. Literary translation theory is necessarily combined with literary works.

Because translation is a recreational activity, literary translation is, among all types of translation, of unique characteristic for its inseparable of beauty, connection with literary creation. Literature originates from the appreciation and it exists and develops for the spiritual needs of human aesthetic consciousness. Writers portray social life through imagination instead of imitation, and literary depiction always means more than real life. This special connection between literature and life determines the basic essence and main features of literature. Social life is the only resource of literary creation, and writers can never produce impressive works unless they have got enough social experiences; while in literary translation, translators work to represent the feelings and thoughts which hardly be achieved by simple language transformation in original texts.

The ancient Chinese poet Jia Dao already noticed the hardness in deciding whether to use "push" or "knock" in his lines, let alone the translator's decision in transformed languages. Hard as the work is, literary translation has been proved possible and can be done well.

Since translators need first to read the original texts, then to feel and comprehend them, and finally to give faithful representations of them, it is safe to say translators are actually writing in target languages while they are doing literary translation.

When literary works as source texts transferred from its source culture to face different target culture and target readers, the interpretation is mainly decided by the translators. As a matter of fact, the theme of the original text and the plot it covers lost the subjectivity to some degree when it is given to the translator, so what its function can be played is to provide a framework or material in-process. Literary theories help original readers' understanding and interpretation from critical point of view, also it can influence the translators to understand original text.

Translators should retain the overall style and power of the source language, and that translation should be considered literary creation as well. British King Alfred compares the creative work of the translators to house building, which is both vivid and believable: With the help of a variety of tools, I take from the trees what I want, through my creative laboring, to build beautiful houses and cities. To King Alfred, translation is really an activity full of flexible strategies and tactics, and the creation in it was often casual adjustments to changing circumstances. Russian literary translators and translation theorists insist that translators should possess the gift of being writers, and translators and writers have many more similarities than differences. The author's creation is of no constraints, while the translator must, in his creation, deal with linguistic interference and other hindrances. In their minds, literary translation should follow the principle of creation, and literary translation is a kind of creative activity, which is to achieve the same artistic effect instead of seeking language resemblance. The artistic schools of translation studies in Russia are opposed to adopt linguistic approach in studying translation for they consider it the most important in literary translation to pursue and convey the aesthetic value of the source text. It is true that linguistic features deserve attention, but linguistic correspondence has never been, and should never be taken as the aim of literary translation. Instead, artistic correspondence and equal aesthetic value are the guarantee of the faithful representation of the artistic appeal of the original writing. To be away from the linguistic expression of the source text is actually to better serve the objective of going near it, and language in itself is a type of creation, and colorful versions come into being when different creative approaches are employed. Therefore the Russian theorists assert that translation is another form of literary creation, and all the criteria set for the evaluation of literary creation are suitable for the use of literary translation.

In some critic views, translators are like painters, cultivate a style of his own so that they deserve the name of artists. Translators are co-operators of artistic work, and they try every means to rebuild the spiritual world of the original writing, so it is never an exaggeration to say that literary translation is on an equality with literary creation, and it is always marked with creative essence. Another well-known American poet and translator Ezra Pound combines his writing and translation in such a perfect way that his work has been rather popular among a great number of readers. Pound gets inspiration from ancient Chinese poems, and he puts special emphasis on the background information and the overall image, which helps to establish his fame in both fields of literary writing and literary translation. Sometimes his translations can hardly be labeled translations since they are in fact creative writings, and readers often find his notion of "the vitality of language" well conveyed in his literary translations.

China has witnessed the effort of the literary translators in their pursuit of creating qualified translations. Zhu Ziqing equals poetry translation to poetry writing for the reason that new sense of language, new poetic style, new sentence structure, and new metaphor are produced in the translations. Qian Zhongshu, for example, puts forward the highest criterion of literary translation: To make the translation an inspired one. Though the criterion does not sound very concrete and might not be easy to handle, the direction toward which translators should work is rather clear, and the ability to do creative writing is highly requested. Xu Yuanchong, also known as a noted literary translator, has accumulated a wealth of experience in literary translation. Among all his notions concerning literary translation, "artistic creation" is the one that deserves close attention, and he even says that the creation on the part of the translator might make up for the loss in the translation, and that only when the translation is rich in creation, could it be called a lofty art. He predicts that the new century is going to be an age of world literature, and only when the translated texts have acquired the qualification of literary writing can they win world recognition. Meanwhile, he is confident that the position of literary translation will be promoted to that of literary writing, and the creative essence will surely be universally recognized.

1.7 THE FUNCTION OF LITERATURE TEXT AND LITERARY THEORY

Critics continually debate literature's chief function. Tracing their arguments to Plato, many contend that literature's primary function is moral, its chief value being usefulness for hidden or undisclosed purposes. But others, like Aristotle, hold that a work of art can be analyzed and broken down into its various parts, with each part contributing to the overall enjoyment of the work itself. For these critics, the value of a text is found within it or inseparably inked to the work itself. In its most simple terms, the debate centers around two concerns: Is literature's chief function to teach (extrinsic) or to entertain (intrinsic)? In other words, can or do we read a text for the sheer fun of it, or must we always be studying and learning from what we read?

Such questions and their various answers lead us directly to literary theory, for literary theory concerns itself not only with ontological questions (whether a text really exists), but also with epistemological issues (how we know or ways of knowing). When we ask, then, if literature's chief function is to entertain or to teach, we are really asking epistemological questions. Whether we read a text to learn from it or to be entertained, we can say that we know that text once having read it.

We can know a text in two distinct ways. The first method involves the typical literature classroom analysis. When we have studied, analyzed, and critiqued a text and arrived at an interpretation, we can then confidently assert we know the text. On the other hand, when we stay up all night turning the pages of a mystery novel to discover who the murderer is, we can also say that we know the text, for we have spent time devouring its pages, lost in secondary world, consumed by its character, and by novel's end eagerly seeking the resolution of its tensions. Both methods — one whose chief goal is to learn and the others' being entertainment — involve similar yet distinct epistemological ways of knowing.

The French verbs **savoir** and **connaitre** can both be translated as "to know" and highlight the difference between these two epistemological ways of knowing a text. **Savoir** means to analyze (from the Greek analuein, to undo) and to study. It is used to refer to knowing something that is the object of study and assumes that the object, such as a text, can be examined, analyzed, and critiqued. Knowledge or learning is ultimate goal.

Connaitre, on the other hand, implies that we intimately know or have experienced the text.

Interestingly, **Connaitre** is used for knowing people and refers to our knowing an author's canon. Knowing people and knowing a literary canon imply intimacy, learning the ins and outs of each one of them. And it is such intimacy that one often experiences while reading a mystery novel all night long to know how to analyze a text, to discuss its literary elements, and to apply the various methodologies of literary criticism means that we know at text (**savoir**). To have experienced the text, to have cried with or about its characters, to have lost time and sleep immersed in the secondary world of the text, and to have felt our emotions stirred also means that we know that text (**connaitre**). From one way of knowing we learn facts or information, and from the other we encounter and participate in an intimate experience.

At times, however, we have actually known the text from both these perspectives, **savoir** and **connaitre**. While analyzing and critiquing a text (savoir), we have at times (and perhaps more often than not) simultaneously experienced it, becoming emotionally involved with its characters' choices and destinies (connaitre) and imagining ourselves to be these characters, or at least recognizing some of our own characteristics dramatized by the characters.

Thus, to say that we know a text is not a simple statement. Underlying our private and public reactions and our scholarly critiques and analyses is our literary theory, the fountainhead of our most intimate and our most public declarations. The formal study of literary theory therefore enables us to plain our responses to any text and allows us to articulate the function of literature in an academic and a personal way.

REFERENCES

[1] BERNARD G. The Enjoyment of Literature[M].New York:Crown,1975.

[2] BONNIE S, LARRY S. A Guide to Literary Criticism and Research[M].Fort Worth:Holt,1992.

[3] HOLMAN C H, WILLIAM H. A Handbook to Literature[M]. New York: Macmillan, 1992.

[4] DAVID D. Critical Approaches to Literature[M]. New York: Longman, 1981.

[5] FRANK L, THOMAS MCL, eds. Critical Terms for Literary Study[M]. Chicago: University of Chicago Press, 1990.

[6] JAMES W S. The Joy of Reading: A Guide to Becoming a Better Reader[M]. Portland: Multnomah Press, 1978.

[7] JAMES W S. The Universe Next Door[M]. Downers Grove: Inter Varsity, 1988.

[8] LOUISE M R. The Reader, the Text, the Poem: The Translational Theory of the Literary Work[M]. Carbondale: Southern Illinois University Press, 1978.

[9] MARK TWAIN. The Adventures of Huckleberry Finn[M]. New York: Harcourt, 1961.

[10] MARLIES D, W STACY JOHNSON. An Introduction to Literary Criticism[M]. Boston: D.C. Heath, 1961.

[11] MONROE C B, ROBERT W D, GLENN H L. Theme and Form: An Introduction to Literature[M]. Englewood Cliffs: Prentice-Hall, 1969.

[12] SHIRLEY F S, ed al. Literary Theories in Praxis[M]. Philadelphia: University of Pennsylvania Press, 1987.

[13] TERRY E. Literary Theory: An Introduction[M]. Minneapolis: University of Minnesota Press, 1983.

CHAPTER II   BEGINNING THE FORMAL STUDY OF LITERARY THEORY

This chapter has stressed the importance of literary theory and criticism and its relationship to literature and the interpretative processes. And it has also articulated the underlying premises as to why a study of literary theory is essential:

· Literary theory assumes that there is no such thing as an innocent reading of a text. Whether our responses are emotional and spontaneous or well reasoned and highly structured, all such interactions with and to a text are based on some underlying factors that cause us to respond to the text in a particular fashion. What elicits these responses or how a reader makes sense out of a text is at the heart of literary theory.

· Because our reactions to any text have theoretical bases, all readers must have a literary theory. The methods we use to frame our personal interpretations of any text directly involve us in the process of literary criticism and theory, automatically making us practicing literary critics.

· Because many readers' literary theory is more often than not unconscious, incomplete, ill–informed, and electric, their interpretations can easily be unsound, and haphazard. A well–defined, logical, and clearly articulated literary theory enables readers to consciously develop their own personal methods of interpretation, permitting them to order, clarify, and justify their appraisals of a text in a consistent and logical manner.

It is the goal of this text to enable readers to make such conscious, informed, and intelligent choices concerning their own methods of literary interpretation and to understand their personal and public reactions to a text. To accomplish this goal, this text will introduce readers to literary theory and criticism, its historical development, and the various theoretical positions or schools of criticism that enable readers to become knowledgeable critics of their own and others' interpretations. By becoming acquainted with diverse and often contradictory approaches to a text, readers will broaden their perspectives not only about themselves but also about others and the world in which they live.

Questions about the value, structure, and even definition of literature undoubtedly arose in all cultures as people heard or read works of art. Such practical criticism probably began with the initial hearing or reading of the first literary works. It is the Greeks of the fifth century B.C., however, who first articulated and developed the philosophy of art and life that serves as the foundation for most theoretical and practical criticism. These Athenians questioned the very act of reading and writing itself, while pondering the purpose of literature. By so doing, these early critics began a debate concerning the nature and function of literature that continues to the present day. What they inaugurated was the formal study of literary criticism.

From the fifth century B.C. to the present, Critics such as Plato, Dante, Wordsworth, and a host of others have developed principles of criticism that have had a major influence on the ongoing discussion of literary theory and criticism. By examining these critics' ideas, we can gain an understanding of and participate in this critical debate while acquiring an appreciation for and a working knowledge of both practical and theoretical criticism.

2.1 CLASSICAL CRITICISM

2.1.1 PLATO (ca. 427−347 B.C.)

Alfred North Whitehead, a modern British philosopher, once quipped that "all of Western philosophy is but a footnote to Plato."[1] Although others have indeed contributed to Western thought, it was Plato's ideas expressed in his *Ion, Crito, the Republic*, and other works, that laid the foundation for many, if not most, of the pivotal issues of philosophy and literature: The concepts of truth, beauty, and goodness; the nature of reality; the structure of society; the nature and relations of being (ontology); questions about how we know what we know (epistemology); and ethics and morality. Since Plato's day, such ideas have been debated, changed, debunked, or simply accepted. None, however, have been ignored.

Before Plato, only fragmentary comments about the nature or value of literature can be found. In the plays and writings of the comic dramatist Aristophanes, a contemporary of Plato, a few tidbits of practical criticism arise, but no clearly articulated literary theory. It is Plato who systematically begins the study of literary theory and criticism.

The core of Platonic thought resides in Plato's doctrine of essences, ideas, or forms. Ultimate

---

① Whitehead A N. Western Philosophy as "footnotes to Plato"[EB/OL].[2018-03-16]. https://www.age-of-the-sage.org/ philosophy.

reality, he states, is spiritual. This spiritual realm, which Plato calls the One, is composed of "ideal" forms or absolutes that exist whether or not any mind posits their existence or reflects their attributes. It is these ideals form that give shape to our physical world, for our material world is nothing more than a shadowy replica of the absolute forms found in the spiritual realm. In the material world, we can therefore recognize a chair as a chair because the ideal chair exists in this spiritual realm and preceded the existence of the material chair. Without the existence of the ideal chair, the physical chair, which is nothing more than a shadowy replica of the ideal chair, could not exist.

Such an emphasis on philosophical ideals earmarks the beginning of the first articulated literary theory and becomes the foundation for literary criticism. Before Plato and his Academy, Greek culture ordered its world through poetry and poetic imagination; that is, by reading such works as *The Iliad and The Odyssey*, the Greeks saw good characters in action performing good deeds. From such story, they formulated their theories of goodness and other similar standards, thereby using the presentational mode for discovering truth: Observing good characters acting justly, honorably, and courageously and inculcating these characteristics within themselves. With the advent of Plato and his Academy, however, philosophical inquiry and abstract thinking usurped the narrative as a method for discovering truth. Not by accident, then, Plato places above his school door the words, "Let no one enter here who is not a geometer"[1] (a master of geometry: The skilled in formal logic and reasoning). All his students had to value the art of reason and abstraction, as opposed to the presentational mode, for discovering truth.

Such abstract reasoning and formal logic not only usurps literature's role as an evaluating mode for discerning truth but actually condemns it. If ultimate reality rests in the spiritual realm and the material world is only a shadowy replica of the world of ideals, then according to Plato and his followers, poets (those who compose imaginative literature) are merely imitating when they write about any object in the material world. Accordingly, Plato declares that a poet's craft is "an inferior who marries an inferior and has inferior offspring,"[2] for the poet, declares Plato, is one who has now two steps or degrees removed from ultimate, reality. These imitators of mere shadows, contends Plato, cannot be trusted.

---

[1]   SUZANNE B. Frequently Asked Questions about Plato[EB/OL].(2004-01-04) [2016-05-18]. http://plato-dialogues.org/faq/faq009.htm.

[2]   SUZANNE B. Frequently Asked Questions about Plato[EB/OL].(2004-01-04) [2016-05-18]. http://plato-dialogues.org/faq/faq009.htm.

While condemning poets for producing art that is nothing more than a copy of a copy, Plato also agrees that the poets produce their art irrational Lyceum. It therefore lacks the unity and coherence of Aristotle's other works, but it remains one of the most important critical influences on literary theory and criticism.

Aristotle's *Poetics* has become the cornerstone of Western literary criticism. By applying his analytic abilities to a definition of tragedy，Aristotle began in the Poetics a discussion of the components of a literary work that continues to the present day. Unfortunately, many critics and scholars mistakenly assume that the *Poetics* is a how-to manual, defining and setting the standards for literature (particularly tragedy) for all time. However, Aristotle's purpose was not to formulate a series of absolute rules for evaluating a tragedy, but to state the general principles of tragedy as he viewed them in his time while responding to many of Plato's doctrines and arguments.

Even his title, *the Poetics* reveals Aristotle's purpose, for in Greek the word **poetikes** means "things that are made or crafted".[①] Like a biologist, Aristotle dissects tragedy to discover its component or crafted parts.

At the beginning of the poetics, Aristotle notes that "epic poetry, tragedy, comedy, dithyrambic poetry, and most forms of flute and lyre playing all happen to be, in general imitations."[②] All seemingly differ in how and what they imitate, but Aristotle agrees with Plato that all the arts are imitations. In particular, the art of poetry exists because people are imitative creatures who enjoy such imitation. Whereas Plato contends that such pleasure can undermine the structure of society and all its values, Aristotle strongly disagrees. His disagreement is basically a metaphysical argument concerning the nature of imitation itself. Whereas Plato posits that imitation is two steps removed from the truth or realm of the ideal (the poet imitating an object that is itself an imitation of an ideal form), Aristotle contends poetry is more universal, more general than things as they are. For "it is not the function of the poet to relate what has happened but what may happen — what is possible according to the law of probability or necessity. It is the historian, not the poet, who writes of what could happen. Poetry, therefore, is a more philosophical and a higher thing than history: For poetry tends to express the universal, history the particular." In arguing that poets present things not as they are should be, Aristotle rebuffs Plato's concept that the poet is merely imitating an imitation, for Aristotle's poet, with his

---

① ARISTOTLE, The Poetics[M]. Coradella Collegiate Bookshelf. 2011:1.
② ARISTOTLE, The Poetics[M]. Coradella Collegiate Bookshelf. 2011:1.

emphasis on the universal, actually attains nearer to the ideal than does Plato's.

But not all imitations by poets are the same, for "writers of great dignity imitated the noble actions of noble heroes; the less dignified sort of writers imitated the actions of inferior men." For Aristotle, "comedy is an imitation of base men...characterized not by every kind of vice but specifically by the 'ridiculous,' some error or ugliness that is painless and has no harmful effects."[1] It is to *tragedy* written by poets imitating noble actions and heroes Aristotle turns his attention.

Aristotle's complex definition of tragedy has perplexed and frustrated many readers:

> Tragedy is then, an imitation of a noble and complete action, having the proper magnitude; it employs language that has been artistically enhanced by each of the kinds of linguistic adornment, applied separately in the various parts of the play; it is presented in dramatic, not narrative form, and achieves, through the representation of pitiable and fearful incidents, the catharsis of such pitiable and fearful incidents.

When put in context with other ideas in the Poetics, such as a complex a middle, and tragedy is put in context with other ideas in the Poetics, such a complex definition highlights Aristotle's chief contributions to literary criticism:

> · Tragedy, or a work of art, is an imitation of nature that reflects a high form of art exhibiting noble characters and noble deeds, the act of imitation itself giving us pleasure.

> · Art possesses form; that is, tragedy, unlike life, has a beginning, a middle, and an end with each of the parts being related to every other part. A tragedy is an organic whole, with all its various parts interrelated.

> · In tragedy, concern for form must be given to the characters as well as the structure of the play, for the tragic hero must be "a man who is not eminently good and just, yet whose misfortune is brought about not by vice or depravity, but by some errors or frailty. He must be one who is highly renowned and prosperous." In addition, all tragic heroes must have a tragic flaw, or hamartia, that leads to their downfall in such a way as not to offend the audience's sense of justice.

> · The tragedy must have an emotional effect on its audience and "through pity and fear" effect a catharsis; that is, by the play's end, the audience's emotions should be

---

[1]   ARISTOTLE. The Poetics[M]. Coradella Collegiate Bookshelf. 2011:9-14.

purged, purified, or clarified (what Aristotle really meant by catharsis is debatable).

· The universal, not the particular, should be stressed, for unlike history, which deals with what happens, poetry (for tragedy) deals with what could happen and is therefore closer to perfection or truth.

· The poet must give close attention to diction or language itself, be it in verse, prose, or song, but ultimately it is the thoughts expressed through language that are of utmost concern.

Interestingly, nowhere in the **Poetics** does Aristotle address the didactic value of poetry or literature. Unlike Plato, whose chief concern is the subject matter of poetry and its effects on the reader, Aristotle emphasizes literary form or structure, examining the component parts of a tragedy and how these parts must work together to produce a unified whole.

From the writings of philosopher-artists, Plato and Aristotle, arise the concerns, questions, and debates that have spearheaded the development of most literary schools of criticism. By addressing different aspects of these fifth-century Greeks' ideas and concepts, a variety of literary critics from the Middle Ages to the present have formulated theories of literary criticism that force us to ask different but legitimate questions of a text. But the shadows of Plato and Aristotle loom over much of what these later theorists espouse.

2.1.2 HORACE (65–8 B.C.)

With the passing of the glory that was Greece and its philosopher-artists came the grandeur of Rome and its chief stylist, Quintus Horatius Flaccus, or simply Horace. Friend of Emperor Augustus and many other members of the Roman aristocracy, Horace enjoyed the wealth and influence of these associates. In a letter to the sons of one of his friends and patrons, Maecenas, Horace articulated what became the official canon of literary taste during the Middle Ages, the Renaissance, and much of the Neoclassical period. By reading this letter and his *Ars Poetica*, or *The Art of Poetry*, any Roman aristocrat, any medieval knight, and even Alexander Pope himself could learn the standards of good or proper literature.

Although Horace was probably acquainted with Aristotle's works, his concerns are quite different. Whereas both Plato and Aristotle decree that poets must, and do, imitate nature, Horace declares that poets must imitate other poets, particularly those of the past. Less concerned with metaphysics than his predecessors, Horace establishes the practical do's and don'ts for a writer.

To be considered a good writer, he maintains, one should write about traditional subjects in unique ways. In addition, the poet should avoid all extremes in subject matter, word choice, vocabulary, and style. Gaining mastery in these areas could be achieved by reading and following the examples of the classical Greek and Roman authors. For example, because authors of antiquity began their epics in the middle of things, all epics must begin in medias res. Above all, writers should avoid appearing ridiculous and must therefore aim their sights low, not attempting to be a new Virgil or Homer.

Literature's ultimate aim, declares Horace, is "dulce et utile" or to be sweet and useful; the best writings, he argues, both teach and delight. To achieve this goal, poets must understand their audience: The learned reader may want to be instructed, whereas others may simply read to be amused. The poet's task is to combine usefulness and delight in the same literary work.

Often oversimplified and misunderstood, Horace opts to give the would-be writer practical guidelines for the author's craft-while leaving unattended and unchallenged many of the philosophical concerns of Plato and Aristotle. For Horace, a poet's greatest reward is the adulation of the public.

2.1.3 LONGINUS (FIRST CENTURY A.D.)

Although his date of birth and national origin remain controversial, Longinus garners an important place in literary history for his treatise "On the Sublime." Probably a Greek, Longinus often peppers his Greek and Latin writings with Hebrew quotations, making him the first literary critic to borrow from a different literary tradition and earning him the title of the first comparative critic in literary history.

Unlike Plato, Aristotle, and Horace, who focus respectively on a work's essence, the constituent parts of a work, and literary taste, Longinus concentrates on single elements of a text, and he is the first critic to define a literary classic.

One cannot accurately judge a literary work, he argues, unless one is exceedingly well read. A well-read critic can evaluate and recognize what is great or what Homer calls sublime: Sublime bears a repeated examination, and which it is difficult to withstand, while sublime is itself great and the memory of it cannot be effaced. Homer asserts that all readers are innately capable of recognizing the sublime, for Nature has informed us to be no base or ignoble animals, and from which our soul is nourished with unconquerable elevated love more divine than we are. When our intellects, our emotions, and our wills harmoniously respond to a given work of art, we know we have been touched by the sublime.

Until the late seventeenth century, few people considered Longinus' *On the Sublime* was important or had even read it. By the eighteenth century, its significance was recognized, and it was quoted and debated by most public authors. Emphasizing the author, the work itself, and the reader's response, Longinus' critical method foreshadows New Criticism, reader-response, and other schools of twentieth-century criticism.

2.1.4 DANTE ALIGHIERI (1265—1321)

Born in Florence, Italy, during the Middle Ages, Dante is the only known significant contributor to literary criticism since Longinus and the appearance of his "On the Sublime" approximately 1000 years earlier. Like Longinus, Dante's concern is the proper language for poetry.

Banished from his native Florence for political reasons, Dante wrote many of his works in exile, including his masterpiece *The Divine Comedy*. As an introduction to the third and last section of this *Commedia*, the *Paradiso*, Dante wrote a letter to Can Grande della Scala explaining his literary theory. Known today as *Letter to Can Grande della Scala*, this work decrees that the language spoken by the people (the vulgar tongue or the vernacular) is an appropriate and beautiful language for writing.

Until the publication of Dante's works, Latin was the universal language, and all important works — such as histories, Church documents, and even government decrees — were written in this official Church tongue. Only frivolous or popular works appeared in the "vulgar" language of the common people. But in his *Letter*, Dante asserts and establishes that the vernacular is an excellent vehicle for works of literature.

In the Letter, Dante also notes that he uses multiple levels of interpretation or symbolic meaning in *The Divine Comedy*. Since the time of Augustine and throughout the Middle Ages, the church fathers had followed a tradition of allegoric reading of scripture that interpreted many of the Old Testament laws and stories as symbolic or allegories of Christ's actions. Such a semiotic interpretation — reading of signs — had been applied only to scripture. Until Dante's *Commedia* no secular work had used these principles of symbolic interpretation.

Praising the lyric poem and ignoring a discussion of genres, Dante established himself as the leading, if not the only, significant critic of the Middle Ages. Because he declared the common tongue is an acceptable vehicle of expression for literature, literary works found an ever-increasing audience.

2.1.5   SIR PHILIP SIRNEY (1554—1586)

The paucity of literary criticism and theory during the Middle Ages is more than made up for by the abundance of critical activity during the Renaissance. One critic of this period far excels all others: Sir Philip Sidney.

The representative scholar, writer, and gentleman of Renaissance England, Sidney is usually considered the first great English critic-poet. His *An Apology for Poetry* (sometimes called *Defence of Poesy*) is the definitive formulation of Renaissance literary theory and the first influential piece of literary criticism in England history. With Sidney begins the English tradition and history of literary criticism.

As evidenced in *An Apology for Poetry*, Sidney is eclectic, borrowing and often amending the theories of Plato, Aristotle, Horace, and a few of his contemporary Italian critics. He begins his criticism by quoting from Aristotle. In his opinion, poetry is an art of imitation, because Aristotle uses **mimesis**, which means a representing, counterfeiting, also perform the function to teach and delight. Like Aristotle, Sidney values poetry over history, law, and philosophy, but he takes Aristotle's idea one step further by declaring that poetry, above all the other arts and sciences, embodies truth.

Unlike his classical forefathers, Sidney best personifies the Renaissance period when he dictates his literary precepts. After ranking the different literary genres and declaring all to be instructive, he declares poetry to excel all. He mocks other genres (tragicomedy, for example) and adds more dictates to Aristotelian tragedy by insisting on unity of action, time, and place.

Throughout *An Apology for Poetry*, Sidney stalwartly defends poetry against those who view it as a mindless or immoral activity. At the essay's end, a passionate and somewhat platonically inspired poet places a curse on all those who do not love poetry. Echoes of such emotionality reverberate throughout the centuries in English literature, especially in British Romantic writings.

2.1.6   JOHN DRYDEN (1631—1700)

Poet laureate, dramatist, and critic John Dryden, more than any other any other English writer, embodies the spirit and ideals of Neoclassicism, the literary age that follows Sidney and the Renaissance. Dr. Samuel Johnson attributes the improvement to Dryden, who sticks to the principle of classicism of its completion of our meter, the refinement of our language, and much of the correctness of our sentiments. The most prolific writer of the Restoration, Dryden excelled in almost all genres. His lasting contribution to literary criticism, *An Essay of Dramatic Poesy*, highlights his genius in most of these genres.

The structure of Dryden's *An Essay of Dramatic Poesy* reflects his brilliance: During a naval battle between the English and the Dutch, four men are floating down a barge on the Thames River, each supporting a different aesthetic theory among those prominently espoused in Renaissance and Neoclassical literary criticism. The Platonic and Aristotelian debate concerning art's being an imitation of nature begins the discussion. Nature, argues one debater, must be imitated directly, whereas another declares that writers should imitate the classical authors such as Homer, for such ancient writers were the best imitators of nature. Through the voice of Neander, Dryden presents the benefits of both positions.

A lengthy discussion ensues over the Aristotelian concept of the three unities of time, place, and action within a drama. Should the plot of a drama take place during one 24-hour cycle (time)? And in one location (place)? Should it be only a single plot with no subplots (action)? The position that a drama must keep the three unities unquestionably wins the debate.

Other concerns center on:

· The language or diction of a play, with the concluding emphasis being placed on "proper" speech.

· Issues of decorum; that is, whether violent acts should appear on the stage, with the final speaker declaring it would be quite "improper".

· The differences between the English and French theaters, with the English drama winning out for its diversity, its use of the stage, and its Shakespearian tradition.

· The value of rhymed as opposed to blank verse in the drama, with rhymed verse being the victor — although Dryden later recanted this position and wrote many of his tragedies in blank verse.

2.1.7 ALEXANDER POPE (1688—1744)

Born into a Roman Catholic family in a Protestant-controlled England, born a healthy infant but quickly deformed and twisted in body by spinal tuberculosis, and born at the beginning of the Neoclassical Age and becoming its literary voice by age 20, Alexander Pope embodies in his writings eighteenth-century thought and literary criticism. His early poems such as *The Rape of the Lock*, *Eloisa to Abelard*, and *Pastorals* establish him as a major British poet, but with the publication of his Essay on Criticism, he becomes for all practical purposes the "literary pope" of England.

Unlike previous literary critics and theorists, Pope in this essay directly addresses the critic rather than the poet while simultaneously codifying Neoclassical literary theory and criticism. Toward the end of the essay, however, he does speak to both critics and poets.

According to Pope, the golden age of criticism is the classical age, the age of Homer, Aristotle, Horace, and Longinus. They are the writers who discovered the rules and laws of a harmonious and ordered nature. It is the critic and poet's task first to know and then to copy these authors and not nature, because to copy nature is to copy the classical authors.

Pope asserts that the chief requirement of a good poet is natural genius coupled with a knowledge of the classics and an understanding of the rules of poetry(literature). Such knowledge must be tempered with politeness and grace, for truth sometimes shows its superiority and this sense beloved only when it is well-cultivated.

Natural genius and good breeding being established, the critic/poet must then give heed to certain rules, says Pope. To be a good critic or poet, one must follow the established traditions as defined by the ancients. Not surprisingly, Pope spells out what these rules are and how they should be applied to eighteenth-century verse. Great concern for poetic diction, the establishment of the heroic couplet as a standard for verse, and the personification of abstract ideas, for example, became fixed standards, whereas emotional outbreaks and free verse were extraordinaire and considered unrefined.

Governed by rules, restraint, and good taste, poetry, as defined by Pope, seeks to reaffirm truths or absolutes already discovered by the classical writers. The critic's task is clear: To validate and maintain classical values in the ever-shifting winds of cultural change. In effect, the critic becomes the custodian and defender of good taste and cultural values.

By affirming the imitation of the classical writers and through them of nature itself, and by establishing the acceptable or standard criteria of poetic language, Pope grounds his criticism in both the mimetic (imitation) and rhetoric (patterns structure) literary theories. By the end of the 1700s, however, a major shift in literary theory occurs.

2.2 ROMANTIC CIRITICSM

2.2.1 WILLIAM WORDSWORTH (1770—1850)

By the close of the eighteenth century, the world had witnessed several major political rebellions — among them the American and French revolutions — along with exceptional social upheavals and prominent changes in Philosophical thought. During this age of rebellion, a paradigmatic shift occurred in how people viewed their world. Whereas the eighteenth-century valued order and reason, the emerging nineteenth-century worldview emphasized intuition as a proper guide to truth. The eighteenth-century mind likened the world to a great machine with all its parts operating harmoniously, but to the nineteenth-century perception the world was a living organism that was always growing and eternally becoming. Whereas the city housed the centers of art and literature and set the standards of good taste for the rationalistic mind of the eighteenth century, the emerging nineteenth-century citizen saw a rural setting as a place where people could discover their inner selves. Devaluing the empirical and rationalistic methodologies of the previous century, the nineteenth-century thinker believed that truth could be attained by tapping into the core of our humanity or our transcendental natures.

Such radical changes found their spokesperson in William Wordsworth. Born in Cockermouth, Cunberlandshire, and raised in the Lake District of England, Wordsworth completed his formal education at St. John's College, Cambridge, in 1791. After completing his grand tour of the Continent, he published Descriptive Sketches and then met one of his literary admirers and soon-to-be friends and coauthors, Samuel T. Coleridge. In 1798 Wordsworth and Coleridge published *Lyrical Ballads*, a collection of poems that heralded the beginning of British romanticism. In the ensuing 15-year period, Wordsworth wrote most of his best poetries, including *Poems in Two Volumes*, *The Excursion*, *Miscellaneous Poems*, and *The Prelude*. But it is *Lyrical Ballads* that ushers in the Romantic age in English literature.

In an explanatory Preface written as an introduction to the second edition of *Lyrical Ballads*, Wordsworth espouses a new vision of poetry and the beginnings of a radical change in literary theory. His purpose is to choose incidents and situations from common life, and describe them in language really used by common people, even commonplace can bring excitement of creation because they are true and loyal to life. Like Aristotle, Sidney, and Pope, Wordsworth concerns himself with the elements and subject matter of literature, but changes the emphasis: Common men and women people in his poetry, not kings, queens, and aristocrats, for in humble and rustic life the poet finds that the rustic life is so natural and real that it can make people attain self-cultivation and promote its maturity. The essential nature of heart can be less restrained, when the poet speak in a more plainer and emphatic language.

Not only does Wordsworth suggest a radical change in subject matter, but he also dramatically shifts focus concerning poetry's "proper language." Unlike Pope and his predecessors, Wordsworth chooses daily language people used — everyday speech, not the inflated poetic diction of heroic couplets, complicated rhyme schemes, and convoluted figures of speech placed in the mouths of the typical eighteenth-century character. Wordsworth's rustics, such as Michael and Luke in his poetic narrative "Michael", speak in the simple, everyday diction of their trade.

In addition to reshaping the focus of poetry's subject and language, Wordsworth redefines poetry itself: "For all good poetry is the spontaneous overflow of powerful feelings."[1] Unlike Sidney, Dante, and Pope, who decree that poetry should be restrained, controlled, and reasoned, Wordsworth now highlights poetry's emotional quality. Imagination, not reason or disciplined thought, becomes its core.

After altering poetry's subject matter, language, and definition, Wordsworth redefines the role of the poet. The poet is no longer the preserver of civilized values or proper taste, but "he is a man speaking to men: a man...endowed with more lively sensibility, more enthusiasm and tenderness, who has a greater knowledge of human nature and a more comprehensive soul than are supposed to be common among mankind." And this poet "has acquired a greater readiness and power in expressing what he thinks and feels, and especially those thoughts and feelings which, by his own choice, or from the structure of his own mind, arise in him without immediate external excitement."[2] Such a poet need no longer follow a prescribed set of rules, for this artist may freely express his or her own individualism, valuing and writing about feelings that are peculiarly the artist's.

Because Wordsworth defines poetry as the spontaneous overflow of powerful feelings, and displayed by the poet's emotion recollected in tranquility. His new kind of poet crafts a poem by internalizing a scene, circumstance, or happening and "recollects" that occasion with its

---

[1] WORDSWORTH W, TAYLOR S. Lyrical Ballads[M]. Penguin Classics, 1999-1.

[2] WORDSWORTH W, TAYLOR S. Lyrical Ballads[M]. Penguin Classics, 1999-1.

accompanying emotions at a later time when the artist can shape that remembrance into words. Poetry, then, is unlike biology or one of the other sciences, for it deals not with something that can be dissected or broken down into its constituent parts, but primarily with the imagination and feelings, intuition, not reason, reigns.

But what of the reader? What part does the audience play in such a process? Toward the end of the *Preface*, Wordsworth writes, "I have one request to make of my reader which is, that in judging these poems he would decide by his own feelings genuinely, and not by reflection upon what will probably be the judgment of others,"[①] Wordsworth apparently hopes that his readers' responses and opinions of his poems will not depend on critics who freely dispense their evaluations. Wordsworth wants his readers to rely on their own feelings and their own imaginations as they grapple with the same emotions the poet felt when he first saw and then later "recollected in tranquility" the subject or circumstances of the poem itself. Through poetry, declares Wordsworth, the poet and the reader share such emotions.

This subjective experience of sharing emotions leads Wordsworth away from the preceding centuries' mimetic and rhetorical theories of criticism and toward a new development in literary theory: The expressive school, which emphasizes the individuality of the artist and the reader's privilege to share in this individuality. By expressing such individuality and valuing the emotions and the imagination as legitimate concerns in poetry, Wordsworth lays the foundation for English romanticism and broadens the scope of literary criticism and theory for both the nineteenth and twentieth centuries.

2.2.2 HIPPOLYTE ADOLPHE TAINE(1828—1893)

Wordsworth's romanticism, with its stress on intuition as a guide to learning ultimate truth and its belief that emotions and the imagination from the core of poetry's content, dominated literature and literary criticism throughout the first three decades of the nineteenth century, and its influence still continues today. With the rise of the Victorian era in the 1830s, reason, science, and a sense of historical determinism began to supplant romantic thought. The growing sense of historical and scientific determinism finally found its authoritative voice and culminating influence, in literary criticism and many other disciplines, in Charles Darwin and his text *The Origin of Species*, published in 1859. Humankind was now demystified, for we finally knew our

---

① WORDSWORTH W, TAYLOR S. Lyrical Ballads[M]. Penguin Classics, 1999-1.

origins and understood our physiological development; science, it seemed, had provided us with the key to our past and an understanding of the present, and would help us determine our future if we relied on the scientific method in all our human endeavors.

Science's methodology, its philosophical assumptions, and its practical applications found an admiring adherent and a strong voice in French historian and literary critic Hippolyte Taine. Born in Vouziers, France, Hippolyte Taine was a brilliant but unorthodox student at the Ecole Normale Superieure in Paris. After finishing his formal education, he taught in various schools throughout France, continuing his investigations in both aesthetics and history. During the 1850s, he published various philosophical and aesthetic treatises, but his chief contribution to literary criticism and history is *The History of English Literature*, published in 1863. In this work, Taine crystallizes what is now known as the historical approach to literary analysis.

In the introduction to *The History of English Literature*, Taine uses a scientific simile to explain his approach to literary criticism:

What is your first remark on turning over the great, stiff leaves of a folio, the yellow sheets of a manuscript, — a poem, a code of laws, a declaration of faith? This, you say was not created alone. It is but a mould, like fossil shell, an imprint, like one of those shapes embossed in stone by an animal which lived and perished. Under the shell there was an animal, and behind the document there was a man. Why do you study the shell, except to represent to yourself the animal? So do you study the document only in order to know the man.

For Taine, then, a text is like a fossil shell that naturally contains the likeness of its inhabiter, who in this case is the author. To study only the text (discovering its date of composition or the accuracy of its historical references or allusions, for example) without considering the author and his or her inner psyche would therefore result in an incomplete analysis. An investigation of both the text and the author, Taine believed, would result in an accurate understanding of the literary work.

To understand any literary text, Taine asserts that we must examine the environmental causes that joined together in its creation. He divides such influence into three main categories: race, milieu, and moment. By race, Taine posits that author of the same race inherited and learned person characteristics, Taine believes we will then be able to understand more fully the author's text. In addition, we must also examine the author's milieu or surroundings. English citizens, he believed, respond differently to life than do French or Irish citizens. Accordingly, by examining the culture of the author, Taine asserts that we would understand more fully the intellectual and cultural concerns that inevitably surface in an author's text. And lastly, Taine maintains that we must investigate an author's epoch or moment — that is, the time period in which the text was written. Such information reveals the dominant ideas, or worldviews held by people at that particular time and therefore helps us identify and understand the characters' actions, motivations, and concerns more fully than if we did not have such information.

Ultimately, for Taine the text becomes a literary object that can be dissected to discover its meaning. By examining the actual text itself, the circumstances of place and race, and the historical times in which the text was written, we will realize, Taine asserts, that no text is written in a vacuum, but is instead the result of its history.[①]

2.2.3　MATTHEW ARNOLD (1822—1888)

In the "Preface to Lyrical Ballads," Wordsworth asserts that "poetry is the breath and finer spirit of all knowledge; it is the impassioned expression which is the countenance of all science."[②] Such a lofty statement concerning the nature and role of poetry finds an advocate in Matthew Arnold, the self-appointed voice for English Victorianism, the literary epoch immediately following Wordsworth's romanticism.

Born during the Romantic era, Matthew Arnold was the son of an English educator. Following in his family's tradition, Arnold attended Oxford, and upon graduation accepted a teaching position at Oriel College. He spent most of his professional life (nearly 35 years) as an inspector of schools. By age 35 he had already written the majority of his poetry, including *Dover Beach*, *The Scholar-Gipsy*, and *Sohrab and Rustum*, some of his most famous works.

During Arnold's early career, reactions against Wordsworth's romanticism and its adherents began to occur. Writers, philosophers, and scientists began to give more credence to empirical and rationalistic methods for discovering the nature of their world than to the Wordsworthian concepts of emotion, individualism, and intuition as pathways to truth. With the publication of Charles Darwin's *The Origin of Species* in 1859 and the writings of Herbert Spencer and philosopher David Friedrich Strauss, science seemingly usurped the place of Wordsworth's religion of nature and the beliefs of most other traditional religions, while philosophy became too esoteric

---

① TAINE H. History of English Literature (II) [M]. LAUN H, trans. New York: Gebbie Publishing, 1863-33.
② WORDSWORTH W, TAYLOR S. Lyrical Ballads[M]. New York: Penguin Classics, 1999-2.

and therefore less relevant as a vehicle for understanding reality for the average Victorian. Into this void stepped Arnold, proclaiming that poetry can provide the necessary truths, values, and guidelines for society.

Fundamental to Arnold's literary theory and criticism is his reapplication of classical criteria to literature. Quotes and borrowed ideas from Plato, Aristotle, Longinus, and other classical writers pepper his criticism. From Aristotle's *Poetics*, for example, Arnold adapts his idea that the best poetry is of a "higher truth and seriousness" than history, or any other human subject or activity, for that matter. Like Plato, Arnold believes that literature reflects the society in which it is written and thereby heralds its values and concerns. Like Longinus, he attempts to define a classic and decrees that such a work belongs to the "highest" or "best class." And in attempting to support many of his other ideas, he also cites the later "classical" writers such as Dante, Shakespeare, and Milton.

For Arnold, poetry — not religion, science, or philosophy — is humankind's crowning activity. In his opinion, he believes more and more people will discover mankind need to turn to poetry to interpret life for themselves, for poetry is human's spiritual origin. National spirit deeply rooted in the fertile soil of a harmonious culture, culture is the carrier of the spirit as well as the origins of civilization of which poetry is the main constitutes. Without poetry, our world will show its incompleteness; and other disciplines, such as science, philosophy will be replaced by poetry. And in the best of this poetry, he declares, we find "in the eminent degree, truth and seriousness."[1] Arnold equating "seriousness" with moral excellence, Arnold asserts that the best poetry can and does provide standards of excellence, a yardstick by which both Arnold and his society should judge themselves.

In his pivotal essays *The Study of Poetry* and *The Function of Criticism at the Present Time*, Arnold crystallizes his critical position. Like Plato's critic, Arnold reaffirms but slightly amends the social role of criticism: creating " a current of true and fresh ideas."[2] To accomplish this goal, the critic must avoid becoming embroiled in politics or any other activity that would lead to a form of bias, for the critic must view society disinterestedly, keeping aloof from the world's mundane affairs. In turn, such aloofness will benefit all of society, for the critic will be able to pave the way for high culture — a prerequisite for the poet and the writing of the best poetry.

---

[1] TAINE. History of English Literature Hippolyte[EB/OL.] [2018-03-10].https://www.taodocs.com/p-35822582.html.

[2] TAINE. History of English Literature Hippolyte[EB/OL.] [2018-03-10].https://www.taodocs.com/p-35822582.html.

But how may the best poetry be achieved or discovered? By establishing objective criteria whereby we can judge whether any poem contains or achieves, in Aristotelian terms, "higher truth or seriousness." The critic's task is "to have always in one's mind lines and expressions of the great masters, and to apply them as a touchstone to other poetry." By comparing the newly written lines to classical poems that contain elements of the "sublime," the critic will instantly know whether a new poem is good or bad.

In practice, such apparent objectivity in criticism becomes quite subjective. Whose judgments, for example, shall we follow? Shall lines written by Homer and Dante be considered excellent? How about Sidney's or even Aristophanes'? Need the critic rank all past poets in an attempt to discover who is great and who is not in order to create a basis for such comparisons and value judgments? And whose moral values shall become the yardstick whereby we judge poetry? Arnold's only?

Such "objective" touchstone theory redefines the task of the literary critic and introduces a subjective approach in literary criticism. No longer the interpreter of a literary work, the critic, now functions as an authority on values, culture, and tastes. This new literary watchdog must guard and defend high culture and its literature while simultaneously defining what high culture and literature really are.

Decreeing the critic to be the preserver of society's values and poetry to be its most important activity, Arnold became the recognized spokesperson for Victorian England and its literature. By taking Wordsworth's concept of the poet one step further, Arnold separated both the critic and the poet from society in order to create a type of poetry and criticism that could supposedly rescue society from its baser elements and preserve its most noble characteristics.

2.2.4　HENRY JAMES (1843—1916)

While Arnold was decreeing how poetry would rescue humanity from its baser elements and would help lead us all to truth, literary works were also being written in other genres, particularly the novel. Throughout both the Romantic and Victorian eras, for example, people in England and America were reading such works as *Wuthering Heights*, *Vanity Fair*, *The House of the Seven Gables*, and *Great Expectations*, However, few were providing for either the writers or the readers of this genre a body of theory or criticism as was being formulated for poetry. As Henry James notes in his critical essay "The Art of Fiction" in 1884, the English novel "had no air of having a theory, a conviction, a consciousness of itself behind it — of being the expression of an artistic faith, the result of choice and comparison."[1] It was left to James himself to provide us with such a theory.

Born in New York City in 1843, Henry James enjoyed the privileges of education, travel, and money. Throughout his early life, he and his family (including his brother William, the father of American pragmatic philosophy) traveled to the capitals Europe, visiting the sites and meeting the leading writers and scholars of the day. Having all things European injected into his early life and thoughts, James believed he wanted to be a lawyer and enrolled in Harvard Law School. He quickly discovered that writing, not law, captivated him and abandoned law school for a career in writing. By 1875, the early call of Europe on his life had to be answered, and James, a bachelor for life, settled permanently in Europe and began in earnest his writing career.

Noted for his short stories — *The Real Thing, The Beast in the Jungle,* and *The jolly Corner,* to name a few — and his novels — *The American, The Portrait of a Lady, The Bostonians,* and *The Turn of the Screw, among others* — *James's favorite theme is the conflict he perceives* between Europe and America. The seasoned aristocracy with its refined manners and taste is often infiltrated in his stories by the naive American, who seemingly lacks refined culture and discernment. In addition to being a practicing writer, James is also concern with developing a theory of writing, particularly for the novel. And in his critical essay "The Art of Fiction" he provides us with the first well-articulated theory of the novel in English literature.

In *The Art of Fiction,* James states that "a novel is in its broadest definition — a personal, a direct impression of life: that, to begin with, constitutes its value, which is greater or less according to the intensity of the impression"; furthermore, "the only obligation to which in advance we may hold a novel, without incurring the accusation of being arbitrary, is that it be interesting. The ways in which it is at liberty to accomplish this result are innumerable."[2] From the start, James's theory rejects the romantic notion of either Wordsworth or Coleridge that the reader suspends disbelief while reading a text. For James, a text must first be realistic, a representation of life as it is and one that is recognizable to its readers. Bad novels, declares James, are either romantic or scientific; good novels show us life in action and, above all else, are interesting.

---

① JAMES H. The Art of Fiction[EB/OL]. [2018-03-10]. https://www.exampleessays.com/viewpaper/13731.html.
② JAMES H. The Art of Fiction[EB/OL]. [2018-03-10]. https://www.exampleessays.com/viewpaper/13731.html.

Bad novels, James continues, are written by bad authors, whereas good novels are written by good authors. Unlike weak authors, good writers are good thinkers who can select, evaluate, and imaginatively use the "stuff of life" (the facts or pictures of reality) in their work. These writers also recognize that a work of art is organic, the work itself is not simply the amassing of realistic data from real-life experiences, but has a life of its own that grows according to its own principles or themes. The writer must acknowledge this fact and distance himself or herself from directly telling the story. Shunning the omniscient narrator as the technical narrative point of view for relating the story, James asserts that a more indirect point of view is essential so that the author shows characters, actions, and emotions to the reader rather than telling us about them. By showing rather than telling us about his characters and their actions, James believes that he creates a greater illusion of reality than if he presents his story through one point of view or one character. Ultimately, however, the reader must decide the worth of the text, and nothing will ever take the place of the good old fashion 'liking of ' a work of art or not liking it: the most improved criticism will not abolish that primitive and ultimate test.

Thanks to Henry James, the genre of the novel became a respectable topic for literary critics. With his emphasis on realism and "the stuff of life", James formulated a theory of fiction that is still discussed and debated today.

2.3 MODERN LITERARY CRITICISM

Matthew Arnold's death in 1888 (and to a lesser degree Henry James's death in 1916) marks a transitional period in literary criticism. Like Dryden, Pope, and Wordsworth before him, Arnold was the recognized authority and leading literary critic of his day, and it is his theories and criticism that embody the major ideas of his era. With the passing of Arnold ends the predominance of any one person or set of ideas representing a broad time period or literary movement. After Arnold, literary theory and criticism became splintered and more diversified, with no one voice speaking ex cathedra or no one theory tenaciously held by all. At the end of the nineteenth century, most critics emphasized either a biographical or historical approach to the text. Using Taine's historical interests in a text and Henry James's newly articulated theory of the novel, many critics investigated a text as if it were the embodiment of its author or a historical artifact. No single, universally recognized voice dominates literary theory in the years that follow Arnold or James. Instead, many distinctive literary voices give rise to a host of differing and exciting ways to examine a text.

What follows in the twentieth century is a variety of schools of criticism, with each school asking legitimate, relevant, but different questions concerning a text. Most of these schools abandon the holistic approach to literary study, which investigates, analyzes, and interprets all elements of the artistic situation, in favor of concentrating on one or more specific aspects. For example, modernism (and in particular the New Criticism, the first critical movement of the twentieth century), wishes to break from the past and seemingly disavow the cultural influences on a work of literature. The text, these critics declare, will interpret the text. On the other hand, New Historicism, one of the newest schools of thought to appear, argues that most critics' historical consciousness must be reawakened, for in reality the fictional text and its historical and cultural milieu are amazingly similar. For these critics, a reader can never fully discern the truth about a historical or a literary text; for truth itself is perceived differently from one era to another. The text-only criticism of the early twentieth and mid-century therefore appears biased and incomplete to these New Historians.

In the remaining chapters of this book, we will examine eleven of the most prominent schools of twentieth-century interpretation. For each of these diverse schools we will note the tenets of their philosophy that underlie their literary theory. Most, if not all, have borrowed ideas, principles, and concerns from the literary critics and theories already discussed. We will examine closely what they borrow from these past schools of criticism, what they amend, and what concepts they add. We will also note each school's historical development, examining, how new schools of criticism often appear as a reaction to previously existing ones.

After explaining each school's historical development, its working assumptions, and its methodology, we will then examine both a student-written and a professional essay that interprets a text from the point of view of that particular school of criticism under discussion. A close examination of such essays will allow us to see how the theories of the various schools of criticism can be applied directly to a text while simultaneously highlighting the various emphases of each critical school.

By becoming acquainted with the various schools of criticism, we can begin to examine our own theory of interpretation and to articulate our own principles of criticism. We will then come to realize that there is no such thing as an innocent reading of a text, for all readings presupposed either a conscious or unconscious, articulated and well-informed, or piecemeal and uninformed reading of a literary work. An informed and intelligent reading is the better option.

REFERENCES

[1]A C BRADLEY. Oxford Lectures on Poetry[M]. London: Macmillan, 1909.

[2]A E TAYLOR. Plato[M]. Ann Arbor: U of Michigan Press, 1960.

[3]ALLEN G W. Literary Satire and Theory: A Study of Horace, Boileau, and Pope[M]. New York: Garland, 1985.

[4]ARISTOTLE. Poetics[M]. INGRAM B, Trans. Oxford: Clarendon, 1920.

[5]ARISTOTLE. Poetics[M]. Trans. LEON G. Englewood Cliffs: Prentice-Hall, 1968.

[6]ARTHUR F. The Unity of Pope's Essay on Criticism[J]. Philological Quarterly 1960:435-56.

[7]AUSTIN W. English Poetic Thenjo 1825-1865[M]. Princeton: Princeton University Press, 1950.

[8]AUSTIN W. Alexander Pope as Critic and Humanist[M]. Princeton: Princeton University Press, 1929.

[9]BATE W J. From Classic to Romantic[M]. Cambridge: Harvard University Press, 1946.

[10]CAROLINE G. Horace in the English Literature of the Eighteenth Century[M]. New Haven: Yale University Press 1918.

[11]C D THORPE. Coleridge as Aesthetician and Critic[J]. Journal of the History of Ideas 1944: 387-414.

[12]CHARLES S S. Dante Studies[M]. 2 vols. Cambridge: Harvard University Press, 1958.

[13]DANTE A. Eleven Letters[M]. Trans. CHARLES S L. Boston: Houghton, 1892.

[14]DANTE A. The Divine Comedy[M]. Princeton: Princeton University Press 1975.

[15]D A RUSSELL, ed. "Longinus" on the Sublime[M]. Oxford: Clarendon, 1964.

[16]DAVID P. Arnold and the Function of Literature[J]. ELH 18 (1951): 287-309.

[17]DEATHCOTE W G. Poetry and the Criticism of Life[M]. New York: Russell, 1963.

[18]DEBORAH M. Aristotle: The Power of Perception[J]. Chicago: University of Chicago Press, 1987.

[19]DUSTIN G. Alexander Pope: The Poet in the Poems[M]. Princeton: Princeton University Press, 1978.

[20]E D HIRSCH. Wordsworth al Schelling[M]. New Haven: Yale University Press, 1950.

[21]ELDER O. Aristotle's Poetics and English Literature[M]. Chicago: of Chicago Press 1965.

[22]ELDER O. The Argument of Longinus's On the Sublime[J]. On Value Judgments in the Arts and Other Essays. Chicago: University of Chicago Press, 1976.

[23]E PECHTER. Dryden's Classical Theory of Literature[M]. London: Cambridge University Press, 1975.

[24]ERICH A. Dante: Poet of the Secular World[M]. Trans. R. MANHEIM. Chicago: Chicago University Press, 1961.

[25]FOREST G R. The Shape of Things Known: Sidney's Apology in Its Philosophical Tradition[M]. Cambridge: Harvard University Press, 1972.

[26]FRANCIS F. On the Poetics[J]. Tulane Drama Review 4 (1960): 23-32.

[27]FRANK S. Pope and Horace: Studies in Imitation[M]. New York: Cambridge University Press, 1985.

[28]GEORGE W. John Dryden: Of Dramatic Poesy and Other Critical Essays[M]. 2 vols. London: J. Dent, 1962.

[29]GERALD F E. Aristotle's Poetics: The Argument[M]. Cambridge: Harvard University Press, 1957.

[30]GERALD F E.Plato and Aristotle on Poetry[M]. Chapel Hill: University of North Carolina Press, 1986.

[31]G M GRUBE. Plato's Thought[M]. London: Methuen, 1935.

[32]H A MASON. An Introduction to Literary Criticism by Way of Sidney's Apology for Poetrie[J]. Cambridge Quarterly 12. 2-3(1984): 79-173.

[33]HENRY J. The Art of the Novel: Critical Prefaces[M]. New York: Scribner, 1932.

[34]HENRY J J. The Egotistical Sublime: A History of Wordstworth's Imagination[M]. London: Chatto & Windus, 1970.

[35]HERBERT L H. Theory and Practice in Henry James[M]. Ann Arbor: Edwards, 1926.

[36]HIPPOLYTE A T. The History of English Literature[M]. 4 vols. Trans. H V LAUN. Philadelphia: David McKay, 1908.

[37]JAMES A D. The Meaning of Delight in Sidney's Defense of Poesy[J]. Studies in the Literary Imagination 15(1982):85-97.

[38]J B MISHRA. John Dryden: His Theory and Practice of Drama[M]. New Delhi: Bahir, 1978.

[39]J F D'ALTON. Horace and His Age[M]. London: Longman Green, 1917.

[40]JOHN C. The Language of Criticism[M]. London: Methuen, 1960.

[41]JOHN C, LOVELL E J. English Romanticism: The Grounds of Belief[M]. London: Macmillan, 1983.

[42]JOHN S E. The Touchstones of Matthew Arnold[M]. New York: Bookman Associates, 1955.

[43]JOHN S H, ed. The Romantic Imagination: A Casebook[M]. London: Macmillan, 1977.

[44]JULES B. Boileau and Longinus[M]. Geneva: Droz, 1953.

[45]LANE C. The Poetics of Aristotle: Its Meaning and Influence[M]. New York: Cooper Square, 1963.

[46]LIONEL T. Matthew Arnold[M]. New York: Norton, 1939.

[47]L S Sharma. Coleridge: His Contribution to English Criticism[M]. New Delhi: Arnold-Heinemann, 1981.

[48]MARVIN T H. The Fusion of Horatian and Aristotelian Literary Criticism[M].Urbana: University of Illinois Press, 1946.

[49]MATTHEW A. Essays in Criticism: First Series[M]. New York: Macmillan, 1895.

[50]MORRIS R. Henry James's Criticism[M]. Cambridge: Harvard University Press, 1929.

[51]NOWELL C S, ed. Wordsworth's Literary Criticism[M]. Bristol: Bristol Classical Press,1980.

[52]PAUL H. Coleridge's Poetics[M]. Oxford: Blackwell, 1983.

[53]PAUL S. Witt Plato Said[M]. Chicago: University of Chicago Press, 1933.

[54]PHILIP R. Classical Theories of Allegory and Christian Culture[M]. Pittsburgh: Duquesne University Press, 1981.

[55]PLATO. The Republic[M]. Tans. B. Jowett. Oxford, UK: Clarendon, 1888.

[56]R HOLLANDER. Allegory in Dante's Commedia[M]. Princeton: Princeton University Press, 1969.

[57]ROBERT D H. Dryden's Criticism[M]. Ithaca: Cornell University Press, 1970.

[58]RUPERT C L. Plato's Theory of Art[M]. New York: Humanities Press, 1953.

[59]SANDI B D. The Literary Criticism of Henry James[M]. Athens: Ohio University Press, 1981.

[60]S H BUTCHER. Aristotle's Theory of Poetry and Fine Art[M]. London: Macmillan,1902.

[61]S MONK. The Sublime: A Study of Critical Theories in XVIII-Century England[M]. Ann Arbor: University of Michigan Press, 1960.

[62]SUSAN S L. The Narrative Act: Point of View in Prose Fiction[M]. Princeton: Princeton University Press, 1981.

[63]T R HENN. Longinus and English Criticism[M]. Cambridge: Cambridge University Press, 1934.

[64]T S ELIOT. John Dryden: The Poet, the Dramatist, the Critic Three Essays[M]. New York: Haskell House, 1966.

[65]W. J. BOWEN. Wordsworth as Critic[M]. Toronto: Toronto University Press, 1971.

PART II   SCHOOLS OF LITERATRY CRITICISM

CHAPTER III   NEW CRITICISM

3.1   INTRODUCTION

Stopping by Woods on a Snowy Evening

Whose woods these are I think I know,

His house is in the village though.

He will not see me stopping here,

To watch his woods fill up with snow.

My little horse must think it queer,

To stop without a farmhouse near,

Between the woods and frozen lake,

The darkest evening of the year.

He gives his harness bells a shake,

To ask if there is some mistake.

The only other sound's the sweep,

Of easy wind and downy flake.

The woods are lovely, dark and deep.

But I have promises to keep,

And miles to go before I sleep.

And miles to go before I sleep

— Robert Frost

If John Frost's poem *Stopping by Woods on a Snowy Evening* were to be taught in most high school or introductory level college English courses, the instructor would probably begin the discussion with a set of questions that contain most, if not all, of the following: What is the meaning of the title? What is the title's relationship to the rest of the poem? Who is the he in stanza 3? What is darkest? What does the word "woods" refer to ? Are there other words in the text that need to be defined? What words connote sharpness? How are these words related to the woods discussed in the poem? Is Frost discussing any particular woods, Can this word be an allusion to some other woods in the canon of Western literature? Is frost establishing any other relationships between words or concepts in the text? What of the poem's physical structure? Does the arrangement of the words, phrases, or sentences help establish relationships among them? What is the poem's tone? How do you know this is the tone? What tensions does the poet create in the poem? What ambiguities? Based on the answers to these questions, what does the poem mean? In other words, what is the poem's form or its overall meaning and interpretation?

Upon close examination of these discussion questions, a distinct pattern or methodology quickly becomes evident. This interpretive model begins with a close analysis of the poem's individual words, including both denotative and connotative meanings, and then moves to a discussion of possible allusions within the text. Following this discussion, the critic searches for any patterns developed through individual words, phrases, sentences, figures of speech, and allusions. The critic's sharp eye also notes any symbols, either public or private, used by the poet. Other elements for analysis include point of view, tone, and any other poetic device that will help the reader understand the dramatic situation. After ascertaining how all the above information interrelates and coalesces in the poem, the critic can then declare what the poem means. The poem's overall meaning or form, then, depends solely on the text in front of the reader. No library research, no studying of the author's life and times, and no other extraneous information is needed, for the poem itself contains all the necessary information to discover its meaning.

This method of analysis became the dominant school of thought during the first two thirds of the twentieth century in most high school and college literature classes, English departments, and English and American scholarship. Known as New Criticism, this approach to literary analysis provides the reader with a formula for arriving at the correct interpretation of a text using only the text itself. Such a formulaic approach gives both the beginning student of literature and academicians a seemingly objective approach for discovering a text's meaning. Using New Criticism's clearly articulated methodology, any intelligent reader, say the New Critics, can uncover a text's hitherto hidden meaning.

New Criticism's theoretical ideas, terminology, and critical methods are, more often than not, disparaged by present-day critics, who themselves are introducing new ideas concerning literary theory. Despite its current unpopularity, New Criticism stands as one of the most important English-speaking contributions to literary critical analysis. Its easily repeatable principles, teachability, and seemingly undying popularity in the English classroom and in some scholarly English journals have enabled New Criticism to enrich theoretical and practical criticism while helping generations of readers to become close readers of texts.

The name New Criticism came into popular use to describe this approach to understanding literature with the 1941 publication of John Crowe Ransom's *The New Criticism*, which contained Ransom's personal analysis of several of his contemporary theorists and critics. Ransom himself was a Southern poet, a critic, and one of the leading advocates of this evolving movement. While teaching at Vanderbilt University in the 1920s, along with several other professors and students, Ransom formed the Fugitives, a group that believed and practiced similar interpretative approaches to a text. Other sympathetic groups, such as the Southern Agrarians at Nashville, soon formed. In The New Criticism Ransom articulates the principles of these various groups and calls for an ontological critic, one who will recognize that poem (used as synonym in New Criticism for any literary work) is a concrete entity like Leonardo da Vinci's *Mona Lisa* or the score of Handel's *Messiah* or even any chemical element such as iron or gold. Like these concrete objects, a poem can be analyzed to discover its true or correct meaning independent of its author's intention, or the emotional state, or the values and beliefs of either its author or reader. Because this belief rests at the center of this movement's critical ideas, it is not surprising, then, that the title of Ransom's book quickly became the official calling card for this approach to literary analysis.

Called modernism, formalism, aesthetic criticism, textual criticism, or ontological criticism throughout its long and successful history, New Criticism does not represent a coherent body of critical theory and methodology espoused by all its followers. At best, New Criticism and its adherents (called New Critics) are an eclectic group, each challenging, borrowing, and changing terminology, theory, and practices from one another while asserting a common core of basic ideas. Their ultimate unity stems from their opposition to the prevailing methods of literary analysis found in academia in the first part of the twentieth century.

3.2　HISTORICAL DEVELOPMENT

At the beginning of the twentieth century (often dubbed the start of the modernist period, or modernism), historical and biographical research dominated scholarship. Criticism's function, many believed, was to discover the historical context of the text and to ascertain how the authors' lives influenced their writings. Such extrinsic analysis (examining elements outside the text to uncover the text's meaning) became the norm in the English departments of many American universities and colleges. Other forms of criticism and interpretation were often intermingled with this emphasis on history and biography. For example, some critics believed we should appreciate the text for its beauty. For these impressionistic critics, how we feel and what we personally see in a work of art are what really matters. Others were more philosophical, arguing a naturalistic view of life that emphasizes the importance of scientific thought in literary analysis. For advocates of naturalism, human beings are simply animals who are caught in a world that operates on definable scientific principles and who respond somewhat instinctively to their environment and internal drives. Still other critics, the New Humanists, valued the moral qualities of art. Declaring that human experience is basically ethical, these critics demanded that literary analysis be based on the moral values exhibited in a text. Finally, remnants of nineteenth-century romanticism asserted themselves. For the romantic scholar, literary study concerns itself with the artists' feelings and attitudes exhibited in their works. Known as the expressive school, this romantic view values the individual artist's experiences as evidenced in the text.

Along with impressionism, the new humanism, and naturalism, this romantic view of life and art was rejected by the New Critics. In declaring the objective existence of the poem, the New Critics assert that only the poem itself can be objectively evaluated, not the feelings, attitudes, values, and beliefs of the author and the reader. Because they concern themselves primarily with an examination of the work itself and not its historical context or biographical elements, the New Critics belong to a broad classification of literary criticism called formalism. Being formalists, the

New Critics espouse what many call "the text and text alone" approach to literary analysis.

Such an approach to textual criticism automatically leads to many divergent views concerning the elements that constitute what the New Critics call the poem. Because many of the practitioners of this formalistic criticism disagree with each other concerning the various elements that make up the poem and hold differing approaches to textual analysis, it is difficult to cite a definitive list of critics who consider themselves New Critics. However, we can group together critics who hold some of the same New Critical assumptions concerning poetic analysis. Among this group are John Crowe Ransom, Rene Wellek, W. K. Wimsatt, R.P. Blackmur, I. A. Richards, Robert Penn Warren, and Cleanth Brooks. Thanks to the publication of the 1938 college text *Understanding Poetry* by Brooks and Warren, New Criticism emerged in American universities as the leading form of textual analysis throughout the late 1930s until the early 1960s.

Although New Criticism emerged as a powerful force in the 1940s, its roots stem back to the early 1900s. Two British critics and authors, T. S. Eliot and I. A. Richards, helped lay the foundation for this form of formalistic analysis. From Eliot, New Criticism borrows its insistence that criticism be directed toward the poem, not the poet. The poet, declares Eliot, does not infuse the poem with his or her personality and emotions, but uses language in such a way as to incorporate within the poem the impersonal feelings and emotions common to all humankind. Poetry is not, then, the feeling of the poet's emotions, but an escape from them. Because the poem is the impersonal formulation of common feelings and emotions, the successful poem unites the poet's impressions and ideas with those common to all humanity, producing a text that is not a mere reflection of the poet's personal feelings.

The New Critics also borrow Eliot's belief that the reader of poetry must be instructed concerning literary technique. A good reader perceives the poem structurally, maintains Eliot, resulting in good criticism. Such a reader must necessarily be trained in good poetry (especially the poetry of the Elizabethans, John Donne, and other metaphysical poets) and be well acquainted with established poetic traditions. A poor reader, on the other hand, simply expresses his or her personal reactions and emotions concerning a text. Such a reader is untrained in literary technique and craft. Following Eliot's lead, the New Critics declare that there are both good and bad readers, and good and bad criticism. A poor reader and poor criticism, for example, may argue that a poem can mean anything its reader or its author wishes it to mean. On the other hand, a good critic and good criticism would assert that only through a detailed structural analysis of a poem can the correct interpretation arise.

Eliot also lends New Criticism some of its technical vocabulary. Thanks to Eliot, for example, the term objective correlative has become a staple in poetic jargon. According to Eliot, the only way of expressing emotion through art is by finding an objective correlative: A set of objects, a situation, a chain of events, or reactions that can effectively awaken in the reader the emotional response the author desires without being a direct statement of that emotion. When the external facts are thus presented in the poem, they somehow come together and immediately evoke an emotion. The New Critics readily adopted and advanced such an impersonal theory concerning the arousing of emotions in poetry.

From Eliot's British contemporary, I. A. Richards, a psychologist and literary critic, New Criticism borrows a term that has become synonymous with its methods of analysis: *Practical Criticism*. In an experiment at Cambridge University, Richards distributed to his students copies of poems without such information as the authors, dates, and oddities of spelling and punctuation, and asked them to record their responses. From these data he identified the difficulties that poetry presents to its readers: matters of interpretation, poetic techniques, and specific meanings. From this analysis Richards devised an intricate system of arriving at a poem's meaning, including a minute scrutiny of the text. It is this close scrutiny or close reading of a text that has become synonymous with New Criticism.

From Eliot, Richards, and other critics, then, New Criticism borrows, amends, and adds its own ideas and concerns. Although few of its advocates would agree on many tenets, definitions, and techniques, there exists a core of assumptions that allow us to identify adherents of this critical approach to texts.

3.3 ASSUMPTIONS

New Criticism begins by assuming that the study of imaginative literature is valuable; to study poetry or any literary work is to engage oneself in an (the effects produced on an individual when contemplating a work of art) that can lead to truth. However, the truth discoverable through an aesthetic experience is distinguishable from the truth that science provides us. Science speaks in a propositional way, telling us whether a statement is demonstrably either true or false. Pure water, says science, freezes at 32 degrees Fahrenheit, not 30 or 31. Poetic truth, on the other hand, involves the use of imagination and intuition, a form of truth that according to the New Critics is discernible only in poetry. In the aesthetic experience alone we are cut off from mundane or practical concerns, from mere rhetorical, doctrinal, or propositional statements. Through an examination of the poem itself, we can ascertain truths that cannot be perceived through the language and logic of science. Both science and poetry, then, provide different but valid sources of knowledge.

Like many other critical theories, New Criticism's theory begins by defining its object of concern, in this case a poem. (New Critics use the word *poem* synonymously with work of art; however, their methodology works most efficiently with poetry rather than any other genre.) New Critics assert that a poem has ontological status; that is, it possesses its own being and exists like any other object. In effect, a poem becomes an artifact, an objective, self-contained, autonomous entity with its own structure. As W. K Wimsatt declares, a poem becomes a verbal icon.

Having declared a poem an object in its own right, the New Critics then develop their objective theory of art. For them, the meaning of a poem must not be equated with its author's feelings or stated or implied intentions. To believe that a poem's meaning is nothing more than an expression of the private experiences or intentions of its author is to commit a fundamental error of interpretation the New Critics call the Intentional Fallacy. Because they believe that the poem is an object, they claim that every poem must also be a public text that can be understood by applying the standards of public discourse, not simply the private experience, concerns, and vocabulary of its author.

That the poem is somehow related to its author cannot be denied. In his essay *Tradition and the Individual Talent*, T. S. Eliot states the New Critical position concerning this relationship between the author and his or her work. The basis of Eliot's argument is an analogy. We all know, he says, that certain chemical reactions occur in the presence of a catalyst, an element that causes but is not affected by the reaction. For example, if we place hydrogen peroxide, a common household disinfectant, in a clear bottle and expose it to the sun's rays, we will no longer have hydrogen peroxide. Acting as a catalyst, the sun's rays cause a chemical reaction to occur, breaking down the hydrogen peroxide into its various parts while the sun's rays remain unaffected.

Similarly, the poet's mind serves as a catalyst for the reaction that yields the poem. During the creative process, the poet's mind, serving as the catalyst, brings together the experiences of the author's personality (not the author's personality traits or attributes), into an external object and a new creation: The poem. It is not the personality traits of the author that coalesce to form the poem, but the experiences of the author's personality. In apparently distinguishing between the personality and the mind of the poet, Eliot asserts that the created entity, the poem, is about the experiences of the author that are similar to all of our experiences. By structuring these sentences, the poem allows us to examine them objectively.

Dismissing the poet's stated or supposed intentions as a means of discovering the text's meaning. The New Critics give little credence to the biographical or contextual history of a poem. If the Intentional Fallacy be correct, then unearthing biographical data will not help us ascertain a poem's meaning. Likewise, trying to place a poem in its social or political context will tell us much social or political history about the time when the poem was authored; although such information may indeed help in understanding the poem, its real meaning cannot reside in this extrinsic or outside the-text information.

Of particular importance to the New Critics, however, are individual words' etymology. Because the words of a poem sometimes change meaning from one time period to another, the critic often needs to conduct historical research, discovering what individual words meant at the time the poem was written. *The Oxford English Dictionary* (a dictionary that cites a word's various historical meanings chronologically) becomes one of the critic's best friends.

Placing little emphasis on the author, the social context, or a text's historical situation as a source for discovering a poem's meaning, the New Critics also assert that a reader's emotional response to the text is neither important nor equivalent to its interpretation. Such an error in judgment, called the Affective Fallacy, confuses what a poem is (its meaning) with what it does. If we derive our standard of criticism, say the New Critics, from the psychological effects of the poem, we are then left with impressionism or worse yet, relativism, believing that a poem has innumerable valid interpretations.

Where, then, can we find the poem's meaning? According to the New Critics, it does not reside in the author, the historical or social context of the poem, or even in the reader. Because the poem itself is an artifact or an objective entity, its meaning must reside within its own structure. Like all other objects, a poem and its structure can be analyzed scientifically. Accordingly, careful scrutiny reveals that a poem's structure operates according to a complex series of laws. By closely analyzing this structure, the New Critics believe that they have devised a methodology and a standard of excellence that we can apply to all poems to discover their correct meanings. It is the critic's job, they conclude, to ascertain the structure of the poem, to see how it operates to achieve its unity and to discover how meaning evolves directly from the poem itself.

According to New Criticism, the poet is an organizer of the content of human experience. Structuring the poem around these often confusing and sometimes contradictory experiences of life, the poet crafts the poem in such a way that the text stirs its readers' emotions and causes its readers to reflect on the poem's contents. As an artisan, the poet is most concerned with effectively developing the poem's structure, for the artist realizes that the meaning of a text emerges from its structure. The poet's chief concern, maintain the New Critics, is how meaning is achieved through the various and sometimes conflicting elements operating in the poem itself.

The chief characteristic of the poem and therefore its structure is coherence or interrelatedness. Borrowing their ideas from the writings of Samuel T. Coleridge, the New Critics posit the organic unity of a poem — that is the concept that all parts of a poem are interrelated and interconnected, with each part reflecting and helping to support the poem's central idea. Such organic unity allows for the harmonization of conflicting ideas, feelings and attitudes, and results in the poem's oneness. Superior poetry, declare the New Critics, achieves such oneness through paradox, irony, and ambiguity. Because such tensions are necessarily a part of everyone's life, it is only fitting and appropriate, say the New Critics, that superior poetry presents these human experiences while at the same time showing how these tensions resolved within the poem to achieve its organic unity.

Because the poem's chief characteristic is its oneness, New Critics believe that a poem's form and content are inseparable. For the New Critics, however, form is more than the external structure of a poem, for a poem's form encompasses but rises above the usual definition of poetic structure (that is, whether the poem be a Shakespearian or Petrarchan sonnet, or a lyric, or any other poetic structure having meter, rhyme, or some other poetic patterns). In New Criticism, form is the overall effect the poem creates. Because all the various parts of the poem combine to create this poem's form is unique. When all the elements of a poem work together to form a single, unified effect — the poem's form — New Critics declare that the poet has written a successful poem, one that has organic unity.

Because all good and successful poems have organic unity, it would be inconceivable to try to separate a poem's form and its content, maintain the New Critics. How can we separate what a poem says from how it says it? Because all the elements of a poem, both structural and aesthetic, work together to achieve a poem's effect or form, it is impossible to discuss the overall meaning of a poem by isolating or separating form and content.

To the New Critic, it is therefore inconceivable to believe that a poem's interpretation is equal to a mere paraphrased version of the text. Labeling such an erroneous belief the Heresy of Paraphrase, New Critics maintain that a poem is not simply a statement that is either true or false, but a bundle of harmonized tensions and resolved stresses, more like a ballet or musical composition than a statement of prose. No simple paraphrase can equal the meaning of the poem, for the poem itself resists through its inner tensions any prose statement that attempts to capsulize its meaning. Paraphrases may help readers in their initial understanding of the poem, but such prose statements must be considered working hypotheses that may or may not lead to a true understanding of the poem's meaning. In no way should paraphrased statements about a poem be considered equivalent to the poem's structure or form, insist the New Critics.

3.4 METHODOLOGY

Believing in the thematic and structural unity of a poem, New Critics search for meaning within the text's structure by finding the tensions and conflicts that must eventually be resolved into a harmonious whole and inevitably lead to the creation of the poem's chief effect. Such a search first leads New Critics to the poem's diction or word choice. Unlike scientific discourse with its precision of terminology, poetic diction often has multiple meanings can immediately set up a series of tensions within the text. For example, many words have both a denotation, or dictionary meaning, and connotation(s) or implied meanings. A word's denotation may be in direct conflict with its connotative meaning determined by the context of the poem. In addition, it may be difficult to differentiate between the various denotations of a word. For example, if someone writes that "a fat head enjoys the fat of the land," the reader must note the various denotative and connotative differences of the word *fat*. At the start of poetic analysis, then, conflicts or tensions exist by the very nature of poetic diction. This tension New Critics call ambiguity. At the end of a close reading of the text, however, all such ambiguities must be resolved.

Even on a surface level of understanding or upon a first reading, a poem, from a New Critic's perspective, is a reconciliation of conflicts, of opposing meanings and tensions. Its form and content are indivisible, so it is the critic's job to analyze the poetic diction to ascertain such tensions. Although various New Critics give a variety of names to the poetic elements that make up a poem's structure, all agree that the poem's meaning is derived from the oscillating tensions conflicts that are bought to the surface through the poetic diction. For example, Cleanth Brooks claims that the chief elements in a poem are paradox and irony, two closely related terms that imply that a word or phrase is qualified or even undercut by its context. Other critics use the word tension to describe the opposition or conflicts operating within the text. For these critics, tension implies the conflicts between a word's denotation and its connotation, between a literal detail and a figurative one, and between an abstract and a concrete detail.

Because conflict, ambiguity, or tension controls the poem's structure, the meaning of the poem can be discovered only by analyzing contextually the poetic elements and diction. Because context governs meaning, meanings of individual words or phrases are therefore context-related and unique to the poem in which they occur. It is the job of the critic, then, to unravel the various apparent conflicts and tensions within each poem and to show that ultimately the poem has organic unity, thereby showing that all parts of the poem are interrelated and support the poem's chief paradox. This paradox, what the New Critics often call form or overall effect, can usually be expressed in one sentence that contains the main tension and the resolution of that tension. It is this key idea to which all other elements of the poem must relate.

Although most New Critics would agree that the process of discovering the poem's form is not necessarily linear (for advanced readers often see ambiguities and ironies upon a first reading of a text), New Criticism provides the reader with a distinct methodology to help uncover this chief tension. Such guided steps allow both novices and advanced literary scholars together to enter the discussion of a text's ultimate meaning, each contributing to the poems interpretation. From a New Critical perspective, one begins this journey of discovering a text's correct interpretation by reading the poem several times and by carefully noting the work's title (if it has one) and its relationship to the text. Then, by following the prescribed steps listed here, a reader can ascertain a text's meaning. The more practice one has at following this methodology and the more opportunities one has to be guided by an advanced reader and critic, the more adept one will undoubtedly become at textual analysis.

(1) Examine the text's diction. Consider the denotation, connotations, and logical roots of all words in the text.

(2) Examine all allusions found within the text by tracing their roots to the primary text or

source, if possible.

(3) Analyze all images, symbols and figures of speech within the text. Note the relationships, if any, among the elements, both within the same category (between images, for example) and among the various elements (between an image and a symbol, for example).

(4) Examine and analyze the various structural patterns that may appear within the text, including the technical aspects of prosody. Note how the poet manipulates metrical devices, grammatical constrictions, tonal patterns, and syntactic patterns of words, phrases, or sentences. Determine how these various patterns interrelate with each other and with all elements discussed in steps 1 to 3.

(5) Consider such elements as tone, theme, point of view, and any other element — dialogue, foreshadowing, narration, parody, setting, and so forth — that directly relates to the text's dramatic situation.

(6) Look for interrelationships of all elements, noting where tensions, ambiguities or paradoxes arise.

(7) After carefully examining all elements, state the poem's chief overarching tension and explain how the poem achieves its dominant effect by resolving all such tensions.

Because all poems are unique, the process of uncovering the poem's chief tension is also unique. By using the prescribed methodology of New Criticism, New Critics believe that readers can justify their interpretations of a text by information gleaned from the text alone while enjoying the aesthetic process that allows them to articulate the text's meaning.

According to such New Critical principles, a good critic examines a poem's structure by scrutinizing its poetic elements, rooting out and showing its inner tensions, and demonstrating how the poem supports its overall meaning by reconciling these tensions into a unified whole. By implication, bad critics are those who insist on imposing extrinsic evidence such as historical or biographical information on a text to discover its meaning. These critics fail to realize that the text itself elicits its own meaning. They flounder in their analysis, declare the New Critics, because such critics believe more often than not that a text can have multiple meanings.

Asserting that a poem has ontological status, the New Critics believe that a text has one and only one correct interpretation and that the poem itself provides all the necessary information for revealing its meaning. By scrutinizing the text and thus giving it a close reading, and by providing readers with a set of norms that will assist them in discovering the correct interpretation of the text, New Criticism provides a teachable, workable framework for literary analysis.

3.5   QUESTIONS FOR ANALYSIS

To apply the assumptions and methodology of New Criticism to a given text, one can begin by asking the following questions:

If the text has a title, what is the relationship of the title to the rest of the poem?

Before answering this question, New Critical theory and practice assume that the critic has read the text several times.

· What words, if any, need to be defined?

· What words' etymological roots need to be explored?

· What relationships or patterns do you see among any words in the text?

· What are the various connotative meanings' words in the text may have? Do these various shades of meaning help establish relationships or patterns in the text?

· What allusions, if any, are in the text? Trace these allusions to their appropriate sources and explore how the origins of the allusion help elucidate meaning in this particular text.

· What symbols, images, and figures of speech are used? What is the relationship between any symbols or images? Between an image and another image? Between a figure of speech and an image? A symbol?

· What elements of prosody can you note and discuss? Look for rhyme, meter, and stanza patterns.

· What is the tone of the work?

· From what point of view is the content of the text being told?

· What tensions, ambiguities, or paradoxes arise within the text?

· What do you believe the chief paradox or irony is in the text?

· How do all the elements of the text support and develop the text's chief paradox?

3.6   SAMPLE ESSAYS

In the sample essay that follows, note how her writing style highlights the principles and practices of New Critical theory. For example, observe how many times she quotes directly from Dizigui's text, noting the various kinds of quoting (single words, phrases, and entire lines). Also recognize the literary vocabulary (elements) Brooks uses and assumes his audience understands:

metaphors, irony, paradox, point of view, apostrophe, central paradox, motifs, organic context, and other dramatic terms. And finally, note the style of New Critical writing. Such essays are usually written in the first person and are authoritative. Note particularly such phrases and clauses as "In my opinion," "He misses the point," and "I can see no other interpretation of the lines." After your reading of the student's essay, be able to explain what is believed to the central paradox is in the text and how all the various elements of the text support the author's argument.

PROFESSIONAL ESSAY

On Metaphor Translation Study in *The Analects*: Comparative Analysis of Roger T. Ames's and Ku Hongming's Versions

Although there are ample metaphors in *The Analects*, the author finds that few articles are concerned with its metaphor translation, and the previous study focused more on the book review, comparative study of translated texts, key concept words, historical and cultural communication. Few people do research on metaphor and its translation from the conceptual blending. Thus, taking metaphors in *The Analects* as the main linguistic data, the author attempts to analyze metaphoric meaning, explore the gains and losses of the two translations, and compare the blending results of the two translations using the conceptual blending theory.

The Analects can benefit the conceptual blending of metaphor in the target readers' system. Thus, the author hopes to employ the network model to analyze the in-space and out-space relations between the three conceptual blending systems (author's, translator's and reader's systems) involved in metaphor translation, thus providing a theoretical foundation for the following sample analysis.

As the representative work of Confucianism, metaphor in this book not only sets forth Confucius thought, but embraces the knowledge ranging from nature, astronomy, geography, physiology to military field. The above-mentioned knowledge adds difficulties to the comprehension of metaphor; therefore, translators have to integrate different information, select and blend relations between various spaces, which is exactly the study focus of conceptual blending network.

Besides, due to the strong Chinese cultural feature in this book, translators have to convey the images of the metaphor to embody Chinese culture as well as the metaphor meaning, therefore, translators may confront different choices in the selection and blending of the relations between various mental spaces, which is the content conceptual blending network deals with. The author attempts to analyze Ames's and Ku's blending methods of metaphor translation in the hope of providing reference for future study on metaphor translation.

Literature Review

Metaphor Research at Home and Abroad

The representative theory of this idea is "substitution theory" and "analogy theory". points out in the Poetics: Use one word that indicates one object to refer to another object, then that word becomes a metaphor word, and it can be used in the following cases: Use one category to one kind, one kind to one category, one kind to another kind and mutual analogy. In this sense, metaphor is generalized into substitution, to the effect that one word takes the place of another word in the same domain, and one object replaces another irrelevant object.

Some Chinese scholar makes a further analysis of Aristotle's explanation. According to Hu, the above-said cases respectively equal to the following ones: The superordinate replaces the hyponym; the hyponym replaces superordinate; one word in the same class to another. In addition, Aristotle states that simile is also a kind of metaphor.

Roman rhetorician Quintilian puts forward Substitution Theory based on Aristotle's definition on metaphor. He claims that metaphor is rhetoric phenomenon where one word is to replace another one in the same domain in accordance with the similarity between the tenor and vehicle. This theory deems metaphor as an unnecessary rhetoric device of sentence, but metaphor possesses an incomparable effect in literature, as a result, this theory has its limitation.

Another ramification of Aristotle's metaphor thought is Analogy Theory. It underlines that feature comparison between the source domain and the target domain constitutes the basic process of metaphor understanding, and metaphor is also a relation established after the comparison of similarities between words from different domains.

Harris also thinks metaphor is a kind of comparison in which one object gains recognition from another object. The defect of this theory is also very obvious in that metaphor is not just a simple comparison between two objects, but a selective projection with the aim of giving insight into the essence of metaphoric conception by the metaphoric language. In general, this rhetoric approach to metaphor is limited to the research of the metaphor phenomenon, and fails to incorporate metaphor into the wider background where human cognition, mind and communicative activity happen, thus concealing the cognitive mechanism and essence of metaphor entirely. To some extent, these limitations get in the way of the research of metaphor translation, misleading people to follow the semantic classification and explore the conventional translation method such as literal translation, free translation.

Cognitive Approach to Metaphor

In the 1930s, English rhetorician Richards put forward Interaction Theory in *Philosophy of Rhetoric*. He claims that metaphor appears as a result of the mutual interaction between the tenor and vehicle. While using metaphor, people hold two kinds of thought on the objects in mind, but express them with one word or phrase.

The primary function of metaphor is to extend language as well as reality, in which two elements interact and produce new meanings. Black further develops and modifies interaction theory, to shed light on that new cognition is generated by changing the relation between the subject and the item. Therefore, metaphor wears creativity apart from similarity.

Although interaction theory explains the mode people understand the ground, but this theory holds that the speaker must make sure all the conceptions he or she expresses are suitable for or agree with the key concepts. Besides, the dominant role played by metaphor users is neglected in constructing and interpreting process. Metaphor construction and interpretation process should be associated with the process and the schema in which people make adjustments and assimilate the object to the subject. Lakoff & Johnson really establish the status of metaphor in the field of cognition by virtue of the book *The Metaphors We Lived By*, ushering in a new channel to study metaphor. They claim that metaphor is not a superficial linguistic phenomenon, but a deep cognitive mechanism. Metaphor enables us to organize our thought better, construct linguistic framework, thus producing new linguistic expression. Metaphor makes the abstract conception specific; and conceptual metaphor comes into being when one conceptual domain is projected to another one. Lakoff and Turner make a clear definition of the concept of "mapping": a set of correspondences between two conceptual domains.

Lakoff's thought can be generalized into the following five aspects: (1) Metaphor exists anywhere, not only in the language, but our minds and behaviors; (2) Metaphor is cognitive in essence, and is a way of thinking embodied in language; (3) Metaphor is systematic for the reason that one metaphoric concept can stimulate vast harmonious language expression, while different metaphoric concept constitutes a coherent network system together influencing our language and minds; (4) Metaphor is made up of two domains: Source domain and target domain, and the schematic structure of source domain is mapped into the target domain to construct and understand the target domain; (5) Metaphor mapping is rooted in our experience.

Mapping theory offsets the limitation of interaction theory in explaining the metaphor cognition. It not only describes the features of interaction process, but explains the systematicness and directivity, thus making great advances in metaphor theory development and leading people to further understand the working mechanism of metaphor.

Fauconnier and Turner develop conceptual blending theory on the basis of mapping theory. Fauconnier integrates metaphor mechanism with other languages and cognitive phenomenon to create the conceptual blending theory. It is a positive supplement of mapping theory of Lakoff. This theory uncovers the online construction process and reasoning mechanism of sense. According to this theory, metaphor meaning is the result of the interaction between the source space, target space and generic space.

By document retrieval, we can find the research achievements on metaphor translation are mainly reflected in the following aspects: The translatability of metaphor, translation strategies and principle and criterion of metaphor.

Dagut points out that the translatability of metaphor depends on to which extent the target readers understand the cultural experience and semantic association contained, in Chitoran claims that common cognition that people can rely on to translate exists in different languages; Horny thinks there exists relative translatability and a certain limitation in metaphor on account of the cultural blank and cultural conflict between different nationalities; Zhao Yanchun also expounds the translatability of metaphor from the perspective of relevance theory. Tan Yesheng, Ge Jinrong points out that the cognitive space based on the conceptual metaphor system of two cultures serves as the foundation of metaphor translatability and its communicative law, Peter Newmark first conducts systematic research on it in literature translation. He puts forward the translation method on conventional metaphor: (1) Retain the same metaphor image, that is to translate literally on the condition that the readers feel comfortable; (2) Change the metaphor into simile; (3) Replace it with the corresponding metaphor in target language; (4) Maintain the same image and simplify the ground (the similarity); (5) Employ explanatory translation. Schaffner generalizes metaphor translation strategy into: substitution (the source metaphor is changed into target metaphor); paraphrase (metaphor is changed into sheer meaning), deletion. His method mainly deals with the one-way study from the source language to the target language, which is equivalent to literal translation, free translation and omission. From the perspective of cognitive semantics, Shu Dingfang (2000) classifies metaphor into four types of semantic structures in accordance with the features of semantic contradiction, the mappings of tenor, vehicle, and ground. Liu Fagong considers that vehicle image conversion is one of the criteria in traditional Chinese-English metaphor translation. He puts forward the following principles in regard to how to maintain the metaphor image: (1) Keep the features of metaphor; (2) Connect the related cultural connotation of Chinese and English metaphors; (3) Make up for the lacking cultural vehicle according to the context. Another criterion is that the vehicle is known in the source text and the target text. As to how the Chinese-English metaphor translation goes, he concludes in the following:

First of all, to apply and understand the Chinese metaphor, secondly, to search for the English metaphor expression form that keeps consistent with Chinese metaphoric connotation; thirdly, to check whether the vehicle's cultural image in source text is converted into the translation from the perspective of vehicle image conversion, thus guaranteeing the quality of Chinese-English metaphor translation.

Deng Yu proposed three principles about metaphor translation's adaptation to culture from the perspective of culture and cognition: (1) Regard metaphor translation as a double cognitive process, thus conveying the exact cultural meaning; (2) Find the unity of conception and form in target language, consider the target reader's acceptance with the aim of promoting cultural fusion; (3) Keep the metaphor character, and reach the aesthetic criterion.

Some studies have been made on metaphors in *The Analects*, which center around the two aspects: Xu Qianshi and Liu Baochun make a systematic classification of metaphors in this book from the perspective of the traditional rhetoric; Chi Changhai and Lin Rong explore the Confucian thought in terms of language. However, several theses can be seen by combination of metaphors and translation. Li Hongmei makes a comparison of The Analects translations in light of metaphor translation; Ji Wenyue also makes a comparative analysis of *The Analects* translations from the angle of conceptual metaphor; Zhou Chunjie compares and appreciates the meaning communication of "Man" — structural metaphor, "Heaven" — ontological metaphor and "Up-down" — oriental metaphor on the basis of metaphor operation process, and draws a conclusion that a successful metaphor translation must make sure that the mapped vehicle image in target language is consistent with that in source language on the condition that the interpretation of the metaphor is right; Li Gang and Chen Yong analyzes the political metaphor in four English versions and discusses the method to treat the source domain of political metaphors.

Theoretical Framework

Conceptual Blending Theory (CBT) is the result of critical development of traditional linguistics theory. It has a history of more than 30 years in foreign countries, while in China, only about 15 years. It developed from "conceptual metaphor theory", but its prototype is "mental space theory". CBT has become a crucial paradigm for the research on cognitive linguistics, and gradually integrated with other paradigms with the aim of developing into a comprehensive research field.

In 2002, Fauconnier and Turner cooperated to release the book *The Way We Think*. They state that conceptual blending is a basic kind of cognitive mental mechanism with a complicated operation process. One of the fundamental task of cognitive linguistics is to discover the principles and mechanisms in the process of conceptual blending. They both claim that its dynamic structural principles refer to cross-space mapping, selective mapping into blending space and emergent structure generated in blending space; the above-said is the constitutive principles of conceptual blending; in fact, conceptual blending is also restrained by principles from another layer called governing principles, which present various strategies for the refinement of emergent structure. They both point out that governing principle is reflected in other aspects, such as the elaboration and integration of structures and modes, reinforcement of various relations, the keeping of the links in the network, the distinction in blending space and the relevance in the whole emergent space. The focus of all the principles, be it constitutive or governing principle, is to gain the conceptual blending of human scale, which refers to the immediate perception and action in the framework we are familiar with.

In general, Wang Dongfeng articulated CBT is a systematic elaboration for the inter-mapping of various mental spaces and their related interaction and effect in the speech communication process, the aim of which is to reveal the cognitive iceberg behind the on-line construction of speech meaning.

Conceptual blending, an important cognitive ability owned by human beings, exists in various cognitive activities, especially creative thinking process. It happens in a conceptual network composed of a series of mental spaces, including at least two or more input spaces, generic space formed by the universality of input spaces, blending space constituted by the selective mapping from input spaces and emergent structure generated from blending space. Input 1 and Input 2 are constituted by information elements from two independent cognitive domains respectively; generic space is an abstract and general projection of the common elements from the two input spaces. By analogy, a cross-domain mapping appears between the two input spaces, that is to say, the corresponding elements match with each other from the two input spaces.

Under the constraint of generic space, elements from the two input spaces are projected into the blending space selectively, thus generating an emergent structure. Here, three operations are involved into the blending and construction of blending space, including "composition", "completion" and "elaboration". In the blending process, elements from the input spaces are composed and produce a relationship that is unavailable in the blending space; the composed structure can be refined by absorbing a large quantity of conceptual blending theory that is also limited by a series of governing principles.

Fauconnier and Turner conclude nine principles including compressing, network, unpacking, max-VIP relationship, topology, VIP relationship strengthening, well-formed principle, integration, and relevant principle.

For example, compressing principle refers to that human beings have to constantly compress important relations to construct and understand the meaning in the cognitive process, and conceptual blending is a perfect tool to compress these important relations.

Well-formed principle means that the existed mode or framework is able to better the frame work in the blending space. That is to say, the structure in the blending space needs to comply with existed grammatical rules or language structure. Integration principle means conceptual blending must form an integrative, harmonious blending scene which can act as a complete unit.

Relevance principle requires that any element in blending space relationship can establish relationships and interact with that in other spaces to operate the blending space, and the important relationships between input spaces must be reflected in the blending space.

Conceptual Blending and Metaphor Translation

From the perspective of conceptual blending, translation process involves three independent conceptual systems: The author system, the translator system and target reader system. According to the rule of the recursion in conceptual blending, the blending result of the previous one can be regarded as the element of the next blending and involve itself into the next round of blending. Therefore, the blending space in the source author system becomes the input space 1 in the translator system, and the blending space in the translator system becomes the input 1 in the target reader system (Table 1).

Table 1 Three Conceptual Blending Systems in Metaphor Translation

Conceptual blending system	Author's System	Translator's system	Target reader's system
Input space 1	Source domain	Blending space of the author system	Blending space of the translator system
Input space 2	Context	Translator's background knowledge	Reader's background knowledge
Generic space	Culture of the source language	Universality between source and target language and culture	Cognitive similarities Between the translator and the reader
Blending space	Metaphor meaning	Blended metaphor	Reader's blended text

Conceptual Blending in Translator's System

The cognitive language operation in translation is embodied in the "unpacking" of the source text and the "reconstruction" of the target language. This is true of metaphor translation. In metaphor translation, the understanding of the metaphor is reflected in the unpacking process and the expression of the translation is reflected in the blending process. That is to say, what translator should do at first is to "unpack" the metaphor, thus forming his own psychological schema of the metaphor; then he should express the interpreted psychological schema in target language. In fact, understanding and expression are two independent conceptual blending systems, and metaphor translation can be deemed as a process from the source language blending to target language blending.

In the process of expression, given that the similarity between languages differs to various extents, the possibility of translation does not mean the feasibility. Although human live in the same world, various history, culture and living environment get in the way of the generic space built among different language communities. Therefore, the blending results in this process vary on account of mapping methods.

Adaptation of CBT to Metaphor Translation in *The Analects*

Firstly, metaphor is the study object of CBT in terms of language cognition. People's cognition and interpretation of metaphor is based on the similarities of related spaces. This is true of conceptual blending network, which explains metaphor's sense-making and construction process as well as cognitive subject's understanding process. The author's intention and Confucian thought, are thus standard to evaluate the correctness of the two translators' understanding.

Secondly, conceptual blending theory studies are the reconstruction process after the meaning blending, and this is also true of the metaphor translation process of The Analects. Metaphor translation in this book not only aims to convey the image in the source text, present Chinese cultural features, but express the implication in the source text. In this sense, the translator needs to blend or integrate information from diverse aspects, select and fuse elements in different mental spaces and their relations, which is just the research content of conceptual blending theory.

Besides, conceptual blending theory also uncovers the fact that the variable factors accounting for different translations from the same text lie in the difference of grammar and usual practice in languages, as well as that of blending process of the described conceptual structure. In the source text's unpacking and the target text's reconstruction process, extra information is involved, which is a subjective selection of translation. Therefore, various translations appear and this also explains the reason for the contradiction of free translation and literal translation in equivalence. Under the metaphor framework, translation is actually a reproduction process where the conceptual structure of the metaphor reappears in the target language; therefore, the objective of "equivalence" can be attainable as long as that structure of the communicative event is retained in target language. In this sense, we can analyze the blending results of different translations from the perspective of conceptual blending in which generic space plays an important role in the determination of different translations.

Metaphor and *The Analects*

The translated texts this thesis selected are *The Analects* by Ames and *The Discourses and Sayings* of Confucius by Gu Hongming. Ames's version is a bilingual one with Chinese and English. This book consists of the following parts: Preface, contents, text, notes, translator's introduction, terms, bilingual table of translated nouns or terms. Ames's book is deemed as the common edition in English world. Ku's version is also a bilingual one with Chinese and English published by Yunnan People's Publishing House. The content mainly includes the bilingual texts in this book. But Ku's version is also a fabulous one for his creative translation. The reason for the selection of the two versions is their obvious differences in terms of translator's academic background, translation purpose and target readers, thus facilitating the comparative study of the translation.

First, in terms of translator's academic background: Ku is a language genius who has a good command of English, Germany and French. He has a thorough knowledge of the Western and traditional China. He is also the first person to introduce Chinese classics to foreign countries. By virtue of his solid foundation in Chinese Classics and excellent language ability, Ku's rendering can help foreign readers to understand Confucian thoughts. Ames is an exceptionally talented sinologist, as well as an influential translator and researcher on Chinese classic thought, whose achievement lies in philosophy. His working experience in the Hawaii University gave him access to sinology books and materials of Chinese classic thoughts; besides, he translated and introduced Chinese poems based upon his knowledge of Chinese philosophy. In addition, his renderings of *The Analects*, *Xiaojing* and *Dao De Jing* are the common versions in English world.

In terms of translation purposes: Ku precisely makes clear his translation purpose. First, he criticizes Legge's version for the lack of literature cultivation and the sense of weirdness it poses to the western readers. Thus, Ku's translation is intended for the common readers in order to eliminate the foreignness of English readers; second, against the background he lived in, he tries to revolt against the Western's invasion of Chinese culture, remove the Western despise of Chinese nation and its tradition, thus acquainting themselves with the authentic Chinese civilization and according to the due understanding and respect; last but not least, his text selection of *The Analects* demonstrates his theory of "saving the West with Chinese culture" in the hope of healing the world civilization with Chinese reasonable and ethical culture equipment.

Ames clearly set forth his purpose of writing, there is no doubt that he attempts to study profound Chinese culture and introduce them to the western world.

In terms of target readers, Ames's version is much easier to read due to its modern style. It plays a significant role in English world, benefiting the common readers as well as the scholars for its reference to some specific Chinese knowledge in annotations. Ames points out that, in spite of the inanimate words in *The Analects*, he realizes the literariness implied readers who consider this book in it, therefore, he strives to meet the demands of being read as a literary text. He quotes some western proverbs to help the Western readers to understand the doctrines of Confucius, thus spreading Confucian thought. Given Ku's translation purpose, his version is intended for the most common western readers.

Statistics of Metaphor Sentences in *The Analects*

With the development of metaphor, different scholars have made various definitions on it. The author believes that metaphor is a way of perceiving world embodied in language. From the perspective of CBT, metaphor is actually a blending result of two or more mental spaces, and human's cognitive and cultural experiences serve as the generic space in the network model. This study searches for 56 metaphor sentences in total reading the texts again and again. It is apparent that metaphor sentences in this book are distributed in a scattered way. The three chapters Zi Han, Zi Zhang and Shu Er account for the most of the metaphors. In Zi Han chapter, Confucius shows his concern for the lapse of time, social instability and his pity for unrecognized talents such as Hui's young death by use of metaphors; in Zi Zhang chapter, are used to comment on the merit and fault of Confucius and his disciples, metaphors especially to highlight Confucius' insurmountable culture; in other chapters, the metaphors are also employed to describe the importance of morality in political governance, trust in socialization and so on (Table 2).

Table 2 The distribution of metaphor sentences *in The Analects*

Chapter	Number of Metaphor	Chapter	Number of Metaphor
Xue Er I	1	Wei Zheng II	3
Ba Yi III	1	Li Ren IV	2
Gong Yechan V	3	YongYe VI	4
Shu Er VII	5	Tai Bo VIII	3
ZI Han IV	6	Xiang Dang X	3
Wei Ling gong XV	2	Ji Shi XVI	2
YangHuo XVII	4	Wei Zi XVIII	1
Zi Zhang XIX	5	Yao Yue XX	0

By analyzing these metaphors, the author finds them focused on the comments on some persons, political creeds in governance, behaving oneself and virtue's improvement. Therefore, the author classifies them into "man's" metaphor and "cultivation" metaphor in the hope of selecting metaphor samples which can represent all the metaphors to the utmost.

On the basis of daily life, metaphoric language in this book is simple and natural. When used to comment on the current affairs, expound the right way of doing things, and elaborate the reasons or describe human's temperament, these metaphors become elegant and attain a higher artistic and literary realm. In the following part, we will try to analyze the metaphors' features and functions in *The Analects*.

It is apparent that the source domain mostly comes from the objects or phenomena with strong cultural color in nature people can accept. In the early stage of human's development, due to the lack of strong expressive power, with people themselves as reference, metaphor is basically what people see and feel about the surrounding.

Metaphors in this book are characterized by explaining the vehicle with simple analogy, objects which is called "Neng Jin Qu Pi" in Chinese people are familiar with in daily life, and "Jin" reflects it is accepted by users and receivers; and "Pi" serves as vehicle which must be familiar to people without strangeness.

First, similarities between people and objects are used to comment people, enriching the person with exuberant feelings and making the description of people true to life. In Chapter 2 Wei Zheng (为政), Confucius describes Junzi (the wise man) by comparing implement with the aim of highlighting the requirement for Junzi's versatile moral qualities. When judging Zigong, Confucius also compares him to one implement which only acts as a container, thus offering his criticism in an implicit way. But Zigong is one top language talent of Confucius; therefore, Confucius compares him to a noble vessel filling sacrifice offerings called "Hu Lian", thus expressing his positive remark on Zigong's talents. Zaiyu is also a talent of Confucius; however, Confucius expresses his strong dissatisfaction for his sleeping in the daytime with "rotten wood" and "wall built by dung". As for Zilu, Confucius evaluates his scholarship level with "entering the hall but the inner room", thus giving a fair and objective evaluation on his culture. Confucius thinks highly of Shiyu's integrity arrow, reaching the unity of form and spirit. Certainly, by use of the straightness of this feature is also true of Confucius' disciples' comments on him. For example, Confucius wooden bell which is used to convene the mass; in this way, they convey their admiration for him, but give a precise comment on his common people.

Second, common objects and simple truth are borrowed to make a comparison with the aim of carrying forward the Confucian morality. Although this book brims with simple words, the metaphors indicate profound meanings and give the mass conspicuous warnings. Confucius uses the common phenomenon " the pole star remains in its position while the lesser ones circle around it" to compare with the ruler's way of governance, thus pointing out the importance of De (virtue) the rulers should embrace in office. As is often the case, the "carriage" fails to go ahead without the linking bar, and Confucius borrows this simple truth to expound the significance of honesty a man should have. It is a common fact that wind blows down the grass, but Confucius uses it to precisely convey the relationship between the ruler and the mass with the requirement that the ruler must behave himself and win trust of the mass by virtues.

Third, vehicle is extracted from daily life, and colloquial and intelligible words and phrases are employed to expound compelling truth. Confucius thinks that craftsman must refine his tools to do his job, while wise man must be willing to get along with those with virtues. Here, he draws the common vehicle from "refined tools" to refer to the men with virtues. The plants which only sprout without bloom, bloom without fruit can be seen anywhere, and Confucius uses them to imply the harm of giving up halfway in scholarship, which contains a profound philosophy.

As is mentioned in chapter 4, vast metaphors are including ruler, Junzi, Confucius and his disciples and so on, which can be employed to comment persons. Enlightened by the classification of Alice Deignan, man's metaphor can be further divided into the following four kinds: Animal metaphor, plant metaphor, container metaphor and other metaphors. Among them, the images in animal metaphor include tiger, rhino, turtle, phoenix, male and female animal; plant metaphor deals with crop, pine and cypress, gourd, grass, wood; container metaphor involves vessel, goblet (Hu), Hu lian (a noble vessel), Dou and Xiao (vessels to measure grains in ancient time); other images include jade, mountain and river, hill, the Yellow River, drum, sword and so on. In all these metaphors, container metaphor is the most representative one.

As metaphor mind and its conceptual system derive from life experience, it can not be formed spontaneously free from the social and cultural environment. Due to various cultural backgrounds, people from each community shape different aesthetic attitudes to some phenomena and matters. Abundant Chinese food culture contributes to a great variety of appliances. As early as the Neolithic Age, many basic appliances we used appeared; until Shang and Zhou Dynasties, tableware gained a rapid development because of the appearance of bronze smelting technology. Although the material and shape of all the table wares and cooking utensils have changed constantly with times, their functions are restrained to initial use. At most, containers are served as ones to hold something. Therefore, Confucius uses "Hulian" (a good vessel) to describe Zigong (a disciple of Confucius); in this way, he not only gives a positive affirmation for Zigong's ability partially, but indicates that Zigong is not a versatile talent he appreciates. During the Spring and Autumn and the Warring period, as the food became increasingly sumptuous, the old tablewares disappeared, and new tablewares appeared constantly. In Confucius times, the shape of Hu (a kind of goblet) changed a lot and completely lost its previous form. Confucius had a frustrated office life.

Although he had learned in every way, and saw through the political situation of Lu State, his inability to consider the situation resulted in his failure in political struggles, even if he made an attempt to realize his aspirations by traveling through various states. While complaining the turbulent society, Confucius also raised doubts to governors of that time, thus producing the exclamation "Hu is not the previous Hu".

Sample Analysis

> Sample 1：
> 原文：君子不器。
> 译文：
> The Master said, "A gentleman is not an implement." (Ames's version)
> Confucius remarked, "A wise man will not make himself into a mere machine fit
> only to do one kind of work." (Ku Hongming' version)

By comparing the features of "Qi (container)" and "Junzi", Confucius explicitly comes up with the cultivation realm Junzi is expected to reach in ancient China: Junzi ought to be erudite. In this metaphor, input space 1 is the cognitive domain "container", and input space 2 is the cognitive domain "Junzi". The framework and elements in the two domains are different, and the diverging cognitive spaces compel cognitive subject to analyze the two input spaces with the help of other background knowledge and relevant elements. In virtue of background knowledge, cognitive subject can infer that the implement at most serves as a container, thus the framework of input space 1 goes like this: The implement only has one function. Unlike the gentleman in the western countries, "Junzi" that Confucius refers to weakens the importance of origin and underlines the nobility in morality and behavior. Thus the framework of input space 2 goes like that Junzi bears versatile moral qualities. No similarity is found in the generic space by comparison of the two input spaces, and a contrast forms between "one function of container" and "breadth of Junzi's moral qualities". Based on its own emergent logic, the blending space integrates the projected elements and structure again, and produces the emergent meaning, thus realizing the final elaboration and highlighting the profound meaning inside the metaphor: Confucius advocates that "Junzi" should be erudite with versatile moralities.

By unpacking the translations, we can deduce and check each metaphor from the translations. First, input space 1 of the translator is compared with the blending space of the author, and it is clear that input spaces 1 from two translators are consistent with the author's emergent structure, which means two translators comprehend the source metaphor precisely. Important element" 君子 "possesses so rich Chinese cultural color that corresponding elements cannot be found in input space 2. Ku translates it into "wise man" instead of "gentleman" by way of transplantation, so as to expound the difference between Junzi and "gentleman". Ames's version "gentleman" may mislead the readers to blend an incorrect concept "a gentleman of a noble origin" and violates the maximum relevance principle. In this way, Ku's version of "Junzi" seems more reasonable. As for " 不器 ", Ames translates it word for word.

Although the literal meaning of " 不器 " can be conveyed, the readers tend to misunderstand the translation. Therefore, Ames gives a proper explanation in annotations, thus highlighting the metaphor meaning. Ames's annotation obeys the principle of VIP relationship strengthening principle, producing a closer relationship among elements and a more natural mapping. As well, Ku also gives an extension of "器", a mere machine fit only to do one kind of work. Here, "器" is translated into "machine", for all it is different from the original meaning "container", and the meaning it conveys is right. Ku also violates the maximum relevance principle while choosing the important element " 器 " in input space 2, but obeys VIP relationship strengthening principle.

Sample 2:

原文：子曰："为政以德，譬如北辰居其所而众星拱之。"——《为政·论语》

译文：

The Master said, "He who rules by moral force is like polestar, which remains in its place while all the lesser stars do homage to it." (Ames's version)

Confucius remarked, "He who rules people, depending upon the moral sentiment, is like the Pole–star, which keeps its place while all the other stars revolve round it.

(Ku Hungming's version)

It is easy to infer the content of input spaces in the metaphor. Input space 1 is the mental space "polestar and other lesser stars", including elements "polestar, keep its place, other stars, revolve"; input space 2 is one concerning "ruler's governance", including elements "ruler, govern by De, the mass, show respect". By the dynamic integration of mind, cognitive subject can extract the abstract structure from the two input spaces into the generic space, that is "important people or object, action, other people and objects, effect". Therefore, the shared framework of the four mental spaces goes that important people or objects impose effect on others by action. By activation of background knowledge, cognitive subject can know that other lesser stars will stick around polestar which keeps in its place and glitters in the sky. Here, the composed elements and relations are projected into the blending space and matches develop like "ruler-polestar, the mass — the lesser stars, governed by De — keep in its place and glitter, revolve — show respect". In the blending space, by positive and dynamic reasoning, cognitive subject can further infer the underlying mappings. Rulers is the polestar in the sky which keeps still and glitters in the place, however, he can win the respect from others by setting a model and governing with De. It can be concluded that the source domain polestar gains affirmation and prominence, and ruler enjoys the same important position like polestar in the sky.

By unpacking the translations and reconstructing the various mental spaces of translators, it can be inferred that two translators understand the metaphor well. Selected elements from the author's system conform to maximum relevance principle.

Given that " 德 " has a typical Chinese cultural color, translators find it hard to get an equal mapping from input space 2. Ames chooses to use Chinese "pinyin" with annotations in the following "Terms", in that readers can get the total meaning of this word and the underlying cultural information involved in Chinese with reference to annotations. In this way, it conforms to maximum relevance principle ("moral force") and " 德 " as well as VIP relationship strengthening principle (" 德 " and "de" a force power closely akin to what we call character and contrasted with physical force), thus achieving a balance among various principles in CBT. Ames's translation can convey the meaning and enable English readers to access Chinese culture " 德 ". In comparison, Ku's translation "moral sentiment" may be insufficient for English readers to fully understand the cultural information involved in Chinese, but can also blend the metaphor meaning. In terms of the wording, Ames's "lesser stars" better highlights the important position polestar holds in the text. Given that most people have a knowledge concerning "polestar" in cognitive experience, Ames directly personifies other stars by using "do homage to it", thus helping English readers understand the importance of governance with De. Generally speaking, input space 1 and input space 2 in the two translators' cognitive system keep consistent and mapping between them is smooth, so the blending system of the two translators' system is close to the source text and English readers can also blend the concept well.

Sample 3:

原文：子在川上曰："逝者如斯夫！不舍昼夜。"——《子罕·论语》

译文：

Confucius once standing by a stream, remarked. "How all things in nature are passing away even like this−ceasing neither day or night!"　　(Ames's version)

Once when the Master was standing by a stream, he said, "Could one but go on and on like this, never ceasing day or night!"　　(Ku Hungming's version)

In this metaphor, cognitive subject can shape two mental spaces: Input space 1 is " the running water" and input space 2 is an abstract concept "time"; generic space reflects the similarity between "water" and "time" —, "moving forward", thus making is possible to produce a cross-space mapping. The framework of input space 1 "water moves forward" and element "time" from input space 2 are projected into the blending theory, and element "time" in input space 2 replaces "water" in input space/generating metaphoric meaning based on original framework. In this way, meaning appears that time elapses like running water.

By compressing, various mental spaces of translators' system can be reconstructed. As mentioned in the above table, two translators translates " 逝者 " into "all things in nature" and one but respectively, slightly contradicting the emergent structure of the author's system. However, as for readers who carry out conception reconstruct, Ames's and Ku's versions also serve as an acceptable input space 1 in reader's system.

Although two translators fail to obey maximum relevance principle, no reason is given for much criticism under the principle of strengthening important relations. With regard to the relationship of elements, Waley translates" 奔流而去 "into " pass away", which is more precise than Ku's "go on and on" in terms of accuracy of words.

Conclusion

Major Findings

Metaphor translation in *The Analects* is actually a conceptual blending process and conceptual blending network is of great significance in the retention of the metaphor meaning.

First, a correct understanding of the metaphor is the prerequisite to know the work's theme in that metaphor meaning contains the author's intention which is also a reflection of the era. By analysis of the source metaphor text of *The Analects*, we can apply the space mental network model of CBT to the metaphoric meaning construction in this book, and the blending result of the author's system standard to evaluate the correctness of translators' understanding can serve as metaphoric meaning. By sample analysis, it is found that Ames and Ku Hungming have understood the metaphoric meaning well.

Second, governing principles of CBT can help us deconstruct various mental spaces in translator's system, and make an evaluation on the quality of the translation by virtue of governing principles of CBT, in which well-formed principle is a fundamental one. Maximum relevance principle and VIP relationship strengthening principle are two important ones to check the gains and losses in the translations.

Third, conceptual blending network also offers a reasonable explanation for the inequality of metaphor translation. Difference between Ames's and Ku's translations lies in cultural and knowledge background during the deconstruction and reconstruction process, as well as the dynamic changes in the generic space of the translator's system.

In brief, translators' different blending methods of metaphor are a subjective selection process, which can give inspirations to future study of metaphor translation methods. Ames's metaphor translation is the result of the source text as well as double projections from the source text and translator spaces, and maintains the cultural elements to the utmost; while Ku's one focuses on the projection from translator's space by use of cultural transplantation and domestication. Since the two translations are intended for different target readers as a result of translators' translation purpose, their blending results can both facilitate target readers' conceptual blending of metaphor to various extents.

Limitations and Suggestions

First, this study mainly analyzes the text by using space network theory, governing principles instead of the whole theory; second, due to the limitations of time, material collected and personal ability, interpretations of some metaphors may be insufficient, therefore, intelligible parts of CBT are selected when analyzing texts.

Certainly, further study of CBT is to be continued, and other aspects of this theory can be tentatively applied to the metaphor translation in combination with other disciplines. Although CBT has developed for about 15 years in China, and become important branch in cognitive linguistics, the application and development potential of it remains to be tested. Hopefully, the author will apply other aspects of CBT to a further study of classic metaphor translation.

REFERENCES

[1]ALLEN T. Reason in Madness[M]. New York: Putnam, 1941.

[2]ALLEN T, LEWIS P S. "What I Owe to Cleanth Brooks" in The Possibilities of Order: Cleanth Brooks and His Work[M]. Baton Rouge: Louisiana State University Press 1976.

[3]AMES R, ROSEMENT H. The Analects of Confucius: A Philosophical Translation[M]. New York: Balattine Publishing Group.1999:30.

[4]CLEANTH B. Modern Poetry and the Tradition[M]. Chapel Hill: University of North Carolina Press, 1939.

[5]CLEANTH B. The Well-Thought Urn: Studies in the Structure of Poetry[M]. New York: Harcourt, 1947.

[6]CLEANTH B. My Credo: Formalist Critics[J]. Kenyon Review 13 (1951): 72-81.

[7]CLEANTH B. In Search of the New Criticism[J]. American Scholar 53 (Winter 1983/84): 41-53.

[8]CLEANTH B, ROBERT B H. Understanding Drama: Twelve Plays[M]. New York: Holt, 1948.

[9]CLEANTH B, ROBERT P W. Understanding Poetry: An Anthology for College Students[M]. New York: Holt, 1939.

[10]FRANK L. After the New Criticism[M]. Chicago: University of Chicago Press, 1980.

[11]KU HONGMING, The Discourses and Sayings of Confucius[M]. Kunming:Yunnan Renming Publisher.2011.

[12]RICHARDS I A. Principles of Literary Criticism[M]. New York: Harcourt, 1924.

[13]RICHARDS I A. Practical Criticism[M]. New York: Harcourt, 1929.

[14]JEROME P I A S. Richard's Theory of Literature[M]. New Haven: Yale University Press, 1969.

[15]J N PATNAIK. The Aesthetics of the New Criticism[M]. New Delhi: Intellectual Publishing House, 1982.

[16]JOHN C R. The New Criticism[M]. New York: New Directions, 1941.

[17]JOHN C R. The World's Body[M]. Baton Rouge: Louisiana State University Press, 1968.

[18]JOHN C R. Beating the Bushes: Selected Essays: 1941-1970[M]. New York: New Directions, 1972.

[19]LEWIS P S, ed. The Possibilities of Order: Cleanth Brooks and His Work[M]. Baton Rouge: Louisiana State University Press, 1976.

[20]MARK J. The Cultural Politics of the New Criticism[M]. Cambridge: Cambridge University Press, 1993.

[21]MARK S. Technique as Discovery[J]. Hudson Review 1 (Spring 1948): 67-87.

[22]MURRAY K. The New Apologists for Poetry[M]. Minneapolis: University of Minnesota Press, 1956.

[23]RENÉ W. The New Criticism: Pro and Contra[J]. Critical Inquiry 4 (Summer 1978): 611-24.

[24]RENÉ W, AUSTIN W. Theory of Literature[M]. San Diego: Harcourt Brace Jovanovich, 1977.

[25]ROBERT P W. Pure and Impure Poetry[J]. Kenyon Review 5 (Spring 1943): 229-54.

[26]TIMOTHY B. American Formalism and the Problem of Interpretation[M]. Houston: Rice University Press, 1986.

[27]T S ELIOT. "Tradition and the Individual Talent." The Sacred Wood[M]. London: Methuen, 1928.

[28]T S ELIOT. "The Function of Criticism." Selected Essays[M]. New York: Harcourt, 1950.

[29]T S ELIOT. Notes Towards the Definition of Culture[M]. London: Faber, 1965.

[30]WILLIAM E C. The Crisis in Criticism: Theory, Literature, and Reform in English Studies[M]. Baltimore: John Hopkins University Press, 1984.

[31]WILLIAM ELTON. Seven Types of Ambiguity[M]. New York: Noonday Press,1958.

[32]WILLIAM EMPSON. A Glossary of the New Criticism[M]. Chicago: Modern Poetry Association, 1949.

[33]WILLIAM J H. Kant and the Southern New Critics[M]. Austin: University of Texas Press, 1963.

[34]WIMSATT W K. The Verbal Icon[M]. Lexington: U of Kentucky Press, 1954.

[35]WIMSATT W K, MONROE B. "The Affective Fallacy" in The Verbal Icon: Studies in the Meaning of Poetry[M]. Lexington: University of Kentucky Press, 1954, 21-39.

[36]WIMSATT W K, CLEANTH B. Literary Criticism: A Short History[M]. New York: Knopf, 1957.

[37]YVOR W. In Defense of Reason[M]. Denver: Swallow, 1947.

CHAPTER IV   READER-RESPONSE CRITICISM

The old man was thin and gaunt with deep wrinkles in the back of his neck. The brown blotches of the benevolent skin cancer the sun brings from its reflection on the tropic sea were on his cheeks. The blotches ran well down the sides of his face and his hands had the deep-creased scars from handling heavy fish on the cords. But none of these scars were fresh. They were as old as erosions in a fishless desert.

Everything about him was old except his eyes and they were the same color as the sea and were cheerful and undefeated.

— The Old Man and The Sea E. M. Hemingway

4.1 INTRODUCTION

In a college-level introductory literature course, several class members are voicing their interpretations of Chapter 1 of *The Old Man and The Sea*, part of which is quoted at the beginning of this chapter. Student A declares that Santiago's struggle is obvious; he is simply debating whether he should listen to his feelings going on sailing again, or listen to his fellows to give up. This chapter asserts that Student A illustrates the novel's unifying theme: The old fisherman's struggle of obeying his innately good feelings versus obeying the abstract commandments of an institutionalized system, his society. What unites all the chapters in the text and is now highlighted and set background in this chapter, maintains Student A, is Santiago's realization that his inner feelings are correct and his society-dominated conscience is wrong. He accordingly opts for declaring his strong humanity and thus sticks to his willpower.

Student B objects, declaring that Student A's interpretation is not relevant to the 1990s. Student A is correct, claims Student B, when she notes that the old man chooses to obey his conscience and disavow his allegiance to society' dictates. This is indeed the writer's chief purpose in his novel. But the novel's significance rests in how it can be applied today. Prejudice, she contends, still exists in our college town. We, like the hero, must see the humanness in all our citizens.

Student C observes that Student A and B have both made valid criticism. What they have overlooked, however, is the change that now takes place in Santiago himself. No longer will we see an old fisherman who will be abandoned by his fellows or even consider hurting himself in any way, maintains Student C. We now have a Santiago who has positioned himself against his society and will not retreat. In the rest of the novel, declares Student C, we will observe this more maturely and directed Santiago as he responds to collective needs.

With a quiver in his voice, Student D remarks that the old man reminds of his youth. Like his young experience, says Student D, the old man likes the challenge no matter where he finds it. Being on the side of the oppressed, he chooses to guard his friend's dignity and self-worth.

Each of the four students sees something slightly different in Hemingway's passage. Consciously or unconsciously, each of their interpretations rests on different theoretical assumptions and their corresponding interpretative methodologies. Of the four interpretations, Student A's is the most distinct theoretical approach to the passage. Seeing an overall textual unity, Student A presupposes that the text is autonomous; it must interpret itself with little or no help from historical, societal, or any other extrinsic factors, with all its parts relating back to its central theme. Using the tenets of New Criticism, Student A posits the organic unity of the text. For this student, learning and applying literary terminology and searching for the correct interpretation are of utmost importance.

Unlike Student A, who applies a given set of criteria to the text in an attempt to discover its meaning, Students B, C, and D become participants in the interpretive process, actively bringing their own experiences to bear upon the text's meaning. Student B's interpretation, for example, highlights the theoretical difference between a text meaning (the author's intentions) and its significance or relevance to present-day readers. Student C's approach begins filling in the gaps in the text, hypothesizing how the old man will act in the pages yet unread based on his decision not to write to Jim's owner. Whether Student C is correct or not, and whether she will have to change some of her ideas concerning the mass, remains open. And Student D's theoretical framework objectifies the text and its meaning based on the reader's personal experiences with prejudice.

Although Students B, C, and D differ in their various approaches, none views the text as an objective entity that contains its own meaning (as does Student A). For these students, the text does not and cannot interpret itself. To determine a text's meaning, these students believe they must become active readers and participants in the interpretive process. Their various theoretical assumptions and methodologies are used to discover a text's meaning and exemplify reader-response criticism.

4.2 HISTORICAL DEVELOPMENT

Although reader-response criticism rose to prominence in literary analysis in the early 1970s and still influences much contemporary criticism, its historical roots can be traced to the 1920s and 1930s. Such precise dating, however, is artificial, for readers have obviously been responding to what they have read and experienced since the dawn of literature itself. Even the classical writers Plato and Aristotle were aware of and concerned about the reader's (or viewer's) reactions. Plato, for example, asserts that watching a play could so inflame the passions of the audience that the viewers would forget that they were rational beings and allow passion, not reason, to rule their actions. Similarly, in *the Poetics* Aristotle voices concern about the effects a play will have on the audience's emotions. Will it arouse the spectators' pity or fear? Will these emotions purge the viewer? Will they cleanse a spectator of all emotions by the play's end? Such interest in audience response to the artistic creation dominates much literary criticism.

Underlying both Plato's and Aristotle's concerns about audience response, and the concern of many critics who follow in their paths, is the assumption that the audience (or the reader) is passive. As if watching a play or reading a book were a spectator sport, readers sit passively, absorbing the contents of the artistic creation and allowing it to dominate their thoughts and actions. From this point of view, the reader brings little to the play or text. The text provides all that is needed to interpret itself.

From Plato's time until the beginning of the Romantic Movement in British literature at the beginning of the 1800s, such a passive view of the reader predominated. Although many critics recognized that a text did indeed have an effect on its readers, criticism concerned itself primarily with the text. With the advent of romanticism, emphasis shifted from the text to the author. The author now became the genius who could assimilate truths that were unacknowledged or unseen by the general populace. And as the nineteenth century progressed, concern for the author continued, with literary criticism stressing the importance of the author's life, times, and social context as chief aids in textual analysis.

But by the 1920s, emphasis in textual analysis once again shifted to the text. With the advent of the New Criticism, the text became autonomous — an objective entity that could be analyzed and dissected. If studied thoroughly, the New Critics believed, the text would reveal its own meaning. Extrinsic factors such as historical or social context mattered little. Now considered a verbal icon, the text itself, declared the New Critics, contains what we need to discover its meaning. We need only master the technical vocabulary and the correct techniques to unlock its meaning.

While positing the autonomy of the text, the New Critics did acknowledge the effects a text could have on its readers. Studying the effects of a literary work, they decreed, was not the same as studying the text itself, however. This emphasis on the objective nature of the text once again created a passive reader who did not bring personal experiences or private emotions to bear on textual analysis.

4.2.1   I. A. Richards

In the midst of New Criticism's rise to dominance in textual analysis which would last for more than 30 years, one of its two founding fathers, I A. Richards (T. S. Eliot being the other), became interested in the reading process itself. Using a decidedly reader-response approach to textual analysis, Richards distributed to his classes at Cambridge University copies of short poems of widely diverse aesthetic and literary value without citing their authors and titles and with various editorial changes that updated spelling and punctuation. He then asked his students to record their free responses and evaluations of each of these short texts. What surprised Richards was the wide variety of seemingly incompatible and contradictory responses.

After collecting and analyzing these responses, Richards published his findings, along with his own interpretations of the short texts, in *Principles of Literary Criticism*. Underlying Richard's text is his assumption that science, not poetry or any other literary genre, leads to truth — that is, science's view of the world is the correct one. Poems, on the other hand, can produce only "pseudo-statements" concerning the nature of reality. But such pseudo-statement, declares Richards, are essential to the overall psychological health of each individual. In fact, according to Richards, human beings are basically bundles of desires called appetites. In order to achieve psychic health, one must balance these desires by creating a personally acceptable vision of the world. Richards observes that religion was once able to provide this vision, but has lost its effectiveness to do so. Borrowing from the thoughts of nineteenth-century poet Matthew Arnold, Richards decrees that poetry, above all other art forms, can beset harmonize and satisfy humankind's appetites and thereby create fulfilling and intellectually acceptable worldview.

After creating such an affective system of analysis, which gives credence to a reader's emotional response to a text, Richards abandons this reader-response approach in his own analysis of his students' responses. Like the New Critics who were to follow him in the next several decades, he declares that the poem itself contains all the necessary information to arrive at the "right" or "more adequate" interpretation. Through textual analysis — that is, by closely examining the poem's diction, imagery, and overall unity — Richards believes a reader can arrive at a better or more correct interpretation of a poem than relying on sheerly personal responses to a text.

Despite his departing from his initial reader-response methodology, Richards recognized the contextual nature of reading poems, for he acknowledged that a reader brings to the text a vast array of ideas amassed through life's experiences, including previous literary experiences, and applies such information to the text. By so doing, the reader is no longer the passive receiver of knowledge but an active participant in the creation of a text's meaning.

4.2.2 Louise M. Rosenblatt

In the 1930s, Louise M. Rosenblatt further developed Richards's earlier assumptions concerning the contextual nature of the reading process. In her text *Literature as Exploration*, Rosenblatt asserts that both the reader and the text must work together to produce meaning. Unlike the New Critics, she shifts the emphasis of textual analysis away from the text alone and views the reader and the text as partners in the interpretive process.

In the late 1930s, however, Rosenblatt's ideas seemed revolutionary, too abstract, and simply off the beaten, critical path. Although New Criticism dominated literary practice for the next 30 years or so, Rosenblatt continued to develop her ideas, culminating her critical work with the publication of *The Reader, the Text, the poem*. In this work, she clarifies her earlier ideas and presents what has become one of the main critical positions held by many theorists and practical critics today.

According to Rosenblatt, the reading process involved a reader and a text. Both the reader and the text interact or share a trans-actional experience. The text acts as a stimulus for eliciting various past experiences, thoughts, and ideas from the reader, those found in both our everyday existence and in past reading experiences. Simultaneously, the text shapes the reader's experiences, selecting, limiting, and ordering the ideas that best conform to the text. Through this trans-actional experience, the reader and the text produce a new creation, a poem. For Rosenblatt and many other reader-response critics, a poem is now defined as the result of an event that takes place during the reading process, or what Rosenblatt calls the aesthetic transaction. No longer synonymous with the word text, a poem is created each time a reader interacts with a text, be that interaction a first reading or any of countless re-readings of the same text.

For Rosenblatt, readers can and do read in one of two ways: Efficiently or aesthetically. When we read for information — for example, when we read the directions for heating a can of soup — we are engaging in efferent reading. During this process we are interested only in newly gained information, not the actual words themselves. When we engage in aesthetic reading, we experience the text. We note its word, its sounds, its patterns, and so on. In essence, we live through the trans-actional experience of creating the poem.

When reading aesthetically, we involve ourselves in an elaborate encounter of give-and-take with the text. Although the text may allow for many interpretations by eliciting and highlighting different past experiences of the reader, it simultaneously limits the valid meanings a poem can acquire. For Rosenblatt, a poem's meaning is not therefore a smorgasbord of endless interpretations, but a trans-actional experience in which several different yet probable meanings emerge and thereby create a variety of "poems".

What differentiates Rosenblatt's and all reader-response critics from other critical approaches (especially New Criticism) is their diverting the emphasis away from the text as the sole determiner of meaning to the significance of the reader as an essential participant in the reading process and the creation of meaning. Such a shift negates the formalists' assumption that the text is autonomous and can therefore be scientifically analyzed to discover its meaning. No longer, then, is the reader passive, merely applying a long list of learned, poetic devices to a text in the hope of discovering its intricate patterns of paradox and irony, which, in turn, will lead to a supposed correct interpretation. For reader-response critics, the reader now becomes an active participant along with the text in creating meaning. It is from the literacy experience (an event that occurs when a reader and print interact), they believe, that meaning evolves.

4.3 ASSUMPTIONS

Like most approaches to literary analysis, reader-response criticism does not provide us with a unified body of theory or a single methodological approach for textual analysis. What those who call themselves reader-response critics, reader-critics, or audience-oriented critics share is a concern for the reader. Believing that a literary work's interpretation is created when a reader and a text interact or transact, these critics assert that the proper study of textual analysis must consider both the reader and the text, not simply a text in isolation. For these critics, the reader + the text = meaning. Only in context with a reader actively involved in the reading process with the text, they decree, can meaning emerge.

Meaning, reader-response critics declare, is context dependent and intricately associated with the reading process. Like literary theory as a whole, several theoretical models and their practical applications exist to explain the reading process, or how we make sense of printed material. Using these various models, we can group these multiple approaches to the literacy experience into three broad categories. Each category emphasizes a somewhat different philosophy, a body of assumptions, and a methodology to explain what these various critics believe happens when a reader interacts with printed material.

Although each model espouses a different approach to textual analysis, all hold to some of the same presuppositions and concerns and ask similar questions. For example, all focus directly on the reading process. What happens, they ask, when a person picks up printed material and reads it? Put another way, their chief interest is what occurs when a text and a reader interact. During this interaction, reader-response critics investigate and theorize whether the reader, the text, or some combination finally determines the text's interpretation. Is it the reader who manipulates the text, they ponder, or does the text manipulate the reader to produce meaning? Do some words, phrases, or images trigger in the reader's mind a specific interpretation, or does the reader approach the text with a conscious or unconscious collection of learned reading strategies that systematically impose an interpretation on the text?

Such questions lead reader-response critics to a further narrowing and developing of terminology. For example, they ask, what is a text? Are they simply the words or symbols on a page? How, they ask, can we differentiate between what is actually in the text and what is in the mind of the reader? And who is this reader, anyway? Are there various kinds of readers? Is it possible that different texts presuppose different kinds of readers?

What about a reader's response to a text? Are the responses equivalent to the text's meaning? Can one reader's response be more correct than some other reader's, or are all responses equally valid? Although readers respond to the same text in a variety of ways, they ask, why do many readers individually arrive at the same conclusions or interpretations of the same text?

Reader-response critics also ask questions about another person: the author. What part, if any, does the author play in a work's interpretation? Can the author's attitudes toward the reader actually influence a work's meaning? And if a reader knows the author's clearly stated intentions for a text, does this information have any part in creating the text's meaning, or should an author's intentions for a work simply be ignored?

The concerns of reader-response critics can best be summarized in one question: What happens during the reading process? The answer to this question is perplexing, for it involves investigating such factors as:

The reader, including this or her worldview, background, purpose for reading, knowledge of the world, knowledge of words, and other such factors.

The text, with all its various linguistic elements.

Meaning, or how the text and the reader interact so that the reader can make sense of the printed material.

How reader-response critics define and explain each of these elements determines their approaches to textual analysis. Furthermore, such answers also help determine what constitutes a valid interpretation of a text for each critic.

Although many reader-response critics allow for a wide range of legitimate response to a text, most agree that reader-response criticism does not mean that any and all interpretations are valid or of equal importance. The boundaries and restrictions placed on possible interpretations of a text vary, depending upon how the critic defines the various elements of the reading process. It is these definitions and assumptions that allow us to group reader-response critics into several broad subgroups.

4.4 METHODOLOGY

Although reader-response critics use a wide variety of critical approaches — from those espousing their own particular and modified form of New Criticism to postmodern practitioners such as deconstructionists — most adherents of reader-response theory and practice fall into three distinct groups. Although members of each group may differ slightly, each particular group espouses its own distinct theoretical and methodological concerns. Student B's interpretation at the beginning of this chapter represents the focus of the first group.

Like all reader-response critics, this group believes that the reader must be an active participant in the creation of meaning, but for these critics the text has more control over the interpretative process than does the reader. A few of these critics lean toward New Critical theory, asserting that some interpretations are more valid than others. Other differentiate between a text's meaning and its significance. For them, the text's meaning can be synonymous with its author's intention, while its significance can change from one context or historical period to another. But the majority of critics in this first group belong to the school known as structuralism.

Structuralism

Basing their ideas on the writings of Ferdinand de Saussure, the father of modern linguistics, structuralists often approach textual analysis as if it were a science. Their proponents — Roland Barthes, Gerard Genette, Roman Jakobson, Claude Levi-Strauss, Gerald Prince, and Jonathan Culler in his early works — look for specific codes within the text that allow meaning to occur. These codes or signs embedded in the text are part of a large system that allows meaning to occur in all facets of society, including literature. For example, when we are driving a car and we see a red light hanging above an intersection, we have learned that we must stop our car. And if we hear a fire engine or an ambulance siren, we have also learned that we must pull over to the side of the road. Both the red light and the sirens are signs or codes in our society that provide us with ways of interpreting and ordering our word.

According to structuralist critics, a reader brings to the text a predetermined system of ascertaining meaning (a complex system of signs or codes like the sirens and the red light) and applies this sign system directly to the text. The text becomes important because it contains signs or signals to the reader that have established and acceptable interpretations. Many structuralists are therefore more concerned about the overall system of meaning a given society has developed than with textual analysis itself, and concentrate on what a reader needs to know about interpreting any sign (such as a road sign or a word) in the context of acceptable societal standards. Because of this emphasis, structuralists seem to push both the text and the reader to the background and highlight a linguistic theory of communication and interpretation. Because structuralism has become a springboard for many other modern theories of literary criticism, its significance to literary theory and practical criticism will be explored at length in Chapter 5.

Meanwhile, the ideas of one leading structuralist, Gerard Prince, will illustrate the methodology of structuralism.

Gerard Prince In the 1970s, Gerard Prince helped develop a specific kind of structuralism known as narratology, the process of analyzing a story using all the elements involved in its telling. Such as narrator, voice, style, verb tense, personal pronouns, audience and so forth. Prince noted that critics often ask questions concerning the story's technical narrative point of view (omniscient, limited, first person, etc.) but rarely do they ask about the person to whom the narrator is speaking, the narratee. Usually the narratee is not the actual person reading the text, for Prince argues that the narrative itself — that is, the story — produces the narratee. By first observing and then analyzing various signs in the text — such as pronoun reference; direct address ("Dear reader"); gender, race, and social class references; and writing style — Prince believes it is possible not only to identify the narratee but also to classify stories based on the different kinds of narrates created by the texts themselves. Such narratees may include the real reader (person actually reading the book), the virtual reader (the reader to whom the author believes he or she is writing), and the ideal reader (the one who explicitly and implicitly understands all the nuances, terminology, and structure of a text).

Although such an approach relies heavily on textual analysis, Prince's concerns about the reader place him in the reader-response school of criticism. Other structuralists, such as Jonathan Culler, who distance themselves from Prince and such close reliance on the text to generate meanings will be discussed in Chapter 5.

Phenomenology

Student C represents the second mayor group of reader-response critics. For the most part, these critics follow Rosenblatt's assumption that the reader is involved in a trans-actional experience when interpreting a text. Both the text and the reader, they declare, play roughly equal parts in the interpretive process. For them, reading is an event that culminates in the creation of the poem.

Many adherents in this group — George Poulet, Wolfgang Iser, Hans Robert Jauss, Roman Ingarden, and Gaston Bachelard — are often associated with phenomenology. Phenomenology is a modern philosophical tendency that emphasizes the perceiver. Objects can have meaning, phenomenologists maintain, only if an active consciousness (a perceiver) absorbs or notes their existence. In other words, objects exist if and only if we register them on our consciousness. Rosenblatt's definition of a poem directly applies this theory to literary study. The true poem can exist only in the reader's consciousness, not on the printed page. When reader and text interact, the poem and therefore meaning are created; they exist only in the consciousness of the reader. Reading and textual analysis now become an aesthetic experience whereby both the reader and the text combine in the consciousness of the reader to create the poem. As in Student C's interpretation at the beginning of the chapter, the reader's imagination must work, filling in the gaps in the text and conjecturing about characters' actions, personality traits, and motives. The ideas and practices of two reader-response critics, Hans Robert Jauss and and Wolfgang Iser, illustrate phenomenology's methodology.

German critic Hans Robert Jass emphasized that a text's social history must be considered in interpreting the text. Unlike New Critical scholars, Jauss declares that critics must examine how any given text was accepted or received by its contemporary readers. Espousing a particular kind of reader-response criticism known as reception theory, Jauss asserts that readers from any given historical period devise for themselves the criteria whereby they will judge a text. Using the term horizons of expectation to include all of a historical period's critical vocabulary and assessment of a text, Jauss points out that how any text is evaluated from one historical period to another (from the Enlightenment to the Romantic period, for example), necessarily changes. For example, Alexander Pope's poetry was heralded as the most nearly perfect poetry of its day, for heroic couplets and poetry that followed prescribed forms were judged as superior. During the Romantic period, however, with its emphasis on content, not form, the critics' reception of Pope's poetry was not as great.

Accordingly, Jauss argues because each historical period establishes its own horizons of expectation, the overall value and meaning of any text can never become fixed or universal, for readers from any historical period establish for themselves what they value in a text. A text, then, does not have one and only one correct interpretation, for its supposed meaning changes from one historical period to another. A final assessment about any literary work thus becomes impossible.

For Jauss, the reader's reception or understanding and evaluation of a text matter greatly. Although the text itself remains important in the interpretative process, the reader, declares Jauss, plays an essential role.

Wolfgang Iser

German phenomenologist Wolfgang Iser borrows and amends Jauss's ideas. Iser believes that any object — a stone, a house, or a poem — does not achieve meaning until an active consciousness recognizes or registers this object. It is thus impossible to separate what is known (the object) from the mind that knows it (human consciousness). Using these phenomenological ideas as the basis for his reader-response theory and practice, Iser declares that the critic's job is not to dissect or explain the text, for once a text is read, the object and the reader (the perceiver) are essentially one. Instead, the critic's role is to examine and explain the text's effect on the reader.

Iser, however, differentiates between two kinds of readers: The "implied reader" who "embodies all those predispositions necessary for a literary work to exercise its effect — predispositions laid down, not by an empirical side outside reality but by the ext itself. Consequently, the implied reader… has his or her roots firmly planted in the structure of the text", as opposed to the actual reader, the person who physically picks up the text and reads it. It is this reader who comes to the text shaped by cultural and personal norms and prejudices. By positing the implied reader, Iser affirms the necessity of examining the text in the interpretive process while declaring the validity of an individual reader's response to the text by acknowledging the actual reader.

Like Jauss, Iser disavows the New Critical stance that a text has one and only one correct meaning and asserts that a text has many possible interpretations. For Iser, texts in and of themselves do not possess meaning. When a text is concertized by the reader (the phenomenological concept whereby the text registers on the readers consciousness), the read automatically views the text form his or her personal worldview. However, because texts do not tell the reader everything that needs to be known about a character, a situation, a relationship, and other such textual elements, readers must automatically fill in these gaps, using their knowledge base grounded in their worldviews. In addition, each reader creates his or her horizons of expectation — that is, a reader's expectation about what will or may happen next. (Note that Iser's use of this term is more individual-oriented than that Jauss, who coined it). These horizons of expectation change frequently, for the center of all stories is conflict or dramatic tension, often resulting in sudden loss, pain, unexpected joy or fear, and at times great fulfillment. Such changes cause a reader to modify his or her horizons of expectation to fit a text's particular situation.

For example, when in Chapter 31 of *the Adventures of Huckleberry Finn Huck* declares that he will not write a letter to Miss Walson telling her Jim's location, Huck openly chooses to side with Jim against the precepts of Huck's society. A reader may then assume that Huck will treat Jim differently, for now Jim, the slave has a chance to become a free man. According to Iser, the reader has now established horizons of expectation. When the reader, however, observes in just a few short chapters later that Tom Sawyer has talked Huck into chaining Jim to a table, the reader may need to reformulate his or her previous horizons of expectation, for Huck is not treating Jim as a free man but once again as a slave.

In making sense of the text, filling in the text's gaps, and continually adopting new horizons of expectation, the reader uses his or her own value system, personal and public experiences, and philosophical beliefs. When, according to Iser, each reader makes "concrete" the text, each concretization is therefore personal allowing the new creation — the text's meaning and effect on the reader — to be unique.

For Iser the reader is an active, essential player in the text's interpretation, writing part of the text as the story is read and concretized and becoming its coauthor.

Subjective Criticism

Student D represents the third group of reader-response critics, who place the greatest emphasis on the reader in the interpretive process. For these psychological or subjective critics, the reader's thoughts, beliefs, and experiences play a greater part than the actual text in shaping a work's meaning. Led by Norman Holland and David Bleich, these critics assert that we can create and find our self-identities in the reading process.

Norman Holland

Using Freudian psychoanalysis as the foundation for his theory and practices formulated in the early 1970s, Norman Holland believes that at birth we receive from our mothers a primary identity. Through our life's experiences we personalize this identity, transforming it into our own individualized identity theme, which becomes the lens through which we see the world, Textual interpretation then becomes a matter of working out our own fears, desires, and needs to help maintain our psychological health.

Like Rosenblatt, Holland asserts that the reading Process is a transaction between the text and the reader. The text is indeed important, for it contains its own themes, its own unity and its own structure. A reader, however, transforms a text into a private world, a place where one works out (through the ego) his or her fantasies, which are mediated by the text so that they will be socially acceptable.

For Holland, all interpretations are therefore subjective. Unlike New Criticism, his reader-response approach asserts that there is no such thing as a correct interpretation. From his perspective, there are as many valid interpretations as there are readers, for the act of interpretation is a subjective experience.

David Bleich

The founder of subjective criticism David Bleich (1978) agrees with Holland's psychological understanding of the interpretive process, but Bleich devalues the role the text plays, denying its objective existence. Meaning, Bleich argues, does not reside in the text but is developed when the reader works in cooperation with other readers to achieve the text's collective meaning (what Bleich calls the interpretation). Only when each reader is able to articulate his or her individual responses within a group about the text, can the group work together, negotiate meaning. Such "communally motivated negotiations" ultimately determine the text's meaning.

For Bleich, the starting point for interpretation is the reader's responses to a text, not the text itself. According to Bleich, however, these responses do not constitute the text's meaning, for meaning cannot be found within a text or within responses to the text. Rather, a text's meaning must be developed from and out of his reader's responses, working in conjunction with other readers' responses and with past literary and life experiences. In other words, Bleich differentiates between the reader's response to a text (which for Bleich can never be equated to a reader's interpretation) and the reader's interpretation or meaning, which must be developed communally in a classroom or similar setting.

The key to developing a text's meaning is the working out of one's responses to a text so that these responses can be challenged and amended and then accepted by one's social group. Subjective critics such as Bleich assert that when reading a text a reader may respond to something in the text in a bizarre and personal way. These private responses will, through discussion, be pruned away by members of the reader's social group. Finally the group will decide what the acceptable interpretation of the text is. Like Student D's interpretation cited at the beginning of this chapter, the reader responds personally to some specific element in the text and then seeks to objectify this personal response and declares it to be an interpretation of the text. Only through negotiations with other readers (and other texts), however, can one develop the text's meaning.

A Two–Step Methodology

Although reader-response critics all believe the reader plays a part in discovering a text's meaning, just how small or large a part is debatable. Espousing various theoretical assumptions, these critics must necessarily have different methodologies with regard to textual analysis. According to contemporary critic Steven Mailloux, however, they all share that a work gives a reader a task or something to do, and the reader's response or answer to that task.

For example, Student D cited at the beginning of this chapter obviously saw something in the text that triggered his memories of his friend George. His task is to discover what in the text triggered his memory and why. He moves, then, from the text to his own thoughts, memories, and past experiences. These personal experiences temporarily overshadow the text, but he realizes that his personal reactions must in some way become acceptable to his peers. He therefore compares George to Huck and himself to Jim and thereby objectifies his personal feelings while having his interpretation deemed socially respectable inn his interpretative community — a term coined by reader-response critic Stanley Fish to designate a group of readers who share the same interpretative strategies.

Because the term *reader-response criticism* allows for so much divergence in theory and methods, many twentieth-century schools of criticism such as deconstruction, feminism, Marxism, and New Historicism declare their membership in this broad classification. Each of these approaches to textual analysis provides its own ideological basis to reader-response theory and develops its unique methods of practical criticism. Such an eclectic membership ensures the continued growth and ongoing development of reader-response criticism.

4.5 QUESTIONS FOR ANALYSIS

Because reader-response critics use a variety of methodologies, no particular list of questions can encompass all their concerns. By asking the following questions of a text, however, one can participate in both the theory and practice of reader-response criticism:

· Who is the actual reader?

· Who is the implied reader?

· Who is the ideal reader?

· Who is the narratee?

· What are some gaps you see in the text?

· Can you list several horizons of expectations and show how they change from a particular text's beginning to its conclusion?

· Using Jauss's definition of horizons of expectations, can you develop first on your own and then with your classmates an interpretation of a particular text?

· Can you identify your identity theme as you develop your personal interpretation of the text?

· Using Bleich's subjective criticism, can you state the difference between your response to a text and your interpretation?

· In a classroom setting, develop your class's interpretive strategies for arriving at the meaning of a text.

4.6   SAMPLE ESSAYS

After reading the sample essay that follows, be able to identify the narratee and the implied and the ideal reader. In addition, be able to identify which one of the various subgroups of reader-response criticism the author of the essay uses to write this essay Is the text, the reader plus the text, or the reader of most importance for this critic in her methodology and philosophy? In addition, can you point out the various personal strategies or moves the author makes to arrive at her interpretation? Also note the style of the essay. From what technical narrative point of view does the author write the essay? Why? Finally, what is the tone of the essay? How does the author establish this tone, and do you believe it is effective?

In the sample professional essay that follows, be able to explain how Norman Holland uses his own theoretical model of reader-response criticism in writing this essay. In other words, explain how the author uses his own identity theme in his interpretation. In addition, be able to identify the Reader-response vocabulary the author uses throughout the essay. Does the author redefine these terms or does he use them as a New Critic word? Finally, be able to discuss the particulars of Bakhtin's style. Does the author's writing style differ from a New Critic's style? If so, explain. If not, explain.

4.7   SAMPLE ESSAYS

On English Translation Versions of *Dao De Jing* from Bakhtin's Theory of Dialogue —
A Case Study of Roger T. Ames's, Arther Waley and Lin Yutang

Bakhtin's theory of dialogue is initiatory in exploring the reader's role in the authoring process of a text, and establishing a co-authorship between the reader and the author. It is of great significance to the translation study, especially to the study of the target reader's role in the practice of translation. However, the theory also has its shortcoming. As a philosopher, Bakhtin elaborates his theory and thoughts of dialogue in an abstract rather than specific way, and he does not deepen the discussion of the relationship between the author and the reader. Nevertheless, the essential spirit of the dialogic relationship can still be detected in his vast and profound thoughts and be applied to the study of the target reader's role in literary translation.

With the development of translation theory and practice, more and more translation theorists and scholars agree on the point that translation is primarily an act of cross-cultural communication, which involves two main stages, namely the translator's interpretation of the source text and representation of the target text. The translator first acts as a reader of the source text and then plays the role of the author of the target text. Enlightened by the dialogic relationship between the author and the reader, it is not difficult to infer that in the representation stage of translation, there exists a dialogic relationship between the translator and the target reader, the translated version being the medium of their dialogue. Translation is not just a process that happens in the translator's mind; a reader also decides to accept or reject the translation. The reader's acceptance is the final stage of the whole translation activity. Therefore, this process of representation entails the translator's endeavor to cater to the target reader's "conceptual horizon". The role of the target reader in the authoring period of the target text is precisely manifested by the translator's consideration of the translation activities that are various and cover literary, political, technical, and routine-work translation based on the source materials. Literary translation is what is concerned about in this thesis. Toury deems it is not restricted to "the translation of texts which are regarded as literary in the source culture," but in a broad sense refers to "the translation of a text in such a way that the product be acceptable as literary to the recipient culture." Different from other types of translation, literary translation is more than transfer of information. Literary works stress aesthetic values as well as informative value. Here by "aesthetic values", it means linguistic and literary aesthetics and unanimous ideology as well. That is the main difference from other kinds of translations. It is known that the aesthetic values with regard to a sign or a phenomenon in the source text are based on the conceptual system assumed to be common to both the author and the source text readers. However, in the process of intercultural interaction, i.e. translation, the source text author belongs to the source culture and the target reader belongs to the target culture. Since conceptual systems are conditioned by cultural norms and conventions, the aesthetic values of the source text are probably different from those of the target reader. This means that one phenomenon, linguistic or social. Conforming to so in literary translation, the translator needs to make some shifts on the source text especially when the aesthetic distance between the work and the target reader's "conceptual horizon" is too large and therefore the readers perhaps cannot derive the aesthetic pleasure from the translated version. Otherwise, the translated version is hard for the target reader to accept, let alone understand it and therefore realize the communication between the translator and the target reader. Naturally, it produced little effect at that time. Why is Lu's translation, faithful to the source texts, not accepted by the target Chinese reader? The reason lies in the strangeness of the language style and literary genre in Lu's translation. Lu Xun employed abstruse classical Chinese that is difficult to understand for the Chinese reader at that time; moreover, he attempted to introduce the new genre of short story to the target Chinese readers by employing short stories in the collection. However, at that time, what was popular in China was the popular classical Chinese versions, like Lin Shu's, and the target readers at that time were not accustomed to the genre of short story. On such occasions, the target reader would be intimidated or thwarted by the awkward wording and the strange genre in the translation and leave it aside. In this way, it is barely possible to impart the target reader with the information of the target text, let alone aesthetics appreciation.

Though the source work *Evolution and Ethics and Other Essays* by Henry Huxley is not a literary work, Yan Fu employed the refined and graceful language of pre-Han dynasty, that is, the old literary style of Tongcheng School, when he translated *Evolution and Ethics* and Other Essays. His choice of the old literary style in his translation *Evolution and Ethics* was closely related to his consideration of his intended readers, i.e. the intelligentsia and officialdom. In late nineteenth century, the classical Chinese prose enjoyed a high prestige in China's literary system. Almost all the celebrated scholars were expert in writing in the style of classical prose and enjoyed reading such prose. It was natural that Yan Fu chose classical Chinese of pre-Han dynasty to attract his target readers to read his translation. In addition, techniques of illuminating prefaces and additional notes were employed to naturalize the foreign texts. According to Wang Kefei, Yan Fu had added 28 notes — over 21,000 words to the version of *Evolution and Ethics*, which accounted for over two fifths of the total length. To have done so, Yan Fu was to ensure the acceptability of his introduction of western learning to his elite readers, i.e. the intelligentsia and the officialdom. Each translator is forced to consider the target readers' aesthetic tendency and their acceptability. Just as in Lefevere's view, the translator should pay great attention to the influence of "poetics" that consists of two components, one of which is an inventory of the literary devices, genres, motifs, prototypical characters and situations, and symbols. In literature, this component of "poetics" is represented by the means of literary writing that takes a leading role in the literary system. The translator tends to rewrite the source text with the poetics of the target reader so as to cater to readers of the translated text. The influence of the target reader's aesthetic values can also be well seen in Pan Xizi's and Lin Shu's translations of *Joan Haste* by the English novelist Haggard Sir Henry Rider.

A translator should pay more attention to the "poetics"and the ideology of the target language reader. And in case the translator has doubts about how to make a better compromise between the source text and the target readers, he should always try to cater to the readers and their expectations.

Types of Target Readers in Literary Translation

"No translator should begin to work without first knowing who is the intended audience". In literary translation, different target readers possess different abilities of decoding information and different aesthetic values, therefore demanding different translated versions. There are many statements about the analysis and classification of the target readers in literary translation and translation theories. In China, Lu Xun in one of his letters to Qu Qiubai, roughly categorized the people in the target society into three groups: Those well-educated; those receiving some education; and those almost illiterate. The last group can be excluded for their being outside the scope of readers. For the second group, "rewriting" is the more suitable strategy, while it is acceptable to add some new expressions and new grammar in the translated version. As for the first group, he insisted that the translation should be rather faithful than expressive. In the West, Theodore Savory, an English scholar, in his *The Art of Translation*，distinguished "readers of translations" into "at least four groups": the reader who knows nothing at all of the original language; the student who is learning the language of the original; the reader who knew the language in the past but who has now forgotten almost the whole of his early knowledge; and the scholar who knows it still. And for the four kinds of readers, the translator should have "alternative kinds of translations" to "fit them naturally and completely". He said, "The ignoramus is happy with the free translation; it satisfies his curiosity and he reads it easily, without the pain of thought. The student is best helped by the most literal translation that can be made in accurate English; it helps him to grasp the implications of the different constructions of the language that he is studying and points out the correct usage of its less familiar words. The third prefers the translation that sounds like a translation; it brings back more keenly the memories of his early scholarship and gives him a subconscious impression that almost he is reading the original language. And the fourth, who knows both the matter and the style of the original, may perhaps find pleasure in occasional touches of scholarship..." Of course, there are other classifications of target readers. Fu Sinian classified the target text readers into two groups, namely, common readers and scholars Mao Dun divided readers into two categories, namely ordinary readers and literary apprentice. With the increase of the number of readers who have received higher education, divided the readers into two groups: professional readers and common readers. Recently, Gu Zhengkun offered a clearer demarcation between seven groups of readers: those who know nothing about a foreign language, those who know much about it, those who are expert in it, academic scholars, special practitioners in a certain field, average entertainers and knowledge-learners. No matter how readers are categorized, it is quite evident that a work can by no means satisfy every reader. The translator can only aim his work at a group of particular readers. It is of great necessity for the translator to adopt different translation strategies in alteration in accordance with different target readers. For example, the translator of children's literature has to consider children's education level and acceptability, and make necessary shifts in wording, grammar, plot, etc. in the translated version. Each version has gathered a certain group of readers around. This fact shows that in the same period, different target readers have different requirements to the translated version. Furthermore, the requirements of target readers are in a dynamic development. As time goes on, target readers ask for a different translated version, since their knowledge and aesthetic values have grown different from those of the readers before them. Take one sentence from *Dao De Jing* for example,

In Chapter 10, "爱民治国，能无为乎？" ①

Stephen Mitchell: Can you love people and lad them without imposing your will?

Gu Zhengkun: If you are to love the people and govern a state, Can you avoid *taking ill action*?

Roger T. Ames: In loving the people and governing the kingdom, can you rule *without interference*?

Xu Yuanchong: Can a people-loving ruler not interfere in the state affair?

"Wu Wei" is one of the main philosophy concepts of *Laotzu*. *Laotzu* advocates that the ruler of a nation should take 无为 (Wuwei) as a principle to rule a nation. 无为 (Wuwei), its literal meaning is doing noting and keep thing as what it is. But in these translations, it can be seen that the phrase 无为 is concretized in the target context. It can refer to the rulers not taking ill action in ruling a nation, or not imposing his own will on the nation or not interfering the life of people. Although the expression is different, it can concretely convey what 无为 (Wuwei) means and the target readers may understand it more easily.

In the translation of *Dao De Jing*, there are some concepts which cannot find out special term to express it but the special meaning of the concepts can vividly convey the meaning of the concepts, so in the translation of *Dao De Jing* some translators choose capitalizing initial words to solve such translation problem. On one hand, these capitalizing initial words can remind readers they are concepts put forward by Laotzu, on the other hand, the meaning of these concepts are presented by themselves and the target readers do not need to make many efforts to comprehend it and gain the context effect easily. The special manifestation of this kind of translation method is concluded as follows:

"What the *Dao De Jing* has to offer, on the other hand, is much simpler. It encourages the cultivation of a disposition that is captured in what we have chosen to call its wu-forms. The Wu-forms free up the energy required to sustain the abstract cognitive and moral sensibilities of technical philosophy, allowing this energy, now unmediated by concepts, theories, and contrived moral precepts, to be expressed as those concrete feelings that inspire the ordinary business of the day. It is through these concrete feelings that one is able to know the world and to optimize the human experience." The abstraction of the concrete ethical dimension of such feeling melted into

---

① WANG BI. Annotation to Dao De Jing[EB/OL]. [2018-03-10].https://www.daodejing.org/10.html.

a formal moralist vocabulary that is rehearsed in Chapter 38 of *Dao De Jing*:

上德不德，是以有德；下德不失德，是以无德。上德无为而无以为；下德无为而有以为。上仁为之而无以为；上义为之而有以为。上礼为之而莫之应，则攘臂而扔之。故失道而后德，失德而后仁，失仁而后义，失义而后礼。夫礼者，忠信之薄，而乱之首。前识者，道之华，而愚之始。是以大丈夫处其厚，不居其薄；处其实，不居其华。故去彼取此。

It is because the most excellent (De) do not strive to excel (De)

That they are of the highest efficacy (De).

And it is because the least excellent do not leave off striving to excel

That they have no efficacy. Persons of the highest efficacy neither do things coercively.

Nor would they have any motivation for doing so.

Persons who are most authoritative (Ren) do things coercively

And yet are not motivated in doing so.

Persons who are most appropriate (Yi) do things coercively

And indeed do have a motive for doing so.

Persons who are exemplars of ritual propriety (if) do things coercively

And when no one pays them any heed,

They yank up their sleeves and drag others along with them.

Thus, only when we have lost sight of way-making (Dao) is there excellence,

Only when we have lost sight of excellence is there authoritative conduct,

Only when we have lost sight of authoritative conduct is there appropriateness,

And only when we have lost sight of appropriateness is there ritual propriety.

As for ritual propriety, it is the thinnest veneer of doing one's best and making good on one's word,

And it is the first sign of trouble.

"Foreknowledge" is tinsel decorating the way,

And is the first sign of ignorance.

It is for this reason that persons of consequence:

Set store by the substance rather than the veneer

And by the fruit rather than the flower.[1]

Hence, eschewing one they take the other.[2]

The moral precepts described in the first two stanzas emerge as objects of reverence, but as hallowed as they might become, they are anemic when compared to the love and life of concrete, spontaneous feelings.

Roger T. Ames's version conforms to modern Chinese readers' aesthetic tendency, easy and smooth and facilitating the target reader's comprehension and appreciation. However, with the development of cross-cultural communications between China and the West, the Chinese reader hopes to know more about vocabulary and syntax with authentic foreign flavor, and to read literary translation works with the language style different from their own. So when retranslating the famous western literary works, many translators transliterate the names of people and places, and employ fewer idiomatic idioms and four-character patterns as long as the target reader can understand the version well.

Let's take another example concerning Zhang Guruo's translation to show this. The stage of mental comfort to which they had arrived at this hour was one wherein their souls seemed to expand beyond their skins, spreading their personalities warmly through the room. If Zhang's translation is more idiomatic and more exquisite and is popularly accepted by modern readers, then contemporary readers seem to show a greater preference for these versions, which is more faithful to the source text and saves "foreign flavor" of the scene. The above discussion shows that the target readers are different synchronically and diachronically, and have different aesthetic values; therefore, the translator should, before translating, make clear for whom his translation is intended. Only by keeping his intended target readers in mind, can the author effectively foresee their aesthetic values and employ proper translation strategies to meet the "conceptual horizon" of his intended readers. In other words, only when the translator has an accurate understanding of the target reader, can he choose appropriate expressions for his translated version and can he realize his dialogue with the target reader. Therefore, the target reader the translator's version

---

① WANG BI. Annotation to Dao De Jing[EB/OL]. [2018-03-10]. https://www.daodejing.org/10.html.

② AMES R, YOUNG W. Lao Tzu: Text, Notes, and Comments[M]. Taibei: Chengwen Publisher. 1981:126.

aims at exerts a great influence on the translator's authoring of the target text in translation. From this point of view, it also goes no saying that the assessment of a translated literary work should to some extent refer to the type of target readers; However, one translated version aims at point should be made clear that translating is after all different from writing, in which the writer tries to create something new. A translator is, as Dryden described, "dancing on ropes with fettered legs"; he is restricted by the original work all the time and shows faithfulness to the source text in different degrees. For example, from the end of 19th century to the mid 20th century, constrained by the target readers' relatively limited knowledge of other nations and the communicative purpose of translation, it is dangerous to impose alien cultural knowledge and aesthetic values on the target reader. Under such conditions, many translators domesticated the foreign literary works in many cases to make the versions better understood. With the promotion of international communications and the increase of educational levels in contemporary times, as Yang Xiaorong points out, the readers who read foreign literary works hope and desire to obtain the culture knowledge of different countries, appreciate the views of different countries and satisfy the different aesthetic requirements through their imaginative thinking. People are more and more keen on "foreignized" literary translated works rather than "domesticated" ones, though there still exist differences among different nations. For the translator, to domesticate or to foreignize in the practice of translation depends on the extent to which the relevant cultural knowledge and aesthetic tendency drawn from the source text are shared by the target readers in different versions and in different periods. The key point is to make the target text understood by the target reader, and to promote the dialogue between the translator and the target reader.

The Target Reader's Knowledge of Alien Culture-loaded Words

A word has not only a designative meaning but also a connotative meaning that is closely related with a nation's culture. Cultural differences are closely related to religious faith, social system, geographical condition, literary tradition, set of value system and conception of beauty, etc. There are vast differences between the English culture and the Chinese culture in these specific aspects. Consequently, discrepancies of the meanings of words are always existing. A person's comprehension of a word depends largely on his own cultural knowledge, consciously or unconsciously.

The source text reader has the same cultural background as the source text author, so he can grasp the deep-leveled meaning of a culture-loaded word. However, the target language reader differs from the original reader in their cultural background. When target readers confront a culture-loaded word whose cultural background is foreign to them, and whose cultural frame of reference alters, they are less prepared to make sense of the meaning of signs under a totally different cultural context. Some signs bring nice connotations in one nation, whereas neutral or derogatory emotions in another, for example. Consequently, confusion and misunderstanding are apt to set off between the source text and the target reader; and transference of information and cultural exchange in interlingual communication will to a substantial extent be hampered and the dialogue between the translator and the target reader fails. Therefore, the target reader's knowledge level about the foreign culture is an important element to be considered in the translating process. The translator has to make some formal adjustments or add annotations in the translated version.

Words, which are identical in designative meanings, but different in connotative meanings, are one kind which may mislead the target reader when encountered in the translated version. An example which can convincingly tell the difference between English and Chinese of seemingly corresponding words. Some idioms also fall into our consideration of the words with different connotations, since by definition, they are usually structurally fixed and semantically opaque, and function as a single unit of meaning. In most cases, a native reader of the source text can figure out the literal and figurative meanings in the light of his national culture. However, if the target reader finds exotic cultural elements in the idioms of a translated text, he will, in accordance with the context perceive it based on his own 'conceptual horizon' and may get a misunderstanding or even find himself at a loss. The translator should take into consideration the reader's knowledge of idioms, as well as the vividness and expressiveness of the idioms in translated literary works, especially when dealing with superficially identical or similar idioms that are in fact different in connotations.

In the following part, the paper will discuss the influence of the target reader's knowledge of these words on translation in two aspects, namely allusions and other signs or expressions resulting from national peculiarity.

Allusions are treasures in each nation's historical culture because they are rich in national language expressions and have distinct cultural connotations. But such allusions are not always easy to understand. In literature, allusion is "an implied or indirect reference to a person, event, thing, or a part of another text." And "most are based on the assumption that there is a body of knowledge that is shared by the author and the reader and that therefore the reader will understand the author's referent."[1] It is no wonder that many of them can bring great handicaps to the interpretation on the part of the target readers, who are unfamiliar with the source culture, if these allusions are not properly handled. Such allusions may stem from various sources, which may be literary works, religious works, legends, fables, historical events, games and place names, etc. In the process of translation, if the translator has a good prediction of the reader's knowledge about these allusions, the target readers will have a better understanding of the translated version. Otherwise, the readers will miss or misunderstand the intention of the version. "When the old man at the frontier lost his horse, he thought it might be a good thing...". Considering that the allegory in the example is strange to the target reader, the translator annotates the whole story after literal translation. When the western reader gets familiar with Chinese allegories years later, the translator can spare the effort of the annotation.

Owing to the substantial cultural distance, this expression sounds meaningless and unnatural in Chinese if translated "大方若隅，大器晚成，大音希声；大象无形，道隐无名，夫唯道善始且善成。[2]" literally as following:

The greatest square has no corners,

The greatest vessel is last to be attended to,

The greatest sound is ever so faint,

The greatest image has no shape.

Way-making is so profuse as to be nameless.

It is only way-making that is as efficacious in the beginnings of things.

As it is in their completion.[3]

Keeping the target reader in mind, the translator has to make certain formal adjustment on this semantically exotic expression as to surmount the cultural boundaries.

Besides allusions, there are many words and expressions in both English and Chinese which bear with them features unique to the two cultures. Their meanings are closely associated with their customs, festivals, life experiences, philosophical thinking, academic schools or simply idiomatic usage, etc. By comparing the two cultures concerned in translating, the translator is to

---

① GRACE Y. Literary Devices Allusion[EB/OL]. [2017-05-12]. https://www.britannica.com/art/allusion.

② WANG BI. Annotation to Dao De Jing[EB/OL]. [2018-03-10].https://www.daodejing.org/10.html.

③ AMES R, YOUNG W. Lao Tzu: Text, Notes, and Comments[M]. Tanbei: Chengwen Publisher. 1981:226.

make a decision with regard to reproduction or adaptation of these culture-specific phenomena. For the cultural phenomena in the source text not yet familiar to the target reader, the translator needs to make it understood by adding the cultural background information to the translation or make other adjustments.

With the development of society and the increase of people's educational level, more and more readers have a strong curiosity for an alien culture. They are eager to read something with authentic foreign flavor and to know about the life and emotion of an alien people. The development of global communication also provides the reader a broad social environment to understand such information. When the reader finds that the information is not familiar to him or can not be understood within his "conceptual horizon", he may, according to Bakhtin's theory of dialogue, try to find the answer by active understanding. To the extreme, "It is clear that a country's reading public do not appreciate a translation made in the style of their own language... What is appreciated is the inverse: Carrying the possibilities oftheir language to the extreme of the intelligible so that the ways of speaking appropriate to the translated author seem to cross into theirs." This is true; however, it implies that the translation should be within the scope of "the intelligible". That is to say, no matter how an exotic version the target reader looks forward to, it still has intelligibility as its prerequisite. On the whole, the original text is aimed for its native readers. The target reader's lacking of cultural knowledge possessed by the native readers will affect their comprehensions of the translated text in different degrees. The translator has to have a full consideration of the target reader's knowledge about alien culture, so as to make the target reader understand what the translator says in the version, thus to realize their dialogues.

The Target Reader's Linguistic and Literary Aesthetic Tendency

The target reader in a certain period, influenced by the habit and tradition of his own national literature, will show a certain aesthetic tendency in the language style, idiomatic language usage and literary norms. To attract the reader, the translated version should conform to the aesthetic requirements of the target reader in language and literary norms.

The Target Reader's Linguistic Aesthetic Tendency

In a certain period, readers enjoy reading translated literary works written in the language dominating at that time. Archaic or strange language styles will produce a negative effect on the target reader to the translated works. If a version is to be accepted and understood by the target reader, then the version must conform to the target reader's aesthetic tendency in the language style. In early modern times, translators, when facing a foreign literary work, encountered at first the alternative of choosing as a target language classical Chinese, vernacular Chinese or an intermediary kind between these two. Yan Fu's employment of the refined and graceful language before the Han Dynasty in his translation *Evolution and Ethics* as mentioned above is a good example. Another example is Lin Shu. At that time, ancient Chinese was used and Mandarin Chinese had not come into being, so in his translations, the language is "relatively popular, casual and elastic" classical Chinese.

The language is changing with the development of the society. After May 4th Movement in 1919, Mandarin Chinese came into being but far from perfect and mature. Some translators like Qu Qiubai advocated creating modern vernacular Chinese through translation. Lu Xun held the idea that the translation would enrich vernacular Chinese language by means of learning from western vocabulary and grammar. In addition, Fu Lei and Zhou Zuoren argued that the translator might use some classical Chinese in translating literary works to compensate for the immaturity of vernacular Chinese. In such situation, in Fu Donghua's translation of Margaret Mitchell's *Gone with the Wind*, the mixture of the vernacular language and classical Chinese characterizes the language style. In contemporary age, the language style enters into a new stage, demanding contemporary language style in the translated version. The difference of the Chinese language and English in ways of idiomatic expressions results in the target reader's different aesthetic tendencies in the way of expressions. For example, English is a hypotactic language that uses various cohesive ties and stresses overt cohesion, intact structure and sentence formation; while Chinese is a paratactic language that seldom uses cohesive ties and emphasizes covert coherence, logical sequence and sentence meaning. If the English text with conjunctive or conjunctions is literally translated into Chinese, the version may seem sloppy, or even ambiguous; if a paratactic Chinese proposition is literally translated into English, the version may be full of grammatical problems or even meaningless.

The literally translated version fails not only in obtaining the style of the original, but also in conforming to the target reader's aesthetic tendency for concise style in literary description. Considering the Chinese reader's aesthetic tendency, the following Chinese version may be more welcomed. As for the use of ancient language style, George Steiner has wonderful remark. He puts it:"…archaism to some degree and a displacement of style towards the past are pervasive in the history and craft of translation. The translator of a foreign classic, of the 'classics' properly speaking, of scriptural and liturgical writings, of historians in other languages, of philosophic works, avoids the current idiom. Explicitly or by an examined habit, with stated intent or almost subconsciously, he will write in a vocabulary and grammar which predate those of his own day."[1] "The bulk of literary, historical, philosophical translation, even where it concerns fiction, political writings, or plays intended for production, shows symptoms of retreat from current speech." He gives "two principal reasons for archaism". "The first is implicit in the dynamics and techniques of understanding. In seeking to penetrate the sense and logic of form of the original, the translator proceeds archaeologically or etiologically. He attempts to work back to the rudiments and first causes of invention in his author. But there is also a second, tactical motive. The translator labors to secure a natural habitat for the alien presence which he has imported into his own tongue and cultural setting." To sum up, viewed historically, readers' aesthetic tendencies are different in different times and change with the development of economy, culture and political environment. The acceptability of a version to some extent depends on its language style and idiomatic language expression, so the version should conform to the requirement of the time in the linguistic level. In the translation practice, the translator should fully take into consideration the target reader and employ the language style conforming to the target reader's aesthetic tendency, thus to make the version accepted and the dialogue between the translator and the target reader come true. His target reader's literary aesthetics originates from the writing tradition and norms of literary works in the target literary system. The literary traditions, norms and conventions dominating at the time of translation effect the target reader's aesthetic tendency in the norms of a literary work.

The Target Reader's Literary Aesthetic Tendency

The target reader's literary aesthetics originates from the writing tradition and norms of literary works in the target literary system. The literary tradition, norms and conventions dominating at the time of translation affect the target reader's aesthetic tendency in the norms of a literary work. Those conforming to the literary tradition and norms of the target reader are much easier to be accepted than those that are not. According to Bakhtin's dialogue of theory, the translator is required to take into consideration the target reader's "conceptual horizon" concerned

---

① KHARMANDAR A. Steiner's Hermeneutic Motion in Translation: A New Reading [EB/OL].(2016-3-12) [2018-03-10]. https://papers.ssrn.com/sol3/papers.cfm?abstract_id=2779016.

with literary norms, the more exactly, the better their literary aesthetic tendency will be. It happens no translator decides that foreign texts are not always models. If the translator belongs to the same society, he will be consciously or unconsciously affected by the target reader, and his appropriate translation will influence the literary tradition, norms and conventions dominating at that time; if not, he must be aware of it and take appropriate measures consciously to make his version accepted and understood. The translators make other adaptation to avoid conflicting with the target reader's aesthetic tendency.

It cannot be dismissed simply as inexactness since different translators in the same period adopt the same method as to the same narrating mode — replacing the first-person narrator with the third-person narrator. To get the bottom of the matter, it is because the traditional Chinese narration seldom employs the first-person narrator. To make the version easily accepted and understood better by the Chinese readers, the translators make a change in then narrating person. From about 1890 to 1919, the European poetry translated into Chinese usually assumes the aspect of Si Yanshi or Wu Yanshi, a Chinese classical poetic genre with four or five characters in each line. As to the introduction of an alien type of literature, the translator should spare no effort to take some measures to make the version understood well. As Andre Lefevere argues that "The genre that is dominant in the target culture defines to a great extent the reader's horizon of expectation with regard to the translated work that tries to take its place in that target culture. If it does not conform to the demands of the genre that dominate the target culture, its reception is likely to be rendered more difficult..."[①] It is really difficult for the reader to follow the sequence of events. To make the version accepted and understood, the translator adds more than 400 footnotes, most of which is suggestive of the shift of time to remind the reader of that. The same thing happens to Mr. and Mrs. Xiao Qian's translation Ulysses by James Joyce. In the Chinese version by Mr. and Mrs. Xiao Qian, about 5840 annotations are added for the explanation. With little knowledge of the new literary type and the powerful traditional literary convention identified by the readers, the target version would be difficult to be accepted and understood without any explanation, in which case the version becomes meaningless and the communication between the translator and the reader fails. Their annotatons in the version results from their consideration of the Chinese reader's aesthetic tendency in literary tradition and norms.

---

① GUO YING, BAI BIN. An Analysis toward Andre Lefevere's Translation Theories[EB/OL].(2016-3-12) [2018-03-16]. http://en.cnki.com.cn/Article_en/CJFDTOTAL-QQHD200802035.htm.

The target reader's aesthetic tendency in literary norms also has a great influence on the translator's choice of specific translation methods. For example,

上善若水。水善利万物而不争，处众人之所恶，故几于道。居善地；心善渊；与善仁；言善信；正善治；事善能；动善时。夫唯不争，故无尤。①

The highest efficacy is like water.

It is because water benefits everything.

Yet vies to dwell in places loathed by the crowd.

That it comes nearest to proper way-making.

In dwelling, the question is where is the right place.②

In thinking and feeling, it is how deeply.

In giving, it is how much like nature's boundary.

In speaking, it is how credibly.

In governing, it is now effectively.

In serving, it is how capably.

In acting, it is how timely.

It is only because there is no contentiousness in proper way-making,

That it incurs no blame.

The translators were afraid that these descriptions would bore the readers, since traditional Chinese fiction tended to rely on dialogue and action to reveal a character's mental state rather than long passages of psychological analysis. In the same way, scenic description was rarely used to enhance the creation of atmosphere in traditional Chinese fiction and only in a very few novels, the target reader's linguistic aesthetic tendency is determined to be affected by the dominant literary norms in which he is nurtured. The translator is responsible to take into consideration the reader's aesthetic tendency in language and literary norms in the practice of translation.

The Target Reader's Aesthetic Tendency in Ideology

Lin Jun in his *A Course book for English-Chinese Translation* discusses the manipulation of ideology in translation and borrows another Marxist critic, Terry Eagleton's definition of ideology. It is important to grasp the precise meaning of Marxist ideology. "Ideology is not

---

① WANG BI. Annotation to Dao De Jing[EB/OL].[2018-03-10].https://www.daodejing.org/10.html.

② JIAHUI LUO. Eagleton's Concept on Literary Ideology[J]. Read and Writing Periodical,2010(9):9.

in the first a set of doctrines. It signifies the way men live out their roles in class-society, the values, ideas and images which tie them to their social function and so prevent them from a true knowledge of society as a whole." According to Marxism, in every period, from the economic base, emerges as upper structure including certain forms of law and politics, a certain kind of state whose essential function is to legitimate the power of the social class which owns the means of economic production. But the superstructure contains more than this: It also consists of certain definite forms of social consciousness (political, religious, ethical, aesthetic and so on), which is what Marxism designates as ideology. The target reader's ideology could influence translation in many aspects from the choice of source materials to the choice of translation strategy and methods. This thesis is going to study the influence of target reader's ideology on translation mainly from two aspects: Ethical ideology and political attitude.

The Target Reader's Ethical Ideology

Each society has its deep-rooted ethics, which manipulates the people's words and deeds and forms a certain "conceptual horizon" concerned with ethics. Usually, the ethics of a culture are characterized to a certain degree by exclusiveness, and cannot tolerate threats from what it regards as unethical or immoral elements introduced by a foreign culture. And the degree of ethical tolerance is varied between cultures and different periods. The more conservative the culture is, the more ethically exclusive it becomes. China is a society with a more than two thousand years' history of feudalism. Hence, the Chinese are relatively conservative and sensitive in ethics. In contrast, the western societies, which have experienced the Renaissance that aims at liberating human being and approaching the nature, show more respect to human nature rather than traditional moral doctrines. It is no wonder that an ethical behavior in the West may be thought immoral in China. The different degrees of liberty in ethics will inevitably influence the target reader's acceptance of the literary works, especially of the translated literature. Hence the translator has to pay attention to the different degrees of liberty between the target reader's ethics and that of the source culture. The higher degree of liberty in ethics of the target reader, the higher acceptance ability the reader possessed, and the more tending to the source culture the translator's translation strategy is; and vice versa.

Literary translation in this thesis is in a broad sense and refers to the translation of a text in such a way that the product can be acceptable as literary to the recipient culture. Literary translation involves not only transference of information, but also aesthetic appreciation in such aspects as language style, literary norms, ethics and political ideology.

People are accustomed to basing their interpretations, judgments or preferences on their own "conceptual horizon". This requires the translator to side with the target reader's conceptual system. The translator who realizes this should take full consideration of the target readers and deliberately manage it in the practice of translation, so as to make the translated version properly understood and smoothly accepted by the target readers.

This paper presents the target reader's influence on literary translation mainly from three aspects, namely the target reader's level of cultural knowledge, linguistic and literary aesthetic tendency, and ethic and political ideology. It is safe to draw a conclusion that the target reader plays an indispensable role in the authoring process of a translated literary work and should, by no means, be neglected. This is also the main reason why we have different translated versions of the same source work targeted at different readers.

Moreover, with more and more contact among different cultures people now are more open-minded and culturally competent. They long to know about literary works abroad. They search them out to satisfy their curiosity or for the novelty of the experience. Hence, the target reader's favoring authentic foreign flavor and their cognitive ability should also be paid close attention to. Manipulated by the changing "conceptual horizon" of the target readers, literary works are re-translated at different demands at different time. This is one of the major reasons why we have different translated versions of the same source work at different times. Viewed from this point, the assessment of a translated literary work should also take into account the factor of the target reader the translator aims at.

REFERENCES

[1]DAVID B. Readings and Feelings: An Introduction to Subjective Criticism[M]. New York: Harper, 1977.

[2]DAVID B. Subjective Criticism[M]. Baltimore: Johns Hopkins University Press, 1978.

[3]ELIZABETH F. The Return of the Render Reader-Response Criticism[M]. New York: Methuen, 1987.

[4]GERALD P. "Introduction to the Study of the Naratee," in Reader-Response Criticism: From Formalism to

Past-Structuralism[M]. Ed. JANE O T. Baltimore: Johns Hopkins University Press, 1980:177-196.

[5]GERALD P. Reading Interpretation, Response[J]. Special Section of Genre.1977: 363-453.

[6]HANS R J. Aesthetic Experience and Literary Hermeneutics[M]. Minneapolis: University of Minnesota Press, 1982.

[7]LOUISE M R. Towards a Transactional Theory of Reading[J]. Journal of Reading Behavior.1969:31-47.

[8]NORMAN N H. The Dynamics of Literary Response[M]. New York: Oxford University Press, 1968.

[9]NORMAN N H. Poems in Persons: An Introduction to the Psychoanalysis of Literature[M]. New York: Norton, 1973.

[10]NORMAN N H. Unity, Identity, Text, Self[J]. PMLA.1975: 813-22.

[11]NORMAN N H. Holland's Guide to Psychoanalytic Psychology and Literature-and-Psychology[M]. Oxford: Oxford University Press 1990.

[12]NORMAN N H. "A Portrait as Rebellion: A Reader-Response Perspective." in "A Portrait of the Artist as a Young Man": Complete, Authoritative Text with Biographical and Historical Contexts, Critical History, and Essays from Five Contemporary Critical Perspectives[M]. Ed. R B KERSHNER. Boston: Bedford Books-St. Martin's, 1993, 279-294.

[13]ROBERT C H. Reception Theory: A Critical Introduction[M]. New York: Methuen, 1984.

[14]ROLAND B. "From Work to Text." In The Rustle of Language[M]. Berkeley: University of California Press, 1989.

[15]STANLEY E F. Literature in the Reader: Affective Stylistics[J]. New Literary History.1970:123-61.

[16]STANLEY E F. Self-Consuming Artifacts: The Experience of Seventeenth-Century Literature[M]. Berkeley: University of California Press, 1972.

[17]STANLEY E F. Is There a Text in This Class? The Authority of Interpretive Communities[M]. Cambridge: Harvard University Press, 1980.

[18]STEPHEN B. "On the Value of Hamlet," in Reinterpretation of Elizabethan Drama[M]. Ed. NORMAN R. New York: Columbia University Press, 1969, 77-99.

[19]STEVEN M. Reader-Response Criticism? [J]. Genre.1977: 413-431.

[20]STEVEN M. Learning to Read: Interpretation and Render-Response Criticism[J]. Studies in the Literary Imagination.1979: 93-108.

[21]STEVEN M. Interpretive Conventions: The Reader in the Study of American Fiction[M]. Ithaca: Cornell University Press , 1982.

[22]SUSAN R S, INGE C, eds. The Reader in the Text: Essays on Audience and Interpretation[M]. Princeton:

Princeton University Press , 1980.

[23]UMBERTO E. The Role of the Reader: Explorations in the Semiotics of Texts[M]. Bloomington: Indiana University Press , 1979.

[24]WALTER S J. Orality and Literacy[M]. New York: Methuen, 1982.

[25]WAYNE C B. The Rhetoric Fiction[M]. Chicago: University of Chicago Press, 1978.

[26]WOLFGANG I. The Implied Reader: Patterns of Communication in Prose Fiction from Bunyan to Beckett[M]. Baltimore: Johns Hopkins University Press , 1974.

[27]WOLFGANG I. The Act of Rending: A Theory of Aesthetic Response[M]. Baltimore: Johns Hopkins University Press , 1978.

[28]WOLFGANG I. Prospecting: From Reader Response to Literary Anthropology[M]. Baltimore: Johns Hopkins University Press , 1989.

CHAPTER V   STRUCTUALISM

5.1   INTRODUCTION

There is a case that took place for interview of postgraduate to an entrance exam. Having narrowed his list of candidates to two, the supervisor of a department at a very famous university instructed her secretary to invite each applicant for an interview. Both candidates seemed equally qualified for the position. Applicant A had graduated from an Ivy League university, earning a B.S. in accounting and business, while applicant B, also undergraduate of institution, earned a B.S. in business administration. Each had received outstanding references from his professors and major mentors. And each scored in the 95th percentile on the Graduate Record Examination. The supervisor's choice, no doubt, would be difficult.

On the day of the interview, applicant A arrived wearing a gray suit, a white cotton shirt, a subdued but somewhat bright yellow tie, a pair of highly polished black Oxfords, and an appropriate smile and short haircut. Applicant B arrived a few minutes after applicant A's interview had begun. Wearing a green, fatigue shirt, a pair of stonewashed jeans, and a pair of black suede Birkenstocks, candidate B brushed back his long hair and wondered why the first applicant's interview was lasting more than an hour. After another 15 minutes had passed, applicant A finally exited through the main doors, and the secretary ushered applicant B into the director's office. Eighteen minutes later, applicant B passed by the secretary's desk and left the building, his interview apparently over.

Shortly thereafter, the supervisor buzzed for her secretary to come to her office. Upon his entering, the supervisor responded, "Please send applicant A the letter of admission. He will represent our business well. Also, mail applicant B an 'I'm sorry, but...' letter. Evidently he doesn't understand our image, our values, and our standards. Jeans, no tie, and long hair, in this office and for this company! Never!"

Applicant A's ability to grasp what his future supervisor valued earned him his chance. Through the language of fashion (language being used in a broad sense to convey a system of codes or signs that convey meaning), applicant A demonstrated to the supervisor his understanding of the study plan and its concern for dress and physical appearance. Applicant B, however, silently signaled his lack of understanding of the study's values and public image through his tireless and seemingly inappropriate attire. Whereas applicant B failed to master those fashion codes that represented his understanding of the supervisor's standards, applicant A demonstrated his command of language of fashion and his potential to learn similar intricate systems or languages used in such areas as economics, education, the sciences, and social life in general. Through his mastery of these codes and his ability (either consciously or unconsciously) to analyze and use them correctly in a given situation, applicant A demonstrated his knowledge of structuralism.

Flourishing in the 1960s, structuralism is an approach to literary analysis grounded in structural linguistics, the science of language. By using the techniques, methodologies, and vocabulary of linguistics, structuralism offers a scientific view of how we achieve meaning not only in literary works but also in all forms of communication and social behavior.

To understand structuralism, we must trace its historical roots to the linguistic writings and theories of Ferdinand de Saussure, a Swiss professor and linguist of the late nineteenth and early twentieth century. His scientific investigations of language and language theory provide the basis for structuralism's unique approach to literary analysis.

5.2 HISTORICAL DEVELOPMENT

5.2.1 Pre-Saussurean Linguistics

Throughout the nineteenth and early twentieth centuries, philology, not linguistics, was the science of language. Its practitioners, philologists, described, compared, and analyzed the languages of the world to discover similarities and relationships. Their approaches to language study was diachronic; that is, they traced language change throughout long expanses of time, discovering how a particular phenomenon such as a word or sound in one language had changed etymologically or phonologically throughout several centuries, and whether a similar change could be noted in other languages. Using cause-and-effect relationships as the basis for their research, the philologist main emphasis was the historical development of languages.

Such an emphasis reflected the nineteenth-century philologists' theoretical assumptions of the nature of language. Language, they believed, mirrored the structure of the world it imitated and therefore had no structure of its own. Known as the mimetic theory of language, this hypothesis asserts that words (either spoken or written) are symbols for things in the world, each word having its own referent —— the object, concept, or idea that represents or symbolizes that word. According to this theory, the symbol (a word) equals a thing: Symbol (word)=Thing.

5.2.2 Saussure's Linguistic Revolution

In the first decade of the 1900s, a Swiss philologist and teacher Frdinand de Saussure (1857—1913), began questioning these long-held ideas and by so doing, triggered a reformation in language study. Through his research and innovative theories, Saussure changed the direction and subject matter of linguistic studies. His Course it General Linguistics, a compilation of his 1906—1911 lecture notes published posthumously by his students, is one of the seminal works of modern linguistics and forms the basis for structuralist literary theory and practical criticism. Through the efforts of this father of modern linguistics, nineteenth-century philology evolved into the more multifaceted science of twentieth-century linguistics.

Saussure began his linguistic revolution by affirming the validity and necessity of the diachronic approach to language study used by such nineteenth-century philologists as the Grimm brothers and Karl Verner. Using this diachronic approach, these linguists discovered the principles governing consonantal pronunciation changes that occurred in Indo-European languages (the language group to which English belongs) over many centuries. Without abandoning a diachronic examination of language, Saussure introduced the synchronic approach, which focuses attention on studying a language at one particular time — a single moment — and emphasizes how the whole state of a particular language functions, rather than tracing the historical development of a single element, as would a diachronic analysis. By highlighting the activity of a whole language system and how it operates rather than its evolution, Saussure drew attention to the nature and composition of language and its constituent parts. For example, along with examining the phonological antecedents of the English sound b, as in the word boy (a diachronic analysis), Saussure opened a new avenue of investigation, asking how the b sound is related to other sounds in use at the same time by speakers of Modern English (a synchronic analysis). This new concern necessitated a rethinking of language theory and a re-evaluation of the aims of language research, and finally resulted in Saussure's articulating the basic principles of modern linguistics.

Unlike many of his contemporary linguists, Saussure rejected the mimetic theory of language structure. In its place, he asserted that language is determined primarily by its own internally structured and highly systematized rules. These rules govern all aspect of language including the sounds its speakers identify as meaningful, various combinations of these sound into words, and how these words may be arranged to produce meaningful communication within a given language.

5.2.3　Structure of Language

According to Saussure, all languages are governed by their own internal rules, which do not mirror or imitate the structure of the world. The basic building block of language is the phoneme — the smallest meaningful (significant) sound in a language. The number of phonemes differs from language to language, with the least number of total phonemes for any one language being in the mid-teens, and the most in the mid-sixties. American English, for example, consists of approximately 43~45 phonemes, depending on the dialect being spoken. Although native speakers of American English are capable of producing phonemes found in other languages, it is these 45 distinct sounds that serve as the building blocks for their language. For example, the first sound heard in the word pint is the /p/ phoneme, the second /i/, and the last /n/. A phoneme that can be identified in writing by enclosing the grapheme — the writer symbol that represents the phoneme's sound — in virgules, or diagonal lines.

Although each phoneme makes a distinct sound that is meaningful and recognizable to speakers of a particular language, in actuality a phoneme is composed of a family of nearly identical speech sounds called allophones. For instance, in the word pit, the first phoneme is /p/, and in the word spin, the second phoneme is also /p/. Although the /p/ appears in both word its pronunciation is slightly different. To validate this statement, simply hold the palm of your hand about two inches from your mouth and pronounce the word pit followed immediately by the word spin. You will quickly note the difference. These slightly different pronunciations of the same phoneme are simply two different allophones of the phoneme /p/.

How phonemes and allophones arrange themselves to produce meaningful speech in any language is not arbitrary, but is governed by a prescribe set of rules developed through time by the speakers of a language. For example, in Modern American English (1755— present), no English word in end with the two phonemes /m/ and /b/. In Middle English (1100—1500), these phonemes could combine to form the two terminal sounds of a word, resulting, for example, in the word lamb, where the /m/ and /b/ were both pronounced. Over time, the rules of spoken English have so changed that when lamb appears in Modern English, /b/ has no phonemic value. The study of these rules governing the meaningful units of sound in a linguistic system is called phonology, whereas the study of the production of these sounds is phonetics.

In addition to phonemes another major building block of language is the morpheme — the smallest part of a word that has lexical or grammatical significance (lexical referring to the base or root meaning of a word and grammatical serving to express relationships between words or groups of words, such as the inflections -ed, -s, and -ing). Like the phoneme, the number of lexical and grammatical morphemes varies from language to language. In American English, lexical morphemes far outnumber grammatical morphemes (10 or so). For instance, in the word reaper, (reap) is a lexical morpheme, meaning "to ripple flax" and (-er) is a grammatical morpheme, meaning "one who." (Note that in print morphemes are placed in braces.) All words must have a lexical morpheme (hence their great number), whereas not every word need have a grammatical morpheme. How the various lexical and grammatical morphemes combine to form words Is highly rule governed and is known in modern linguistics as the study of morphology.

Another major building block in the structure of language is the actual arrangement of words in a sentence or syntax. Just as the placement of phoneme and morphemes in individual words is a rule-governed activity, so is the arrangement of words in a sentence. For example, although native speakers of English would understand the sentence "John threw the ball into the air," such speakers would have difficulty ascertaining the meaning of "Threw the air into the ball John." Why? Native speakers of a language have mastered which strings of morphemes are permitted by syntactic rules and which are not. Those that do not conform to these rules do not form English sentences and are called ungrammatical. Those that do conform to the established syntactic structures are called sentences or grammatical sentences. In most English sentences, for example, the subject ("John") precedes the verb ("threw"), followed by the complement ("the ball into the air"). Although this structure can at times be modified, such changes must follow tightly prescribed rules of syntax if a speaker of English is to be understood.

Having established the basic building blocks of a sentence — phonemes, morphemes, and syntax-Language provides us with one additional body of rules to govern the various interpretations or shades of meaning such combinations of words can evoke: Semantics, Unlike morphemes, whose meaning can be found in the dictionary or word stock of a language its-lexicon-the semantic features or properties of words are not so easily defined. Consider, for example the following sentences:

"Charles is a nut."

"I found a letter on Willard Avenue."

"Get a grip, Heidi."

In order to understand each of these sentences, a speaker or reader needs to understand the semantic features that govern an English sentence. For each of the above sentences has several possible interpretations. In the first sentence, the speaker must grasp the concept of metaphor, in the second, lexical ambiguity, and in the third, idiomatic structures. Unless these semantic features are consciously or unconsciously understood by the reader or listener, problems of interpretation may arise. Like the other building blocks of language, an understanding of semantics is necessary for clear communication in any language.

5.2.4 Langue and Parole

By age five or six, native speakers of English or any other language have consciously and unconsciously mastered their Language's complex system of rules or its grammar — their language's phonology, morphology, syntax, and semantics — which enables them to participate in language communication. They have not, however, mastered such advanced elements as all the semantic features of their language, nor have they mastered its prescriptive grammar, the rules of English grammar often invented by eighteenth century and nineteenth century purists who believed that there were certain constructions that all educated people should know, such as using the nominative form of a pronoun after an intransitive linking verb, as in the sentence, "It is I." But what these five-year-old or six-year-old native speakers of a language have learned Saussure calls langue, the structure of the language that is mastered and shared by all its speakers.

Whereas langue emphasizes the social aspect of language and an understanding of the overall language system, an individual's actual speech utterances and writing Saussure calls parole. A speaker can generate countless examples of individual utterances, but these are all governed by the language's system, but the speaker can generate countless, its langue. It is the task of the linguist, Saussure believes, to infer a language's langue from the analysis of many instances of parole. In other words, for Saussure, the proper study of linguistics is the system (langue), not the individual utterances of its speakers (parole).

5.3   Saussure's Redefinition of a Word

Having established that languages are systems that operate according to verifiable rules and that they must be investigated both diachronically and synchronically, Saussure then re-examined philology's definition of a word. Rejecting the long-held belief that a word is a symbol that equals a thing (its referent), Saussure proposed that words are signs made up of two parts: The signifier (a written or spoken mark) and a signified (a concept): sign=signifier/signified.

For example, when we hear the sound ball, the sound is the signifier and the concept of a ball that comes to our minds is the signified. Like the two sides of a sheet of paper, the linguistic sign is the union of these two elements. As oxygen combines with hydrogen to form water, Saussure says, so those of its parts. Accordingly, for Saussure a word does not represent a referent in the objective world, but a sign. Unlike previous generations of philologists who believed that we perceive things (word=thing) and then translate them into units or meaning. Saussure revolutionizes linguistics by asserting that we perceive signs.

Furthermore, the linguistic sign, declares Saussure, is arbitrary: the relationship between the signifier (ball) and the signified (the concept of ball) is a matter of convention. The speakers of a language have simply agreed that the written or spoken sounds or marks represented by ball equal the concept ball. With few exceptions, proclaims Saussure, there is no natural link between the signifier and the signified, nor is there any natural relationship between the linguistic sign and what it represents.

If as Saussure maintains, there is no natural link between the linguistic sign and the reality it represents, how do we know the difference between one sign and another? In other words, how does language create meaning? We know what a sign means, says Saussure, because it differs from all other signs. By comparing and contrasting one sign with other signs, we learn to distinguish each individual sign. Individual signs, then can have meaning (or signify) only within their own langue.

For Saussure, meaning is therefore relational and a matter of difference. Within the system of sound markers that make up our language, we know *ball*, for instance, because we differentiate it from *hall*, *tail*, and *pipe*. Likewise, we know the concept *bug* because it differs from the concepts *truck*, *grass*, and *kite*. Saussure hold the view that only difference exists in language. Because signs are arbitrary, conventional, and differential, Saussure concludes that the proper study of language is not an examination of isolated entities but the system of relationships among them. He asserts, for example, that individual words cannot have meaning by themselves. Because language is a system of rules governing sounds, words, and other components, individual words obtain their meaning only within that system. To know language and how it functions, he declares, we must study the system (langue), not individual utterances (parole) that operate according to the rules of langue.

For Saussure, language is the primary sign system whereby we structure our world. Language's structure, he believes, is like that of any other sign system of social behavior, such as fashion, table manners, and sports. Like language, all such expressions of social behavior generate meaning through a system of signs. Saussure proposed a new science called semiology that would study how we create meaning through these signs in all social behavioral systems. Because language was the chief and most characteristic of all these systems, Saussure declared, it was to be the main branch of semiology. The investigation of all other sign systems would be patterned after that of language, for like language's signs, the meaning of all signs was arbitrary, conventional, and differential.

Although semiology never became an important new science as Saussure envisioned, a similar science was being proposed in America almost simultaneously by philosopher and teacher Charles Sanders Peirce. Called semiotics, this science borrowed linguistic methods used by Saussure and applied them to all meaningful cultural phenomena. Meaning in society, this science of signs declares, can be studied systematically, in terms of both how this meaning occurs and the structures that allow it to operate. Distinguishing among the various kinds of signs, semiotics as a field of study continues to develop today. Because it uses structuralist methods borrowed from Saussure, the terms semiotics and structuralism are often used interchangeably, although the former denotes a particular field of study whereas the latter is more an approach and method of analysis.

5.4 ASSUMPTIONS

Borrowing linguistic vocabulary, theory, and methods from Saussure and to a smaller degree from Peirce, structuralists — their studies being variously called structuralism, semiotics, stylistics, and narratology, to name a few — believe that codes, signs, and rules govern all human social and cultural practices, including communication. Whether that communication is the language of fashion, sports, education, friendships, or literature, each is a systematized combination of codes (signs) governed by rules. Structuralists want to discover these codes which they believe give meaning to all our social and cultural customs and behavior. The proper study of meaning and therefore reality, they assert, is an investigation of the system behind the individual practices themselves. To discover how all the parts fit together and function is their aim.

Structuralists find meaning, then, in the relationship among the various components of a system. When applied to literature, this principle becomes revolutionary. The proper study of literature, for the structuralists, involves an inquiry into the conditions surrounding the act of interpretation itself (how literature conveys meaning), not an in-depth investigation of individual work. Because an individual work can express only the values and belief of the system of which it is a part, structuralists emphasize the system (langue) whereby texts relate to each other, not an examination of an isolated text (parole). They believe that a study of the system of rules that govern literary interpretation becomes the critic's primary task.

Such a belief presupposes that the structure of literature is similar to the structure of language. Like language, so say the structuralists, literature is a self-enclosed system of rules that is composed of language. And also like language, literature needs no outside referent but its own rule-governed but socially constrained system. Before structuralism, literary theorists discussed the literary conventions — that is, the various genres or types of literature such as the novel, the short story, or poetry. Each genre, it was believed, had its own conventions or acknowledged and acceptable way of reflecting and interpreting life. For example, in poetry a poet could write in non-sentences, using symbols and other forms of figurative language to state a theme or to make a point. For these pre-structuralist theorists, the proper study of literature was an examination of these conventions and of how individual texts used these conventions to make meaning or how readers used these conventions to interpret the text. Structuralists, however, seek out the system of codes that they believe convey a text's meaning. For them, how a text conveys meaning rather than what meaning is conveyed at the center of their interpretative methodology: For example, how a symbol or metaphor imparts meaning is now of special interest. For instance, in Nathaniel Hawthorne's "Young Goodman Brown," most readers assume that the darkness of the forest equates with evil and images of light represent safety of particular interest to the structuralist is how darkness comes to represent evil. A structuralist would ask why darkness more often than not represents evil in any text and what sign system or code is operating that allows readers to interpret darkness as evil intertextuality or in all or most texts they read. For the structuralist, how a symbol or any other literary device functions becomes of chief importance, not how literary devices imitate reality or express feelings.

In addition to emphasizing the system of literature and not individual text, structuralism claims to demystify literature. By explaining literature as a system of signs encased in a cultural frame that allows that system to operate, no longer, says structuralism, can a literary work be considered a mystical or magical relationship between the author and the reader, the place where author and reader share emotions, ideas, and truth. A scientific and an objective analysis of how readers interpret texts, not a transcendental or intuitive response to any one text, leads to meaning. Similarly, an author's intentions can no longer be equated to the text's overall meaning, for meaning is determined by the system that governs the writer, not an individual author's own quirks. And no longer can the text be autonomous, an object whose meaning is contained solely within itself. All texts, declare structuralists, are part of the shared system of meaning that is intertextual not text specific; that is, all texts refer readers to other texts. Meaning can therefore be expressed only through this shared system of relations, not in an author's stated intentions or the reader's private or public experiences.

Declaring both isolated text and author to be of little importance, structuralism attempts to strip literature of its magical powers or so-called hidden meanings that can be discovered only by a small, elite group of highly trained specialists. Meaning can be found by analyzing the system of rules what make up literature itself.

5.5 METHODOLOGIES

Like all other approaches to textual analysis, structuralism follows neither one methodological strategy nor one set of ideological assumptions. Although most structuralists use many of Saussure's ideas in formulating their theoretical assumptions and foundations for their literary theories, how these assumptions are applied to textual analysis varies greatly. A brief examination of five structuralists or subgroups will help highlight structuralism's varied approaches to textual analysis.

5.5.1 Claude Levi-Strauss

One of the first scholar/researchers to implement Saussure's principles of linguistics to narrative discourse in the 1950s and 1960s was anthropologist Claude Levi-Strauss. Attracted to the rich symbols in myths, Levi-Strauss spent years studying many of the world's myths. Myth, he assumed, possessed a structure like language. Each individual myth was therefore an example of parole. What he wanted to discover was myth's langue, or its overall structure that allows individual examples (parole) to function and have meaning.

After reading countless myths, Levi-Strauss identified recurrent themes running through all of them. Such themes transcended culture and time, speaking directly to the minds and hearts of all people. These basic structures which he called "mythemes" were similar to the primary building blocks of language, the phonemes. Like phonemes, these "mythemes" find meaning in and through their relationships within the mythic structure. And as with phonemes, such relationships often involve oppositions. For example, the /b/ and /p/ phonemes are similar in that they are pronounced by using the lips to suddenly stop a stream of air. They differ or "oppose" one another in only one aspect: Whether the air passing through the wind pipe does or does not vibrate the vocal cords (vibrating vocal cords produce/b/, non-vibrating cords produce /p/ during actual speech). Similarly, a mytheme finds its meaning through opposition. Hating or loving ones parents, falling in love with someone who does or who does not love you, and cherishing or abandoning one's children all exemplify the dual or opposing nature of my themes. The rules that govern how these mythemes may be combined constitute myth's structure or grammar. The meaning of any individual myth, then, depends on the interaction and order of the mythemes within the story. Out of this structural pattern comes the myth's meaning.

When applied to a specific literary work, the intertextuality of myth becomes evident. For example, in Shakespeare's King Lear, King Lear overestimates the value and support of children when he trusts Regan and Goneril, his two oldest daughters, to take care of him in his old age. He also underestimates the value and support of children when he banishes his youngest and most-loved daughter, Cordelia. Like the binary opposition that occurs between the /b/ and /p/ phonemes, the binary opposition of underestimating versus overestimating love automatically occurs when reading the text, for such my themes have occurred in countless other texts and immediately ignite emotions within the reader.

As we unconsciously master our language's langue, we also master myth's structure. Our ability to grasp this structure, says Levi-Strauss, is innate. Like language, myths are simply another way we classify and organize our world.

5.5.2 Roland Barthes

Researching and writing in response to Levi-Strauss was his contemporary, eminent French structuralist Roland Barthes. His contribution to structuralist theory is best summed up in the title of his most famous text, S/Z. In Balzac's Sarrasine, Barthes noted that the first s is pronounced as the "s" in snake, and the second as the z in zoo. Both phonemes, /s/ and /z/ are a minimal pair — that is, both are produced by the same articulatory organs and in the same place in the mouth, the different being that /s/ is unvoiced (no vibration of vocal cords) and /z/ is voiced (vibration of vocal cords when air is blowing through the breath channel). Like all minimal pairs — /p/and /b/, /t/and /d/, and /k/and /g/, for example — this pair operates in what Barthes calls binary opposition. Even within a phoneme, binary opposition exists, for a phoneme is, as Saussure reminded us, a class of nearly identical sounds called allophones that differ phonetically — that is, by slightly changing the pronunciation but not altering the recognizable phoneme. Borrowing and further developing Saussure's work, Bathes then declares that all language is its own self-enclosed system based on binary operations.

Bathes then applies his assumption that meaning develops through difference to all social contexts, including fashions, familial relations, dining, and literature, to name a few. When applied to literature, an individual text is simply a message — a parole — that must be interpreted by using the appropriate codes or signs or binary operations that form the basis of the entire system, the langue. Only through recognizing the codes or binary operations within the text, says Barthes, can we explain the message encoded within the text. For example, in Nathaniel Hawthorne's "Young Goodman Brown" most readers intuitively know that Young Goodman Brown will come face to face with evil when he enters the forest. Why? Because one code or binary operation that we all know is that light implies good and dark evil. Thus, Brown enters the "dark" forest and leaves the "light" of his home, only to find the false "light" of evil emanating from the artificial light — the fires that light the baptismal service of those being inducted into Satan's legions. By finding other binary oppositions within the text and showing how these oppositions interrelated, the structuralist can then decode the text, thereby explaining its meaning.

Such a process dismisses the importance of the author, any historical or literary period, or particular textual elements or genres. Rather than discovering any element of truth within a text, this methodology shows the process of decoding a text in relationship to the codes provided by the structure of language itself.

5.5.3   Vladimir Propp

Expanding Levi-Strauss's linguistic model of myths, a group of structuralists called narratologists began another kind of structuralism: Structuralist narratology, the science of narrative. Like Saussure and Levi-Strauss, these structuralists illustrate how a story's meaning develops from its overall structure, its langue, rather than each individual story isolated theme. Using this idea as his starting point, Russian linguist Vladimir Propp investigated Russian fairy tales to decode their langue. According to his analysis, which appears in his work *The Morphology of the Folktale*, all folk or fairy tales are based on 31 fixed elements, or what Propp calls "functions", which occur in a given sequence. Each function identifies predictable patterns or functions that central characters, such as the hero, the villain, or the helper will enact to further the plot of the story. Any story may use any number of these elements, such as "accepting the call to adventure" "recognizing the hero" and "punishing the villain" but each element occurs in its logical and proper sequence.

Applying Propp's narratological principles to specific literary works is both fun and easy. For example, in *Twain's Adventures of Huckleberry Finn*, Huck, the protagonist or hero, is given a task to do: Free Jim. His evil enemy or villain society, tries to stop him. But throughout the novel various helpers appear to propel the plot forward, until the hero's task is complete, and he frees Jim and flees from his enemy.

5.5.4   Tzvetan Tororov and Gerard Genette

Another narratologist, Bulgarian Tzvetan Todorov, declares that all stories are composed of grammatical units. For Todorov, the syntax of narrative or how the various grammatical elements of a story combine is essential. By applying a rather intricate grammatical model to narrative — dividing by text into the semantic syntactic and verbal aspects — Todorov believes he can discover the narrative's langue and establish a grammar of narrative. He begins by asserting that the grammatical clause and, in turn, the subject and verb, is the basic interpretative unit of each sentence and can be linguistically analyzed and further dissected into a variety of grammatical categories to show how all narratives are structured. An individual text (parole) interests Todorov as a means to describe the overall properties of literature in general (langue).

Other narratologists such as Gerard Genette and Roland Barthes have also developed methods of analyzing a story's structure to uncover its meaning, each building on the former work of another narratologist and adding an additional element or two of his own. Genette, for example, believes that tropes or figures of speech require a reader's special attention. Barthes, on the other hand, points us back to Tordorov and provides us with more linguistic terminology to dissect a story.

Although these narratologists provide us with various approaches to texts, all furnish us with a metalanguage — words used to describe language — so that we can understand how a text means, not what it means.

5.5.5 Jonathan Culler

By the mid-1970s, Jonathan Culler became the voice of structuralism in America and took structuralism in yet another direction. In Structuralist Poetics, Culler declared that abstract linguistic models used by narralogists tended to focus on Parole, spending too much time analyzing individual stories, poems, and novels. What was needed, he believed, was a return to an investigation of langue, Saussure's main premise.

According to Culler, readers, when given a chance, will somehow make sense out of the most bizarre text. Somehow, readers possess literary competence. Through experiences with texts, Culler asserts, they have internalized a set of rules that govern their acts of interpretation. Instead of analyzing individual interpretations of a work, Culler insists, we must spend our time analyzing the act of interpretation itself. We must shift the focus from the text to the reader. How, asks Culler, does the interpretation take place in the first place? What system underlies the very act of reading that allows any other system to operate?

Unlike other structuralists, Culler presents a theory of reading. What, he asks, is the internalized system of literary competence readers use to interpret a work? In other words, how do they read? What system guides them through the process of interpreting the work, of making sense of the spoken or printed word?

In Structuralist Poetics Culler asserts what three elements undergird any reading, for instance, of a poem:

A poem should be unified.

It should be thematically significant.

This significance can take the form of reflection in poetry.

Accordingly, Culler then seeks to establish the system, the langue, that undergirds the reading process. By focusing on the act of interpretation itself to discover literature's language, Culler believes he is returning structuralism to its Saussurean roots.

5.5.6 A Model of Interpretation

Many structuralist theories abound, but a core of structuralists believe that the primary signifying system is best found as a series of binary oppositions that the reader organizes, values, and then uses to interpret the text. Each binary operation can be pictured as a fraction, the top half (the numerator) being what is more valued than its related bottom half (the denominator). Accordingly, in the binary operation light/dark, the reader has learned to value light over dark, and in the binary operation good/evil the reader has similarly valued good over evil. How the reader maps out and organizes the various binary operations and their relationships found within the text but already existing in the mind of the reader determines for that particular reader the text's interpretation.

No matter what its methodology, structuralism emphasizes form and structure, not actual content of a text. Although individual texts must be analyzed, structuralists are more interested in the rule-governed system that underlies texts than in the texts themselves. How a text's underlying structural codes combine to produce the text's meaning rather than a reader's personal interpretation is structuralism chief interest.

5.6 QUESTIONS FOR ANALYSIS

What are the various binary oppositions or operations that operate in Nathaniel Hawthorne's "Young Goodman Brown" or any other story of your choosing. After you map out these oppositions, show how the text means, not what it means.

What mythemes are evident in Robert Browning's "My Last Duchess"? How do these mythemes show the intertextuality of this particular text with other literary texts you have read?

How do the various semantic features contained in a text of your choosing directly relate to the codes, signs, or binary oppositions you find in the text?

Using a text of your choosing, can you apply at least three different methods of structuralism to arrive at how the text achieves its meaning? In the final analysis, is there a difference in how the text achieves its meaning among the three methodologies?

Can you choose another sign system — sports, music, classroom etiquette — and explain the codes that generate meaning?

5.7 SAMPLE ESSAYS

Decoding Confucius: An Educator and a Statesman

The semiotic study of a literary text is not wholly unlike traditional interpretation or rhetorical analysis, nor is it meant to replace these other modes of response to literary works. But the semiotic critic situates the text somewhat differently, privileges different dimensions of the text, and uses a critical methodology adapted to the semiotic enterprise. Most interpretative methods privilege the "meaning" of the text. Hermeneutic critics seek authorial or intentional meaning; the New Critics seek the ambiguities of "textual" meaning; the "reader response" critics allow readers to make meaning. With respect to meaning the semiotic critic is situated differently. Such a critic looks for the generic or discursive structures that enable and constrain meaning.

Under semiotic inspection neither the author nor the reader is free to make meaning. Regardless of their lives as individuals, as author and reader they are traversed by codes that enable their communicative adventures at the cost of setting limits to the messages they can exchange. A literary text, then, is not simply a set of words, but (as Roland Barthes demonstrated in S/Z, though not necessarily in just that way) a network of codes that enables the marks on the page to be read as a text of particular sort.

In decoding narrative texts, the semiotic method is based on two simple but powerful analytical tools: The distinction between story and discourse, on the one hand, and that between text and events on the other. The distinction between story and discourse is grounded in a linguistic observation by Emile Benveniste to the effect that some languages (notably French and Greek) have a special tense of the verb used for the narration of past events. This tense, the artist, emphasizes the relationship between the utterance and the situation the utterance refers to, between the narration and the events narrated. This is par excellence the mode of written transcriptions of events: Histoire or "story." Benveniste contrasts this with the mode of *discours* or "discourse," in which the present contact between speaker and listener is emphasized. Discourse is rhetorical, and related to oral persuasion.

Story is referential and related to written documentation. Discourse is now; story is then. Story speaks of he and she; discourse is a matter of you and me, I and thou.

In any fictional text, then, we can discern certain features that are of the story: Reports on actions, mentions of times and places, and the like. We can also find elements that are of the discourse; evaluations, reflections, language that suggests an authorial or at least narratorial presence who is addressing a reader or narratee with a persuasive aim in mind. When we are told that someone in the work "good or bad", we can detect more of story in the verb and more of discourse in the adverb. Some literary texts, those of ShiJi, for example, are highly supposed to be a vivid record of historical character and events. However, the text of dialogue is common in the ancient which prevails between the philosophers and their disciples in the world. To read Confucius's classics is to enter into a personal relationship with someone who resembles the writer 's private correspondence. Confucius, on the other hand, often seems to have made a strong effort to eliminate discourse but enlighten the reader to realize the nature law — an effort that is apparent in "The Analects" (*Lunyu*) .

The distinction between daily commonplace and discourse is closely related to another with which it is sometimes confused, and that is the distinction between the *recit* and *diegesis* of a narrative. In this case. we are meant to distinguish between the whole text of a narration as a text, on the one hand, and the events narrated as events on the other. We can take over the Greek term, *diegesis*, for the system of characters and events, and simply anglicize the other term as recital; or just refer to the "text" when we mean the words and the "diegesis" for what they encourage us to create as a fiction.

The text itself may be analyzed into components of dialogue and discourse, but it may also be considered in relation to the diegesis. One of the primary qualities of those texts we understand as fiction is that they generate a diegetic order that has an astonishing independence from its text. To put it simply, once a story is told it can be recreated in a recognizable way by a totally new set of words — in another language, for instance — or in another medium altogether. The implications of this for analysis are profound. Let us explore some of them.

A textual diegesis draws its nourishment not simply from the words of its texts but from its immediate culture and its literary tradition. The magical words "once upon a time" in English set in motion a machine of considerable momentum which can hardly be turned off without the equally magical "they lived happily ever after" or some near equivalent. The diegetic processes of "realistic" narrative are no less insistent. "*Lun Yu*, by its location in Confucius's main text , and a few key words — Ren, Xiao, Tian, Junzi, Zhong, Xin, Shi — allows us to supply the crucial notions of human being, government and family that the diegesis requires.

This process is so crucial that we should perhaps stop and explore its implications. The words on the page are not the story. The text is not the diegesis. The text is constructed by the reader from the words on the page by an inferential process — a skill that can be developed. The reader's role is in a sense creative — without it, no text exists — but it is also constrained by rules of inference that set limits to the legitimacy of the readers' constructions. Any interpretive dispute may be properly brought back to the "words on the page", of course, but these words never speak their own meaning. The essence of writing, as opposed to speech, is that the reader speaks the written words, the words that the writer has abandoned. A keen sense of this situation motivates the various sorts, of "envoi" that writers supplied for their books in the early days of printing. They felt that their books were mute and would be spoken by others.

In reading a narrative, then, we translate a text into a diegisis according to codes we have internalized. This is simply the narrative version of the normal reading process. As E. D. Hirsch has recently reminded us, for almost a century research in reading Fillenbaum in 1966, Sachs in 1967, Johnson-Laird in 1970, Levelt and Kampen in 1975, and Brewer in 1975— specific citations can be found in Hirsch) has shown us that memory stores not the words of texts but their concepts, not the signifiers but the signified. When we read a narrative text, then, we process it is a diegesis. If we retell the story, it will be in our own words. To the extent that the distinction between poetry and fiction is a useful one, it is based on the notion of poetry as monumental, fixed in the words of the text and therefore untranslatable; while documentary text has proved highly translatable because its essence is not in its language but in its diegetic structure. As fiction approaches the condition of poetry, its precise words become more important; as poetry moves toward narrative, its specific language decreases in importance. However, documentary text combined the features both of them. Since many quotations are from *the Book of Songs* (anthroposophy of Poems).

In reading fiction, then, we actually translate from the text to a diegesis, substituting narrative units (characters, scenes, events, and so on) for verbal units (nouns, adjectives, phrases, clauses, etc.) And we perform other changes as well. We organize the material we receive so as to make it memorable, which means that we systematize it as much as possible. In the diegetic system we construct, time flows at a uniform rate; events occur in chronological order; people and places have the qualities expected of them — unless the text specifies otherwise. A writer may relocate the Eiffel Tower to Chicago but unless we are told this we will assume that a scene below that tower takes place in Paris — a Paris equipped with all the other items accorded it in our cultural paradigm.

Places and other entities with recognizable proper names (Napoleon, Waterloo, Broadway) enter the diegesis coded by culture. The events reported in a narrative text, however, will be stored in accordance with a syntactic code based on a chronological structure. The text may present the events that compose a story in any order, plunging in *medias res* or following through from beginning to end, but the diegesis always seeks to arrange them in chronological sequence. The text may expand a minute into pages or cram years into a single sentence, for its own ends, but the minutes and years remain minutes and years of diegetic time all the same. In short, the text may discuss what it chooses, but once a diegesis is set in motion no text can every completely control it. "How many children had Lady Macbeth?" is not simply the query of a naive interpreter but the expression of a normal diegetic impulse. Where authors and texts delight in equivocation, the reader needs certainty and closure to complete the diegetic processing of textual materials. From this conflict of interests comes a tension that many modern writers exploit.

Pure diegetic narration constructs the basic structure of the novel and sets the anti-herotone for the characterization and theme-probe. The semiotician takes the reader's diegetic impulse and establishes it as a principle of structuralismt. The logic of diegetic structure provides a norm, a benchmark for the study of textual strategies, enabling us to explore the dialogue between the text and diegesis, looking for points of stress, where the text changes its ways in order to control the diegetic material for its own ends. The keys to both affect and intention may be found at these points. Does the text return obsessively to one episode of the diegetic history? Does it disturb diegetic order to tell about something important to its own discursive ends? Does it omit something that diegetic inertia deems important? Does it change its viewpoint on diegetic events? Does it conceal things? Does it force evaluations through the rhetoric of its discourse? The calm inertia of diegetic process, moved by the weight of culture and tradition and the needs of memory itself, offers a stable background for the mapping of textual strategies. And our most aesthetically ambitious texts will be those that find in most necessary to put their own stamp on diegetic process.

Confucius's "The Analects" presents itself as exceptional reticent. The familiar dialogue style, which Gerard Genette has called "behaviorist," seems to efface itself, to offer us a pure diegesis. Teacher and pupil — a kindred heart dialogue as they used to say in their days — about life, about human; a negation that proclaims the text's realistic or naturalistic status? But there is already a tension here, between the open form of the slice of life and the neat closure of the fairy tale, which emerges most clearly if we compare the progress of diegetic time with the movement of the text. We can do this in a crude way by mapping the hours, days, and weeks of diegetic time against the paragraphs of the text. There are some paragraphs are the first: From waiting for a bosom friend to share common ideals, then from probing into theory to practice. After that done, an ordinary person can cultivate himself to be a virtuous man when he keeps composed even if was misconceived by others. The narrative thus increases its speed throughout, and achieves its effect of culmination by the use of the parallel sentence in the first paragraph. The text might easily have contented itself with recounting the fact that to be a man and a student, there is approach we should take, only when we find it can we enjoy our life.

Before trying to answer that question we would do well to consider some other features of the text/diegesis relationship. From the first paragraph on, it is noticeable that one of the two main characters in the diegesis has a name in the text while the other is always referred to by a pronoun. Why should this be? The answer emerges when we correlate this detail with other features of the text/diegesis relationship. The text, as we have observed, is reticent, as if it, too, is Confucius, the master. So through the dialogue between the teacher and his diciples, questions of being a human, of study, of friends and so forth can be raised. All the questions are thought-provoking. But it is more reticent about some things than others. In the first paragraph, the main character is introduced in the first sentence. The text is completely reticent about how he feels about life and himself, though the implication is that he finds himself peaceful in loneliness. How he seems to his confidant friend or how he feels about himself are not considered relevant. This is a selective reticence. Our vision is subjectively with him (as the personal pronoun implies), while Confucius is seen more objectively (as the proper name implies). The final implication of paragraph 1 is that his lofty sentiment exercised by daily study and practice. But the reticent text makes the reader responsible for closing that little gap in the diegesis.

This matter of the point of view taken by the text can be established more clearly with the use of a sort of litmus test developed by Roland Barthes. If we rewrite the text substituting the first-person pronoun for the third, we can tell whether or not we are dealing with what Barthes calls a "personal system", a covert, first-person narration (see "Introduction to the Structural Analysis of Narrative", in Image-Music-Text, p.112).In the case of *The Analects*, where we have more third-person characters of apparently equal consequence, we must read twice to find out what we need to know. Actually, the issue is settled conclusively after the 20 chapters, which are all I will present here:

The first two paragraphs of "The Analects" rewritten — for example "the student Zixia" transposed to "I":

My views of the substance of learning. I said, "If a man withdraws his mind from the love of beauty, and applies it as sincerely to the love of the virtuous; if, in serving his parents, he can exert his utmost strength; if, in serving his prince, he can devote his life; if, in his intercourse with his friends, his words are sincere: — Although men say that he has not learned, I will certainly say that he has."

An illustration of the successive steps in self-cultivation. I said, "What do you pronounce concerning the poor man who yet does not flatter, and the rich man who is not proud?" The Master replied, " They will do; but they are not equal to him, who, though poor, is yet cheerful, and to him, who, though rich, loves the rules of propriety."

Tsze-kung replied, "It is said in the Book of Poetry, 'As you cut and then file, as you carve and then polish.' — The meaning is the same, I apprehend, as that which you have just expressed."

The Master said, "With one like Ts'ze, I can begin to talk about the odes. I told you one point, and you knew its proper sequence."

"He" transposes to "I" perfectly, in the second rewriting the first person itself enters the discourse with a shocking abruptness, since the earlier sentences seem to have been from the outside's point of view. The stress becomes greater in the last sentence of the first paragraph, which has been constructed to indicate how the argumentation appeared to him, not how the student seemed to himself. With the first-person narrator informing us of how well the student feel about life, and finally describing his thoughts to welcome the master. In this rewriting there is simply too great a tension between the angle of vision and the person of the voice. The discourse remains its coherence. But the first rewriting is completely coherent because in it voice and vision coincide. It is really his narrative all the way. The third-person narration of the original text is a disguise, a mask of pseudo-objectivity worn by the text for its own rhetorical purpose.

The discourse of this text, as I have suggested, is marked by its reticence, but this reticence of the text is contrasted with a certain amount of talkativeness in the diegesis. Master, of course, want to give a teaching by action rather than by words, or more than that, by mind. But the record want "everyone to know about" their relationship. Implication: Everyone here can be the student listening to Confucius's teaching. There is absolutely no direct discourse in the text, but there are 20 chapters devoted to sayings and one student to recounting a dialogue. Here, too, we find reticence juxtaposed to talkativeness. The style of the discourse becomes unusually paratactic — even for the recorder — whenever the meaning are presented. They were all about our life, and how to conduct oneself, how to play roles well in family and in the world. The repetitive "hows" and "the Master said" suggest an authoritative prose style even without direct quotation. Above all, they indicate a seriousness but liveliness lack of reticence.

Curiously, the conditions are represented not only as things it is "understood" that Confucius will and will not do but also as the natural law he wants to say or not. It is not difficult to imagine a man being willing to involved into society and promote his systematic thought of Confucianism, to work, and to carry it out in order to reach to a millennium of peace and complacency, but it is hard to imagine any governors of the vessels and kingdom who do not want to accept the education of "Ren". The text seems to be reporting on the diegesis in a most waxed a waned way here. This is not simply reticence but irony. There is a strong implication that he is being pushed too far, even having his wisdom and knowledge. If there were any kings can understand Confucius, the narration of *The Analects* would be changed.

Finally, the final chapter arrives. First appeared the great sagacious emperor Yao and Shun, In reporting it the text clearly allows Confucius' political ambition to shine through once again, complete with repetition of the phrase about governing quality:

Priciples and ways of Yâo, Shun, Yü, T'ang, and Wû.

(1) Yâo said, "Oh! you, Shun, the Heaven-determined order of succession now rests in your person. Sincerely hold fast the due Mean. If there shall be distress and want within the four seas, the Heavenly revenue will come to a perpetual end."

(2) Shun also used the same language in giving charge to Yû.

(3) T'ang said, "I, the child Lî, presume to use a dark-colored victim, and presume to announce to Thee, O most great and sovereign God, that the sinner I dare not pardon, and thy ministers, O God, I do not keep in obscurity. The examination of them is by thy mind, O God. If, in my person, I commit offenses, they are not to be attributed to you, the people of the myriad regions. If you in the myriad regions commit offenses, these offenses must rest on my person."

(4) Châu conferred great gifts, and the good were enriched.

(5) "Although he has his near relatives, they are not equal to my virtuous men. The people

are throwing blame upon me, the One man."

(6) He carefully attended to the weights and measures, examined the body of the laws, restored the discarded officers, and the good government of the kingdom took its course.

(7) He revived states that had been extinguished, restored families whose line of succession had been broken, and called to office those who had retired into obscurity, so that throughout the kingdom the hearts of the people turned towards him.

(8) What he attached chief importance to were the food of the people, the duties of mourning, and sacrifices.

(9) By his generosity, he won all. By his sincerity, he made the people repose trust in him. By his earnest activity, his achievements were great. By his justice, all were delighted.

Whose discourse is this, whose story, whose diegesis, whose world? It is Masters, of course, who taught a whole generation of readers to prepare for a world where master may be our friends. Up to this point in the second sentence we are not aware that there has been a change of topic from that which closed the earlier chapter. The language of oral retentiveness coincides neatly with that of written words. To some degree, we should comprehend the implication of the text, As Lao Tze put it on another occasion: Tao is beyond words, if we express it with language, maybe we lose what essence of Tao.

Having come this far with a semiotic analysis, we can begin to distinguish it more precisely from New Critical exegesis. In doing so, we must begin by admitting that the two approaches share a certain number of interpretive gestures. We must also recognize that no two semiotic analyses or New Critical exegeses are likely to be identical. The major differences in the two critical approaches can be traced to their different conceptions of the object of study: For New Criticism, the work; for semiotics, the text. As a work, "The Analects" must be seen as complete, unified, shaped into an aesthetic object, a verbal icon. The pedagogical implications of this are important.

By the New Critical standards, the narrator is impersonal and reliable. The words on the page are all we have, and they tell us of a scholarly by no means serious, prudent and wise master who speak with governors. But semi-optic analysis has already suggested alternatives to this view. Seen as a text that presents a diegesis, this interpretation of *The Analects* is far from completeness. There are gaps in the diegesis, reticence in the text, and a highly manipulative use of covert first-person narrative. There are signs of equality, understanding and respect in the text, too, that suggest not an omniscient impersonal author but a normal, flawed human being-like the rest of us — exists as the student behind the words on the page.

REFERENCES

[1]CAMPBELL T. Beyond Structuralism[J]. Genre 10. no.1977: 131-55.

[2]CLAUDE L. Structural Anthropology[M]. Trans. C JACOBSON, B G SCHOPF. London: Allen Lanne, 1968.

[3]DAVID C. A Dictionary of Linguistics and Phonetics[M]. 2nd ed. Cambridge: Basil Blackwell, 1985.

[4]DAVID L. Working with Structuralism: Essays and Reviews on Nineteenth-and-Twentieth-Century Literature[M]. Boston: Routledge & Kegan Paul, 1981.

[5]DAVID L. Working with Structuralism[M]. London: Routledge, 1986.

[6]DAVID R, ed. Structuralism: An Introduction[M]. Oxford: Clarendon, 1973.

[7]DOROTHY B S. Structuralism for the Non-Specialist: A Glossary and a Bibliography[J]. College English 1975): 160-66.

[8]EVE T B. Structuralism and the Logic of Dissent[M]. Chicago: University of llinois Press, 1989.

[9]FERDINAND DE SAUSSURE. Course in General Linguistics[M]. Trans. W Baskin. London: Collino, 1974.

[10]FREDRIC J. The Prison-House of Language: A Critical Account of Structuralism and Russian Formalism[M]. Princeton: Princeton University Press, 1972.

[11]GERARD G. Narrative Discourse[M]. Oxford: Blackwell, 1980.

[12]GERALD P. Narratology: The Form and Functioning of Narrative[M]. New York: Mouton, 1982.

[13]JACQUES E, ed. Structuralism[M]. Garden City: Doubleday, 1970.

[14]JOHN S. Structuralism and Since[M]. New York: Oxford University Press, 1979.

[15]JONATHAN C. Structuralist Poetics: Structuralism, Linguistics and the Study of Literature[M]. London: Routledge, 1975.

[16]JONATHAN C. Ferdinand de Saussure[M]. Baltimore: Penguin, 1976.

[17]JONATHAN C. The Pursuit of Signs: Semiotics, Literature, Deconstruction[M]. Ithaca: Cornell University Press, 1981.

[18]MARSHALL B, ed. On Signs[M]. Baltimore: Johns Hopkins University Press, 1985.

[19]MICHAEL L, ed. Introduction to Structuralism[M]. New York: Harper, 1972.

[20]MURRAY K, L S DEMBO, eds. Directions for Criticism: Structuralism and Its Alternatives[M]. Madison:

University of Wisconsin Press, 1977.

[21]RICHARD M, EUGENIO D, eds. The Structuralist Controversy[M]. Baltimore: Johns Hopkins University Press, 1970.

[22]RICHARD T D G, M FERMANDE, eds. The Structuralists from Marx to Lévi-Strauss[M]. Garden City: Doubleday, 1972.

[23]ROBERT D. Story, Sign, and Self: Phenomenology and Structuralism as Literary Critical Methods[M]. Philadelphia: Fortress, 1978.

[24]ROBERT E I, ed. Semiotics: An Introductory Reader[M]. London: Hutchinson, 1986.

[25]ROBERT S. Structuralism in Literature: An Introduction[M]. New Haven: Yale University Press, 1974.

[26]ROBERT S. Semiotics and Interpretation[M]. New Haven: Yale University Press, 1982.

[27]ROGER T A. Translation and Translating: Theory and Practice[M]. Beijing: Foreign Language Teaching and Research Press, 2001

[28]ROLAND B. Elements of Semiology[M]. Trans. A. LAVERS, C SMITH. London: Cape, 1967.

[29]ROLAND B. S/Z[M]. Trans. R MILLER. New York: Hill & Wang, 1971.

[30]ROLAND B. Critical Essays[M]. Trans. R HOWARD. Evanston: Northwestern University Press, 1972.

[31]ROLAND B. Selected Writings[M]. London: Fontana, 1983.

[32]ROMAN J. Fundamentals of Language[M]. Paris: Mouton, 1975.

[33]STEVEN C. "Structuralism and Post-structuralism: From the Centre to the Margin" in Encyclopedia of Literature and Criticism[M]. London: Routledge, 1990.

[34]TERENCE H. Structuralism and Semiotics[M]. London: Methuen, 1977.

[35]TZVETAN T. The Fantastic: A Structural Approach to a Literary Genre[M]. Ithaca: Cornell University Press, 1973.

[36]TZVETAN T. The Poetics of Prose[M]. Trans. RICHARD H. Ithaca: Cornell University Press, 1977.

[37]VLADIMIR P. The Morphology of the Folktale[M]. Austin: Texas University Press, 1968.

PART III FROM MODERNISM TO POST-MODERNISM

For many historians and literary theorists, the Enlightenment or the Age of Reason (eighteenth century) is synonymous with modernism. That its roots predate this time period is unquestioned, with some even dating to 1492 (Columbus's journeys to the Americas) and its overall spirit lasting until the middle of the twentieth century. At the center of this view of the world lie two prominent beliefs: That reason is humankind's best guide to life and science, above all other human endeavors, could lead humanity to a new promised land. Philosophically, modernism rests on the foundations laid by René Descartes, a French philosopher, scientist, and mathematician. Ultimately, declares Descartes, the only thing one cannot doubt is one's own existence. Certainty and knowledge begin with the self. "I think, therefore I am" thus becomes the only solid foundation on which knowledge and a theory of knowledge can be built. For Descartes, the rational essence freed from superstition, from human passions, and from one's often irrational imagination will allow humankind to discover truth about the physical world.

As Descartes's teachings elevated to new heights humankind's ability to reason and an individual's rational essence, the scientific writings and discoveries of Francis Bacon and Sir Isaac Newton allowed science to be likewise coronated. Thanks to Francis Bacon, the scientific method has become part of everyone's elementary and high school education. It is through experimentation, in the doing of experiments, in making inductive generalizations, and in verifying the results that one can discover truths about the physical world. And thanks to Sir Isaac Newton, the physical world is no longer a mystery but a mechanism that operates according to a system of laws that can be understood by any thinking, rational human being who is willing to apply the principles of the scientific method to the physical universe.

Armed with an unparalleled confidence in man kinds capacity to reason — the ability to inquire and to grasp necessary conditions essential for seeking out such undoubtable truths as provided by mathematics — and the assurance that science can lead the way to a complete understanding of the physical world, the modern or Enlightenment scholar was imbued with a spirit of progress. Anything the enlightened mind set as its goal, so these scholars believed, was attainable. Through reason and science, all poverty, all ignorance, and all injustice would finally be banished.

Of all enlightenment people, Benjamin Franklin may best exemplify the characteristics of modernity. Gleaned from self-portraits contained in his *Autobiography*, Franklin is the archetypal modern philosopher and scientist. Self-assured, Franklin declares that he literally pulled himself up by his own bootstraps, overcoming poverty and ignorance through education to become America's first internationally known and respected scientist, philosopher, statesman. Believing in the power and strength of the individual mind, he delighted in the natural world and decided early in life to know all possible aspects of his universe. Accordingly, he abandoned superstitions and myths and placed his trust in science to lead him to truths about his world. Through observations, experiments, and conclusions drawn upon the data discovered from using the scientific method, Franklin believed he could obtain and know the necessary truths to guide him through life.

Like Descartes, Franklin does not abandon religion and replace it with science. Holding to the tenets of Deism, he rejects miracles, myths, and much of what he called religious superstitions. What he does not reject is a belief in the existence of God. He asserts, however, that God leaves it to humanity, to each individual, to become masters of his or her own fate. According to Franklin, individuals must find salvation within themselves. By using one's God-given talents of reason and rational abilities coupled with the principles of science, each person, declares Franklin, can experience and enjoy human progress.

For Franklin and other enlightened minds, truth is to be discovered scientifically, not through the unruly and passionate imagination or through one's feelings or intuition. And what is to be known and discovered via the scientific method is reality: The physical world. All people, declares Franklin, must know this world objectively and must learn how to investigate it to discover its truths.

Self-assured, self-conscious, and self-made, Franklin concludes that all people possess essential nature. It is humanity's moral duty to investigate this nature contained within ourselves and to investigate our environment through rational thinking and the methods of science so that we can learn and share the truths of the universe. By devoting ourselves to science and to the magnificent results that will necessarily follow, Franklin proclaims that human progress is inevitable and will usher in a new golden age.

Franklin and modernity's spirit of progress permeated humankind's beliefs well into the twentieth century. For seven centuries modernity's chief tenets — that reality can be known and investigated and that humanity possesses an essential nature characterized by rational thought — became the central ideas on which many philosophers, scientists, educators, and writers constructed their worldviews. In particular, writers and literary theoreticians — New Critics, structuralists, and others — believed that texts had some kind of objective existence and therefore could be studied and analyzed with appropriate conclusions to follow from such analyses. Whether a text's actual value and meaning were intrinsic or extrinsic was debatable; nevertheless, an aesthetic text's meaning could be discovered. With the advent of deconstruction, the first poststructuralist or postmodern school of criticism, the belief in the objective reality not only of texts but also of objective reality itself becomes questionable.

CHAPTER VI   DECONSTRUCTION

6.1   STRUCTURALISM AND POSTSTRUCTURALISM: TWO VIEWS OF THE WORLD

Throughout the 1950s and 1960s, a variety of different forms of structuralism dominated European and American literary theory: The French structuralism of Roland Barthes, the Russian structuralist narratology of Vladimir Propp, and Jonathan Culler's American brand of structuralist poetics, to name a few. The application of structuralist principles varies from one theoretician to another, but all believe that language is the primary means of signification (how we achieve meaning) and that language comprises its own rule-governed system to achieve such meaning. Although language is the primary sign system, it is not the only one. Fashions, sports, dining, and other activities all have their own "language" or codes whereby the participants know that is expected of them in a particular situation. When dining at a restaurant, for example, connoisseurs of fine dining know that it is inappropriate to drink from a finger bowl. Similarly, football fans know that it is appropriate to shout, scream, and holler to support their team.

From a structuralist perspective, such expectations highlight that all social and cultural practices are governed by rules of codes. Wanting to discover these rules, structuralists declare that the proper study of reality and meaning is the system behind such individual practices, not the individual practices themselves. Like football or fine dining, the act of reading is also a cultural and a social practice that contains its own codes. Meaning in a text resides in these codes, which the reader has mastered before he or she even picks up an actual text. For the structuralist, the proper study of literature is an inquiry into the conditions surrounding the act of interpretation itself, not an investigation of the individual text.

Holding to the principles of Ferdinand de Saussure, the founding father of structuralism, structuralists seek to discover the overall system (langue) that accounts for an individual interpretation (parole) of a text. Meaning and the reasons for meaning can be both ascertained and discovered.

With the advent of deconstruction theory and practice in the late 1960s, however, the structuralist assumption that a text's meaning can be discovered through an examination of its structural codes was challenged and replaced by the maxim of undecidability: A text has many meanings and therefore no definitive interpretation. Rather than providing answers about the meaning of texts or a methodology for discovering how a text meant, deconstruction asks a new set of questions, endeavoring to show that what a text claims it says and what it actually says are discernibly different. By casting doubt on most previously held theories, deconstruction declares that a text has an almost infinite number of possible interpretations. And the interpretations themselves, declare some deconstructionists are just as creative and important as the text being interpreted.

With the advent of deconstruction and its challenge to structuralism and other preexisting theories, a paradigmatic shift occurs in literary theory. Before deconstruction, literary critics — New Critics, some reader-response theorists, structuralists, and others — found meaning within the literary text or the codes of the various sign systems within the world of the text and the reader. The most innovative of these theorists, the structuralists, provided new and exciting ways to discover meaning, but none the less, these theorists maintained that meaning could be found. Underlying all of these pre-deconstructionists' views of world is a set of assumptions called modernism (or the modern world view) that provides the philosophical, ethical, and scientific bases for humankind for about 300 years. With the coming of deconstruction, these long-held beliefs were challenged, creating post-structuralism, a new basis for understanding and guiding humanity (its name denotes that it historically comes after, or post, structuralism). Often historians, anthropologists, literary theorists and other scholars use the term postmodernism synonymously with **deconstruction** and **poststructuralism**, although the term postmodernism was coined in the 1930s and has broader historical implications outside the realm of literary theory than do the terms **poststructuralism** and **deconstruction**. To place in context the somewhat turbulent reception of the first of several poststructural schools of criticism — deconstruction theory and practice — a working understanding of modernism and postmodernism is necessary.

Poststructuralism or Postmodernism

What is truth? How can truth be discovered? What is reality? Is there an objective reality on which we can all agree? If so, how can we best investigate this reality so that all humanity can understand the world in which we live and prosper from such knowledge? Until the late 1960s (with a few notable exceptions), the worldview espoused by modernity and symbolized by Benjamin Franklin provided acceptable and workable answers to these questions. For Franklin and other modern thinkers, the primary form of discourse is like a map. The map itself is a representation of reality as known, discovered, and detailed by humanity. By looking at a map a traveler could see a delineated view of the world and therefore an accurate picture of reality itself: The mountains, rivers, plains, cities, deserts, and forests. By placing his or her trust in this representation of reality, the traveler could plot a journey, feeling confident in the accuracy of the map and its depictions. For the modern mind, objective reality as pictured on the map was knowable and discoverable by any intelligent person who wished to do so.

With the advent of deconstruction, Jacque Derrida's poststructural view of the world in the mid-1960s, modernity's understanding of reality is challenged and turned on its head. For Derrida and other postmodernists, no such thing as objective reality exists. For these thinkers, all definitions and depictions of truth are subjective, simply creations of the minds of humanity. Truth itself is relative, depending on the various cultural and social influences in one's life. Because these poststructuralist thinkers assert that many truths exist, not one, they declare that modernity's concept of one objective reality must be disavowed and replaced by many different concepts, each being a valid and reliable interpretation and construction of reality.

Postmodernist thinkers reject modernity's representation of discourse (the map) and replace it with the collage. Unlike the fixed, objective nature of a map, a collage's meaning is always changing. Whereas the viewer of map relies on and obtains meaning and direction. from the map itself, the viewer of a collage actually participates in the production of meaning. And unlike a map, which allows one interpretation of reality, a collage permits many possible meanings, for the viewer can simply juxtapose a variety of combinations of images, thereby constantly changing the meaning of the collage. Each viewer, then, creates his or her own subjective picture of reality.

To say postmodernism popped onto the American literary scene with the coming of Derrida to America in 1966 would be inaccurate. Although historians disagree as to who actually coined the term, scholars generally agree that it first appeared in the 1930s. Previously, however, its seeds had already germinated in the writings of Friedrich Nietzsche(1844~1900). As Nietzsche's Zarathustra, the protagonist of *Thus Spake Zarathustra*, proclaims the death of God, the death knell begins to sound for objective reality and ultimate truth. World Wars I and II, a decline in the influence of Christianity and individualism, and the appearance of a new group of theologians led by Thomas Altizer, who in the 1950s echoed Nietzsche's words that God is dead, all spelled the demise of objective reality and the autonomous scholar who seeks to discover ultimate reality.

Beginning in the 1960s and continuing to the present, the voices of French philosopher Jacques Derrida, French cultural historian Michel Foucault, aesthetician Jean-Francois Lyotard, and ardent American pragmatist Richard Rorty, professor of humanities at the University of Virginia, all declare univocally the death of objective truth. These leading voices of postmodernism assert that modernity failed because it searched for an external point of reference — God, reason, and science, among others — on which to build its philosophy. For these postmodern thinkers, there is no such point of reference, for there is no ultimate truth or inherently unifying element in the universe and thus no ultimate reality.

According to postmodernism, all that is left is difference. We must acknowledge, they say, that each person shapes his or her own concepts of reality. Reality becomes a human construct that is shaped by each individual's dominant social group. There is no center and no one objective reality, but as many realities as there are people. Each person's interpretation of reality is necessarily different. No one has a claim to absolute truth; therefore, tolerance of each other's points of view is the postmodern maxim.

Because postmodern philosophy is constantly being shaped, reshaped, defined, and articulated by its present followers, no one voice can adequately represent it or serve as its archetypal spokesperson, as Franklin does for modernity. By synthesizing the beliefs of Derrida, Foucault, Lyotard, and Rorty, however, we can hypothesize what this representative postmodern thinker would possibly espouse:

I believe, like my forebears before me, that we, as a race of people will see progress, but only if we all cooperate. The age of the lone scholar, working diligently in the laboratory, is over. Cooperation among scholars from all fields is vital. Gone are the days of individualism. Gone are the days of conquest. Now is the time for tolerance, understanding, and collaboration.

Because our knowledge always was and always will be incomplete, we must focus on a new concept: Holism. We must realize that we all need each other including all our various perspectives on the nature of reality. We must also recognize that our rationality, our thinking process, is only one of many avenues that can lead to an understanding of our world. Our emotions, feelings, and intuition can also provide us with valid interpretations and guidelines for living.

And we have finally come to realize that no such thing as objective reality exists; there is no ultimate truth, for truth is perspectival, depending on the community and social group in which we live. Because many truths exist, we must learn to accept each other's ideas concerning truth, and we must learn to live side by side, in a pluralistic society, learning from each other while celebrating our differences.

We must stop trying to discover the undiscoverable — absolute truth — and openly acknowledge that what may be right for one person may not be right for another. Acceptance, not criticism; open-mindedness, not closed-mindedness; tolerance, not bigotry; and love, not hatred must become the guiding principles of our lives. When we stop condemning ourselves and others for 'not having truth', then we can spend more time interpreting our lives and giving them meaning, as together we work and play.

When such principles are applied to literary interpretation, the postmodernist realizes that no such thing as "the" meaning or the correct meaning of an aesthetic text exists. As in a collage, meaning develops as the reader reacts with the text, for meaning does not reside within the text itself. And because each reader's view of truth is of perspective, the interpretation of a text that emerges when a reader interacts with a text will necessarily be different from every other reader's interpretation. For each text, then, there exists an almost infinite number of interpretations, or at least as many interpretations as there are readers.

6.2 HISTORICAL DEVELOPMENT

6.2.1 Beginnings of Deconstruction

Coined by its founding father, Jacques Derrida, deconstruction first emerged on the American literary stage in 1966 when Derrida, a French philosopher and teacher, read his paper "Structure, Sign, and Play" at a Johns Hopkins University symposium. By questioning and disputing in this paper the metaphysical assumptions held to be true by Western philosophy since the time of Plato, Derrida inaugurated what many critics believe to be the most intricate and challenging methods of textual analysis as yet to appear.

Derrida himself, however, would not want deconstruction dubbed a critical theory, a school of criticism, a mode or method of literary criticism, or a philosophy. Nowhere in Derrida's writings does he state the encompassing tenets of his critical approach, nor does he ever present a codified body of deconstructive theory or methodology. Although he gives his views in bits and pieces throughout his canon, he believes that he cannot develop a formalized statement of his rules for reading, interpretation, and writing. Unlike a unified treatise, Derrida claims, his approach to reading (and literary analysis) is more a strategic device than a methodology, more a strategy or approach to literature than a school or theory of criticism. Such theories of criticism, he believes, must identify with a body of knowledge that they claim to be true or to contain truth. It is this assertion (that truth or a core of metaphysical ideals actually exists and can be believed, articulated, and supported) that Derrida and deconstruction wish to dispute and "deconstruct".

Because deconstruction uses previously formulated theories from other schools of criticism, coins many words for its newly established ideas, and challenges beliefs long held by Western culture, many students, teachers, and even critics avoid studying it, fearing its supposed complexity. By organizing deconstruction and its assumptions into three workable areas of study rather than plunging directly into some of its complex terminology, we can begin to grasp this approach to textual analysis. In order to understand deconstruction and its strategic approach to a text, then, we must first gain a working knowledge of the historical and philosophical roots of structuralism, a linguistic approach to textual analysis that gained critical attention and popularity in the 1950s and 1960s (See Chapter 5 for a detailed analysis of structuralism). From this school of criticism Derrida borrows the basis of and the starting point for his deconstructive strategy. After examining structuralism, we must investigate the proposed radical changes Derrida makes in Western philosophy and metaphysics. Such changes, Derrida readily admits, turn Western metaphysics on its head. Finally, we must master a set of new terminology coupled with new philosophical assumptions and their corresponding methodological approaches to textual analysis if we wish to understand and use deconstruction's approach to interpreting a text.

6.2.2　Structuralism at a Glance

Derrida begins formulating his strategy of reading by critiquing Ferdinand de Saussure's *Course in General Linguistics*. Saussure, the father of modern linguistics, dramatically shifted the focus of linguistic science in the early twentieth century. It is his ideas concerning language that form the core of structuralism, the critical body of literary theory from which Derrida borrows many of the major philosophical building blocks of deconstruction.

According to Saussure, structural linguistics (and structuralism itself) rests on a few basic principles. First, language is a system of rules, and these rules govern its every aspect, including individual sounds that make up a word (the *t* in *cat*, for example), small units that join together to form a word (garden+er=gardener), grammatical relationships between words (such as the rule that a singular subject must combine with a singular verb, as in *John eats ice cream*), and the relationships among all words in a sentence (such as relationship between the phrase *under a tree* and all remaining words in the sentence *Mary sits under a tree to eat her lunch*). Consciously and unconsciously every speaker of a language learns these rules and knows when they are broken. Speakers of English know, for example, that the sentence *Simon grew up to be a brilliant doctor* seems correct and thereby follows the rules of the English language, but that the sentence *Simon up grew a brilliant doctor is somehow* incorrect and violates the rules of English. These rules that make up a language and that we learn both consciously and unconsciously Saussure dubs langue. Saussure recognizes that individual speakers of a language evidence langue in their individual speech utterances, which he calls parole. It is the task of the linguist, Saussure believes, to infer a language's langue from the analysis of many instances of parole.

Emphasizing the systematized nature of language, Saussure then asserts that all languages are composed of basic units or emes. Identifying these paradigms (models) or relationships among symbols (the letters of the alphabet, for example) in a given language is the job of a linguist. This task becomes especially difficult when the emes in the linguist's native language and those in an unfamiliar language under investigation differ. Generally, linguists must first recognize and understand the various emes in their native language. For example, one eme in all languages is the individual sounds that make up words. The number of distinct and significant sounds (or phonemes) that make up a language ranges from the low teens to 60 and above. English, for instance, has approximately 45 phonemes. But telling the difference among sounds and knowing when any alteration in the pronunciation of a phoneme can change the meaning of a group of phonemes (i.e., a word) or when a simple variation in a phoneme's pronunciation is linguistically insignificant can be difficult. For example, in English the letter *t* represents the sound /t/. But is there one distinct pronunciation for this sound whenever and wherever it appears in an English word? Is the *t* in the word *tip*, for instance, pronounced the same as the *t* in *stop*? Obviously not, for the first t is aspirated, or pronounced with a greater force of air than the t in stop. In either word, however, a speaker of English could still identify the /t/as a phoneme, or a distinct sound. If we then replace the *t* in *tip* with a *d*, we now have *dip* the difference between the two words being the sounds /t/ and /d/. upon analysis, we find that these sounds are pronounced in the same location in the mouth but with one difference: /d/ is voiced, or pronounced with the vocal cords vibrating, whereas /t/is unvoiced, with the vocal cords remaining basically still. It is this difference between the sounds /t/ and /d/ allows us to say that /t/ and /d/ are phonemes or distinct sounds in English. Whether the eme (any linguistic category such as a phoneme) is a sound, or a minimal unit of grammar such as the adding of an "-s" in English to form most plurals, or any other distinct category of a language, Saussure's basic premise operates: Within each eme, distinctions depend on differences.

That distinctions or meaning in language depend on differences within each radically changes some fundamental concepts long held by linguists preceding Saussure. Before Saussure, linguists believed that the structure of language was mimetic, merely mimicking the outside world; language, then, had no structure of its own. It simply copied its structure from the reality exhibited in the world in which it was used. Saussure denies that language is intrinsically mimetic and demonstrates that it is determined primarily by its own internal rules, such as phonology (individual sounds), grammar (the principles and rules of a language), and syntax (how words combine within an utterance to form meaning). Furthermore, these rules are highly systematized and structured. But most importantly, Saussure argues that the linguistic sign (Saussure's linguistic replacement for the word *word*) that makes up language itself is both arbitrary and conventional. For example, most languages have different words for the same concept. For instance, the English word *man is homme* in French. And in English we know that the meaning of the word pit exists not because it possesses some innate acoustic quality but because it differs from *hit*, *wit*, and *lit*. In other words, the linguistic sign is composed of two parts: The signifier, or the spoken or written constituent such as the sound /t/ and the orthographic (written) symbol "t", and the signified, the concept signaled by the signifier. It is this relationship between the signifier (the word *dog*, for example) and the signified (the concept or the reality behind the word *dog*) that Saussure maintains is arbitrary and conventional. The linguistic sign, then, is defined by differences that distinguish it from other signs, not by any innate properties.

Believing that our knowledge of the world is shaped by the language that represents it, Saussure insist on the arbitrary relationship between the signifier and the signified. By so doing, he undermines the long held belief that there is some natural link between the word and the thing it represents. For Saussure, meaning in language resides in a systematized combination of sounds that rely chiefly on the differences among these signs, not any innate properties within the signs themselves. It is this concept that meaning in language is determined by the differences among the language signs that Derrida borrows from Saussure as a key building block in the formulation of deconstruction.

6.2.3   Derrida's Interpretation of Saussure's Sign

Derridean deconstruction begins with and emphatically affirms Saussure's decree that language is a system based on differences. Derrida agrees with Saussure that we can know the meaning of **signifiers** through and because of their relationships and their differences among themselves. But unlike Saussure, Derrida also applies this reasoning to the signified. Like the signifier, the signified (or concept) can also be known only through its relationships and its differences among other **signifieds**. Furthermore, declares Derrida, the signified cannot orient or make permanent the meaning of the signifier, for the relationship between the signifier and the signified is both arbitrary and conventional. And, accordingly, **signifieds** often function as **signifiers**. For example, in the sentence I *filled the glass with milk*, the spoken or written word *glass* is a signifier; its signified is *the concept of a container* that can be filled. But in the sentence *The container was filled with glass*, the spoken or written word *container*, a signified in the previous sentence, is now a signifier, its signified being the concept of an object that can be filled.

6.3   ASSUMPTIONS

6.3.1   Transcendental Signified

Believing that signification (how we arrive at meaning from the linguistic signs in language) is both arbitrary and conventional, Derrida now begins his process of turning Western philosophy on its head. He boldly asserts that the entire history of Western metaphysics from Plato to the present is founded upon a classic, fundamental error: The searching for a transcendental signified; an external point of reference on which one may build a concept or philosophy. Once found, this transcendental signified would provide ultimate meaning, being the origin of origins, reflecting itself, and as Derrida says, providing a "reassuring end to the reference from sign to sign". In essence, it would guarantee to those who believe in it that they do exist and have meaning. For example, if we posit that I or self is a transcendental signified, then the concept of self becomes the unifying principle on which I structure my world. Objects, concepts, ideas, or even people take on meaning in my world only if I filter them through my unifying, ultimate signified self.

Unlike other signified, the transcendental signified would have to be understood without being compared to other signifieds or signifiers. In other words, its meaning would originate directly with itself, not differentially or relationally, as does the meaning of all other signifieds or signifiers. These transcendental signifieds would then provide the center of meaning, allowing those who believed in them to structure their ideas of reality round them. Such a center of meaning could not subject itself to structural analysis, for by so doing it would lose its place as a transcendental signified to another center. For example, if I declare the concept *self* to be my transcendental signified and then learn that my mind or self is composed of the id, the ego, and the super ego, I could no longer hold the *self* or I to be my transcendental signified. In the process of discovering the three parts of my conscious and unconscious mind, I have both structurally analyzed and decentered *self*, thus negating it as a transcendental *signified*.

6.3.2 Logocentrism

According to Derrida, Western metaphysics has invented a variety of terms that function as centers: *God, reason, origin, being, essence, truth, humanity, beginning, end, and self* to name a few. Each can operate as a concept that is self-sufficient and self-originating and can serve as a transcendental signified. This Western proclivity for desiring a center Derrida names logocentrism: The belief that there is an ultimate reality or center of truth that can serve as the basis for all our thoughts and actions.

That we can never totally free ourselves from our logocentric habit of thinking and our inherited concept of the universe Derrida readily admits. To *decenter* any transcendental signified is to be caught up automatically in the terminology that allows that centering concept to operate. For example, if the concept *self* functions as my center and I then "discover" my unconscious *self*, I automatically place in motion a binary operation or two opposing concepts: the self and the unconscious *self*. By decentering and questioning the *self*, I cause the *unconscious self* to become the new center. By questioning the old center, I establish a new one.

Such logocentric thinking, declares Derrida, has its origin in Aristotle's principle of noncontradiction: A thing cannot both have a property and not have a property. Thanks to Aristotle, maintains Derrida, Western metaphysics has developed an either-or mentality or logic that inevitably leads to the centering and decentering of transcendental signifields. Such a logocentric way of thinking, asserts Derrida, is natural for Western readers, but problematic.

6.3.3 Binary Oppositions

Because the establishing of one center of unity automatically means that another is de-centered, Derrida concludes that Western metaphysics is based on a system of binary operations or conceptual oppositions. For each center, there exists an opposing center (God / humankind, for example). In addition, Western philosophy holds that in each of these binary operations or two opposing centers, one concept is superior and defines itself by its opposite or inferior center. We know truth, for instance, because we know deception; we know good because we know bad. The creating of these hierarchic binaries is the basis of Western metaphysics to which Derrida objects.

6.3.4 Phonocentrism

Such a fragile basis for believing what is really Derrida wishes to dismantle. In the binary oppositions on which Western metaphysics has built itself from the time of Plato, Derrida declares that one element will always be in a superior position, or privileged, whereas the other becomes inferior, or unprivileged. According to this way of thinking, the first or top elements in the following list of binary oppositions are privileged: man/woman, human/animal, soul/body, good/bad. Most importantly, Derrida decrees that Western thought has long privileged speech over writing. This privileging of speech over writing Derrida calls phonocentrism.

In placing speech in the privileged position phonocentrism treats writing as inferior. We value a speaker's words more than the speaker's writing, says Derrida, for words imply presence. Through the vehicle of spoken words, we supposedly learn directly what a speaker is trying to say. From this point of view, writing becomes a mere copy of speech, an attempt to capture the idea that was once spoken. Whereas speech implies presence, writing signifies absence, thereby placing into action another binary opposition: Presence/absence.

Because phonocentrism is based on the assumption that speech conveys the meaning or direct ideas of a speaker better than writing (a mere copy of speech), phonocentrism assumes a logocentric way of thinking, that the self is the center of meaning and can best ascertain ideas directly from other selves through spoken words. Through speaking, the self declares its presence, its significance, and its being (or existence).

6.3.5　Metaphysics of Presence

Accordingly, Derrida coins the phrase metaphysics of presence to encompass ideas such as logocentrism, phonocentrism, the operation of binary oppositions, and other notions that Western thought holds concerning language and metaphysics. His objective is to demonstrate the shaky foundations on which such beliefs have been established. By deconstructing the basic premises of metaphysics of presence, Derrida believes he gives us a strategy for reading that opens up a variety of new interpretations heretofore unseen by those who are bound by the restraints of Western thought.

6.4　METHODOLOGY

6.4.1　Acknowledging Binary Operations in Western Thought

The first stage in a deconstructive reading is to recognize the existence and operation of binary oppositions in our thinking. One is the most "violent hierarchies" derived from Platonic and Aristotelian thought is speech/writing, with speech being privileged. Consequently, speech is awarded presence, and writing is equated with absence. Being the inferior of the two, writing becomes simply the symbols of speech, a second-hand representation of ideas.

Once the speech/writing hierarchy or any other hierarchy is recognized and acknowledged, Derrida asserts, we can readily reverse its elements. Such a reversal is possible because truth is ever elusive, for we can always decenter the center if any is found. By reversing the hierarchy, Derrida does not wish merely to substitute one hierarchy for another and to involve himself in a negative mode. When the hierarchy is reversed, says Derrida, we can examine the values and beliefs that give rise to both the original hierarchy and the newly created one. Such an examination reveals how the meanings of terms arise from the differences between them.

Arche-writing

In *Of Grammatology*, Derrida spends much time explaining why the speech/writing hierarchy can and must be reversed. In short, he argues for a redefining of the term writing that will allow him to assert that writing is actually a precondition for and prior to speech. According to Derrida's metaphysical reasoning, language is a special kind of writing which he calls archi-écriture or arche-writing.

Using traditional Western metaphysics that is grounded in phonocentricism, Derrida begins his reversal of the speech/writing hierarchy by noting that language and writing share common characteristics. For example, both involve an encoding or inscription. In writing, this coding is obvious, for the written symbols represent various phonemes. And in language or speech, a similar encoding exists, As Saussure has already shown, there exists an arbitrary relationship between the signifier and the signified (between the spoken word cat and the concept of cat itself). Thus, there is no innate relationship between the spoken word and the concept, object, or idea it represents. Nevertheless, once a signifier and a signified join to form a sign, some kind of relationship then exists between these components of the sign. For example, some kind of inscription or encoding has taken place between the spoken word cat (the signifier) and its concept (the signified).

For Derrida both writing and language are means of signification, and ach can be considered a signifying system. Traditional Western metaphysics and Saussurean linguistics equate speech (language) with presence, for speech is accompanied by the presence of a living speaker. The presence of the speaker necessarily links sound and sense and therefore leads to understanding — one usually comprehends the spoken word. Writing, on the other hand, assumes an absence of a speaker. Such absence can produce misunderstanding, for writing is a depersonalized medium that separates the actual utterance of the speaker and his or her audience. This absence can lead to misunderstanding of the signifying system.

But Derrida asserts that we must broaden our understanding of writing. Writing, he declares, cannot be reduced to letters or other symbols inscribed on a page. Rather, it is directly related to what Saussure believed to be the basic element of language: Difference. We know one phoneme or one word because each is different from another. And we know that there is no innate relationship between a signifier and its signified. The phoneme /b/, for example, could have easily become the symbol for the phoneme /d/, just as the coined word bodt could have become the English word ball. It is this free play or element of undecidability in any system of communication totally eludes a speaker's awareness when using language, for the speaker falsely assumes a position as supposed master of his or her speech.

By equating writing with the free play or the element of undecidability at the center of all systems of communication, Derrida declares that writing actually governs language, thereby negating the speech/writing hierarchy of Western metaphysics. Writing now becomes privileged and speech unprivileged, for speech is a kind of writing called arche-writing.

This being so, Derrida then challenges Western philosophy's concept that human consciousness gives birth to language. Without language (or arche-writing), argues Derrida, there can be no consciousness, for consciousness presupposes language. Through arche-writing, we impose human consciousness on the world.

Supplementation

The relationship between any binary hierarchy, however, is always unstable and problematic. It is not Derrida's purpose simply to reverse all binary oppositions that exist in Western thought but rather to show the fragile basis for the establishment of such hierarchies and the possibility of inverting these hierarchies to gain new insights into language and life.

Derrida uses the term **supplement** to refer to the unstable relationship between elements in a binary operation. For example, in the speech/writing opposition, writing supplements speech and in actuality takes the place of speech (arche-writing). In all binary oppositions such supplementation exists. In the truth/deception hierarchy, for example, Western thought would assert the supremacy of truth over deception, attributing to deception a mere supplementary role. Such a logocentric way of thinking asserts the purity of truth over deception. Upon examination, deception more often than not contains at least some truth. And who is to say, asks Derrida, when truth has been spoken, achieved, or even conceived? The purity of truth may simply not exist. In all human activity, then, supplementation operates.

Différance

By realizing that supplementation operates in all of Western metaphysics' binary operations and by inverting the privileged and unprivileged elements, Derrida begins to develop his reading strategy of deconstruction. Once he turns Western metaphysics on its head, he asserts his answer to logocentrism and other Western elements by coining a new word and concept: **différance**. The word itself is derived from the French word **différer,** meaning both to defer, postpone, or delay, and to differ, to be different from. Derrida deliberately coins his word to be ambiguous , taking on both meanings simultaneously. And in French the word is a pun, for it exists only in writing: in speech there is no way to tell the difference between the French word **différence** and Derrida's coined word **différence**.

Understanding what Derrida means by différance is one of the basic keys to understanding deconstruction. Basically, **différance** is Derrida's what-if question. What if no transcendental signified exists? What if there is no presence in whom we can find ultimate truth? What if all our knowledge does not arise from self-identity? What if there is no essence, being, or inherently unifying element in the universe? What then?

The presence of such a transcendental signified would immediately establish the binary operation presence/absence. Because Western metaphysics holds that presence is supreme or privileged and absence unprivileged, Derrida suggests that we temporarily reverse this hierarchy to become absence/presence. By such a reversal, no longer can we posit a transcendental signified. No longer is there some absolute standard or coherent unity from which all knowledge proceeds and develops. All human knowledge and all self-identity must now spring from difference, not sameness, from absence, not presence.

When such a reversal of Western metaphysics' pivotal binary operation occurs, two dramatic results follow: First, all human knowledge becomes referential; that is, we can know something only because it differs from some other bit of knowledge, not because we can compare this knowledge to any absolute or coherent unity (a transcendental signified). Human knowledge, then, must now be based on **différence**. We know something because it differs from something else to which it is related. Nothing can be studied or learned in isolation, for all knowledge becomes context-related. Second, we must also forgo closure; that is, because no transcendental signified exists, all interpretations concerning life, self-identity, and knowledge are possible, probable, and legitimate.

But what is the significance of **différance** in reading texts? If we, like Derrida, assert that **différance** operates in language and therefore also in writing (Derrida sometimes equates **différance** and arche-writing), what are the implications for textual analysis? The most obvious answer is that texts lack presence. Once we do away with the transcendental signified and reverse presence/absence binary operation, texts can no longer have presence; that is, in isolation, texts cannot possess meaning. Because all meaning and knowledge are now based on differences, no text can simply mean one thing. Texts become intertextual. Meaning evolves from the interrelatedness of one text to many other texts. Like language itself, texts are caught in a dynamic, context-related interchange. Never can we state a text's definitive meaning, for it has none. No longer can we declare one interpretation to be right and another wrong, for meaning in a text is always illusive, always dynamic, also transitory.

The search, then, for the text's correct meaning or the author's so-called intentions become meaningless. Because meaning is derived from differences in a dynamic, context-related, ongoing process, all texts have multiple meanings or interpretations. If we assert, as does Derrida, that no transcendental signified exists, then there can exist no absolute or pure meaning supposedly conveyed by authorial intent or professorial dictates. Meaning evolves as we, the readers, interact with the text, with both the readers and the text providing social and cultural context.

6.4.2 Deconstructive Suppositions for Textual Analysis

A deconstructor would thus begin textual analysis assuming that a text has multiple interpretations and that it allows itself to be reread and thus reinterpreted countless times. Because no one correct interpretation of any text exists, the joy of textual analysis resides in discovering new interpretations each time a text is read and reread. Ultimately, a text's meaning is undecidable, for each reading or rereading can elicit different interpretations.

When beginning the interpretative process, deconstructors seek to override their own logocentric and inherited ways of viewing a text. Such revolutionary thinkers find the binary oppositions at work in the text itself. These binary oppositions, they believe, represent established and accepted ideologies that usually posit the existence of transcendental signifieds. These binary operations restrict meaning, for they already assume a fixed interpretation of reality. They assume, for instance, the existence of truth and falsehood, reason and insanity, good and bad. Realizing that these hierarchies presuppose a fixed and a biased way of viewing the world, deconstructors seek out the binary oppositions operating in the text and reverse them. By reversing these hierarchies, deconstructors wish to challenge the fixed views assumed by such hierarchies and the values associated with such rigid beliefs.

By identifying the binary operations that exist in the text, deconstructors can then show the preconceived assumptions on which most of us base our interpretations. For example, we all declare some activity, being, or object to be good or bad, valuable or worthless, significant or insignificant. Such values or ideas automatically operate when we write or read any text. By reversing the hierarchies on which we base our interpretations, deconstructors wish to free us from the constraints of our prejudiced beliefs. Such freedom, they hope, will allow us to see a text from exciting new perspectives that we have never before recognized.

These various perspectives cannot be simultaneously perceived by the reader or even the writer of a text. In Nathaniel Hawthorne's "Young Goodman Brown," for example, many readers believe that the 50-year-old character who shepherds Goodman Brown through his night's visit in the forest is Satan and therefore necessarily an evil character. Brown's own interpretation of this character seems to support this view. According to deconstructionist ideas, at least two binary operations are at work here: good/evil and God/Satan. But what if we reverse these hierarchies? Then the scepteral figure may not be Satan and therefore may not be evil! Such a new perspective may dramatically change our interpretation of the text.

According to deconstructors, we cannot simultaneously see both of these perspectives in the story. To discover where the new hierarchy Satan/God or evil/ good will lead us in our interpretation, we must suspend our first interpretation. We do not, however, forget it, for it is locked in our minds. We simply shift our allegiance to another perspective or level.

Such oscillating between interpretations, levels, or perspectives allows us to see the impossibility of ever choosing a correct interpretation, for meaning is ongoing activity that is always in progress, always based on **différance**. By asking what will happen if we reverse the hierarchies that frame our preconceived ways of thinking, we open ourselves to a never-ending process of interpretation that holds that no hierarchy or binary operation is right and no other is wrong.

6.4.3 Deconstruction: A Net Reading Strategy

Deconstruictors do not wish, then, to set up a new philosophy, a new literary theory of analysis, or a new school of literary criticism. Instead, they present a reading strategy that allows us to make choices concerning the various levels of interpretation we see operating in a text. All levels, they maintain, have validity. They also believe their approach to reading frees them and us from ideological allegiances that restrict our finding meaning in a text.

Because meaning, they believe, emerges through interpretation, even the author does not control a text's interpretation. Although writers may have clearly state intentions concerning their texts, such statements must be given little credence. Like language itself, texts have no outside referents (or transcendental signifieds). What an author thinks he or she says or means in a text may be quite different from what is actually written. Deconstructors therefore look for places in the text where the author misspeaks or loses control of language and says what was supposedly not meant to be said. These "slips of language" often occur in questions, figurative language, and strong declarations. For example, suppose we read the following words: "important Seniors'

Meeting." Although the author thinks that readers will interpret these words to mean that it is important that all seniors be present at this particular meeting, the author may have misspoken, for these words can actually mean that only important seniors should attend this meeting. By examining such slips and the binary operations that govern them, deconstructors are able to demonstrate the undecidability of a text's meaning.

At first glance, a deconstructionist reading strategy may appear to be linear — that is, having a clearly delineated beginning, middle, and end. If this is so, then to apply this strategy to a text, we must do the following:

· Discover the binary operations that govern a text.

· Comment on the values, concepts, and ideas beyond these operations.

· Reverse these present binary operations.

· Dismantle previously held worldviews.

· Accept the possibility of various perspectives or levels of meaning in a text based on the new binary inversions.

· Allow meaning of the text to be undecidable.

Although all these elements operate in a deconstructionist reading, the may not operate in this exact sequence. Because we all tend toward logocentrism when reading, we may not note some logocentric binary operations functioning in the text until we have reversed some obvious binary oppositions and are interpreting the text on several levels. In addition, we must never declare such a reading to be complete or finished, for the process of meaning is ongoing, never allowing us to pledge allegiance to any one view.

Such a reading strategy disturbs most readers and critics, for it is not a neat, completed package whereby if we follow step A through to step Z we arrive at "the" reading of the text. Because texts have no external referents, their meanings depend on the close interaction of the text, the reader, and the social and cultural elements, as does every reading or interpretive process. Denying the organic unity of a text, deconstructors declare the free play of language in a text. Because language itself is reflexive, not mimetic, we can never stop finding meaning in a text, whether we have read it once or a hundred times.

Overall, deconstruction desires an ongoing relationship between the interpreter (the critic) and the text. By examining the text alone, deconstructors hope to ask a set of questions that continually challenges the ideological positions of power and authority that dominate literary criticism. And in the process of discovering meaning in a text, they declare that criticism of a text is just as valuable as the creative writing being read, thus inverting the creative writing/criticism hierarchy.

6.5   AMERICAN DECONSTRUCTORS

After Derrida's introduction of deconstruction to his American audience in 1966, Derrida found several sympathetic listeners who soon became loyal adherents and defenders of his new reading strategy: Romantic scholar Paul de Man, rhetorical deconstructor Hayden White, the sometimes terse metaphysical deconstructor Geoffrey Hartman, the strong voice of Barbara Johnson, and phenomenological critic turned deconstructor J. Hillis Miller. These critics asserted that deconstruction would find a voice and an established place in American literary theory. Although the voices of other post-structural theories such as New Historicism and postcolonial theory now clamor to be heard, deconstruction's philosophical assumptions and practical reading strategies form the basis of many postmodern literary practices.

6.6   QUESTIONS FOR ANALYSIS

Interpret a short story or poem of your choice. After you have completed your interpretation, cite the binary operations that function both within your chosen text and within your thinking to allow you to arrive at your perspective.

Using the same text and interpretation you used for the first question, reverses one of the binary operations and reinterpret the text. When you are finished, reverse two additional binaries and reinterpret the story. What differences exist between the two interpretations?

Using Robert Browning's "My Last Duchess" or a poem of your choice, demonstrates how the author misspeaks, or where the text involves itself in paradox. Be specific. Be able to point to lines, figurative speech, or imaginative language to support your statements.

Using Robert Browning's "My Last Duchess," cite at least four dramatically different interpretations, all based on a deconstructive reading.

Reread the student essay found at the end of Chapter 3, "New Criticism" What elements of the story does the author simply ignore or dismiss? Consider how Derrida's concept of supplementation is operating in this critic's analysis.

Read the student essay located at the end of this chapter. Because this essay approaches textual analysis from a deconstructive point of view, the author must assume that all essays can be so analyzed. On this assumption, deconstruct the student essay, noting where the author of the essay misspeaks and how the essay dismantles itself.

6.7   SAMPLE ESSAYS

In the student essay that follows, note how the author uses the various binary operations she discovers in the text to show how the text misspeaks and dismantles itself. Also note and be able to explain how the binaries used by the author involve the text in paradoxes, Based on the binary oppositions at work in the parable, be able to explain at least four different interpretations. In addition, note how the author tries to divorce herself from logocentric thinking and the metaphysics of presence as she seeks to analyze the parable.

The Creative Treason in Roger T. Ames's English Translation Versions of *Dao De Jing* from the Perspective of Deconstructionism

Dao De Jing is the treasure of Chinese philosophy, and it has numerous translation texts. The paper tries to study the creative treason in the English translation of *Dao De Jing* from deconstructionism perspective. It is known that deconstructionism is a predominant theory in post-modernism theory. It deconstructs the loyalty concept of traditional translation theory, and holds that the writer has been dead, which give translators rights to translate the work. Creative treason is first put forward by French sociologist of literature Robert Escarpit, and he also firms the subjectivity of translators.

The paper mainly aims at dissolving several problems: Firstly, translation is a kind of creative treason activity; secondly, deconstructionism theory and creative treason can be complementary with each other; thirdly, the limitation of creative treason, namely, what kind of treason can be called creative treason? According to the different translation texts of *Dao De Jing*, it induces that only those creative treason which gain the optimal relevance of the source text by changing abstraction into concreteness, capitalizing initial words, literal translation pluses notes, amplification translation, liberal translation, domestication translation, and foreignization translation.

Dao De Jing, five thousand words, is the first complete philosophy work in Chinese philosophy history, which guides people to break the narrow space and widen their thought into the vast universe as well as enlighten people to explore the unknown world. The book concludes how to keep healthy, how to live, politic theory, military theory, cognition theory, life philosophy, natural philosophy, universe philosophy and so on. Some of its ideas like the study on *Dao De Jing* translation versions is prevalent. Many scholars study it from different aspects: someone studies it from the course of English translation of *Dao De Jing*; someone makes analysis and comparison of different English translation of *Dao De Jing*; or study the translation of key words and translation style; meanwhile, someone turns to study the translators and the transformation of the culture image.

However, this paper will study the creative treason of *Dao De Jing*'s English translation versions from the perspective of deconstructionism.

Literature Review

Domestication and foreignization translation methods decrease the embarrassing situation of translation to some extent, but their shortcomings are still obvious. The writer holds that the cultural dispersion experience can harmonize the conflict between domestication and foreignization. The cultural dispersion experience has great effect on the target readers. According to the test result, these overseas students with the cultural dispersion experience can gain much more information than those who do not have this experience when they read translation of *Dao De Jing* either by Chinese translators or foreign translators. He also mentions that the number of overseas students is limited as a whole and the tasks of the translator are still to enhance the cultural cultivation, keep the beauty of meaning, phonetics and form and try best to transform the cultural image in order to make the target readers further understand the Chinese culture.

The Study of *Dao De Jing* Abroad

Julia M. Hardy first does a research on *Dao De Jing* according to the survey of some influential western interpretations. She concludes three periods of the translation of *Dao De Jing* and its characteristics in each phase. Michael LaFargue and Julian Pas, they make a comparison between seventeen major English translations and give some reasons for the differences existing. But their study just focuses on the first sentence of Chapter Four and Chapter Thirteen. The shortcoming of the paper is that they do not pay much attention to the great effect of social and political ideology on the translation and translation activity. Herbert A.Giles(1885),British sinologist, makes a comparison among the four translation texts by John Chalmers, Stanislas Julien, James Legge and Frederic Henry Balfour. He gives detailed analysis on the difference of these versions and puts forward his doubt for the authenticity of the source text of *Dao De Jing*.

Concept Review of Creative Treason

Creative Treason in Sociology of Literature

French sociologist of literature Robert Escarpit is the first person who proposes the concept of creative treason in his book *Sociology of Literature* in the year of 1958; if people are willing to accept the statement that translation is a kind of creative treason, then, translation, the irritating problem would be settled. To say translation is treason, it is because that it puts the sourer text in a totally unexpected reference system (language); translation is a kind of creative treason, and its form in translation is deletion, adding and paraphrase. ... and no matter what the result is for translation, creative treason is obviously the most important medium of literature communication in different languages and the first study object in comparative literature. Translation characteristic, translation theory, the resonance of translators for the source text and the changing of the translation work etc, which are brought by creative treason, not only shows the influence of foreign literature but also shows the literature situation of one country, and all this is the content of translation study. *The Chinese Western Comparative Literature Course* (1988) by Le Daiyun makes a new and special chapter to study medio-translatology in which it makes a brief introduction on the translation history, translation property, principle and its basic character. Meanwhile, it also points out that medio-translatology is a big branch including language comparison, the comparison of the source text and the translation one, but the creative treason will exert great effect on the translation study. The understanding of the translators and the readers are always a kind of recreation, because all the translation texts are read and accepted in an unimaginable re-creative way. The source text must go through this kind of creative treason to expand its vitality and being read and being accepted widely. There are double times of creative treason from translators to the acceptance of readers. The readers always do the re-creative activity in their own way in the reading process. For example, Lu Xun, Mao Dun and Fu Sinian respectively create the image of Nietzsche. This kind of creative treason is produced sometimes due to the limitation of history and literature, such as the difference between national mentality and aesthetics value even some complicated elements like the effect of politic trend which obviously plays a role in free translation and adaptation of translators.

The coauthor of *General Introduction of comparative Literature* by Chen Cun and Xiu

Xiangyu still give detailed study about medio-translatology. The importance of translation not only lies that translation is the mind bridge to combine different nations, but also offers medium for the spread of literary influence.

It can be said that the treason in literature can be viewed as a kind of betrayal to the source text that translators make in translation process in order to approach some kind of subjective intention. And in theory, it is just feasible, in the actual literary translation, creativity and treason cannot be separated and they are harmonious organism. The target text and the source text just equate in some aspects. As a kind of communication, translation is always translators' inclusions and omissions process. Translators make choices according to the intention of the author and the expectation of the readers: Translators seek for the optimal relevance from the ostensive communicative action of the author (namely the source text or artistic conception) then, and they convey this optimal relevance to the readers to reach the optimal relevance between the communicative intention of the author and the expectation of the readers.

In order to realize the optimal relevance of the source text, translators should go through ostensive-inference process twice, the first is that the translators find out the implication of the source text through the information and related context the author offers to gain the optimal relevance between the source text and context. The second process is evaluating the expectation of the readers and conveying the intention of the source text to the readers. Only by this, translators can keep the optimal relevance of the source text in the translation texts and let the readers gain sufficient context effect with the least effort.

Translation study is an important part of comparative literature, and it presents different views from the researcher of comparative literature and the traditional translation study. French comparative literature researcher Paul Van Tieghem, one of the pioneers of comparative literature pays attention to the translation problem. He holds that the study of the translation text mainly lies in two aspects: First, the comparing of the translation text and the source text to see whether there are adding or losing; second, comparing different translation works in different time of the same source text to see its change and the different effect the author has on different time. Paul Van Tieghem exerts a pioneering effect on the translation study, because he classifies translation study into Mesologie study. Although he does not put forward the term creative treason, the two study aspects he offers are important study content of creative treason which constructs the synchronic and diachronic existence of creative treason.

In the 80s and 90s of 20th century, many comparative literature works view creative treason as the main translation study object in China. But the first comparative literature treatise *Introduction To Comparative Literature* (1984) does not mention the creative treason; it just begins the early probe on content and method study of medio-translatology, meanwhile, it points out that medio-translatology includes the translation work study, translation theories and translation history.

Creative treason refers to three aspects: first, the misunderstanding of readers in modern times as for the former works, being contrary to the source text meaning, such as *Gulliver's Travels* by Swift and *Lu Binsun Crusoe* by Defoe are now regarded as children's reading materials. Second, changing the source text meaning of the source text in order to cater for the native readers, such as Pound's adaptation of Chinese poems. Third, the theory mistakes led by the limitation of language in translation produces creative treason.

The word entry on translation also points that:

Translation is a kind of creative treason, and its form in translation is deletion, adding and paraphrasing…and no matter what the result is for translation, creative treason is obviously the most important medium of literature communication in different language and the first study object in comparative literature. Translation characteristic, translation theory, the resonance of translators with the source text and the changing of the translation work etc., which are brought by creative treason, not only shows the influence trace of foreign literature but also shows the literature situation of one country, and all of these are the content of translation study.

Translation is often regarded as creative treason. From one language to another, the work must add or lose some elements and the translators can not completely be loyal to the source text. The translation text will betray the source text no matter in form or content; however, any translation cannot deviate the source text and the re-creation must be the source text-centered. In translation, a work gains its second life by being introduced into a new environment. "Creative translation is not exclusive to literature translation but a basic principle of culture transmission and acceptance. If no creative treason, there would not be culture transmission and acceptance." From oral literature to written literature, the literature works continuously get changed, and enriched. No work can completely convey the intention of the author to readers without any mistakes, because each receiver comprehends and accepts the work from their own experiences. Once a work spreads across time, geography, nation and language, the creative treason gets much clear. "creative treason has surpassed the pure literature acceptance scope, bring different cultures into literary creation by means of different translation strategy". This kind of cognition introduces creative treason into different culture communication and collision; meanwhile, it opens a wide field to further study.

Translation as a Kind of Creativity and Treason

Translation, more or less, is the creative treason of translators; namely, translation is the transition of language which is not confined within the form of source text to reappear the verve and artistic conception of the source text. The content and quintessence of text often relies on some especial language forms, so when the source text enters a new environment via translation, it is necessary to change the superficial form of source text and make good use of the optimal language form of the target language to convey the artistic conception of the source text. Moreover, the special culture carried by special language makes interlingual translation hard to reach semantic equivalence. So translation is not just simply language changing but a creative job. Creative treason is an objective and common phenomenon in translation.

Meanwhile, it reveals that the essence of translation is communication. The translation text is the homologous text of the source text but not the same one. Namely, the same information can be expressed in different ways. Certainly, treason is not meaning of the completely treason from contents to form. Afterall, translation is second creation within the field of source text. It is no doubt that there is a problem on which level of treason can be called creative treason, namely, the limitation of creative treason.

Although creative treason of translation has hotly discussed in recent years, it still lacks criterion and maxim in theory. However, it can be easily found that the optimal relevance in relevance theory can help to solve the problem. Only such treason that reaches the optimal relevance of the source text can be called creative treason. Relevance theory views translation as an ostentive-inference process that aims at explaining the source language. The relevance principle is the core concept of relevance theory. And the context effect and cognition effort are the two elements to construct the relevance theory. Hence, the relevance refers to the balance between the context effect and cognition effort. The relationship of relevance, context effect and cognition effort can be expressed as follows:

$R = C/E$

In the formula, R refers to relevance, C refers to context effect and E refers to cognitive effort. It can be seen from the formula that the larger the context effect is, the less cognitive effort will be made, and much stronger of relevance will be, and vice versa. The optimal relevance just refers to comprehending the utterance with the minimum cognitive effort to gain the sufficient context effect. So, when creative treason takes optimal relevance maxim as its criterion, the treason can be meaningful and translation also avoids translating at random. So, in the view of optimal relevance maxim based creative treason, the target text and the source text just equate in some aspects. As a kind of communication, translation is always the process of translators' inclusions and omissions.

The essence of any translation, either scientific literature translation or arts and literature translation, is to convey the information of one language in another language. However, translation practice shows that there are always gaps between the purpose and the result that translation can reach. Language can produce the vividness that art requires, because it has close relationship with the accumulation of history, culture and life experience of the language users. Due to the historical and cultural accumulation of special language context and life experience of language users, these elements make language users produce rich imagination when they use special vocabulary, which grants the language imagery and vividness. When the literature work produced in some kind of language context is planted into another language context, in order to make the receiver produce the same art effect as the source text, translators must find the appropriate expressions. And these expressions can mobilize and stimulate the translation activity as a creative treason.

In translation, no matter the translation work is superior or inferior to the source text, the phenomenon is decided by the creativity and treason of translation. The creativity of translation shows the subjective endeavor of translator to reproduce the source text by using his creative ability, and the treason in translation is the objective deviation towards the source text in order to reach some subjective aims. But creativity and treason can not be divided in practical translation, they are a harmonious whole. The creative treason is prominently shown in the translation of poems. Because as a special genre poetry combines the highly concise literature forms with infinite rich contents, which makes translators in dilemma — keeping the content, but losing the form and vice versa.

Creative Treason in Translation from Deconstructionism Perspective

From the development of deconstructionism, it can be seen that deconstructionism is a kind of philosophy concept and it has a deep philosophy foundation. When it is combined with translation, it produces a great impact on traditional translation. In traditional translation concept, the writer is the authority who controls the meaning of text and ranks in a high position, because he /she is the main part to create the thought and language of the text and he or she can do the creativity at will. But the translator can not. What the translators can do is to strictly follow the meaning of the writer according to the source text. In the seventeenth century, John Dryden, translation theorist in England, compares the translators as "slaves" who work in slave owner's manor while the labor fruits belong to the owner. So traditional translation theory treats the source text as the owner and the translator must follow the meaning of the source text.

Deconstructionism puts forward query for the authority of the writer. The representative of deconstructionism theory, Roland Barthes, claims in his paper *The Death of Writer* that God the incarnation of text — writer death. The death of writer denies the source text writer and his/ her creativity. Deconstruction proposes that the meaning of text is not fixed in itself but in the production procession of readers' reading which is similar to the theory of Modern Hermeneutics. Modern Hermeneutics affirms the historical existence of human beings determining conscious movement and denies the eternal absolute meaning.

Derrida thinks that the translator can not be in the invisible position, because he/she is human with his/her own acceptation and rejection ability. He points out that there is no authenticity of the source text, and the value of the source text goes on. So the source text gets alive due to the translation text. Hence, the position of the translator should be as equal as the writer. But in translating process, what is the role of the translator? Derrida holds that translators can not be equal with the writer because his/her task is to make efforts than gains from his/her efforts. "The pay" refers to that the translator's action is in the state of comprehension and expounding for the source text, and "The get" means the new meaning that surpass emphasizes the source text by the creative expounding of the translator. The translation school of deconstructionism inherits the activity theory of Benjamin and Derrida, so it accepts that translation is a kind of movement that is full of active cultural explanation and the creativity of the translators.

Derrida agrees that translation can not be replicated, because translation text is not image or replica. In the process of translation, the translator is not only the one that passively conveys the meaning of the source text, but also the one who has his/her own idea, way of expression and word choice for the original.

Deconstructionism theory offers creative treason a powerful theory, and in return creative treason makes up for the shortcoming of deconstructionism. From three traits of creative treason, it can be seen that the creative treason limits the subjectivity of the translators. In this aspect, it makes up for the shortcoming of deconstructionism theory that is the translators have absolutely free right to translation.

The translator must undergo obligation and responsibility, and all these elements make it impossible that the translator conveys the meaning of the source text unvarying, and the translator will add some of his/her subjective comprehension and active expression. The translator is not the megaphone of the source text, but re-appearing the source text to a great extent, sometimes, it can make the source text which is in the situation of "approaching death" to be alive again. So the subjectivity of translators gets great release in the theory of deconstruction.

Translation covers what lacks in the source text and the translation text becomes a complement of the source text. Gentzler thinks that the purpose of Derrida is that he tries to unmask the hinted and findable operation of the traces. Due to the results of difference movement, any text contains the traces of the past and the future, and Derrida expounds the traces as the state of continuous production of difference. Venuti emphasizes that there never has loyalty in translation, but the freedom often exists. Translation never owns its identity, and it always lacks something. Robinson also says that the good translation text is not the one that gives people the feeling that it is written in the target language. Maybe this kind of concept is just an allusion. The loyalty in deconstructionism view shows its comprehension and expound meanings for the source text, "culture" is one of the complicated concepts with different definitions. And the comprehension and communication of meaning is the special connotation of culture. The historicity of creative treason can be interpreted as that creative treason is produced in some historical context with particular historical phenomenon. English scholar Gadenna asserts, interpretation lies in Hermeneutic Effectiveness, and significance exists in the things that the author expresses with a series of signs, so significance can reappear via signs.

Creative treason is a deviation from the source text, but any translator can not ignore the meaning of the source text and comprehend the text from their pre-understandings at will. Deconstructionism negates the source text-centered, and the other is the requirement of self, so comprehension must return to self.

But this kind of return is based on the other, so it must adopt the horizon of the other. Deconstructionism theory offers us a new horizon to see the problem in translation. It also has a great impact on the traditional translation concepts. After all, it relocates the relationship between the source and the translation work, the author and the translator. The translation work no longer submits to the source text, and the source text gets a new life from the translation work which is read and accepted by different readers. Meanwhile, the author is not in the predominant place and the translators try their best to explore the connotation of the source text and re-appearing the source text.

Translators are not only those that passively convey the meaning of the source text, but also those who have their own idea, way of expression and word choice for the source text, which to some extent deconstructs the traditional translation concept of loyalty. Deconstructionism theory advocates the subjective initiative and creativity of the translators, because in the view of deconstructionism theory the meaning of the sign is in the play of difference, only in this way can the translator understand the source text much deeper. Even though, deconstructionism theory offers powerful theoretical support for translators' subjectivity, and it can easily produce an extreme situation that any explanation for the source text will be reasonable. So in this aspect, creative treason can make up for the shortcoming of deconstructionism theory.

Firstly, from the three traits of creative treason, it can be seen that creative treason needs the subjectivity of translators. But meanwhile, translators cannot explain the source text at will, and they often do the translation on the basis of their pre-understandings.

Optimal Relevance Maxim−based Creative Treason in the Translation of *Dao De Jing*

The translation of *Dao De Jing*, the translators use the translation method of literal translation plus notes to solve the problem. On one hand, it remains the culture color, and on the other hand, it makes the readers know the new culture by using the notes which make them gain the largest context effect with the least effort. So this kind of creative treason translation can help the translation text reach the optimal relevance of *Dao De Jing*. And the manifestation of this creative treason in the translation of *Dao De Jing* is concluded as follows.

The Translation of Dao

Dao which is included in the name of book and as the most important key word in *Dao De Jing* is listed in the first one in the glossary of new words. Ames does not agree with the conventional translation of Dao as "the Way" or the transliteration by many translators. His translation strategy is to put the philosophical key word in the content and to add many explanations to make its original meaning clear to readers.

Ames explains the meaning of Dao from the construction of its Chinese character "道". "道" can be divided into two parts: The left part means "to pass over" or "to go over" and the right part means "head", both hair and eye, so it is the "foremost". The meaning of "head" gives the suggestion of "to lead", "to give a heading" or "to lead forth". The following examples will uncover the translation strategies of Ames.

Example 1: 道，可道也，非常道也。(Chapter 1)

Ames: Way-making (Dao) that can be put into words is not really way-making.

The three Daos in the first chapter have different meanings. The first and the third Dao are the philosophical words in Laotzu's thought, while, the second Dao does not mean the same as the first and third one, referring to "to speak or to express". The first and the third Dao are used a proper noun of Laotzu, and they are nouns and the second one is used as a verb, so when doing translation the translator need to identify them and make transformation properly. Ames translates the first and the third as gerund and defines them as way-making. It is an example to see that in Ames's translation, the noun form of Dao is translated into "way-making".

In Chapter 4, take "道盅，而用之又弗盈也" for instance. The translation version is "Way-making being empty, you make use of it but do not fill it up". The character 道 is used as noun, so it is translated as "way-making" to reveal that whatever is most enduring is overtaken in the ceaseless transformation. Another example is from Chapter 25, "人法地，地法天，天法道，道法自然". It is translated as "Human beings emulate the earth, the earth emulates the heavens, the heaven emulates way-making, and way-making emulates what is spontaneously so (Ziran)". Dao is also a noun in the sentence, so it is translated as "way-making". There are still many other examples to illustrate this point, but will be left to be discussed later.

Example 2: 以道佐人主者，不以兵强于天下，其好事还。(Chapter 30, Dao De Jing)

Ames: Those who use way-making (Dao) to minister to the ruler

Does not seek to make him the strongest in the world by force of arms.

With a small difference from the above examples, " 道 " is mostly translated as "way-making" but it adds the transliteration to make the meaning more obvious to the Western readers. The meaning of " 道 " can be expressed by only using "way-making", while the adding of "Dao" can help western readers have a view of the profound Chinese culture. Besides, that is also the translation characteristics of Ames who is used to adopt explanation plus transliteration to make the ancient Chinese more acceptable and active in modern English.

Example 3: 古之为道者，微妙玄达，深不可识。(Chapter 15, Dao De Jing)

Ames: Those of old who were good at forging their way (Dao) in the world;

Subtle and mysterious, dark and penetrating.

In this example, Dao is translated into "way" because of its special usage of " 为 道者 " which means the ones whose career is studying Dao. That is why Dao here is a noun but it is translated into "way" rather than "way-making". It is Ames's style to try to use new ways to translate philosophical terms in his translation activity.

The same condition can be seen from the example from Chapter 81, " 故天之道，利而不害 ; 圣人之道，为而不争 " is translated into "Thus, the way of Tian is to benefit without harming; the way of the sages is to do without contending". Dao here is interpreted as "way" though it is a noun, so as Ames says "All effective transactions are effective transactions", Dao here adopts its extensive meaning to connote a pathway that has been made and hence can be traveled as a "way". It is due to its connotation that Dao is somewhat problematically translated as "the way" or "way".

Considering all the above, the conclusion can be drawn that in Ames's version, Dao is translated into "way-making" and "way" according to its practical usage. Ames's explanation of Dao depends on his special understanding of Chinese philosophy, so it can be adopted in the following translation of *Dao De Jing*. That the domestication translation is the main form of creative treason in translation is not to say it refuses the foreignization translation. To some extent, translation is a fight between domestication translation and foreignization translation. It is a common phenomenon in translation that the target language culture annexes the source language culture and vice versa. And the latter also needs the creativity of the translators. So in the translation of *Dao De Jing* there are some manifestations of this kind translation.

The Translation of De

The central issue of the philosophical work *Dao De Jing* is about the classic of this de and its Dao. Dao and de seem to be in the same field, but de focuses on different aspects. De in *Dao De Jing* brings a political and a cosmic dimension to the effective potency. The cultivation of one's de is realized through one's full participation in the community where he can achieve an excellent role and relationship.

Example 1: 为天下溪，恒德不离，恒德不离复归于婴儿。(Chapter 28, *Dao De Jing*)

Ames: As a river gorge to the world,

You will not lose your real potency (De),

And not losing your own potency,

You return to the state of the new born babe.

It is better not to care about what you can get or lose at the moment because the water flows out in a trickle which takes a long time to exhaust. When people are perfecting themselves, it benefits to purify them at the same time. So the "de" here represents the potency to stay pure. Ames uses transliteration and adding to make it clear. Normal translators will put the transliteration before the explanation, while Ames does it differently, so we can see he translates de into "real potency (De)".

Example 2: 上德不德，是以有德，下德不失德，是以无德。(Chapter 38)

Ames: It is because the most excellent (De) do not strive to excel (De)

That they are of the highest efficacy (De).

And it is because the least excellent do not leave off striving to excel

That they have no efficacy.

There are six des in the sentence, Ames deals with the same term using different translations. They are "excellent (De)", "excel (De)", and "efficacy (De)". Ames concludes them into four des to brief the expression. He insists on using transliteration with explanation to make his translation not that alienated.

Example 3: 含德之厚者，比于赤子。(Chapter 55)

Ames: One who is vital in character (De)

Can be compared with a newborn baby

Like what have discussed above, the translation of de by Ames varies in terms of the condition and the content of the whole sentence. So there is not a definite translation according to the versions given by Ames. In this example, " 德 " is referred to someone who acquires the quality of de, so it is rendered as "character (De)" appropriately. The condition of the translation of Dao and de also goes to other philosophical terms in the context.

" 和 " in Ames's version is translated as "harmony (He)" in Chapter 55 and its verb form of " 和其光 " is translated into "soften the glare" respectively. Ames uses transliteration to deal with 天, because he believes that the normal translation of " 天 " into "heaven" may mislead the western readers to a large degree. Therefore, the translation of " 天 " is "Tian", 天命 as "Tianming" and " 天地 " as "Tiandi" with explanation attached before and after the chapters to give a bridge between the intercommunication of two different cultures.

Besides, the translation of " 自然 " is also using transliteration to translate it as "spontaneously (Ziran)" in Chapter 17, Chapter 25 and Chapter 51.

There are another two versions in Chapter 23 as "natural" as an adjective and "their own course (Ziran)" in Chapter 64. A series of phrases with 无 is listed together to identify them. Ames translates " 无名 " as "naming without fixed reference", " 无事 " as "to be non-interfering in going about your business", " 无为 " as "non-coercive action that is in accordance with the de of things", " 无心 " as "unmediated thinking and feeling", " 无欲 " as "objectless desire", " 无争 " as "striving without contentiousness" and " 无知 " as "unprincipled knowing". These are different terms with one same word — " 无 " in them, so when Ames is translating, he observed the similarities and differences to make his translation faithful to the original form as possible as he can.

In a word, Ames selects to use transliteration with explanation broadly to make sure that the western reader can not only seize the meaning of the text but also does not bring in their western philosophical thinking patterns when they are reading Chinese philosophical book and let try to understand Chinese philosophy by reading and accepting *Dao De Jing*. So he pays high attention to the translation of key terms. Ames's this kind of selection to pursue difference from the previous translation will make it possible for western readers to explore Chinese philosophy from a new perspective without the limitation of their western philosophical ways.

Ideology

Ideology is the main factor that constitutes the pre-understanding. The changing from a natural man to a social man needs the humanization of society and the methods that receiving the humanization is applied in education institution, teaching material, media, accessing system which has close relationship with national authority organization or constructed directly by nation. To some extent, receiving humanization is to accept the humanization of ideology. Ideology often influences man unconsciously. With *Dao De Jing* as his translation target, Ames needs to face much more difficulties than translators translate other modern Chinese works due to the ancient Chinese style and the vagueness and variety which are hard to understand nowadays. To make things worse, a lot of culture-loaded words have existed only in some ancient books that are hard to find. While to comprehend *Dao De Jing* better, Ames must seize the essence of ancient culture at that time and pay high attention to cross-cultural factors like ethnics, conventions, and aesthetic consciousness and the whole cultural system above the linguistic level, so translators must not only deal with the problem of transformation between Chinese and English, but also the dissemination of culture in the original text.

According to creative translation, a translator should make adaptation and selection in cultural dimension to be suitable to the environment. In other words, when the translator is doing translation, he is obliged to bear culture in his mind and has the realization that he needs to make efforts to overcome the cultural barriers to help the process of exchange go smoothly. The most important part of transformation in cultural dimension focuses on the differences of the source language and the target language. Many modern translation researchers such as Itamar Even-Zohar, TheoHermans, Gideon Toury and Andre Lefevere, give up the study model of the source text oriented but turn to the study of translation in the social and cultural background. Therefore, when translators are doing translation, they should take the whole culture system of language into consideration. Although translators have the right to adapt and select in the eco-environment on the basis of "translator-centeredness" theory, translators need also respect and take the source language's culture as well as the target language's culture into account due to the uniqueness of every language.

"Ziran" and Its English Translation

Dao De Jing focuses on the natural balance of all the things in the universe, so it is important to interpret "Ziran" in ancient Chinese philosophy well to help the understanding of other concepts and ideas of Daoism. That maybe is the main reason why Ames listed the translation of "Ziran" in the chapter of glossary of key terms to arouse readers' attention. The word "ran" means the natural state of things rather than their change but their original state. "Zi" is a reflexive pronoun which refers to oneself. In this way, "Ziran" can be translated into "be so of oneself", "nature" and so on. The word "Ziran" appears in the description of water and Dao.

> Example 1: 希言自然，飘风不终朝，骤雨不终日 (Chapter 23, *Dao De Jing*).
>
> Ames: It is natural to speak only rarely,
>
> Violent winds do not last a whole morning.
>
> And torrential rains do not last a whole day.

It is the only place where Ames translates "Ziran" into "natural", which is accepted by translators in the field. "Ziran" here refers to the nature people see and it continues to recover the rules of the nature to lead readers to relate them to human beings. If people want to long live on the earth, they need to observe the rules of nature and bear them in mind when they are carrying out their plans.

> Example 2: 成功遂事，而百姓皆谓我自然 (Chapter 17, *Dao De Jing*).
>
> Ames: With all things accomplished and the work complete
>
> The common people say, "We are spontaneously like this."

In example 2, "Ziran" is translated as "spontaneously like this" because "Ziran"here does not represent the nature but reveals the condition of things happening. This meaning is commonly used in *Dao De Jing*, so readers will run into many of these "Ziran".

> Example 3: 人法地，地法天，天法道，道法自然。(Chapter 52, *Dao De Jing*)
>
> Ames: Human beings emulate the earth,
>
> The earth emulates the heavens,
>
> The heavens emulate way-making,
>
> And way-making emulates what is spontaneously so (Ziran).

In these two stations, "Ziran" is equaled to "spontaneously like this" or "spontaneously and so (Ziran)" that only have some small differences between them. Well there exists the third way of dealing with "Ziran".

> Example 4: 能辅万物之自然而弗敢为。(Chapter 64, *Dao De Jing*)
>
> Ames: Although they are quite capable of helping all things (Wanwu) follow their

own course (Ziran),

They would not think of doing so.

In this chapter, Ames makes some adjustment not to be the same as the previous translation and let the meaning here be unique. It means to express the main idea that people should not interrupt the development of "Wanwu" in the world. What they should do is to let it go and let it develop in its most natural way.

"Wanwu" and Its English Translation

"Wanwu" is a key term listed in the glossary of the source text and the target text can be seen from it. In the past translators often translate "Wanwu" into "creatures", "things", "ten thousand things" or "the myriad living things" based on their own understanding of the concept. There is no standard translation of "Wanwu". If it is translated into "creature" and "things", the range of "Wanwu" will be restricted to the scope of things with life and things without life, which cannot be equal to the real meaning of "Wanwu" in ancient China because the meaning of "Wanwu" refers to things with and without life in the natural world. So there is a fundamental difference of the meaning of "Wanwu" in China and in the English world. The same measurement goes to "the ten thousand things" and "the myriad living things", because they are just like the two versions before translating the concept from the different scope.

Example 1: 万物作而弗始也，焉而弗恃也，成功而弗居也。(Chapter 2, *Dao De Jing*).

Ames: In all that happens (Wanwu),

The sages develop things but do not initiate them.

They act on behalf of things but do not lay any claim to them,

They see things through to fruition but do not take credit for them.

In example 1, the translation of "Wanwu" presents the characteristics of Ames's translation. He used to use explanation plus transliteration to translate these cultural concepts to retain the style of archaic Chinese and combine the expression way of English. "Wanwu" includes everything in the universe and human beings are just a part of it. So "万物" in Chapter 2 refers to everything that happens in the world and they cannot be changed to accord with human beings' mind. Amen translates "Wanwu" according to the real eco-environment rather than translating it in the same way. It can be seen that Ames has made the right choice to translate

"Wanwu" as "all that happens", and the most valuable is that he adds the transliteration version to the end to help the western readers have a way to see the original Chinese style.

Example 2: 道生一, 一生二, 二生三, 三生万物。万物负阴而抱阳冲气以为和。(Chapter 42, *Dao De Jing*)

Ames: Way-making (Dao) gives rise to continuity,

Continuity gives rise to difference,

Difference gives rise to plurality,

And plurality gives rise to the manifold of everything that is happening (Wanwu).

Everything carries *yin* on its shoulders and *yang* in its arms

And blends these vital energies (Qi) together to make them harmonious (He).

There are two "Wanwu" in the same chapter and they represent different things, so Ames deals with them differently. The first "Wanwu" stresses the change from less to more and from simple to plural, so it is translated into "the manifold of everything that is happening (Wanwu)"to make it out from "way-making", "continuity" and "difference".

The second "Wanwu" is translated as "everything", which is the most universal way to deal with it. By comparing the two translation ways, it is obvious that Ames has made wise choice to make the transformation on the culture level more natural.

Example 3: 道者, 万物之注也。(Chapter 62, *Dao De Jing*)

Ames: Way-making (Dao) is the flowing together of all things (Wanwu).

In example 3," 万物 "is rendered as "all things (Wanwu)", which is another way of translation. The most obvious characteristic of Ames's translation is that the versions of many philosophical terms are not settled by varying from sentence to sentence. The translation version of " 万 物 " in example 3 is the most common version in the whole book. Therefore, this way of translating "Wanwu" can also be seen in many other chapters like chapter 8, Chapter 32, Chapter 34, Chapter37, Chapter 51 and Chapter 65. In these chapters, "Wanwu" are treated as "everything (Wanwu)" that is the most common meaning of "Wanwu" as "Wanwu" in these chapters refers to the same thing. " 水善利万物而有静 " in Chapter 8 and " 道者万物之注也 " are translated into everything (Wanwu) and all things (Wanwu) which can be regarded as the same meaning and the same way to make transformation in the cultural dimension.

In the translation of *Dao De Jing*, there are some concepts which can not find out the special term to express it but the special meaning of the concepts can vividly convey the meaning of the concepts, so in the translation of *Dao De Jing* some translators choose capitalizing initial words to solve such translation problem. On one hand, these capitalizing initial words can remind readers they are concepts put forward by Laotzu, on the other hand, the meaning of these concepts are presented by themselves and the target readers do not need to make much efforts to comprehend it and gain the context effect easily.

Creative treason has great effect on the translation. On one hand, translators have to make good use of their creativity to convey the information of the source text; on the other hand, it also changes the direction of the translation criticism, upgrading the value of translation, and promoting the status of the translator. Deconstructionism translation upgrades the state of translators in two aspects.

Firstly, deconstructionism denies the authority of the source text, and the text is in the state of difference, which ignores the determinacy of the meaning of the source text. So the requirement of faithfulness to the source text becomes meaningless. Secondly, deconstructionism holds that it is the translation that endows the source text second life, so deconstructionists ask in retort, "What if one suggested that, without translation, the source text ceased to exist, that the very survival of the source text depends not on any particular quality it contains, but upon those qualities that its translation contains". The understanding of the saying becomes easier due to that the deconstructionism theory views the translation text as the rebirth or afterlife of the source text. In this way, translators gain their right in the translation process and they have the same status as the author. It is the translation that makes the source text survival, so to some extent, the author should thank the translators. Hence, the status of translators has been promoted to a boastful high level.

REFERENCES

[1]A J CASCARDI. Skepticism and Deconstruction[J]. Philosophy and Literature.1984: 1-14.

[2]ALLAN M. Prophets of Extremity: Nietzsche, Heidegger, Foucault, Derrida[M]. Berkeley: University of California Press, 1985.

[3] AMES R, YOUNG W. Lao Tzu: Text, Notes, and Comments[M]. Taibei: Chengwen Publisher,1981.

[4]ANN J. "Structuralism and Post Structuralism." Modern Literary Theory: A Comparative Introduction[M].

Totowa: Barnes, 1982, 84-112.

[5]ATKINS G D. Reading Deconstruction: Deconstructive Reading[M]. Lexington: University Press of Kentucky, 1983.

[6]BARBARA J. The Critical Difference: Essays in the Contemporary Rhetoric of Reading[M]. Baltimore: Johns Hopkins University Press, 1980.

[7]CHRISTOPHER N. Deconstruction: Theory and Practice[M]. New York: Meuthen, 1982..

[8]CHRISTOPHER N. The Deconstructive Turn: Essays in the Rhetoric of Philosophy[M]. New York: Methuen, 1983.

[9]CHRISTOPHER N. Deconstruction and the Interests of Theory. Oklahoma Project for Discourse and Theory 4[M]. Norman: University of Oklahoma Press, 1989.

[10]DANNY J A. "Deconstruction: Critical Strategy/Strategic Criticism" in Contemporary Literary Theory[M]. Eds. G D ATKINS, LAURA M. Amherst: University of Massachusetts Press, 1989, 137-57.

[11]EDWARD W S. The World, the Text, and the Critic[J]. Cambridge: Harvard University Press, 1983.

[12]FERDINAND DE SAUSSURE. Course in General Linguistics[M]. Eds. CHARLES B, ALBERT R. Trans. WADE B. New York: Philosophical Library, 1959.

[13]FERDINAND DE SAUSSURE. Course in General Linguistics[M]. New York: McGraw-Hill, 1966.

[14]GEOFFREY H. Criticism in the Wilderness: The Study of Literature Today[M]. New Haven: Yale University Press, 1980.

[15]GEOFFREY H. Saving the Text: Literature/Derrida/Philosophy[M]. Baltimore: Johns Hopkins University Press, 1981.

[16]GEOFFREY H, et al. Deconstruction and Criticism[M]. New York: Continuum, 1979.

[17]GERALD L B. Structuralism, Enconstruction, and Hermeneutics[J]. Diacritics.1984:12-23.

[18]HAROLD B. A Map of Misreading[M]. New York: Oxford University Press, 1975.

[19]HAROLD B, et al., eds. Deconstruction and Criticism[M]. New York: Seabury Press, 1979.

[20]HAYDEN W. Tropics of Discourse[M]. Baltimore: Johns Hopkins University Press, 1978.

[21]JACQUES D. Of Grammatology[M]. Trans. GAYATRI S. Baltimore: Johns Hopkins University Press, 1974.

[22]JACQUES D. "Structure, Sign, and Play in the Discourse of the Human Sciences" in The Structuralist Controversy: The Languages of Criticism and the Sciences of Man[M]. Eds. RICHARD M, EUGENIO D. Baltimore: Johns Hopkins University Press, 1970, 247-65.

[23]JACQUES D. Speech and Phenomena, and Other Essays on Husserl's Theory of Signs[M]. Trans. DAVID B. A. Evanston: Northwestern University Press, 1978.

[24]JACQUES D. Writing and Difference[M]. Trans. ALAN B. Chicago: University of Chicago Press, 1978.

[25]JACQUES D. "Living On: Border Lines" in Deconstruction and Criticism[M]. New York: Seabury, 1979, 75-175.

[26]JACQUES D. Acts of Literature[M]. 2nd ed. Minneapolis: University of Minnesota Press, 1983.

[27]JACQUES D. A Derrida Reader: Between the Blinds[M]. Ed. PEGGY K. New York: Columbia University Press, 1991.

[28]JACQUES D. Dissemination[M]. Ed. DEREK A. New York: Routledge, 1992.

[29]MILLER J H. Introduction to Charles Dickens's Bleak House[M]. Ed. NORMAN P. Harmonds worth: Penguin, 1971, 11-13.

[30]MILLER J H. Tradition and Differance[J]. Diacritics.1972: 6-13.

[31]MILLER J H. Narrative and History[J]. EHL.1974: 455-73.

[32]MILLER J H. Tropes, Parables and Performatives: Essays in the Contemporary Rhetoric of Reading[M]. Baltimore: Johns Hopkins University Press, 1980.

[33]J H MILLER. Fiction and Repetition: Seven English Novels[M]. Cambridge: Harvard University Press, 1982.

[34]JOHN D C. The Good News About Alterity: Derrida and Theology[J]. Faith and Philosophy 10.4 (1993.10): 453-70.

[35]JOHN M E. Against Deconstruction[M]. Princeton: Princeton University Press, 1989.

[36]JONATHAN A, WLAD G, WALLACE M, eds. "The Yale Critics: Deconstruction in America" in Theory and History of Literature, vol. 6[M]. Minneapolis: University of Minnesota Press, 1983.

[37]JONATHAN C. Structuralist Poetics: Structuralism, Linguistics and the Study of Literature[M]. Ithaca: Cornell University Press, 1975.

[38]JONATHAN C. The Pursuit of Signs: Semiotics, Literature, Deconstruction[M]. Ithaca: Cornell University Press, 1981.

[39]JONATHAN C. On Deconstruction: Theory and Criticism after Structuralism[M]. Ithaca: Cornell University Press, 1982.

[40]MARK C T, ed. Deconstruction in Context: Literature and Philosophy[M]. Chicago: University of Chicago Press, 1986.

[41]ABRAMS M H. The Deconstructive Angel[J]. Critical Inquiry.1977: 425-438.

[42]MICHAEL F. Does Deconstruction Make Any Difference? [M]. Bloomington: Indiana University Press, 1987.

[43]MICHEL F. The Foucault Reader[M]. Ed. PAUL R. New York: Pantheon, 1984.

[44]MICHAEL R. Marxism and Deconstruction[J]. Baltimore: Johns Hopkins University Press, 1982.

[45]PAUL DE MAN. Blindness and Insight: Essays in the Rhetoric of Contemporary Criticism[M]. New York: Oxford University Press, 1971.

[46]PAUL DE MAN. Allegories of Reading[M]. New Haven: Yale University Press, 1979.

[47]PAUL DE MAN. The Rhetoric of Romanticism[M]. New York: Columbia University Press, 1984.

[48]RAJNATH, ed al. Deconstruction: A Critique[M]. New York: Macmillan, 1989.

[49]RALPH F. The Rhetoric of Doubtful Authority: Deconstructive Readings of Self-Questioning Narratives, St. Augustine to Faulkner[M]. Ithaca: Cornell University Press, 1994.

[50]RICHARD R. Consequences of Pragmatism[M]. Minneapolis: University of Minnesota Press, 1982.

[51]RICHARD R. Deconstruction and Circumvention[J]. Critical Inquiry.1984: 1-23.

[52]ROBERT C D, RONALD S, eds. Rhetoric and Form: Deconstruction at Yale[M]. Norman: University of Oklahoma Press, 1985.

[53]ROBERT S. Deconstruction and Criticism[J]. Critical Inquiry.1988: 278-295.

[54]ROBERT Y, ed. Untying the Text: A Post-Structuralist Render[M]. London: Routledge & Kegan Paul, 1981.

[55]RODOLPHE G. Deconstruction as Criticism[J]. Glyph Textual Studies.1979: 177-215.

[56]RODOLPHE G. The Taint of the Mirror[M]. Cambridge: Harvard University Press, 1986.

[57]ROLAND B. S/Z[M]. Trans. RICHARD M. New York: Hill, 1974.

[58]ROLAND B. The Pleasure of the Text[M]. Trans. RICHARD M. New York: Noonday, 1976.

[59]ROLAND B. "The Death of the Author" in Image-Music-Text[M]. Trans. S. HEATH. New York: Hill & Wang, 1977.

[60]SHARON C. A Teacher's Introduction to Deconstruction[M]. Urbana: National Council of Teachers of English, 1989.

[61]SPIVAK G. Reading the World: Literary Studies in the 1980s[J]. College English.1981: 671-679.

[62]TZVETAN T. The Fantastic: A Structural Approach to a Literary Genre[M]. RICHARD, Trans, H. Ithaca: Cornell University Press, 1975.

[63]VINCENT B L. The Laterial Dance: The Deconstructive Criticism of J. Hillis Miller[J]. Critical Inquiry.

1980: 593-607.

[64]VINCENT B L. Deconstructive Criticism: An Advanced Introduction[M]. New York: Columbia University Press 1983.

[65]WILLIAM E C. Deconstruction in America: The Recent Literary Criticism of J. Hillis Miller[J]. College English.1979: 367-382.

CHAPTER VII   PSYCHOANALYTIC CRITICISM

So, if I dream I have you, I have you,

For, all our joys are but fantastical.

And so I scape the pain, for pain is true;

And sleep which locks up sense, doth lock out all.

After such fruition I shall wake,

And, but the waking, nothing shall repent;

And shall to love more thankful sonnets make,

Than if more honour, tears, and pains were spent.

But dearest heart, and dearer image, stay;

Alas, true joys at best are dream enough;

JOHN DONNE, "The Dream", 1635

7.1   INTRODUCTION

Our dreams fascinate, perplex, and often disturb us. Filled with bizarre twists of fate, wild exploits, and highly sexual images, our dreams can bring us pleasure or terrorize us. Sometimes they cause us to question out true feelings, to contemplate our unspoken desires, and even to doubt the nature of reality itself. Do dreams, we wonder, contain any degree of truth, and do they serve any useful function?

Chemist Friedrich August Kekule answers in the affirmative. For years, Kekule was investigating the molecular structure of benzene. One night he saw in a dream a string of atoms shaped like a snake swallowing its tail. Upon awakening. he drew this serpentine figure in his notebook and realized it was the graphic structure of the benzene ring he had been struggling to decipher. When reporting his findings at a scientific meeting in 1890, he stated, to learn to dream, and then it can help us find the truth.

Giuseppe Tartini, an Italian violinist of the eighteenth century, similarly discovered the value of dreams. One night he dreamed the devil came to his bedside and offered to help him finish a rather difficult sonata in exchange for his soul. Tartini agreed, whereupon the devil picked up Tartini's violin and completed the unfinished work. Upon awakening, Tartini jotted down from memory what he had just heard. Known as *The Devil's Trill Sonata*, this piece is Tartini's best known composition.

Like numerous scientists and composers, many writers have claimed that they too have received some of their best ideas from their dreams. Robert Louis Stevenson, for example, maintained that many of his ideas for *Dr. Jekyll and Mr. Hyde* came directly from his nightmares. Similarly, Dante, Goethe, Blake, Bunyan, and a host of others owed much of their writings, they claimed, to their world of dreams. And others, such as Poe, DeQuincey, and Coleridge borrowed from their drug-induced dreams the content of some of their most famous works.

That our dreams and those of others fascinate us cannot be denied. Whether it is their bizarre and often erotic content or even their seemingly prophetic powers, dreams cause us to question and explore the part of our minds over which we have seemingly little control: The unconscious.

Without question, the foremost investigator of the unconscious and its activities is Vienna neurologist and psychologist Sigmund Freud. Beginning with the publication of *The Interpretation of Dreams* in 1900, Freud lays the foundation for a new model of how our minds operate. Hidden from the workings of the conscious mind. the unconscious, he believes, plays a large part in how we act, think, and feel. According to Freud, the best avenue for discovering the content and the activity of the unconscious is through our dreams. It is through the interaction of both the conscious and unconscious working together, argues Freud, that we shape ourselves and our world.

Developing both a body of theory and a practical methodology for his science of the mind, Freud became the founding father of psychoanalysis, a method of treating emotional and psychological disorders. During psychoanalysis, Freud had his parents talk freely in a patient-analyst setting about their early childhood experiences and dreams. When we apply these same methods to our interpretations of works of literature, we engage in psychoanalytic criticism.

Unlike some other schools of criticism, psychoanalytic criticism can exist side by side with any other critical method of interpretation. Because this approach attempts to explain the hows and whys of human actions without developing an aesthetic theory — a systematic, philosophical body of beliefs concerning how meaning occurs in literature — Marxists, feminists, and New historicists, for example, can use psychoanalytic methods in their interpretations without violating their own hermeneutics. Psychoanalytic criticism, then, may best be called an approach to literary interpretation rather than a particular school of criticism.

Although Freud is unquestionably the father of this approach to literary analysis, psychoanalytic criticism has continued to develop in theory and practice throughout the twentieth century. Carl Jung, Freud's rebellious student, borrowed some of Freud's ideas while rejecting many others. Jung branched out into new theories and concerns and established analytical psychology. Using some of Jung's ideas, Northrop Frye, an English professor and literary theorist, developed symbolic or archetypal criticism in the mid-1950s that changed the direction of twentieth-century literary analysis. In the 1960s, French neo-Freudian psychoanalyst Jacques Lacan revised and expanded Freud's theories in light of new linguistic and literary principles, and thereby revitalized psychoanalytic criticism and ensured its continued influence on literary criticism today. And many present-day feminist critics turn to psychoanalytic criticism, using the ideas of Lacan as the basis of their critical methodology.

7.2   HISTORICAL DEVELOPMENT

The theories and practice of Sigmund Freud provide the foundation for psychoanalytic criticism. While working with patients whom he diagnosed as hysterics, Freud theorized that the root of their problems was psychological, not physical. His patients, he believed, had suppressed incestuous desires with which they had unconsciously refused to deal. Suffering from his own neurotic crisis in 1887, Freud underwent self-analysis. Results from this self-analysis coupled with his research and analyses of his patients led Freud to posit that fantasies and wishful thinking, not actual experiences, play a large part in the onset of neuroses.

7.2.1   Models of the Human Psyche: Dynamic Model

Throughout his lifetime Freud developed various models of the human psyche that became the changing bases of his psychoanalytic theory and practice. Early in his career, he posited the dynamic model, asserting that our minds are a dichotomy consisting of the conscious (the rational) and the unconscious (the irrational). The conscious, Freud argued, perceives and records external reality and is the reasoning part of the mind. Unaware of the presence of the unconscious, we operate consciously, believing that our reasoning and analytical skills are solely responsible for our behavior. But Freud is the first to suggest that it is the unconscious, not the conscious, that governs a large part of our actions.

This irrational part of our psyche, the unconscious receives and stores our hidden desires, ambitions, fears, passions, and irrational thoughts. Freud did not coin this term; this honor goes to C. G. Carus. Carus and many of Freud's other contemporaries viewed the unconscious as a static system that simply collects and maintains our memories. Freud dramatically redefined the unconscious, believing if to be a dynamic system that not only contains our biographical memories but also stores our suppressed and unresolved conflicts. For Freud, the unconscious is the storehouse of disguised truths and desires that want to be revealed in and through the conscious. These disguised truths and desires inevitably make themselves known through our dreams, art, literature, play, and accidental slips of the tongue known as **Freudian slips**.

Economic Model

Freud's second model of the human psyche enlarges on but retains most of his ideas housed in the dynamic model. In both models, the conscious and the unconscious battle for control of a person's actions. And the both models a person's unconscious desires force their way to the conscious state. But in the **economic model**, Freud introduces two new concepts that describe and help govern the human psyche, the pleasure principle and the reality principle. According to Freud, the pleasure principle craves only pleasures, and it desires instantaneous satisfaction of instinctual drives, ignoring moral and sexual boundaries established by society. Immediate relief from all pain or suffering is its goal. The pleasure principle is held in check, however, by the **reality principle**, that part of the psyche that recognizes the need for societal standards and regulations on pleasure. Freud believed that both these principles are at war within the human psyche.

Topographic Models

Throughout his career Freud developed yet another model of the human psyche, the **topographic model**. In an earlier version of this model, Freud separated the human psyche into three parts: The conscious, the preconscious, and the unconscious. The conscious is the mind's direct link to external reality, for it perceives and reacts with the external environment, allowing the mind to order its outside world. The preconscious is the storehouse of memories that the conscious part of the mind allows to be brought to consciousness without distinguishing these memories in some form or another. As in his previously devised models, Freud contends that the third part of the psyche, the unconscious, holds the repressed hungers, images, thoughts, and desires of human nature. Because these desires are not housed in the preconscious, they cannot be directly summoned into the conscious state. These repressed impulses must therefore travel in distinguished forms to the conscious part of the psyche and surface in their respective disguises in our dreams, our art, and in other unsuspecting ways in our lives.

But the most famous model of the human psyche is Freud's later version of the topographic model, the **tripartite model**. This model divides the psyche into three parts: The id, the ego, and the superego. The irrational, instinctual, unknown, and unconscious part of the psyche Freud calls the id. Containing our secret desires, our darkest wishes, and our most intense fears, the id wishes only to fulfill the urges of the pleasure principle. In addition, it houses the libido, the source of all our psychosexual desires and all our psychic energy. Unchecked by any controlling will, the id operates on impulse, wanting immediate satisfaction for all its instinctual desires.

The second part of the psyche Freud calls the ego, the rational, logical waking part of the mind, although much of its activities remain in the unconscious. Whereas the id operates according to the pleasure principle, the ego operates in harmony with the reality principle. It is the ego's job to regulate the instinctual desires of the id and to allow these desires to be released in some nondestructive way.

The third part of the psyche, the superego, acts as an internal censor, causing us to make moral judgments in light of social pressures. In contrast to the id, the superego operates according to the morality principle and serves primarily to protect society and us from the id. Representing all of society's moral restrictions, the superego serves as a filtering agent, suppressing the desires and instincts forbidden by society and thrusting them back into the unconscious. Overall, the superego manifests itself through punishment. If allowed to operate at its own discretion, the superego will create an unconscious sense of guilt and fear.

It is left to the ego to mediate between the instinctual (especially sexual) desires of the id and the demands of social pressure issued by the superego. What the ego deems unacceptable it suppresses and deposits in the unconscious. And what it has most often repressed in all of us is our sexual desires of early childhood.

7.2.2 Freud's Pre-Oedipal Developmental Phases

In addition to his various models or the human psyche, Freud developed several stages of human development that are important to the healthy development of one's psyche. According to Freud, in our early childhood all of us go through three over-lapping phases: The oral, and phallic stages. As infants, we experience the **oral phase**: As we suck our mother's breast in order to be fed, our sexuality (or libido) is activated. Our mouths then become an erotogenic zone that will later cause us to enjoy sucking our thumbs and, still later, kissing. In the second or **anal stage**, the anus becomes the object of pleasure when children learn the delights of defecation while simultaneously learning that they are independent persons who are separate from their mothers. During this stage the anus becomes an erotogenic zone, for children become sadistic, expelling and destroying through defecation as a means of expressing both their anger and their excitement upon discovering their independence from their mothers. By withholding feces. children also learn that they can control others. In the final phase, the **phallic stage**, a child's sexual desire or libido is directed toward the genitals when the child learns the pleasure that results from stimulating one's sexual organs.

At this point in a child's development, Freud asserts that the pleasure principle basically controls the child. Being self-centered, sadistic, and assertive, the child cares for nothing but his or her own pleasure. If a child, however, is to grow up as a normal adult, he or she must develop a sense of sexuality, a sense of his maleness or her femaleness. Freud maintains that this awareness can be achieved by a successful handling of either the Oedipus or the Electra complex.

The Oedipus, Castration, and Electra Complexes

The formulation of the Oedipus complex is one of Freud's most significant contributions not only to psychoanalytic criticism but also to all literary criticism in general. Freud borrows the name from the play *Oedipus Rex*, written by Greek playwright Sophocles. In this play, Oedipus, the protagonist, is prophesied to kill his father and marry his mother. His attempts to abort the prophecy fail, and the once-foretold events occur as predicted. According to Freud, the essence of Oedipus' story becomes universal human experience.

Using Sophocles' plot as the basis for his Oedipus complex, Freud asserts that during the late infantile stage (somewhere between ages 3 and 6) all infant males possess an erotic attachment to their mother. Unconsciously, the infant desires to engage in sexual union with his mother. He recognizes, however, a rival for his mother's affection: the father. Already in the phallic stage and therefore sexually aware of his own erogenous organs, the child perceives the father's attention given to the mother as sexual.

If a child's sexual development is to proceed normally, Freud maintains, each must then pass through the castration complex. From observing themselves, their mothers, and perhaps their sisters, little boys know they have a penis like their fathers whereas their mothers and sisters do not. What prevents the male child from continuing to have incestuous desires for his mother is fear of castration by his father. The child therefore represses his sexual desire, identifies with his father, and hopes someday to possess a woman as his father now possesses his mother. Unconsciously, the boy has thus successfully made the transition to manhood.

Whereas a boy must successfully negotiate the Oedipus complex in order to become a normal man, a girl must successfully negotiate the **Electra complex** if she is to make the transition from a girl to a normal woman. Like a boy, a young girl is also erotically attracted to her mother, and like the boy, she too recognizes a rival for her mother's affection: The father. Unconsciously, however, the girl realizes that she is already castrated, as is her mother. Because she knows her father possesses that which she desires, a penis, she turns her desires to him and away from her mother. After the seduction of her father fails, she turns back toward the mother and identifies with her. Her transition into womanhood being complete, the girl realizes that one day she, like her mother, will possess a man. Through her relationships with a man, her unfulfilled desire for a penis (penis envy) will be mitigated, and her sense of lacking will be somewhat appeased.

The process of becoming a man or a woman, Freud maintained, may be long and difficult, but necessary For within this process, the child passes from basing his or her life on the pleasure principle, in which all decisions are based on the immediate gratification of pleasure, to the reality principle in which societal needs and the operation of the superego occur. During this stage, Freud believed that a child's moral development and conscience appear for the first time.

The Significance of Dreams

Even though the passage into manhood, womanhood may be successful, according to Freud the child has stored many painful memories of repressed sexual desires, anger, rage, and guilt in his or her unconscious. Because the conscious and the unconscious are part of the same psyche, the unconscious with its hidden desires and repressed wishes continues to affect the conscious in the form of inferiority feelings, guilt, traditional thoughts and feelings, and dreams and nightmares.

In his magnum opus, *The interpretation of Dreams* (1900), Freud asserts that the unconscious expresses its suppressed wishes and desires. Even though the conscious mind has repressed these desires and has forced them into the unconscious, such wishes may be hard for the conscious psyche to handle without producing feelings of self-hatred or rage. The unconscious then redirects and reshapes these concealed wishes into acceptable social activities , presenting them in the form of images or symbols in our dreams or writings. By so doing, the psyche creates a window to the id by allowing the softened and socially acceptable desires to seep into the conscious state.

The psyche may create this window to the id in a variety of ways. Through the process of displacement, for example, the unconscious may switch a person's hatred for someone named Mr. Apple by onto a rotting apple in a dream. Or through condensation, the psyche may consolidate one's anger to a variety of people and objects into a simple sentence. Whatever the case, through symbols and images, but not directly, the unconscious continually asserts its influence over our motivations and behavior.

When certain repressed feelings or ideas cannot be released adequately through dreams, jokes, or other methods, the ego must act and block any outward response. In so doing, the ego and id become involved in an internal battle that Freud called neurosis. From a fear of heights to a pounding headache, neurosis can create many physical and psychological abnormalities. According to Freud, it is the job of the psychoanalyst to identify the unresolved conflicts that give rise to a patient's neurosis. Through psycho-analytic therapy and dream analysis, the psychotherapist attempts to return the patient to a state of well-being or normalcy.

7.3 LITERATURE AND PSYCHOANLAYSIS

For Freud, the unresolved conflicts that give rise to any neurosis are the stuff of literature. A work of literature, he believes, is the external expression of the author's unconscious mind. Accordingly, the literary work must be treated like a dream, applying psychoanalytic techniques to the text to uncover the author's hidden motivations and repressed desires.

Carl G Jung

Freud's most famous pupil is Carl Gustav Jung (1875~1961), a Swiss physician, psychiatrist, philosopher, and psychologist. Selecting Jung as his favorite "son," Freud appointed him his successor. Toward the end of their 7-year teacher-disciple relationship (1912), however, Jung prophetically wrote to Freud, quoting from Nietzsche's *Thus Spake Zarathustra*, "One repays a teacher badly if one remains only a pupil." A year later, the pupil broke away from his master and eventually became one of the leading forces in the psychoanalytic movement.

Jung's dissatisfaction with some elements of Freudian psychoanalysis arose from theoretical differences with Freud concerning the interpretation of dreams and each psychologist's models of the human psyche. According to Freud, all human behavior, including dreams, is fundamentally sexual, being driven by one's sexual energy or libido. Interpreting dreams almost exclusively in sexual terms, Freud linked most dreams to the Oedipus or Electra complexes. Jung disagreed with Freud's basic premise that all human behavior is sexually driven. More than sexual imagery, Jung argued, appears in dreams. In 1912 Jung published his seminal work *Symbols of Transformation*, which ultimately led to his separation from Freud. In this work, Jung asserts that dreams include mythological images as well as sexual ones. Jung's new ideas caused him to be banished from the psychoanalytic community for the next 5 years. During this time, however, he formulated his own model of the human psyche that would eventually become his most important contribution to psychology and literary criticism.

In forming his model of the human psyche, Jung accepts Freud's assumption that the unconscious exists and that it plays a major role in our conscious decisions. But he rejects Freud's analysis of the contents of the unconscious. According to Jung, the human psyche consists of three parts: The personal conscious, the personal unconscious, and the collective unconscious. The **personal conscious**, or waking state, is the image or thought of which we are aware at any given moment. Like a slide show, every moment of our lives provides us with a new slide. As we view one slide, the previous slide vanishes from our personal consciousness, for nothing can remain in the personal conscious. Although these vanished slides are forgotten by the **personal consciousness**, they are stored and remembered by the personal unconscious. Jung asserts that all conscious thoughts begin in the personal unconscious. Because each person's moment-by-moment slide show is different, everyone's personal unconscious is unique.

But in the depths of the psyche and blocked off from human consciousness lies Jung's third part of his model of the human psyche: The **collective unconscious**. This part of the psyche houses the cumulative knowledge, experiences, and images of the entire human race. According to Jung, People from all over the world respond to certain myths or stories in the same way not because everyone knows and appreciates the same story, but because lying deep in our collective unconscious are the racial memories of humanity's past. These memories exist in the form of archetypes: patterns or images of repeated human experiences such as birth, death, rebirth, the four seasons, and motherhood, to name a few, that express themselves in our stories, dreams, religions, and fantasies. Archetypes are not ready-made ideas, but predispositions, causing us to respond to stimuli in a certain way: Furthermore, they are inherited genetically (a psychic, not a biological, inheritance), making up an identical collective unconsciousness for all humankind. For Jung, these archetypes give form to typical experiences of our ancestors and are the psychic remains of innumerable experiences of the same type, of sentiments that have been repeated countless times in our ancestral history. Occurring in literature in the form of recurrent plot patterns, images, or character types, these archetypes stir profound emotions in the reader because they awaken images stored in the collective unconscious and thereby produce feelings or emotions over which the reader initially has little control.

Jung was the first to suggest that such archetypes directly affect the way we respond to external elements. For example, when we see or read about an infant in diapers surrounded by a litter of puppies licking the child's face, feelings of contentment, warmth, and love seemingly pop up in most of us. These somewhat uncontrollable emotions, Jung would claim, are the results of the stirring of an archetype.

Many anthropologists would argue that archetypes are inherited cultural responses that are passed down from one generation to another in a particular social group. Eventually, such social phenomena become myths or stories that help give meaning and significance to people's lives. Jung would strongly disagree, asserting that myths are symbolic expressions of the inner world, in which unconscious activities of the psyche are displayed. For Jung myths are the means by which archetypes evidence themselves not only in our dreams but also in the personal conscious.

Throughout the 1920s and until his death in 1961, Jung continued developing his methods of **analytical psychology**. When we apply his theories and methods to literature, we engage in **archetypal criticism**. Unquestionably, the foremost archetypal critic of the twentieth century is Northrop Frye.

Northrop Frye

With the publication of his work *Anatomy of Criticism* in 1957. Frye became the primary advocate of the principles of archetypal criticism in literary theory. Although he never declares allegiance to Jung's concept of the collective unconscious, Frye borrows Jung's ideas concerning myths and archetypes and develops a systematic approach to archetypal or **mythic criticism**. Divorcing a text from its social history. Frye maintains that there exists an overall structure or mythic development that can explain the structure and significance of all texts.

Frye believes that all of literature makes up one complete and whole story called the **monomyth**. This monomyth can best be diagrammed as a circle containing four separate phases, with each phase corresponding to a season of the year and to peculiar cycles of human experiences. The Romance phase, which is located at the top of the circle, is our summer story.In this kind of story, all our wishes are fulfilled, and we can achieve total happiness. At the bottom of the circle is winter, or the Anti-romance phase. The opposite of summer, this phase tells the story of bondage, imprisonment, frustration, and fear. Midway between Romance and Anti-romance and to the right of the middle of the circle is spring, or Comedy. This phase relates the story of our rise from Anti-romance and frustration to freedom and happiness. Correspondingly, across the circle is Tragedy, or fall, narrating our fall from the Romance phase and from happiness and freedom to disaster. According to Frye, all stories can be placed somewhere on this diagram.

What Frye provides for us is a schema of all possible kinds of stories. Such a structural framework furnishes the context whereby we can identify stories according to their particular genre, kinds of symbolization, themes, points of view, and other literary elements. In addition, Frye's schematic supplies the background and context for his form of literary criticism and allows us to compare stories on the basis of their relationship among themselves.

With the advent of archetypal criticism and Frye's schematics in the 1950s, few critics used Freudian analysis in their practical criticism. But in the 1960s, French psychoanalyst, neo-Freudian, and poststructuralist critic Jacques Lacan helped revive Freudian criticism and rescued it from its overwhelmingly phallocentric or a male-dominated position

Jacques Lacan

Like Freud, Lacan believes that the unconscious greatly affects our conscious behavior. But unlike Freud, who pictures the unconscious as a chaotic, unstructured, bubbling cauldron of dark passions, hidden desires, and suppressed wishes, Lacan asserts that the unconscious is structured, much like the structure of language. And like language, this highly structured part of the human psyche can be systematically analyzed. What we will learn from such an analysis, claims Lacan, is that all individuals are fragmented: No one is whole. The ideal concept of a wholly unified and psychologically complete individual is just that: An abstraction that is simply not attainable.

Like Freud, Lacan devises a tripartite model of the human psyche. In the Freud's model, the interactions of the id, ego, and superego greatly determine our behavior. Underlying Lacan's model, however, is the basic assumption that language shapes and ultimately structures our unconscious and conscious minds and thus shapes our self-identity.

According to Lacan, the human psyche consists of three parts, or what Lacan calls orders: The **Imaginary**, the **Symbolic**, and the **Real**. As in Freud's tripartite model, each of these orders interacts with the others. From our birth until somewhere around 6 months, we function primarily in the Imaginary Order, or the part of the psyche that contains our wishes, fantasies, and, most importantly, images. In this phase of our psychic development, we are joyfully united as one with our mother, receiving our food, our care, and all our comfort from her. In this preverbal state, we rely on images as a means of perceiving and interpreting the world. Consequently, our image of ourselves is always in flux, for we are not able to differentiate where one image stops and another begins.

Somewhere between the age of 6 and 18 months, we enter what Lacan calls the mirror stage. In this stage we literally see ourselves in a mirror, or we may metaphorically see ourselves in our mothers' image. Seeing this mirror image permits us to perceive images that have discrete boundaries, thereby allowing us to become aware of ourselves as independent beings who are separate from our mothers. This mirror image of ourselves as a whole and complete being is in itself an ideal, for unlike the actual mirror image, we are not in full control of ourselves. For example, we cannot move our bodies as we want or eat when we so desire.

During this mirror stage, we come to recognize certain objects — what Lacan calls a object — as being separate images from ourselves. These include bodily wastes, our mothers' voices and breasts, and our own speech sounds. When these objects or sounds are not present, we yearn for them. According to Lacan, such objects become for us symbols of lack. This sense of lack will continue to plague us for the rest of our lives.

While we are passing through the Imaginary Order, one great consuming passion dominates our existence: The desire for our mother. Mother, we believe, can fulfill all our wishes just as we can fulfill all of hers. But like our mothers before us, we must learn that we are separate entities who can never be totally unified with our mothers. According to Lacan, such total unity and wholeness is in itself an illusion.

Once we learn that we are individual beings who are separate from our mothers, we are ready to enter Lacan's second developmental phase, the **Symbolic Order**. Whereas the mother dominates the Imaginary Order, the father dominates the Symbolic Order. In this phase, we learn language. Lacan, however, would argue that language masters us, for he believes that it is language that shapes our identity as separate beings and molds our psyches. Using linguistic principles formulated by Ferdinand de Saussure, Lacan declares that we differentiate between individual sounds and words on the basis of difference. We know the word might, for example, because it is different from sight, and we know hill because it differs from bill. Knowing and mastering this concept of difference enables to enter and pass through the Symbolic Order successfully.

Lacan contends that in the Symbolic Order we learn to differentiate between male and female. This process of learning gender identity is based on difference and loss. Whereas in the Imaginary Order we delighted in the presence of our mother, in the Symbolic Order we learn that our father comes to represent cultural norms and laws. It is he who stands between us and our mother, and it is he who enforces cultural rules by threatening to castrate us if we do not obey. Because the castration complex is obviously different for boys and girls, the process of completing the Symbolic Order successfully is different for each sex.

For Lacan, what sex we are — male or female — is biologically determined. Our gender or our sexuality, however, is culturally created. For example, society decrees that a little boy should play with cars and a little girl with dolls. And it is the father, the power symbol, who enforces society's rules and ensures we follow them. Both sexes, then, come to understand their own sexuality by observing what they are not, a boy noting that he does not do the things a young girl does and vice versa. Each must recognize that he or she will forever be a splintered self, never again being able to experience the wholeness and joy of being one with his or her mother in the Imaginary Order.

For the boy, entry into the Symbolic Order dictates that he identifies and acknowledges the father as the symbol of society's power and as the object that blocks his desire for sexual union with his mother. For the girl, entry into the Symbolic Order demands that she too acknowledge the father or the male as the symbol of power in society and as her personal superior. Like the boy, she wishes to return to the happy state of union with her mother in the Imaginary Order. Unlike the boy, however, she maintains more access than he to this pre-Oedipal stage as she grows up.

Lacan maintains that entering the Symbolic Order is a form of castration for either sex. For Lacan, castration is symbolic, not literal, and represents each person's loss of wholeness and his or her acceptance of society's rules. For the male it means accepting the father, the power symbol who possesses a phallus or penis. Likewise, the female must not only accept the father figure as dominant but also accept her lack of phallus. Similar to his differentiation between sex and gender, Lacan distinguishes between the penis, the actual biological organ, and the phallus, what becomes for Lacan, in poststructural terms, the transcendental signified — the object that gives meaning to all other objects. In other words, for Lacan the phallus is the ultimate symbol of power. Although neither males or females can ever possess the phallus and therefore can never be complete or whole, males do have a penis, giving them a slight claim to such power.

At the heart of Lacan's theory and his understanding of the human psyche is lack and fragmentation. We have longings for love, for physical pleasure and for countless objects, but nothing can fulfill our desire to return to the Imaginary Order and be at one with our mother. It is this fragmentation, this divided self, that concerns Lacan when he examines a literary text. For Lacan, literary texts hold the possibility of capturing, at least for a moment, our desire to return to the Imaginary Order and to regain that sense of pure joy we felt when were whole and united with our mothers.

In examining a text, Lacan also looks for elements of the third and most remote and unreachable part of the human psyche: the Real Order. On one hand, the Real Order consists of the physical world, including the material universe and everything in it. On the other hand, the Real Order also symbolizes all that a person is not. Or as Lacan would say, the Real Order contains countless *object* a — objects that continually function for us as symbols of primordial lack. Because these objects, and indeed the entire physical universe, can never be parts of us, we therefore can never experience or really know them except through language. And as Lacan contends, it is language that causes our fragmentation in the first place. For Lacan literature's particular ability is to capture **jouissance,** or a brief moment of joy or terror or desire that somehow arises from deep within our unconscious psyche and reminds us of a time of perfect wholeness when we were incapable of differentiating among images from the Real Order. More often than not, these experiences are sexual, although other images and experiences such as birth or death can serve this function. Such moments of joy Lacan often finds in the writings of Poe, Shakespeare, and Joyce.

7.4 THE PRESENT STATE OF PSYCHOANALYTIC CRITICISM

Thanks primarily to Lacan, psychoanalytic criticism has enjoyed new popularity. In particular, feminist critics such as Sandra Gilbert and Susan Gubar (*Madwoman in the Attic*, 1979) and a host of others continue to adapt both Freud and Lacan's theoretical models to show the psychological conflicts and concerns encountered by female writers in a male-dominated world. Others critics such as Felix Guattari continue to challenge both Freud and Lacan's ideas, devising their own models of the human psyche. Without question, however, Freud and his models of the human psyche remain at the core of psychoanalytic criticism.

7.5 ASSUMPTIONS

The foundation for all forms of psychoanalytic criticism irrefutably belongs to Freud and his theories and techniques developed during his psychiatric practice. Whether any practicing psychoanalytic critic uses the ideas of Jung, Frye, Lacan, or any other psychoanalyst, all must acknowledge Freud as the intellectual founding father of this form of criticism.

Central to psychoanalytic criticism is Freud's assumption that all artists, including authors, are neurotic. Unlike most other neurotics, however, the artist escapes many of the outward manifestations and results of neurosis such as madness or self-destruction by finding a pathway back to saneness and wholeness in the act of creating his or her art.

According to Freud, an author's chief motivation or writing any story is to gratify some secret desires, some forbidden wishes that probably developed during the author's infancy and was immediately suppressed and dumped in the unconscious. The outward manifestation of this suppressed wish becomes literary work itself. Freud declares that the literal work is therefore the author's dream or fantasy. By using Freud's psychoanalytic techniques as they are used in dream therapy, psychoanalytic critics believe we can unlock the hidden meanings contained within the story and housed in symbols. Only then can we arrive at an accurate interpretation of the text.

Because Freud believes that the literary text is really an artist's dream or fantasy, the text can and must be analyzed like a dream. For Freud, this means that we must assume that the dream is a disguised wish. All, of our present wishes, Freud believed, originated in some way during infancy. As an infant, we longed to be both sensually and emotionally satisfied. The memory of these satisfied infantile desires provides the fertile ground for our present wishes to occur. All present wishes are therefore re-creations of a past infantile memory — especially elements of the Oedipal phase — brought to the surface of our unconscious and conscious states through sensations, emotions, and other present-day situations.

But the actual wish is often too strong and too forbidden to be acknowledged by the minds censor, the ego. Accordingly, the ego distorts and hides the wish or **latent content** of the dream, thereby allowing the dreamer to remember a somewhat changed and often radically different dream. It is this changed dream or manifest content of the dream that the dreamer tells the dream analyst. In turn, the dream analyst must strip back the various layers of the patient's conversation and carefully analyze the multiple layers of the dream. The analyst's job is much like that of an archaeologist who painstakingly uncovers a valued historical site layer by layer. Like the archaeologist, the analyst must peel back the various layers of a dream until the true wish is uncovered.

Like the dream analyst, the psychoanalytic critic believes that any author's story is a dream that on the surface reveals only the manifest content of the true tale. Hidden and censored throughout the story on various levels lies the latent content of the story, its real meaning or interpretation. Usually this latent content directly relates to some element and memory of the Oedipal phase of our development. By directly applying the techniques used in Freudian dream analysis, the psychoanalytic critic believes the actual, uncensored wish can be brought to the surface, thereby revealing the story's true meaning.

As noted earlier in this chapter, not all psychoanalysts agree with Freud's basic assumptions. For example, Jung believes that mythological as well as sexual images appear in our dreams. Frye borrows this assumption from Jung and develops a schematic for interpreting all dreams and stories. Lacan, another psychoanalytic critic, disavows Freud's assumption that the unconscious is a cauldron of boiling passions and announces that the unconscious is as highly structured as language itself. By analyzing this structure, Lacan declares that no one can achieve wholeness, for we are all and will always remain fragmented individuals who are seeking completeness. However, all of these theorists and their theories relate in some way to Freud's presuppositions.

7.6   METHOLOTHY

First introduced to literary studies in the 1920s and 1930s, Freud's psychoanalytic criticism still survives today. Although its methods have been challenged, revised, and supplemented, psychoanalytic criticism provides a stimulating approach to literary analysis that holds that we humans are complex yet somewhat understandable creatures who often fail to note the influence of the unconscious on our motivations and our everyday actions.

For several decades after its introduction, psychoanalytic criticism focused mainly on the author. Known as psycho-biography, this method of analysis begins by amassing biographical data of an author through biographies, personal letters, lectures, and any other document deemed related in some way to the author. Using these documents and the author's canon, these psychoanalytic critics believed they could theoretically construct the author's personality with all its idiosyncrasies, internal and external conflicts, and most importantly, neuroses. In turn, such a devised theory, they believed, could illuminate an author's individual works, giving rise to the latent content in the author's texts. By gaining an in-depth understanding of the author, these critics assumed they would be better able to interpret an author's canon. Of particular interest to them were the lives and works of Edgar Allan Poe, William Blake, and Leonardo da Vinci.

In the 1950s, psychoanalytic critics turned their attention away from psychobiography to character analysis, studying the various aspects of characters' minds found in an author's canon. Such a view gave rise to a more complex understanding of a literary work. Individual characters within a text now became the focus. Believing that the author had in mind a particular personality for his or her characters, critics also noted that readers develop their own conceptions of each character's personality. A character's motivations and actions, then, became more complex than simply the author's ideas. How the readers interpreted the various characters now became an integral part of the text's interpretation. Whereas the author creates a character, a reader re-creates the same character, bringing to the text and to an individual character all the reader's past experiences and knowledge. The character simultaneously becomes a creation of both the author and of the reader. In order to interpret the story, a psychoanalytic analysis of the author and the reader were thus needed.

Today, many psychoanalytic critics realize that the reader plays a major role in interpreting a work. Understanding ourselves from a Freudian point of view and the context in which we live is therefore essential if we are to interpret a text.

One of the most controversial psychoanalytic techniques used today involves applying Freud's key assumption — that all human behavior is sexually driven — directly to a text. In the hands of novice critics who are often ill or misinformed about Freud's psychoanalytic techniques, everything in a text becomes a sexual image. For these critics, every concave image, such as a flower, cup, cave, or vase, is a female symbol, and any image whose length exceeds its diameter, such as a tower, sword, knife, or pen, becomes a phallic or male symbol. Consequently, a text containing a boat floating into a cave or a pen being placed within a cup is interpreted as a symbol of sexual intercourse. From this perspective, all images and actions within a text must be traced to the author's id, for everything in a text is ultimately the hidden wishes of the author's libido.

Another psychoanalytic approach is archetypal criticism first developed by Jung and then later by Frye. In this form of analysis, critics examine a text to discover the various archetypes that they claim appear in it. According to Jung, these archetypes have the same meaning for all readers. The color red, for example, signifies danger just as water symbolizes life. By showing where and how these archetypes appear in the text and form recognizable patterns, the archetypal critic believes that he or she can discover the text's meaning. To apply this method accurately, a critic must be greatly conversant with Jung's rather complex theory and terminology.

But the most recent type of psychoanalytic criticism to appear is that developed by Lacan. A Lacanian critic would attempt to discover how a text symbolically represents elements of the Real, the Imaginary, and the Symbolic Orders. By identifying the symbolic representations of these orders within the text, the critic would then examine how each of these symbols would demonstrate the fragmentary nature of the self. Such a demonstration would show the reader that all individuals are in actuality splintered selves. The overall purpose, then, of a Lacanian analysis is to teach us that a fully integrated and psychologically whole person does not exist and that we must all accept fragmentation.

Whichever psychoanalytic method a critic chooses to use, he or she must master the psychoanalytic theories and practices of Freud and some of his pupils in order to devise an interpretation that is credible and clear. Although mastering the theory and its appropriate applications may be difficult, the result could be a rewarding discovery of the truth that lies within each of us.

7.7   QUESTIONS FOR ANALYSIS

Because psychoanalytic criticism is based on various models of the mind rather than any aesthetic theory, this critic approach to textual analysis can use methodology of a variety of schools of criticism. Explain how the critical methods of New Criticism, reader-response, and deconstruction can be used in a psychoanalytic reading of a text.

Using Hawthorne's "Young Goodman Brown," analyze the character of Goodman Brown from the Freudian, Jungian, and Lacanian perspectives.

Apply Freud's theories to Robert Browning's "My Last Duchess" and articulate a psychoanalytic interpretation of this poem.

Using a short story or poem of your choice, identify the various images and structural patterns that occur. Then, using your understanding of psychoanalytic criticism, explain the presence of these images and patterns and how each of them relates to an overall psychoanalytic interpretation of the text itself.

Investigate the life of John Keats and apply the principles of psychobiography to his poem "Ode on a Grecian Urn." When your psychobiographical analysis is completed, apply the theories of Freud to this same poem, pointing out and explaining any phallic or yonic symbols that appear in the text.

7.8   SAMPLE ESSAYS

In the student essay that follows, note carefully how the author, David Johnson, applies Freudian psychoanalytic terminology and methodology to arrive at his interpretation. After briefly reviewing basic elements of Freudian psychology, what primary psychoanalytic approach does he use in his analysis? Is the author concentrating his psychoanalysis more on the poet or on the poem? Can you find any evidence that the author interacts with the text and imposes his own personality traits on his interpretation of the text? In your opinion, is this psychoanalytic essay a valid and legitimate interpretation of the text? Be able to defend your response.

In the professional essay that follows, note how the author uses intercultural psychology theory and methodology to arrive at an interpretation of culture-loaded words as they appear in *Lunyu*. In this essay, is the author using a Freudian, Jungian, or Lacanian approach to the text? After deciding which approach the critic is employing, be able to cite the psychoanalytic terminology and methodological principles the critic uses to develop the critical essay.

Professor Essay

On Culture–loaded Words in Roger T. Ames's English Version of Lunyu from Jung's Cultural Psycho-analysis Theory.

Introduction

Confucius is a well-known Chinese educationist, philosopher and statesman. His thinking exerts a far-reaching influence on Chinese culture even on Asian culture, today the study on Confucianism from various aspects has been a hot issue in the academia. This paper is an attempt to study the English version of *Lunyu* translated by Roger T. Ames (1998) according to Whitehead's process philosophy.

Confucius is more a culture transmitter than an innovator. As a thinker, he establishes his own ideological system with Ren (仁) as its focus. As the first great educator and thinker in the history of Chinese thought, he makes it possible for the common people to be instructed, regardless of their family backgrounds. As a statesman, he highlights the governors on how to pursue a harmonious society and administration in good functions through education.

Both at his times and in the following days, Confucius has been enjoying great authority and popularity as the Chinese Sage. His ideas on learning, governing, family, self-cultivation and philosophy have been the rich sources of Chinese culture, gradually making Confucianism stand out among the "Hundred Schools" and have become the orthodox ideology of the state after Emperor Wu (140—87 BC) came to the throne in the Han Dynasty.

Lunyu (known as Analects in the Western world, a name firstly used by James Legge in his translation), stands as the foundation of Confucian thought. Just as the name suggests, it means "Selected Sayings". Lun (论) refers to "discussing and compiling", while Yu (语) implies "discourses and sayings". Therefore, *Lunyu* is the compilation of the sayings (of Confucius and his followers). *Lunyu* contains twenty books, each of which has many chapters, ranging from three to forty-seven. It is commonly said that the chapters are arbitrarily arranged within each book, but the truth is that there is a great coherence; many chapters cluster around specific subjects and themes, such as politics, philosophy, literature and education and moral cultivation, almost all the fundamental concepts of Confucianism such as, "Tian"(天), "Dao" (道), "Ren" (仁) "Xiao" (孝), "Junzi" (君子) etc.The interesting thing is that such specific subject is not indicated from the title of each book, for the title is simply derived from the first few words of the first chapter in respective book, some of which are simply the name of disciples.

The Analects of Confucius (*Lunyu*) has been translated into English since the 17th century, hereafter caused a profound influence on the Western world, in particular for Jame Legge's translation. The Confucian philosophy embodied in *The Analects of Confucius* has been translated and interpreted by the West sinologists and missionaries, and to some degree it was branded with religious interpretation in some translation versions. Great changes took place until the later part of the 20th century with the coming of globalization. Some sinologists and philosophers took different viewpoints and hold various perspectives to research on Confucian thoughts, bringing Confucianism a new look in the new era. Consequently, the study of translations on Confucian classics began to increase in significance in the various fields.

Roger T. Ames's Translation on *Lunyu*

Translation today is perceived as an interdisciplinary field of study and the indissoluble connection between language and the way of life. As pragmatics springs up and develops, shifts from linguistics to a culture turn provides translation studies from new perspectives. Deeper exploration on the nature of translation has presented a shifting pragmatic trend. As a matter of fact, translation, as the activity of cross-cultural communication between two different languages, is a kind of complicated linguistic and cultural phenomenon. In translation, the translator acts as both a receptor and a producer, so their practices are affected by inter-linguistic and extra-linguistic factors.

Roger T. Ames as the modern sinologist, mainly does researches on Oriental philosophy, Confucianism and Taoism, and comparative philosophy. He has involved himself in translation of Chinese philosophical classics and comparative study of Chinese and Western philosophy. In his translation work *The Confucius Analects: A Philosophical Translation Based on the Dingzhou Manuscripts* (with Henry Rosemont, Jr 1998), Ames has devoted his academic life to challenging the ethnocentrism in Western philosophical tradition. For hundred years of study on Oriental culture, some Western translators have found Confucianism compatible with Christianity and conductive to their missionary work, so most of the translations have been done with heavy resort to Christian explanation; therefore Confucianism has been taken as religion rather than philosophy in the West can be partly due to lack of philosophical interpretation. To discover the essential differences between Chinese and Western cultures is absolutely alienated when they study Chinese traditional classics, so the meaning of Eastern philosophical terms can hardly recognized and are often interpreted indiscriminately as western terms. To sum up, misunderstanding and undervaluation in the West on Chinese philosophy can be attributed to two things: one is Western ethnocentrism and cultural chauvinism; the other is cultural reductionism. That is, philosophical terms with Chinese characteristics are simplified in translation, misleading Western readers to acquire the characterization of Chinese philosophy, let alone to be identified and accepted by them. So Ames's translation of Chinese classics is creatively integrated with philosophical interpretation. What he drives at is not a sheer study of Chinese tradition but to lead Westerners to a proper understanding of Chinese thought while revealing the originality of classical Confucian philosophy.

This study proposes a philosophical theoretical model on Confucian classics via Roger T. Ames's English translation of *Lunyu*, aiming at finding the developing trend of Confucius study in the English-Speaking world. The research is expected to bring theoretical and practical values by shedding more light on the translation of *Lunyu*.

This paper starts with the application of process theory, and then select the core terms in *Lunyu* to analyse the different features, covering analyzing the basic viewpoints of the former scholars on Confucius "Ren" "Dao" "De" "Junzi" and the problem of self-cultivation.

Nowadays, high-tech products move forward the material civilization and bring huge economic benefits. However, a lot of social problems and environmental problems come on the heels of that. It is the common vision for us to rebuild a harmonious world and to achieve peace and development. So some socialists, philosophers and educators all over the world probed into the hot issue to take the value and application of Confucianism in modern times into consideration for the purpose of dissolving the global crisis and trying to find a way for series of social problems.

Roger. T. Ames's translation version of *Lunyu* from perspective of philosophy makes it possible to rebuild the Oriental cultural image in the West. Researches on Chinese classics bring a fresh force and thinking to the study of Confucianism in the world as well as deepen the understanding and cognition on Chinese culture. Moreover, it will promote the intercultural communication and construction of global harmonious cultural ecological environment.

Purpose of Study

For a long time, translation of *Lunyu*, regarded as literary translation, is explored merely on its linguistic transference or literal reproduction between different versions by traditional researchers. To some extent, this kind of static and one-side research method restricts the development of translation studies. Translation studies witnesses the trend of interdisciplinary development, and then theories from other disciplines are borrowed into translation study. Today, emphasis on interdiciplinary research on *Lunyu* is even more important in translation multiple environments, which allows different kinds of interpretation and expression to occur.

Even some western translators explored a comparative analysis of the different versions of *Lunyu* from the aspect of philosophy,the translation studies onward make it possible to enlarge our study horizons by virtue of new development of translation theories, thus contributing to further study on translations of *Lunyu*. The research objective can be attained firstly, in light of Process theory, and different translations of *Lunyu* can be investigated comprehensively at the Language-internal and the language-external levels. Secondly, the Process theory can manifest the translators' respective subjectivity according to detailed translations in all "processing" aspects. And thirdly, the Processing theory combines extra-linguistics level with philosophical elements to read Confucian works, which brings new angles in understanding *Lunyu*.

Literature Review

Lunyu is the most important Confucius book which embodies the political, ethical and educational principles of the Confucianism, and its significance could not be substituted by any other ancient book in China. As Confucianism attracts more and more attention in the world, the English versions of *Lunyu* become abundant resources for people all over the world to understand Chinese history, society and culture. In recent years, the study of English translation of *Lunyu* has become a hot issue in academic world.

Chinese researchers' investigations into the English translations of *Lunyu* date back as far as the turn of the 20th century. While with the founding of the People's Republic of China in 1949, there was a temporary pause in this area of this study, since the 1980s, with the resurgence of interest in the English translations of *Lunyu*, quite fruitful progress has been made in this field. In the past decades, domestic research on the English translations of *Lunyu* has been focusing on five aspects: English translation (s), translator (s), the translation of key Confucian terms, transmission and reception, and the editing and publishing of these translations.

Of the five aspects of inquiry, the translations of *The Analects* have attracted the largest share of researchers' attention. This kind of study is usually normative-approach based, with one or more translations as the focus of attention. After a comparison of James Legge's translation and the original, as a result of the sharp contrast between Chinese and English language and customs, as well as the influence of social context of *The Analects*, literal translation, which dominates James Legge's version, can sometimes bring about erroneous editions. Holding James Legge's translation in great esteem, this translation is an impressive example to later generation translators. In the book named *The Geek Culture* Ku Hungming, Huang Xing-tao compares the translation of James Legge and the translation of Ku Hungming, and indicates the translation of Ku exceeded that of James Legge. On the one hand, with immeasurable academic significance, these notes and explanations James Legge's translation is an indispensable reference to later translators of *The Analects*. On the other hand, "as an important component of the whole translation, they pose a formidable obstacle to the smooth and easy appreciation of the meaning of the text". As to James Legge's literal way of translation, it would lead to the violation of English syntactical rules, thus making the translated version unnatural. There are many points in need of improvement.

In addition to comparisons between English translations and the original, comparative studies of different translations have also attracted increasing attention from researchers. After comparing the James Legge's version with that of D.C. Law, some scholars think they each have their strong points and weak points. James Legge's version is more formal in diction and has a certain classic elegance but can be difficult for the young readers to read. The version by D. C. Law, on the other hand, is more colloquial and easier to understand, but at times there may be stylistic deviation from the original. From the angle of translation purpose, Zou Xiuqin (2008) compares James Legge's translation with Ezra Pound's version. And she points out Pound's translation is known as poetic translation, since he used to apply his modern poetics in his translation practice. His three principles of imagism are generally put into his translations, and his *The Analects* is typical of a product representing his poetics of image, expression and musicality. There are other analysis which covers the translations of James Legge, Ezra Pound and Edward Slingerland, and which is conducted from four perspectives, functional theory, culture, linguistics and structuralism. He Gangqiang (2007) makes a comparison of the translations by James Legge and Arthur Waley. In his opinion, from the perspective of reader response theory, Arthur Waley's translation is more readable than that of James Legge. Historically, it is obvious that these two translations should be ranked among the most classic, but considered from today's criteria, the overall quality of these two translations is still far from satisfactory. It is imperative that Chinese translators make collective efforts to bring about a classic translation of their own to contribute to the worldwide popularization of Chinese civilization.The English translators include Leonard A. Lyall. Ku Hungming employed the method of "domestication", using a set of Western sayings, concepts, and idioms to refer to those of Confucius, which made his *The Discourses and Sayings of Confucius* (1898) familiar to Western readers, with no peculiarity and idiosyncrasy. Other English translators include: W E.Soothill, L. Giles, Raymond Dawson, Thomas Cleary, Simon Leys, E. Bruce and A. Taeko Brooks, David Hinton. E. Slingerland.

The Chinese translators include Lin Yutang, Li Tianchen, Lao An, Fan Fu'en & Wen Shaoxia, Lai Bo & Xia Yuhe, Wang Fulin, the Khu brothers, David H. Li, Ding Wangdao and Xu Yuanchong. After the survey of the development of English versions, it is clear that the version by Roger T. Ames and Henry Rosemont is a new one. What's more, it was only in 2003 that the Chinese version of their translation came out.

Theoretical Framework

The founder of Process Philosophy is Alfred North Whitehead (1861—1947), the celebrated British mathematician, logician and scientific philosopher. He called his philosophy "Philosophy of Organism" in his representative work *Process and Reality: an Essay in Cosmology* (1978), centering on events and process. For this reason, the so-called "Process Philosophy" came into being. In other words, the substantiality of the world lies in process that makes the world, so the world exists in the process. The process is the reality and vice versa. In his words, "That the actual world is a process, and that the process is the becoming of actual entities. Thus actual entities are creatures." The top principle of his philosophy is "creativity".

Primary notions of Process Philosophy are divergence from and exceeding of proceeding philosophical ontology. Such notions involve "actual entities", "prehension", "nexus" and "ontological process". In the first three notions, much work has been done to base philosophical thought on the most concrete elements in daily experience. "Actual entities" are the final real things of which the world is made up. There is no going behind actual entities to find anything more real. Whitehead defines it as "prehension". "The essence of actual entity consists solely in the fact that it is a apprehending thing". In terms of its relation with the fact, "The final facts are, all alike, actual entities; and these actual entities are drops of experience, complex and interdependent". Every actual entity is described as an organic process, progressing from one phase to another, with each phase basing a succeeding one.

So Prehension, or Concrete Facts of Relatedness, reveals the relation between "actual entity" and every entity in the cosmos. Just as Whitehead puts it, a prehension produces in itself the general characteristic of an actual entity: It is referent in an external world and in this sense will be said to have a "vector character": it involves emotion and purpose, valuation and causation. In fact, any characteristic of an actual entity is reproduced in a prehension.

Western metaphysics is based on the paradigmatic assumption of creation, concerning itself with what things are, the nature of things, while Chinese metaphysics deals with how they are, how the transcendent force things interact. So western metaphysics pervading "has tended to see reality as substance, the Chinese to see it as relationship". It can be safely concluded that in ontology, process philosophy holds process as reality and reality as process. In epistemology, Whitehead introduces the notion of "prehension" to remove the subjective and objective duality in traditional philosophy. He advocates that the relation between subject and object is a gradually generated concreteness, and human beings and nature should maintain a harmonious co-existence during such process. In this sense, process philosophy is an innovation, surmounting realism and duality in antecedent Western philosophy, and involves a great potentiality to become one of the growing points in modern philosophy. Process Philosophy holds affinity with Chinese culture. To some extent, Whitehead's idea gets closer to Chinese thought than to European thought, for the former roots in process and relevance while the latter in fact and logic. Not only Whitehead himself but nearly all the other process ideologists favor Chinese traditional philosophy and show a growing interest in Chinese culture. The themes of life, motion, and evolution exhibited in classical Chinese culture seem closely linked to process philosophy.

Roger T. Ames asserts that process thinking brings a revolution to world philosophy. Its emphasis on integration, creativity and relevance corresponds to the call of current times for a newly reset world order with peace and harmony as the irrefutable themes. Ames discovers that such process thinking is the shared language for mutual communication, for process thinking crosses all boundaries. Therefore, he bases his study of Chinese philosophy on the similarity between Chinese and Western philosophy. This similarity is a necessity. As Ames says, it is Whitehead's Process Philosophy that provides such categories and language required to analyze Chinese philosophy for Ames. In his opinion, Confucius is a process thinker and the language in *Lunyu* is the language for process thinking. This thought of process runs through Ames's translation of Chinese classics. When interpreting *Lunyu*, Ames resorts to analogy, relating paragraphs to paragraphs, historical events to historical events, and pays close attention to the correlation among certain historical figures and events. Such strategies equal what Whitehead calls "prehension", imbuing interpretations with life experiences both from readers and interpreters, which makes his interpretations of *Lunyu* quite special and unique, making it a works with everlasting vitality and ongoing stories.

Text-Analysis

Tian (天)

Human tendencies are not predetermined or fixed their come-into-being which resides in their constant acting and interacting with the shifting natural, social and cultural circumstances. The inter-dependent and interactive field is brought into focus through human development. In the process of self-cultivation education plays a vital role. The translation of "Tian" is made against the intention of English readers to understand source culture on target cultural terms. When it comes to translation strategy, Ames borrows foreignization by using Chinese pinyin and Chinese characters to introduce Chinese philosophical concepts and terms more than English terms' interpretation.

"Tian" used to be translated into "Heaven" in historical western texts, while Roger T. Ames gives "Tian" such explanation because "Heaven" can evoke the readers' transcendental and religious imagination being so far from Confucian thoughts. According to Confucius, "Tian" is given no transcendental meaning, neither "God" nor "absolute truth" can represent its ontological concept. Ames holds "in the first place, Tian is often used as an abbreviation for Tiandi — 'the heavens and the earth' — suggesting that Tian is not independent of this world." To be exact, "Tian" is rather a designation for what the world is, it is not just a natural world, and it has as its integral part of human, social dimension. So "Tian" as "social force" is inclusive of both nature and culture.

Ames relates "Tian" to the tradition of ancestors' reverence rather than the worship of

God. Tian would seem to stand for a cumulative and continuing cultural legacy focused by the spirits who have come before. In this sense, "Tian" is so novel and irrelevant to Western cultural experience, "Tian" (heaven) and "Ren" (human) become underpinned. One becomes a transmitter-creator, being able to create meaning and value. "Tian" is personified. Continuity and congruence are obtained between the way of heaven and the way of man. "Tian" is not entity to transform and nourish the world, but a living culture, residing in human community. It implies the intimate relationship in the process of human evolution. Since the world is an organic whole in which the myriad event and processes interrelate with one another. "Tian" and "Ren" is not the relationship between "creator" and "the created" but subject-oriented, people-centered and life-centered. Cosmic creation is not an external creator but an internal creator, that is affiliated with the theme of man's creative self-cultivation and self-realization.

Confucius sayings abound showing the faith in subject-oriented, insofar as the monism, the relationship between human and outer world are one in nature. The truth is beauty and good-nature, and beauty truth, which is displayed by the nature law. Consequently, what man should do is to enlighten the innate nature without privately concerned and follow it naturally.

Dao

Confucius treats the relationship between individual and himself, individual and family, and individual and society. The saint coined "Wulun relationship" means five basic relationships among human as a relation division. Ames interprets "Dao" into "the totality of all things".It is a process that requires the language of both "change (bian 变)"and "persistence (tong 通)" to capture its dynamic disposition. It denotes to realize the Dao is to experience, to interpret, and to influence the world in such a way as to reinforce and extend the way of life inherited from one's cultural predecessors. This way of living in the world is to inherit the ancestors' wisdom and spiritual experience and impart them on to the successors.

When "Dao" linked with professional word, it refers to the rule and particular method of the field. Such as "Wangdao" is put into English "kingly government", the rule by practicing virtues. Turning back to the subject and inward to the heart, it repudiates self-cultivation with a preference for doing over knowing. For Confucius, Dao is primarily applied in Rendao (人道).

For Examples:

A way of becoming consummately and authoritatively human.

It is the person who is able to broaden the way, not the way that broadens..

Roger Ames explains here "way" embodies no meaning of the simple road we travel but as a philosophical lexicon as it cognates "Dao (导)", which means to lead, to forge for road-building, so it is processional and dynamic.[①] "Dao" here is not knowledge in the Western sense of the term but resorts to the building of a moral character, a knowledge of the way, and a kind of know-how. In this sense, the goal of classical Confucian philosophy is oriented towards cultivating good behavior and making the world different rather than trying to scholarly apprehend the world or to conquer it.

Ren

Ren, translated herein as "authoritative conduct," "to act authoritatively," or "authoritative person," is the foremost prospect taken up by Confucius, and occurs over one hundred times in the text. According to the lexicon of Chinese character, "Ren" belongs to "huiyi" (会意字), the elements made up of Ren, " 人 " (person), and " 二 " (two). It originally means human being is the most elegant existence in the universe, and " 二 " in ancient Chinese character is the homophone of " 上 " referring to being noble and sublime. So "Ren" can be explained as the man with noble virtues. This underscores the Confucian conceptions. Afterward with the development of simplified character, "Ren" is given interpretation as underlying human communal power because there are two persons in the structure of the character. Ren is most commonly translated as "benevolence," "goodness," or "humanity," Ames uses "the authoritative person" as his translation. In his opinion, Ren is one's entire person with his cultivated cognitive, aesthetic, moral, and religious sensibilities that can be displayed in one's ritualized roles and relationships. And "it is a sum of significant relationships that constitute one as a resolutely social person"."Humanity", suggests a shared cultural quality and essential condition of being human owned, indicating the common traits of the species, so extending to "humanism" opposing so much to theocracy. Yet "Ren" in Confucianism can not be replaced by western terms so easy. It is an aesthetic project, an accomplishment. It is what we grow from, and we are becoming. In light of process philosophy, Ames articulates "Ren" is not a static existence but a changing, dynamic quality. It is not an essential endowed potential, but an interface between one's natural quality and social, cultural environments. Ren is an organic unity residing in these relationships. To understand "school of

---

① AMES R, YOUNG W. Lao Tzu: Text, Notes, and Comments[M]. Chengwen Publisher,1981:46.

Ren" in Confucianism, one should realize to associate "Ren" with history, society, community and oneself. That was expressed many times by the lectures and dialogues between Confucius and his disciple in *Lunyu*. From various aspects, "Ren" rich in connotation can be the guiding ideology of Confucianism.

Junzi

In *Lunyu*, sage is defined as the deified man or the perfect model of virtue with the highest self-realization achieved, who is first in disclosing meaning and value. Roger Ames and Hall translated Junzi into " the exemplary person". "Junzi" is the person whose moral and conductive behavior can set an example for others and help them realize the natural course, so conduct themselves in accordance with nature law as to achieve a harmonious, peaceful and ideal life.

The conventional translations of the term such as "superior man", "noble man" or "gentleman" fail to convey the core sense of "Junzi" being the standard and demanding emulation. In Confucian thought, "Junzi" and "Xiaoren" is a counterpart division for people in spiritual realm. The former is the spontaneous upholding human nature, and the latter is the laborious cultivation. When a person intends to uplift his moral, spiritual cultivation and resides less on the material pursuit, he turns to insight into human inward world and approaches to the state of "Junzi"; while "Xiaoren" focuses on the worldly fame or profits, laying more stress on his own benefits and pleasure than self-improvement and sublimation. There are a lot of sayings in *Lunyu* reveal the distinct difference between "Junzi" and "Xiaoren".

Ames translates from the perspective of philosophy, giving the process-relational paradigm of classical Chinese thought that a person is not an atomic individual solely existence but the sum of relationships or the roles he plays in communal life. Therefore, "Junzi" in *Lunyu* is not superior man with high ranking and surpassing quality or as a lonely righteous recluse, only self-appreciated and cut off the society, but a strong undertaker who is obliged to lead the people to move forward.

Conclusion

On Roger T. Ames's side, to integrate Chinese thought in Chinese classics with practice in the contemporary age is significant to understand *Lunyu* from the perspective of philosophy. Roger Ames casts Chinese ideas that are foreign to Westerners, enabling them to apprehend Chinese philosophical thought. For Chinese philosopher, the reality of a thing is not its essence or identity , or the category but the inter-related and interacting flux of the universe. The age of globalization has witnessed the rising of research on intercultural communication and E plus times has brought out more high techniques to enhance cooperation and dialogue between us. What Ames's intention is to build a relatively positive angle for a better understanding of Chinese classics and the philosophical thought so that the essence of the theory can be combined into practice. Dialogue with Western thought is a job that must be done, and it transcends national or cultural boundaries. In the context of Western philosophy, which leaves little room for Eastern philosophy, we need to learn more. Additional research is recommended on the strategy and norms that Western sinologists have developed in their unique viewpoints and cultural context, and the various translation environment it is faced with.

REFERENCES

[1]ALFRED K. "Freud and His Consequences." Contemporaries[M]. Boston: Little, Brown, 1962.

[2]BERNARD J P. A Psychological Approach to Fiction: Studies in Thackeray, Stendhal, George Eliot, Dostoevsky, and Conrad[M]. Bloomington: Indiana University Press, 1974.

[3]BETTINA L K. A Jungian Approach to Literature[M]. Carbondale: Southern Illinois University Press, 1984.

[4]BICE B, ROGER K. The Works of Jacques Lacan: An Introduction[M]. New York: St. Martin's, 1986.

[5]CARL G J. Symbols of Transformation[M]. 2nd ed. Trans. R F C HULL. Princeton: Princeton University Press, 1967.

[6]JUNG C G. The Collected Works of C. J. Jung, Sir Herbert Read, Michael Fordhan, and Gerhard Adler, eds. 20 vols., plus supplements[M]. New York: Bollingen Foundation, 1953-1983.

[7]CLAUDE L. "The Structural Study of Myth" in Structural Anthropology[M]. Trans. CLAIRE J , BROOKE G S. New York: Basic, 1963, 206-231.

[8]LEWIS C S. "Myth." An Experiment in Criticism[M]. Cambridge: Cambridge University Press, 196, 140-149.

[9]LEWIS C S. "The Anthropological Approach" and "Psycho-analysis and Literary Criticism" in Selected Literary Essays[M]. Ed. WALTER H. Cambridge: Cambridge University Press, 1969.301-311, 286-300.

[10]DAVID C. Freud and the Myth of Origins[J]. New Literary History.1975: 511-528.

[11]EDITH K, WILLIAM P, eds. Literature and Psychoanalysis[M]. New York: Columbia University Press, 1983.

[12]ELIZABETH W. Psychoanalytic Criticism: Theory in Practice[M]. New York: Methuen, 1984.

[13]EMIL G. The Handbook of Dream Analysis[M]. New York: Liveright, 1951.

[14]ERIC E. Childhood and Society[M]. New York: Norton, 1963.

[15]FREDERICK C C, ed. Psychoanalysis and Literary Process[M]. Cambridge: Winthrop, 1970.

[16]FREDERICK C C, ed. Out of My System. New York: Oxford University Press, 1975.

[17]FREDERIC J H. Freudianism and the Literary Mind[M]. 2nd ed. Baton Route: Louisiana State University Press, 1957.

[18]GEOFFREY H. Psychoanalysis and the Question of the Text[M]. Baltimore: Johns Hopkins University Press, 1979.

[19]GEORGE K. Psychoanalytic Theory: An Exploration of Essentials[M]. New York: International Universities Press, 1976.

[20]JANE G. Reading Lacan[M]. Ithaca: Cornell University Press, 1985.

[21]JEAN W. Reconstructing Desire: The Role of the Unconscious in Women's Reading and Writing[M]. Chapel Hill: University of North Carolina Press, 1990.

[22]JOHN P M, WILLIAM J R. The Purloined Poe: Lacan, Derrida, and Psychoanalytic Reading[M]. Baltimore: Johns Hopkins University Press, 1988.

[23]JOSEPH C. The Hero with a Thousand Faces[M]. New York: Pantheon, 1949.

[24]JOSEPH C. The Hero with a Thousand Faces[M]. 2nd ed. Princeton: Princeton University Press, 1968.

[25]JOSEPH C. The Power of Myth[M]. Ed. BETTY S F. New York: Doubleday, 1988.

[26]JOSEPH N, FREDERIC L R. Psychocriticism: An Annotated Bibliography[M]. Westport: Greenwood, 1984.

[27]JOSEPH P S, ed. Literary Criticism and Psychology[M]. University Park: Pennsylvania State University Press, 1976.

[28]JOSEPH R, MAURICE C. The Psychoanalytic Study of Literature[M]. Hillsdale: Analytic, 1985.

[29]JULIET M. "Introduction: I." in Feminine Sexuality: Jacques Lacan and the École Freudienne[M]. Eds. JULIET M and JACQUELINE R. Trans. JACQUELINE R. New York: Norton, 1982, 1-26.

[30]LAURENCE M P. The Interpretation of Dreams: Freud's Theories Revisited[M]. Boston: Hall, 1986.

[31]LEONARD T, ed. The Practice of Psychoanalytic Criticism[M]. Detroit: Wayne State University Press, 1976.

[32]LILLIAN F. Madness in Literature[M]. Princeton: Princeton University Press, 1980.

[33]LIONEL T. Freud and the Crisis of Our Culture[M]. Boston: Beacon, 1955.

[34]MARIE B. The Life and Works of Edgar Allen Poe[M]. Trans. JOHN R. London: Imago, 1949.

[35]MAUD B. Archetypal Patterns in Poetry[M]. New York: Vintage, 1958.

[36]MEREDITH A S. The Literary Use of Psychoanalytic Process[M]. New Haven: Yale University Press, 1981.

[37]NORTHROP F. Anatomy of Criticism[M]. Princeton: Princeton University Press, 1957.

[38]NORMAN N H. The Dynamics of Literary Response[M]. New York: Oxford University Press, 1968.

[39]NORMAN N H. "The 'Unconscious' of Literature" in Contemporary Criticism[M]. Eds. NORMAN B, DAVID P. New York: St Martin's, 1970.

[40]NORMAN N H. Literary Interpretation and the Three Phases of Psychoanalysis[J]. Critical Inquiry.1976: 221-233.

[41]NORMAN N H. The 1[M]. New Haven: Yale University Press, 1985.

[42]PERRY M, et al. Freud: A Collection of Critical Essays[M]. Englewood Cliff: Prentice-Hall, 1981.

[43]PERRY M. Freud: Twentieth Century Views[M]. Englewood Cliffs: Prentice-Hall,1981.

[44]RAINER N. Reading After Freud[M]. New York: Columbia University Press, 1987.

[45]RAY S. The Analytic Attitude[M]. New York: Basic Books, 1982.

[46]RENÉ G. Violence and the Sacred[M]. Trans. PATRICK G. Baltimore: Johns Hopkins University of Massachusetts Press, 1981.

[47]RENÉ G. The Bible Is Not a Myth[J]. Literature and Belief 1984: 7-15.

[48]ROBERT C D, et al. The Fictional Father: Lacanian Readings of the Text[M]. Amherst: University of Massachusetts Press, 1981.

[49]ROBERT C D. Lacan and Narration: The Psychoanalytic Difference in Narrative Theory[M]. Baltimore: Johns Hopkins University Press, 1983.

[50]ROBERT C D . Special issue on Psychoanalysis and Pedagogy[J]. College English 49 6/7 1987.

[51]ROY P B. Sex, Symbolism, and Psychology in Literature[M]. New York: Octagon, 1975.

[52]SANDOR G, ed. Introducing Psychoanalytic Theory[M]. New York: Brunner-Mazel, 1982.

[53]SANDOR G, ed. Reading Freud's Reading[M]. New York: New York University Press, 1994.

[54]SAMUEL N K, ed. Mythologies of the Ancient World[M]. New York: Anchor-Doubleday, 1961.

[55]SANDRA G, SUSAN G. Madwoman in the Attic: The Woman Writer and the Nineteenth Century Literary Imagination[M]. New Haven: Yale University Press, 1979.

[56]SHOSHANA F, ed. Literature and Psychoanalysis: The Question of Reading — Other wise[M]. Baltimore: Johns Hopkins University Press, 1982.

[57]SHOSHANA F, ed. Writing and Madness (Literature/Philosophy/Psychoanalysis)[M]. Trans. MARTHA N E ,

SHOSHANA F. Ithaca: Cornell University Press, 1985.

[58]SHOSHANA F, ed. Jacques Lacan and the Adventure of Insight: Psychoanalysis in Contemporary Culture[M]. Cambridge: Harvard University Press, 1987.

[59]SIGMUND FREUD. Totem and Taboo[M]. Trans. A A BRILL. New York: Moffat, 1918.

[60]SIGMUND FREUD. Introductory Lectures on Psycho-Analysis[M]. Trans. JOAN R. London: Allen, 1922.

[61]SIGMUND FREUD. The Basic Writings of Sigmund Freud[M]. Trans. and ed. A A BRILL. New York: Modem Library, 1938.

[62]SIGMUND FREUD. The Interpretation of Dreams[M].New York: Random House, 1950.

[63]SIGMUND FREUD. Group Psychology and the Analysis of the Ego[M]. Trans. JAMES S. New York: Norton, 1990.

[64]SIMON O L. Fiction and the Unconscious[M]. Boston: Beacon, 1957.

[65]WILBUR S. Five Approaches to Literary Criticism[M]. London: Collier-Macmillan, 1962.

[66]WILLIAM B. "Writers and Madness" in Literature and Psychoanalysis[M].New York: Columbia University Press, 1983.

[67]XINTAO HUANG. Culture Talent Ku Hungming[M]. Beijing: Zhong Hua Press, 1996.

[68]YOULAN FENG. A Short History of Chinese Philosophy[M]. Tianjin:Tianjin Social Science Academy Press, 2007.

[69]ZHAOGUANG GE. History of Chinese Thought[M]. Shanghai: Fudan University Press, 2004.

CHAPTER VIII   FEMINISM

Women–only spaces were made by cultural feminists to challenge negative gendered constructions, where they were ran "by women for women" . Women only events were being criticized because they excluded men and by excluding men, they were being defined as the problem, rather than locating the problem in the structures of patriarchy.

— Bromley Victoria 2012

8.1   INTRODUCTION

In 1972, Judith Viorst, a well-known author of children's literature, published her short, poetic, revised version of the fairy tale *Cinderella*, In "…And Then the Prince Knelt Down and Tried to Put the Glass Slipper on Cinderella's Foot," Viorst writes:

> I really didn't notice that he had a funny nose.
>
> And he certainly looked better all dressed up in fancy clothes.
>
> He's not nearly as attractive as he seemed the other night.
>
> So T think I'll just pretend that this glass slipper feels too tight.

Viorst's recasting of Cinderella may make us smile or laugh or simply wonder what has happened to our childhood version of this story that was read to us countless times by our parents, our teachers, and our friends. Viorst's Cinderella is, after all, certainly not the Cinderella we remember. The Cinderella we have been taught would never think or act the way Viorst's re-creation does. Our Cinderella is beautiful, but poor. Treated cruelly by her ugly stepsisters and her arrogant, scheming, selfish stepmother, our Cinderella dutifully cleans the family home while she quietly weeps, lamenting that she will not be able to attend the upcoming ball to be held at the castle. Bearing with great patience her trials, our Cinderella will triumphantly get her wish, for her fairy godmother comes to her rescue. Now clothed in a magnificent gown, the lovely Cinderella is driven to the ball in a coach fit for a queen. At the ball, she meets her handsome prince, who is immediately overwhelmed by her beauty, grace, and charm. But at the stroke of midnight, the Cinderella we remember must return home, losing her glass slipper in her haste to return to her carriage.

Dressed once again in rages, our childhood Cinderella finds herself once again cooking and cleaning for her ugly stepsisters and her wicked stepmother. Bearing her a lot in life with unspeakable patience, she is scorned and rebuked time and time again by her older siblings. And then one day the prince and his attendants come to her home, seeking the owner of the glass slipper accidentally left on the steps of the castle. After her ugly stepsisters try unsuccessfully to squeeze their big feet into the small slipper, the Cinderella we remember comes face to face with her handsome prince and successfully puts her petite foot into the magical shoe. Immediately the prince recognizes her as the woman of his dreams and proposes marriage. And after their marriage, they live happily ever after.

Viorst's version of this fairy tale characterizes Cinderella a bit differently. In this re-creation, Cinderella now has opinions of her own. In the light of day, she observes that the prince does not seem to be as attractive as he was the other night at the ball. Asserting her own independence, she pretends the glass slipper does not fit. Accordingly, there will be no marriage, for Cinderella herself has decided she does not want to marry the prince.

This new Cinderella refuses to be defined as the non-significant other. Unlike the old Cinderella, she will not allow herself to be shaped by her society. She realizes that her culture has all too often presented her with stereotypes that she and many others like her have so blindly accepted. Beautiful women, her society decrees, are often oppressed and belittled. If, however, these beautiful people will only bear with patience their a lot in life, they will be rewarded. For like the traditional Cinderella, society says that they must accept that in addition to their beauty, they must also be good-natured and meek. After all, ugly women like Cinderella's stepsisters are cruel and heartless while beautiful women like Cinderella must bear patiently their sufferings and accept that they are victims of the circumstances of life. If they accept their lot in life, they will, in time, be rewarded. According to their society's decrees, they will meet some handsome, wealthy princes who will marry them, care for them, and dote over them the rest of their lives.

This re-created Cinderella debunks the false standards and ideas concerning women and their portrayals in both life and literature that have been carefully perpetuated by the traditional Cinderella and her society. Women, says this new Cinderella, should not mindlessly wait around for a handsome prince to come to their rescue. Women must not be like the traditional Cinderella: Dependent creatures who blindly accept the commandments of their patriarchal society. Unlike the traditional Cinderella, women must not weep about their lot in life, but take an active part in creating and determining their own lives and their own futures. They must therefore reject many of their culture's stereotypes of women such as "the wicked stepmother" syndrome that asserts that the established conceptions on woman., such as beautiful girls must be either "princess syndrome" like aggressive, opinionated or weak, tender and dependant. The adaptation of fairy tales reveals feminist writers hope to subvert the distorted image of women by recreate new heroines to speak for women. The new women holds such ideas that firstly, marriage not the only or the ultimate goal for their life, and the aim to get married is not for a long-term meal ticket. Secondly, women are not the mindless, weepy, passive, helpless creatures who are supposed to be stay at home and wait for a man to make her life meaningful. Thirdly, the happiness and success of a woman's life is not determined by her husband and her good-looking. What a woman should concern is not with her look but her mind. So briefly, What feminists want to tell the world is they are not limited by their sex, like any man, they can shape their personhood and protect their resourcefulness, their minds, and their will powers to become what they dream to be. For the re-created Cinderella knows something the old Cinderella never knew: Whereas sex is biologically determined, gender is culturally determined. And like the revised Cinderella, all women must therefore reject the patriarchal standards of society and become persons in their own right. What they must become is a "significant person," not the other.

In essence, this new version of the Cinderella fairy tale crystallizes the central issues of feminism:

Women have long been inferior to man, and given no voices in the important field concerning important issues of society.

By not giving voice and value to women's opinions, responses, and writings, men have therefore suppressed the female, defined what it means to be feminine, and thereby de-voiced, devalued, and trivialized what it means to be a woman.

In effect, men have made women the "non-significant other".

Feminism's goal is to change this degrading view of women so that all women will realize that they are not a "Non-significant Other", but that each woman is a valuable person possessing the same privileges and rights as every man. Women, feminists declare, must define themselves and assert their own voices in the arenas of politics, society, education and the arts. By personally committing themselves to fostering such change, feminists hope to create a society where the male and female voices are equally valued.

8.2 HISTORICAL DEVELOPMENT

According to feminist criticism, the roots of prejudice against women have long been embedded in Western culture. Such gender discrimination may have begun, say some feminists, with the Biblical narrative that places the blame for the fall of humanity on Eve, not Adam. In similar fashion, the ancient Greeks abetted such gender discrimination when Aristotle, one of their leading philosophers and teachers, asserted that "the male is by nature superior, and the female inferior; and the one rules and the other is ruled."

Following Aristotle's lead, religious leaders and philosophers such as Thomas Aquinas and St. Augustine declared that women are really "imperfect men". These imperfect and spiritually weak creatures, they maintained, possess a sensual nature that lures men away from spiritual truths, thereby preventing males from achieving their spiritual potential. And in the centuries to follow, other theologians, philosophers, and scientists continue such gender discrimination. For example, in *The Descent Of Man*, Darwin announces that women are of a characteristic of a past and lower state of civilization. Such beings, he noted, are inferior to men, who are physically, intellectually, and artistically superior.[1]

For century after century, men's voices continued to articulate and determine the social role and cultural and personal significance of women. In the late 1700s, a faint voice crying in the wilderness against such patriarchal opinions arose and began to be heard. Believing that women along with men should have a voice in the public arena, Mary Wollstonecraft authored *A Vindication of the Rights of Women* (1792). Women, she maintained, must stand up for their rights and not allow their male-dominate society to define what it means to be a woman. Women themselves must take the lead and articulate who they are and what role they will play in society. Most importantly, they must reject the patriarchal assumption that women are inferior to men.

It was not until the Progressive era of the early 1900s, however, that the major roots of feminist criticism began to grow. During this time, women gained the right to vote and became prominent activists in the social issues of the day, such as health care, education, politics, and literature. But equality with men in these arenas remained outside their grasp.

---

① Li Zhenling.Feminist Criticism [EB/OL.][2018-03-18].http://www.igc.apc.org/women/feminist.html

Virginia Woolf

Then in 1919, British scholar, teacher, and early feminist Virginia Woolf laid the foundation for present-day feminist criticism in her seminal work *A Room of One's Own*. In this text, Woolf declares that men have and continue to treat women as inferiors. It is the male, she asserts, who defines what it means to be female and who controls the political, economic, social, and literary structures. Agreeing with Samuel T. Coleridge, one of the foremost nineteenth-century literary critics, that great minds possess both male and female characteristics, she hypothesizes in her text the existence of Shakespeare's sister, one who is as gifted a writer as Shakespeare. Her gender, however, prevents her from having "a room of her own". Because she is a woman, she cannot obtain an education or find profitable employment. Her innate artistic talents will therefore never flourish, for she cannot afford her own room. Woolf's symbol of solitude and autonomy needed to seclude one's self from the world and its accompanying social constraints in order to find time to think and write. Ultimately, Shakespeare's sister dies alone without any acknowledgment of her personal genius. Even her grave does not bear her name, for she is buried in a unmarked grave simply because she is female.

Such loss of artistic talent and personal worthiness, says Woolf, is the direct result of society's opinion of women: That they are intellectually inferior to men. Women, Woolf argues, must reject this social construct and establish their own identity. Women must challenge the prevailing, false cultural notions, concerning their gender identity and develop a female discourse that will accurately portray their relationship "to the world of reality and not to the world of men."

If women accept this challenge, Woolf believes that Shakespeare's sister can be resurrected in and through women living today, even those who may be "washing up the dishes and putting the children to bed" right now. But the Great Depression of the 1930s and World War II in the 1940s focused humankind's attention on other matters and delayed the development of such feminist ideals.

Simone de Beavoir

With the 1949 publication of French writer Simone de Beavior's *The Second Sex*, however, feminist interests once again surfaced. Heralded as the foundational work of twentieth-century feminism, Beavoir's text declares that both French and Western societies are patriarchal, controlled by males. Like Woolf before her, Beavoir believed that the male in these societies defines what it means to be human, including, therefore, what it means to be female. Because the female is not male, Beavoir asserted, she becomes "The Other", an object whose existence is defined and interpreted by the male, who is the dominant being in society. Always subordinate to the male, the female finds herself a secondary or nonexistent player in the major social institutions of her culture, such as the church, government, and education systems. According to Beavoir, a woman must break the bonds of her patriarchal society and define herself if she wishes to become a significant human being in her own right and defy male classification as the Other. She must ask herself, "What is a woman?" Beavoir insists that a woman's answer must not be "mankind", for such a term once again allows men to define women. This generic label must therefore be rejected, for it assumes that "humanity is male and man defines woman not in herself but as relative to him."[①]

Beavoir insists that women see themselves as autonomous beings. Women, she maintains, must reject the societal construct that men are the subject or the absolute and that women are the Other. Embedded in this false assumption is the supposition that males have power and define cultural terms and roles. Accordingly, women must define themselves outside the present social construct and reject being labeled as the Other.

Kate Millett

With the advent of the 1960s and its political activism and social concerns, feminist issues found new voices. One such voice was Kate Millett. Within her publication of *Sexual Politics* in 1969, a new wave of feminism began. Millet was one of the first feminists to challenge the ideological social characteristics of both the male and the female. According to Millet, a female is born and a woman is created. In other words, one's sex, be that male or female, is determined at birth. One's gender, however, is a social construct, being created by cultural ideals and norms. Consciously or unconsciously, women and men conform to the cultural ideas established for them by society. Little boys, for example, must be aggressive, self-assertive, and domineering, whereas little girls must be passive, meek, and humble. These cultural norms and expectations are transmitted through television, movies, songs and literature. Conforming to these prescribed

---

① ZHENG HONGYAN. Duplicitous Voice in Jane Austen's Novels: Interpreting Jane Austen from a Feminist Perspective[D]. 2005(4):8-9.

sex roles dictated by society is what Millet calls **sexual politics**. Women, Millett maintains, must revolt against the power center of their culture; male dominance. In order to do so, women must establish female social conventions for themselves by establishing female discourse, literary studies, and feminist criticism.

Feminism in the 1960s and 1970s

Moving from the political to the literary arena throughout the 1960s and 1970s, feminist critics began examining the traditional literary canon and discovered an array of male dominance and prejudice that supported Beavoir and Millet's assertion that males considered the female "The Other", an unnatural or deviant being. First, stereotypes of women abounded in the canon: Women were sex maniacs, goddesses of beauty, mindless entities, or old spinsters. Second, whereas Dickens, Wordsworth, Hawthorne, Thoreau, Twain, and a host of other male authors were "canonized", few female writers achieved such status. Third, for the most part, the roles of female, fictionalized characters were limited to secondary positions, usually occupying minor parts within the stories or simply reverting to the male's stereotypical images of women. And fourth, female scholars such as Virginia Woolf and Simone de Beavoir were ignored, their writings seldom if ever referred to by the male crafters of the literary canon.

Feminist critics of this era asserted that males who created and enjoyed a place of prominence within the canon assumed that all readers were males. Women reading such works could unconsciously be duped into reading as a male. In addition, because most university professors were males, female students were usually trained to read literature as if they were males. But the feminists of the 1960s and 1970s now postulated the existence of a female reader who was affronted by the male prejudices abounding in the canon. Questions concerning the male or female qualities of literary form, style, voice, and theme became the rallying points for feminist criticism, and throughout the late 1970s books that defined women's writings in feminine terms abounded.

Having highlighted the importance of gender, feminist critics then discovered a body of literary works authored by females that their male counterparts decreed inferior and therefore unworthy to be part of the canon. In America, for example, Kate Chopin's late nineteenth-century novel *The Awakening served* as the archetypal rediscovered feminist text of this period, whereas in England Doris Lessing's *The Golden Notebook* (1962) and in France Monique Wittig's *Les*

Guerilleres (1969) fulfilled these roles. Throughout the universities and in the reading populace, readers turned their attention to historical and current works authored by women. Simultaneously, works that attempted to define the feminine imagination, to categorize and explain female literary history, and to attempt to define the female aesthetic of concept of beauty became the focus of feminist critics.

The ongoing debate concerning definitive answers to these key feminist interests continued throughout the 1980s, as it does today.

Elaine Showalter

The predominant voice of feminist criticism throughout the 1980s is that of Elaine Showalter. In her text A Literature of *Their Own*, Showalter chronicles what she believes to be the three historical phases of evolution in female writing: The feminine phase (1840—1880), the feminist phase (1880—1920), and the female phase (1970—present). During the feminine phase, writers such as Charlotte Bronte, George Eliot, and George Sand accepted the prevailing social constructs of their day concerning the role and therefore the definition of women. Accordingly, these female authors wrote under male pseudonyms, hoping to equal the intellectual and artistic achievements of their male counterparts. During the feminist phase, female authors dramatized the plight of the slighted woman. These authors depicted the harsh and often cruel treatment of female characters at the hands of their more powerful male creations. In the female phase of today, women reject the imitation prominent during the feminine phase and the protest that dominated the feminist phase. According to Showalter, feminist critics now concern themselves with developing a peculiarly female understanding of the female experience in art, including a feminine analysis of literary forms and techniques. Such a task necessarily includes the uncovering of **misogyny** in male texts, a term Showalter uses to describe the male hatred of women.

Showalter asserts that female authors were consciously and therefore deliberately excluded from the literary canon by the male professors who first established the canon itself. Authors such as Susan Warner, E. D. N. Southworth, and Mary E. Wilkins Freeman — by far the most popular authors of the second half of the nineteenth century in American fiction — were not deemed worthy to be included in the canon. Showalter urges that such exclusion of the female voice must be stopped. She coins the term gynocritics to build a female framework for analysis of women's literature to develop new models based on the study of female experience, instead of adapting to male models and theories. Through gynocritics, Showalter hopes to expose the false cultural assumptions of women as depicted in literature. By exposing these inaccurate pictures of women, she hopes to establish women as both readers and writers in their own right.

Showalter's term gynocriticism has now become synonymous with the study of women as writers and provides critics with four models concerning the nature of women's writing that help answer some of the chief concerns of feminist criticism: the biological, linguistic, psychoanalytic, and cultural. Each of Showalter's models is sequential, subsuming and developing the preceding model. The biological emphasizes how the female body marks itself upon a text by providing a host of literary images and a personal, intimate tone. The linguistic model concerns itself with the need for a female discourse. This model investigates the differences between how women and men use language. It asserts that women can and do create a language peculiar to their gender and how this language can be used in their writings. The psychoanalytic model, based on an analysis of the female psyche and how such an analysis affects the writing process, emphasizes the flux and fluidity of female writing as opposed to male rigidity and structure. And the cultural model investigates how the society in which female authors work and function shape women's goals, responses, and points of view.

Geographical Strains of Feminism

Because no one critical theory of writing dominates feminist criticism and few theorists agree on a unifying feminist approach to textual analysis, physical geography plays a great part in determining the major interests of various voices of feminist criticism. Three distinct geographical strains of feminism have thus emerged: American, British, and French. According to Elaine Showalter, American feminism is essentially textual stressing repression; British feminism is essentially Marxist stressing oppression; and French feminism is essentially psychoanalytic stressing repression. All groups attempt to rescue women from being considered the Other.

American feminist critic Annette Kolodny helps set the major concern of American feminism: the restoration of the writings of female authors to the literary canon. Believing that literary history is itself a fiction, Kolodny wishes to restore the history of women so that they themselves can tell "her-story," In order to tell and write her-story, however, women must first find a means to gain their voices in the midst of numerous voices — particularly male-clamoring for attention in society.

Like Kolodny, Sandra M. Gilbert and Susan Gubar, authors of *The Madwoman in the Attic: The Woman Writer and the Nineteenth-Century Literary Imagination* (1979), assert that the male voice has for too long been the dominant one in society. Because males have also had the power of the pen and therefore the press, they have been able to define and create images of women as they so choose in their male texts. According to Gilbert and Gubar, such male power has caused "anxiety of authorship" in women, causing them to fear the act of literary creation itself and the act of writing. Such creation, they fear, will isolate them from society and may even destroy them. Gilbert and Gubar's solution is that women develop a "women's sentence" that would encourage literary autonomy. By inventing such a sentence, a woman can thus sentence a man just as for centuries men have been sentencing women to isolation, anxiety, and literary banishment. In effect, by formulating a woman's sentence, women writers can finally free themselves from being defined by men.

Such a sentence could also free women from being reduced to the stereotypical images that all too often appear in literature. According to Gilbert and Gubar these two major images are "the angel in the house" and the "madwoman in the attic." If a woman is depicted as the angel in the house, she supposedly realizes that her physical and material comforts are gifts from her husband. Her goal in life, therefore, is to please her husband, to attend to his every comfort, and to obey him. Through these selfless acts, she finds the utmost contentment by serving her husband and children. If, perchance, a female character should reject this role, the male critics quickly dub her a monster, a freakish anomaly who is obviously sexually fallen.

Gilbert and Gubar assert that both of these images — the angel and the madwoman — are unrealistic images of women in society. One canonizes and places the woman above the world and the other denigrates and places her below the world. And the message, say Gilbert and Gubar, is clear to all women: If you are not an angel, then you are a monster. Such stereotypical male-created images of women in literature must be uncovered, examined, and transcended if women are to achieve literary autonomy.

Whereas American feminism emphasizes repression, British feminism stresses oppression. Essentially Marxist, British feminism refuses to separate art — literature — and life. Denying the existence of any spiritual reality, British feminists view reading, writing, and publishing as facets of material reality. Being part of material reality, literature, like one's job and one's social activities, is part of a great whole, with each part affecting the other. How women are depicted in life, then, directly affects how they are treated in real life. Particularly in the West, women are exploited not only in literature but also in economic and social conditions. From this perspective, the traditional Western family structure helps to subordinate women, causing them to be economically dependent. Such dependency is then reflected in literature. And it is the job of feminist critics, British feminism maintains, to change this unfair social status of women economically and socially and also in texts. For these feminist critics, the goal of criticism is to change society, not simply critique it.

Believing that women are oppressed both in life and art, French feminism, the third geographical division of present-day feminism, typically stresses the repression of women. As a whole, French feminism is closely associated with the theoretical and practical applications of psychoanalysis. At first, the association with psychoanalysis may be a bit puzzling, for the father of psychoanalysis is Sigmund Freud. Believing that the penis is power, Freud viewed women as incomplete males. All women, he thought, were envious of a male's power as symbolized by the penis. Wanting this power, all women possess penis envy, desiring to gain the male phallus and thereby obtain power. The French psychoanalytic critic Jacques Lacan, however, rescues psychoanalysis from some of Freud's misogynistic theories. (For a detailed explanation of Lacan's theories, see "Jacques Lacan," Chapter 7.) According to Lacan, language, not the phallus, ultimately shapes and structures our conscious and unconscious minds and thus shapes our self-identity. And it is language that ultimately denies women the power of language and therefore the power of literature and writing.

Lacan believes that the human psyches consists of three parts, or what he calls orders: the Imaginary, the Symbolic, and the Real. Each of these orders interacts with the others. From birth to 6 months or so, we function primarily in the Imaginary Order, a preverbal state that contains our wishes, fantasies, and physical images. In this state we are basically sexless, for we are not yet capable of differentiating ourselves from our mothers. Once we successfully pass through the Oedipal crisis, we depart from a biological language into a socialized language into the second of the Lacanian orders: the Symbolic Order. Unfortunately, in this Order the male is socialized into the dominant discourse whereas the female is socialized into a subordinated language. Upon entering this Order, the father becomes the dominant image, or the law. In this stage of our psychic development, both the male and the female fear castration at the hands of the father. For the male, castration means obeying and becoming like the father while simultaneously repressing the Imaginary Order that is most closely associated with the female body. The Imaginary Order, with its pre-Oedipal male desires, becomes a direct threat for the male to the third Lacanian Order, the Real Order, or the actual world as perceived by the individual. Similarly, for the female, entrance into the Symbolic Order means submission to law of the father. Such submission means subservience to the male. Being socialized into a subordinated language, the female becomes a second-class citizen. Because language, for Lacan, is a psychological, not biological, construct, women can learn the dominant discourse of both the Symbolic and the Real Orders and become tools of social change.

Other French feminists, such as Julia Kristeva and Hélène Cixous, further develop and apply Lacan's theories to their own form of feminist criticism. Kristeva, for example, posits that the Imaginary Order is characterized by a continuous flow of fluidity or rhythm, which she calls chora. Upon entering the Symbolic Order, both males and females are separated from the chora and repress the feelings of fluidity and rhythm. Similar to a Freudian slip whereby an unconscious thought breaks through the conscious mind, the chora can break through into the Real Order and disturb the male-dominant discourse. On the other hand, Hélène Cixous explores an entirely different mode of discourse that arises from the Imaginary, not the Symbolic, Order. Cixous maintains that there exists a particular kind of female writing that she calls l'écriture féminine. Characterized by fluidity, this particularly feminine discourse, when fully explored, transforms the social and cultural structures within literature.

In addition to the three geographical strains of feminism, other significant feminist strains such as black and lesbian feminism transcend geographical boundaries. For example, Alice Walker, a spokesperson for black feminism, refuses to be associated with traditional feminist criticism and with the term *feminist* itself. She prefers to be called a womanist. On the other hand, French lesbian feminist Monique Wittig rejects the label *woman*, asserting that this term does not include lesbians. She prefers to be called a lesbian, believing that this nomenclature will allow women to have the right and space to name and redefine themselves.

No matter what they emphasize in theory, however, all feminist critics assert that they are on a journey of self-discovery that will lead them to a better understanding of themselves. And once they understand and then define themselves as women, they believe they will be able to change their world.

8.3   ASSUMPTIONS

To the onlooker, feminist theory and practice appear to be a diffuse, loosely connected body of criticism that is more divided than unified, housing more internal, disagreements than unity among its adherents than are found in perhaps any other approach to literary analysis. Because it claims no ultimate spokesperson but many different voices, there is not one but a variety of feminist theories. Behind all these seemingly contradictory voices and theories, however, is a set of principles that unite this criticism.

Although feminist critics' ideas concerning the directions of their criticism vary, feminists possess a collective identity: They are women (and some men) who are struggling to discover who they are, how they arrived at their present situation, and where they are going. In their search, they value differing opinions, thereby giving significance to the personal rather than a group of people or a codified and authoritative collection of texts. Their search, they assert, is political, for their aim is to change the world in which they live, a world that they maintain must be changed if all individuals, all cultures, all subcultures, and both sexes are to be valued as creative, rational people who can all contribute to their societies and their world. Such a revisionist, revolutionary, and ideological stance seeks to understand the place of women in society and to analyze all aspects that affect women as writers and their writings in what feminists believe is a male-dominated world. In this masculine world, the feminists declare that it is man who defines what it means to be human, not woman. Because a woman is not a man, she has become the other, the not-male. Man is the subject, the one who defines meaning; woman is the object, having her existence defined and determined by the male. The man is therefore the significant figure in the male/female relationship and the woman is subordinate.

Such female insignificance did not first appear in the twentieth century, declare feminists such as Jane Tompkins. Long before the existence of our present-day, male-dominated world, most societies have been governed by males. These patriarchal societies, say the feminists, have simply passed down their erroneous beliefs from generation to generation, culminating with the predominant Western assumption that women are less than, not equal to, men. Arbitrarily using the male as the standard, these societies apparently agree with Aristotle's assertion that the female is determined to be female because they certain lack of qualities. Or they support St. Thomas Aquinas' conviction that all women are simply imperfect men. And some still believe that Freud is correct when he argues that female sexuality is based on a lack of a penis, the male sexual organ.

According to feminist critics, by defining the female in relation to the male while simultaneously decreeing the superiority of the male, Western and other cultures have decreed that the female, by nature, is inferior. Once Western culture consciously or unconsciously assimilated this belief into its social structures and allowed it to permeate all levels of its society, females became the oppressed people, inferiors who must be suppressed lest humankind fail to reach its potential.

Feminist critics want to show humankind the errors of such a way of thinking. Women, they declare, are people in their own right; they are not incomplete or inferior men. Despite how often literature and society fictionalize and stereotype women as angels, barmaids, bitches, whores, brainless housewives, or old maids, women must break free from such oppression and define themselves. No longer, assert these critics, can they allow their male-dominated society to define and articulate their roles, values, and opinions.

To free themselves from such oppression, say feminist critics, women must analyze and challenge the established literary canon that has helped shape the images of female inferiority and oppression ingrained in our culture. Women must create an atmosphere that is less oppressive by contesting the long-held patriarchal assumptions concerning their sex. Because no female Aristotle has articulated a philosophy or coined a battle cry for women's equality, all women must muster a variety of resources to clarify, assert, and implement their beliefs. By re-examining the established literary canon, validating what it means to be a woman, and involving themselves in literary theory and its multiple approaches to a text, women can legitimize their responses to texts written by both males and females, their own writings, and their political, economic, and social positions in their culture.

8.4 METHODOLOGY

Just as there is no single feminist theory but many theories, so there exists not one but a variety of feminist approaches to a text. Wanting to challenge and change Western culture's assumption that males are superior to females and therefore are better thinkers, more rational, more serious, and more reflective than women, feminist critics may begin their debunking of male superiority by exposing stereotypes of women found throughout the literary canon. Women, they argue, cannot be simply depicted and classified as either angels or demons, saints or whores, or brainless housewives or eccentric spinsters. Such characterizations must be identified and, challenged throughout the canon, and such abuse of women by male authors must be acknowledged as ways men have consciously or unconsciously demeaned, devalued, and demoralized women.

Having identified the antifeminist characterization that occurs in many texts, the feminist critic may then turn to either the American, English, or a non-Western literary canon, seeking to discover works written by women. This is usually a difficult task because males have authored the majority of texts. The American literary canon, for example, is decidedly male. With the works of Hawthorne, Melville, Poe, and other male notables filling the pages of the canon, little or no room is allowed for the writings of Susan Warner, E. D. N. Southwick, and Mary E. Wilkins Freeman, three of the most widely read authors in nineteenth-century America. Feminists assert that these female authors must be "rediscovered" by having their works republished and reevaluated. When complete, this rediscovery will reveal a valuable body of female authors who share common themes, histories, and often writing styles.

Other feminist critics suggest that we reread the canonized works of male authors from a woman's point of view. Such an analysis is possible, they maintain, by developing a uniquely female consciousness based on female experience rather than the traditional male theories of reading, writing, and critiquing. Known as gynocriticism, this female model of literary analysis offers four areas of investigation:

Images of the female body as presented in a text. Such an anatomical study, for example, would highlight how various parts or the female body such as the uterus and breasts often become significant images in works authored by women.

Female language. Such a concern centers on the differences between male and female language. Because we live in patriarchal societies, would it be fair to assume, wonder feminists, that our language is also male–dominated? Do women speak or write differently from men? Although there is little consensus in the answers to these questions, critics interested in this kind of investigation analyze grammatical constructions, recurring themes, and other linguistic elements.

The female psyche and its relationship to the writing process. Such an analysis applies the psychological works of Freud and Lacan to a text and shows how the physical and psychological development of the female evidences itself in the writing process through penis envy, the Oedipus complex, and other psychological stages.

Culture. By analyzing cultural forces (such as the importance and value of women's roles in a given society), critics who emphasize this area of study investigate how society shapes a woman's understanding of herself, her society, and her world.

8.5 QUESTIONS FOR ANALYSIS

Whatever method of feminist criticism we choose to apply to a text, we can begin textual analysis by asking some general questions.

When we get a text, should we pay attention to the gender of the author

If we get a fiction, can you make sure the identity of the narrator?

What types of roles do women have in the text?

What role the female characters plays in the text? As the heroine or secondary, minor characters?

Is there any stereotypical characterizations of women character created in the text?

What are the attitudes toward women images held by the male characters?

What is the author's attitude toward women in society?

Why should we know the background of the author ?

Is feminine imagery used? If so, what is the significance of such imagery?

Do the female characters in the text show her different way from the male characters?

In your investigation, compare the frequency of speech for the male characters with the frequency of speech for the female characters.

By asking any or all of these questions of a text, we can begin our journey in feminist criticism while helping ourselves to understand better the world in which we live.

REFERENCES

[1]DIAMOND A, EDWARDS L, et al. The Authority of Experience: Essays in Feminist Criticism[M]. Amherst: University of Massachusetts Press, 1977.

[2]ADRIENNE R. On Lies, Secrets, and Silence: Selected Prose 1966-1978[M]. London: Virago, 1980.

[3]ALICE J, PAUL S, et al. Men in Feminism[M]. New York: Methuen, 1987.

[4]ALICE W. Living by the Word: Selected Writings, 1973-1987[M]. New York: Harcourt Brace Jovanovich, 1988.

[5]ANNETTE K. The Lay of the Land. Metaphor as Experience in American Life and Letters[M]. Chapel Hill:

University of North Carolina Press,1975.

[6]ANNETTE K. Some Notes on Defining a "Feminist Literary Criticism"[J]. Critical Inquiry.1975: 75-92.

[7]ANNETTE K. Dancing Through the Minefield: Some Observations on the Theory, Practice, and Politics of a Feminist Literary Criticism[J]. Feminist Studies 6.1(1980): 1-25.

[8]ANN R J. "Writing the Body: Toward an Understanding of I'Ecrittre Féminine" in The New Feminist Criticism: Essays on Women, Literature, and Theory[M]. Ed. ELAINE S. New York: Pantheon, 1985, 361-77.

[9]CATHERINE B, JANE M, eds. "The Feminist Reader" in Essays in Gender and the Politics of Literary Criticism[M] . London: Macmillan, 1989.

[10]CHRIS W. Feminist Practice and Poststructuralist Theory[M]. Oxford: Basil Blackwell, 1987.

[11]CORA K. "Radical Feminism and Literature: Rethinking Millett's Sexual Politics" in Feminist Literary Criticism[M]. Ed. MARY E. New York: Longman, 1991.

[12]DALE M B. Feminist Dialogics: A Theory of Failed Community[M]. Albany: State University of New York Press, 1988.

[13]ELAINE M, ISABELLE D C, eds. New French Feminisms[M]. New York: Schocken, 1981.

[14]ELAINE S. A Literature of Their Own: British Women Novelists from Brontë to Lessing[M]. Princeton: Princeton University Press,1977.

[15]ELAINE S. New Feminist Criticism: Essays on Women, Literature, Theory[M]. New York: Pantheon, 1985.

[16]ELAINE S. Sexual Anarchy: Gender and Culture at the Fin de Siècle[M]. New York: Viking-Penguin, 1990.

[17]ELIZABETH A, ed. Writing and Sexual Difference[M]. Chicago: University of Chicago Press, 1982.

[18]ELIZABETH A, EMILY K. Abel. The Signs Reader: Women, Gender & Scholarship. Introduction[M]. Chicago: University of Chicago Press, 1983.

[19]ELIZABETH A. F, PATROCINIO S, eds. Gender and Reading: Essays on Readers, Texts, and Contexts[M]. Baltimore: Johns Hopkins University Press, 1986.

[20]ELIZABETH M. Crossing the Double-Cross: The Practice of Feminist Criticism[M]. Chapel Hill: University of North Carolina Press, 1986.

[21]ELIZABETH M. (EX)Tensions: Re-Figuring Feminist Criticism[M]. Urbana: University of Illinois Press, 1990.

[22]FRANCETTE P. "The Impossible Referent: Representations of the Androgyne" in Formations of Fantasy[M]. London: Methuen, 198:62-84.

[23]GAYATRI C S. In Other Words: Essays in Cultural Politics[M]. New York: Methuen, 1987.

[24]GAYLE G, COPPELIA K, eds. "Making a Difference" in Feminist Literary Criticism[M]. New York: Methuen, 1985.

[25]GLORIA A, ed. Making Face, Making Soul---Haciendo Caras---Creative and Critical Perspectives of Women of Color[M]. San Francisco: Aunte Lute Foundation Books, 1990.

[26]Hazel V C. Reconstructing Womanhood: The Emergence of the Afro-American Woman Novelist[M]. New York: Oxford University Press, 1987.

[27]HÉLÉNE C. The Character of "Character"[J]. New Literary History 1974: 383-402.

[28]HÉLÉNE C. The Laugh of the Medusa[J]. Trans. KEITH C and PAULA C. Signs 1976: 875-94.

[29]HÉLÉNE C. Castration or Decapitation? [J]. Trans. ANNETTE K. Signs 1981: 41-55.

[30]HÉLÉNE C. Readings: The Poetics of Blanchot, Joyce, Kafka, Kleist, Lispector and Tsvetayeva[M]. Hempstead: Harvester Wheatsheaf, 1992.

[31]HÉLÉNE C, CATHERINE C. The Newly Born Woman[M]. Paris: Union Génèrale d' Editions, 1975.

[32]HESTER E. Contemporary Feminist Thought[M]. London: Unwin, 1984.

[33]HESTER E, ALICE J, eds. The Future of Difference[M]. Boston: G.K. Hall, 1980.

[34]JANE G. The Daughter's Seduction: Feminism and Psychoanalysis[M]. Ithaca: Cornell University Press, 1982.

[35]JANET T. Feminist Literary History[M]. New York: Routledge, 1988.

[36]JANET T. Feminist Literary Theory: A Defence[M]. Oxford: Polity, 1988.

[37]JEAN W. Reconstructing Desire: The Role of the Unconscious in Women's Reading and Writing[M]. Chapel Hill: University of North Carolina Press, 1990.

[38]JOSEPHINE D, ed. Feminist Literary Criticism: Explorations in Theory[M]. Lexington: Kentucky University Press, 1975.

[39]JUDITH F. The Resisting Reader: A Feminist Approach to American Fiction[M]. Bloomington: Indiana University Press, 1978.

[40]JUDITH N, DEBORAH R, ed al. "Feminist Criticism and Social Change" in Set Class and Race in Literature and Culture[M]. New York: Methuen, 1985.

[41]JULIA K. Desire in Language: A Semiotic Approach to Literature and Art. Trans. THOMAS G, ALICE J, LEON S R. Ed. LEON S R. New York: Columbia University Press, 1980.

[42]KATE M. Sexual Politics[M]. New York: Doubleday, 1970.

[43]K JAY, J GLASGOW, eds. Lesbian Texts and Contexts: Radical Revisions[M]. New York: New York University Press, 1986.

[44]K K RUTHVEN. Feminist Literary Studies: An Introduction[M]. New York: Cambridge University Press, 1984.

[45]LEE E, ARLYN D, eds. The Authority of Experience: Essays in Feminist Criticism[M]. Amherst: University of Massachusetts Press, 1977.

[46]LINDA J N. Feminism/Postmodernism[M]. New York: Routledge, 1990.

[47]MAGGIE H, ed. Feminisms: A Reader[M]. Hemel Hempstead: Harvester Wheatsheaf, 1992.

[48]MARGARET W. Luce Irigaray: Philosophy in the Feminine[M]. London: Routledge, 1991.

[49]MARILYN R S, SUSAN RVD, et al. Women's Place in the Academy: Transforming the Liberal Arts Curriculum[M]. Totowa: Rowman & Allanheld, 1985.

[50]MARY E. Thinking About Women[M]. New York: Harcourt, 1968.

[51]MARY E, ed. Feminist Literary Theory: A Reader[M]. Oxford: Basil Blackwell, 1996.

[52]MARY E, ed. Feminist Literary Criticism[M]. New York: Longman, 1991.

[53]MARY S S. Gender and the Writer's Imagination: From Cooper to Wharton[M]. Lexington: University Press of Kentucky, 1987.

[54]MARY W. A Vindication of the Rights of Women[M]. Harmonds worth: Penguin Books, 1975.

[55]MONIQUE W. Les Guerilleres[M]. Trans. DAVID L V. New York: Avon, 1973.

[56]NINA A. Communities of Women: An Idea in Fiction[M]. Cambridge: Harvard University Press, 1978.

[57]NINA B. Women's Fiction: A Guide to Novels by and About Women in America, 1820-1870[M]. Ithaca: Cornell University Press, 1978.

[58]PATRICIA W. Feminine Fictions: Revisiting the Postmodern[M]. New York: Routledge, 1989.

[59]RALPH C, ed. Feminist Directions[J]. New Literary History: A Journal of Theory and Interpretation.

[60]ROBYN R W, DIANE P H, eds. Feminisms: An Anthology of Literary Theory and Criticism[M]. Basingstoke: Macmillan, 1992.

[61]ROSEMARIE T. Feminist Thought: A Comprehensive Introduction[M]. Boulder: Westview, 1989.

[62]ROWENA F. Feminist Criticism: The Common Pursuit[J]. New Literary History: 51-62.

[63]SALLY M, ed. New Lesbian Criticism: Literary and Cultural Readings[M]. Brighton: Harvester Press, 1987.

[64]SANDRA M G, SUSAN G. The Madwoman in the Attic: The Woman Writer and the Nineteenth-Century

Literary Imagination[M]. New Haven: Yale University Press, 1979.

[65]SANDRA M G, SUSAN G. A Classroom Guide to Accompany the Norton Anthology of Literature by Women[M]. New York: Norton, 1985.

[66]SANDRA M G, SUSAN G. No Man's Land: The Place of the Woman Writer in the Twentieth Century. Vol. 1, The War of the Words[M]. New Haven: Yale University Press, 1988.

[67]SANDRA M G, SUSAN G. No Man's Land: The Place of the Woman Writer in the Twentieth Century. Vol. 2, Sex changes[M]. New Haven: Yale University Press, 1988.

[68]SHOSHANA F. Rereading Femininity[J]. Yale French Studies 1981: 19-44.

[69]SIMONE D B. The Second Sex[M]. 1949. Ed. and Trans. H. M. PARSHLEY. New York: Modern Library, 1952.

[70]SUSAN R S. "(Re)writing the Body: The Politics and Poetics of Female Erotocism" in The Female Body in Western Culture[M]. Cambridge: Harvard University Press, 1986, 7-29.

[71]VERENA A C. Hélène Cixous[M]. Hemel Hempstead: Harvester Wheatsheaf, 1992.

[72]VIRGINIA W. A Room of One's Own[M]. London: Hogarth, 1929; London: Grafton, 1987.

[73]VIRGINIA W. Collected Essays[M]. London: Hogarth, 1966.

[74]VIRGINIA W. Women and Writing[M]. London: Women's Press, 1979.

CHAPTER IX CULTURAL POETICS OR NEW HISTORICISM

I walked along the Thames river side, coming across Shakespeare, John Dryden and Bacon, they tell me the greatness of Renaissance and narrate the majestic and glory stories about humanism. All of a sudden, I was swept to the sea, a small cockle shell came into my sight, Robinson Crusoe came to me, giving me his diary on voyage. His drift and wandering in the isolated island impressed me so deeply. I read it and lost myself. And then, a beautiful lady comes up to me, is she Jane Austen? Would she take me out of the loneliness and fly with Keat's nightingale's song to her Mansfield park to feel the ease life at a small county, to feel her sense and sensibility? Is it a dream or reality?

9.1   INTRODUCTION

During the 1940s,1950s, and 1960s, New Criticism, or formalism, was the dominant approach to literary analysis. At this time René Wellek and Austin Warren's text *Theory of Literature* became the Bible of hermeneutics, focusing the interpretive process on the text itself rather than historical, authorial, or reader concerns.

During this high tide of formalism, it would have been common to hear a college lecture like the following in a literature classroom.

9.1.1   A NEW CRITICAL LECTURE

Today, we will quickly review what we learned about Elizabethan beliefs from our last lecture so that we can apply this knowledge to our understanding of Shakespeare's tragedies. As you remember, the Elizabethans believed in the interconnectedness of all life. Having created everything. God imposed on creation a cosmic order. At all costs, this cosmic order was not to be upset. Any element of the created universe that portended change in this order, such as a violent storm, eclipses of the sun or moon, or even disobedient children within the family structure suggested chaos that could lead to anarchy and the destruction of the entire earth. Nothing, believed the Elizabethans, should break any link in this Great Chain of Being, the name given to this created cosmic order. With God and the angels in their place, with the King governing his obedient people in their places, and the animals being subdued and used by humankind in theirs, all would be right in the world and operate as ordained by God.

Having gained an understanding of the Elizabethan worldview, let's turn to Act I, Scene ii, lines 101-12 of *King Lear*. You will recall that in this scene Edmund, the illegitimate son of the Duke of Gloucester, has persuaded the Duke that Edgar, the Duke's legitimate son and heir to the dukedom, wants his father dead so that he may inherit the Duke's title, lands, and wealth. Believing his natural son has betrayed both him and Edmund, the Duke says, 'These late eclipses in the sun and moon portend no good to us. Though the wisdom of nature can reason it thus and thus, yet nature finds itself scourged by the sequent effects. Love cools, friendship falls off, brothers divide.'

What we see in these lines, class, is the Elizabethan worldview in operation, The Duke obviously believes in the inter relatedness of the created cosmic order and the concept of the Great Chain of Being. The significance of the eclipses of the sun and moon therefore rests in their representing change and chaos. Because the Duke believes that the macrocosm (the universe) directly affects the microcosm (the world of humanity on earth), he blames these natural occurrences (the eclipses) for interfering in familial relationships and destroying love between brothers, between father and daughters (King Lear having already banished his most beloved daughter, Cordelia), and between King and servant (Kent, King Lear's loyal courtier also having being expelled from the kingdom).

9.2   OLD HISTORICISM

In this typical formalist lecture, the professor's method of literary analysis represents a good example of both New Criticism and what is known today as the old historicism. In this methodology, history serves as a background to literature. Of primary importance is the text, the art object itself. The historical background of the text is only secondarily important, for it is the aesthetic object — the text — that mirrors the history of its times. The historical context serves only to shed light on the object of primary concern, the text.

Underlying such a methodology is a view of history that declares that history, as written, is an accurate view of what really occurred. Such a view assumes that historians are able to write objectively about any given historical time period and are able to state definitively the truth about that era. Through various means of historical analysis, historians are seemingly capable of discovering the mindset, the worldview, or the beliefs of any group of people. For example, when the professor in our hypothetical lecture states the beliefs of the Elizabethans at the beginning of the lecture, he or she is articulating the Elizabethan worldview — the unified set of presuppositions or assumptions that all Elizabethans supposedly held concerning their world. By applying these assertions to the Elizabethan text *King Lear*, the professor believes he or she can formulate a more accurate interpretation of the play than if the teacher did not know the play's historical context.

9.3   THE NEW HISTORICISM

That historians can articulate a unified and internally consistent worldview of any given people, country, or time period and can reconstruct an accurate and objective picture of any historical event is a key assumption that cultural poetics, one of the most recent approaches to literary analysis, challenges. Appearing as an alternative approach to textual interpretation in the 1970s and early 1980s, cultural poetics — often called New Historicism in America and cultural materialism in Great Britain — declares all history is subjective, written by people whose personal biases affect their interpretations of the past. History, asserts cultural poetics, can never provide us with the truth or give us a totally accurate picture of past events or the worldview of a group of people. Disavowing the old historicism's autonomous view of history, cultural poetics declares that history is one of many **discourses** or ways of seeing and thinking about the world. By highlighting and viewing history as one of many equally important discourses such as sociology and politics and by closely examining how all discourses (including that of textual analysis itself) affect a text's interpretation, cultural poetics or New Historicism claims to provide its adherents with a practice of literary analysis that highlights the interrelatedness of all human activities, admits its own prejudices, and gives a more complete understanding of a text than does the old historicism and other interpretive approaches.

9.3.1   Historical Development

Although the assumptions of cultural poetics and its accompanying practices have been used by critics for several decades, the beginning of New Historicism dates to 1979-80 with the publication of several essays and texts such as *Improvisation and Power* and *Renaissance*

Self-Fashioning, by Renaissance scholar Stephen Greenblatt, and a variety of works by Louis Montrose, Jonathan Dollimore, and others. Wishing to remain open to differing politics, theories, and ideologies, these critics share a similar set of concerns, not a codified theory or school of criticism. Of chief interest is their shared view that from the mid-1800s to the middle of the twentieth century historical methods of literary analysis were erroneous. During this time many scholars believed that history served as background information for textual analysis and that historians were able to objectively reproduce a given historical period and state " how it really was". In disclaiming these assumptions of old historicism and formulating its own theories of history and interpretive analysis, cultural poetics was first and aptly named New Historicism by one of its chief proponents, Stephen Greenblatt, in the introduction to a collection of Renaissance essays in a 1982 volume of the journal Genre. Because of its broader concerns with culture, history, literature, and a host of other factors that help determine a text's meaning, Greenblatt and his followers now believe that the term cultural poetics more aptly describes their approach to textual analysis than does New Historicism.

According to Stephen Greenblatt, cultural poetics was in large part shaped by the institutional character of American literary criticism during the 1960s and 1970s. During this time, one of the dominating influences in literary criticism was formalism, or New Criticism, with its accompanying theoretical assumptions and practical methodology. For example, during Greenblatt's graduate studies at Yale — a place he has since called the cathedral of High Church New Criticism — Greenblatt himself mastered New Critical principles. New Critical scholars, writers, and critics such as T. S. Eliot, Alien Tate, John Crowe Ranson, Cleanth Brooks, and Robert Penn Warren were revered and their methodology widely practiced throughout the country.

Aided early in its development by the publication and wide use of Cleanth Brooks and Robert Penn Warren's textbook *Understanding Poetry* (1939), New Criticism presented scholars and teachers a workable and teachable methodology for interpreting texts. From a theoretical perspective, New Criticism regards a literary text as an artifact or object with an existence of its own, independent of and not necessarily related to its author, its readers, the historical time it depicts, or the historical period in which it was written. From this viewpoint, a text's meaning emerges when readers scrutinize it and it alone. Such a close scrutiny results, the New Critics maintain, in perceiving a text as an organic whole wherein all parts fit together and support one overarching theme. A poem, a play, or a story, then, is highly structured and contains its meaning in itself and reveals that meaning to critic-reader who examines it on its own terms by applying a rigorous and systematic methodology. Such an analysis is particularly rewarding, say the New Critics, for literature offers a unique kind of knowledge that presents us with the deepest truths related to humanity, truths that science is unable to disclose.

What New Criticism did not provide for Greenblatt and other critics was attempt to understand literature from a historical perspective. From a New Critical perspective, the text was what mattered, not its historical context. Consideration of any given text as the result any historical phenomenon was devalued or silenced. In addition, Greenblatt felt that questions about the nature and definition of literature were not encouraged. He and other critics wished to discuss how literature was formed, whose interest it served, and what the term *literature* really meant. Do contemporary issues and the cultural milieu of the times operate together to create literature, they wondered, or is literature simply an art form that will always be with us?

Cultural poetics, then, began to develop as a direct result of New Criticism's dominance of literary criticism and its response or lack thereof to questions about the nature, definition, and function of literature itself. While Greenblatt was asking a different set of literary questions, a variety of new critical theories and theorists appeared on the literary scene. Deconstruction, Marxism, feminism, and Lacanian psychoanalysis also began to challenge the assumptions of New Criticism. Rejecting New Criticism's claim that the meaning of a text can be found, for the most part, in the text alone, these poststructural theories had been developing a variety of theoretical positions concerning the nature of the reading process, the part of the reader plays in that process, and the definition of a text or the actual work of art. It is among this cacophony of voices that cultural poetics arose.

Upon reading sociological and cultural studies by Michel Foucault, Greenblatt and other critics admired and emulated Foucault's tireless questioning of the nature of literature, history, culture, and society; like Foucault, they refused to accept the traditional well-worn answers. From the Marxist scholars (Georg Lukács, Walter Benjamin, Raymond Williams, and others) they learned that history is shaped by the people who live it, and they accepted the Marxist idea of the interconnectedness of all life. What we do with our hands and how we make our money does indeed affect how and what we think, they believed. But unlike many of the post-structualist theories, especially deconstruction, cultural poetics struggled to find a way out of undecidability or aporia, about the nature of reality and the interpretation of a text. Without denying that many factors affect the writing, production, and publication of texts, New Historicists sought to move beyond undecidability rather than simply assert that a text has many possible meanings. In so doing, they challenged the assumptions of the old historicism that presupposed that historians could actually write an objective history of any situation, they redefined the meaning of a text, and they asserted that all critics must acknowledge and openly declare their own biases.

Throughout the 1980s and 1990s, critics such as Catherine Gallagher, Jonathan Dollimore, Jerome McGann, Stephen Greenblatt, and many others voiced their concerns that the study of literature and its relationship to history has been too narrow. Viewing a text as culture in action, these critics blur the distinction between an artistic production and any other kind of social production or event. These cultural poetics critics want us to see that the publication of Swift's "A Modest Proposal" is a political act, for example, while nothing that the ceremony surrounding the inauguration of a United States president is an aesthetic event with all the trappings of symbolism and structure found in any poem. Many similar examples of their critical practices can be found in their chief public voices, the journal representations.

However, no consensus can be found among those who espouse the theory and practice of cultural poetics about theories of art, terminology, and practical methods of interpretation. Cultural poetics, like all other approaches to literary analysis, is best considered a practice of literary interpretation that is still in process, one that is continually redefining and fine tuning its purposes, philosophy, and practices while gaining new followers. Currently, its followers can be divided into two main branches: Cultural materialists and New Historicists. Members of both groups continue to call for a reawakening of our historical consciousness, to declare that history and literature must be analyzed together, to place all texts in their appropriate contexts, and to understand that while we are learning about different societies that provide the historical context for various texts, we are simultaneously learning about ourselves, our own habits, and our own beliefs.

9.3.2 Cultural Materialism

Cultural materialism, the British branch of cultural poetics, is openly Marxist in its theories and overtly political and cultural in its aims. It finds its ideological roots in the writings of Marxist critics Louis Althusser and Raymond Williams. Believing that literature can serve as an agent of change in today's world, cultural materialists that any culture's hegemony is basically unstable. For literature to produce change, a critic must therefore read the works of the established canon "against the grain". By so doing, the critic will expose the political unconscious of the text and help debunk the social and political myths created by the bourgeoisie.

New Historicism

The American branch of cultural poetics is often called New Historicism. Its founding father Stephen Greenblatt, along with a host of other scholars, hold that one's culture permeates both texts and critics. Just as all of society is intricately interwoven, so are critics and texts, both with each other and with the culture in which the critics live and the texts are produced. Because all critics are influenced by the culture in which they live, New Historicists believe that they cannot escape public and private cultural influences. Each critic therefore arrives at a unique interpretation of a text. Less overtly political than its British counterpart, New Historicism continues to be refined and redefined by its many practitioners.

9.4   ASSUMPTIONS

Like other poststructuralist practices, cultural poetics begins by challenging the long-held belief that a text is an autonomous work of art that contains all elements necessary to arrive at a supposedly correct interpretation. Disavowing the old historical assumption that a text simply reflects its historical context — the mimetic view of art and history — and that such historical information provides an interesting and sometimes useful backdrop for literary analysis, cultural poetics redirects our attention to a series of philosophical and practical concerns that it believes will highlight the complex interconnectedness of all human activities. For example, it redefines the definition of a text and of history while simultaneously redefining the relationship between a text and history. Unlike the old historicism, New Historicism asserts that there is an intricate connection between an aesthetic object (a text or any work of art) and society while denying that a text can be evaluated in isolation from its cultural context. It declares that we know the societal concerns of the author, the historical times evidenced in the work, and other cultural elements exhibited in the text before we can devise a valid interpretation. This new approach to textual analysis questions the very act of how we can arrive at meaning for any human activity, such as a text, social event, long-held tradition, or political art.

Michel Foucault

Cultural poetics finds the basis for such concerns and a coherent body of assumptions in the writings of the twentieth-century French archaeologist, historian, and philosopher Michel Foucault. Foucault begins his rather complex and sometimes paradoxical theoretical structure by redefining the concept of history. Unlike many past historians, Foucault declares that history is not linear, for it does not have a definite beginning, middle, and end, nor is it necessarily teleological, purposefully going forward toward some known end. Nor can it be explained as a series of causes and effects that are controlled by some mysterious destiny or an all-powerful deity. For Foucault, history is the complex interrelationship of a variety of discourses or the various ways — artistic, social, political — that people think and talk about their world. How these discourses interact in any given historical period is not random, but dependent on a unifying principle or pattern. Foucault calls the episteme: Through language and thought, each period in history develops its own perceptions of the nature of reality (or what it defines as truth), and sets up its own acceptable and unacceptable standards of behavior, in addition to its criteria for judging what it deems good or bad, and what people articulate, protect, and defend the yardstick whereby all established truths, values, or actions are deemed acceptable.

To unearth the episteme of any given historical period, Foucault borrows techniques and terminology from archaeology. Just as an archaeologist must slowly and meticulously dig through various layers of earth to uncover the symbolic treasures of the past, historians must expose each layer of discourse that comes together to shape a people's episteme. And just as an archaeologist must date each finding and then piece together the artifacts that define and help explain that culture, so must the historian piece together the various discourse and the interconnections among them and with non-discursive practices (any cultural institution, such as a form of government) that will assist in articulating the epistemology.

Seen from this point of view, history is a form of power. Because each era or people develops its own epistemology, in actuality the epistemology controls how that era or group of people views reality. History, then, becomes the study and unearthing of a vast, complex web of interconnecting forces that ultimately determines what takes place in each culture or society.

Why or how epistemology change from one historical period to another is unclear. That they change seemingly without warning is certain. Such a change occurred at the beginning of the nineteenth century — the change from the Age of Reason to romanticism, for example —

and initiated a new epistemology. In this new historical era a variety of different relationships developed among discourses that had not evolved or did exist and were deemed, unacceptable in the previous historical period. Foucault asserts that such radical and abrupt changes that cause breaks from one epistemology to another are neither good nor bad, valid nor invalid. Like the discourses that help produce them, different epistemes exist in their own right; they are neither moral nor immoral, but amoral.

According to Foucault, historians must realize that they influenced and prejudiced by the episodes in which they live. Because their thoughts, customs, habits, and other actions are colored by their own epistemes, historians must realize that they can never be totally objective about their own or any other historical period. To be a historian means one must be able to confront and articulate one's own set of biases before examining the various discourses or material evidence of past events that make up an epistemology of any given period. Such an archaeological uncovering of the various discourses. Foucault believes, will not unearth a monological view of an epistemology that presupposes a single, overarching political vision or design, but a set of inconsistent, irregular, and often contradictory discourses that will explain the development of the episteme, including what elements were accepted, changed, or rejected to form the "truth" and set the acceptable standards for that era.

Clifford Geertz

In addition to borrowing many of its ideas from Foucault, cultural poetics also uses theories and methodologies from cultural anthropologists such as Clifford Geertz. Geertz believes that there is no human nature is innate quality, has nothing with culture, man is social animal which is determined that he is defined by a set of control mechanisms — plans, norms, rules, instructions for the governing of behavior. Each person, then, must be viewed as a cultural production. How each person views society is always unique, for there exists what Geertz calls an "information gap" between what our body tells us and what we have to know in society.

Further Reference

Many terms lying beyond the scope of this dictionary are explained in other reference books, which are listed below under subject headings.

General

J. A. Cuddon. *A Dictionary of Literary Terms* (1977) has extensive lists of examples, and an unusually detailed coverage of Hispanic and Slavic verse-forms. C. Hugh Holman and William Harmon. *A Handbook to Literature* (1986) features longer entries on literary periods, with chronologies and lists of Nobel and Pulitzer prize-winners. Many rather general topics such as *art, belief, and language* are discussed in Roger Fowler (ed.), *A Dictionary of Modern Critical* Terms. A careful historical investigation into shifting senses of terms like creative, culture, and ideology is conducted in Raymond Williams, *Keywords* (1976).

Poetry

Many of the more obscure poetic terms are covered by Cuddon and by Holman and Harmon (see above). The most extensive coverage of poetic terminology is to be found in Alex Preminger (ed.), *Princeton Encyclopedia of Poetry and Poetics*. A shorter selection of entries from this work has been published as the *Princeton Handbook of Poetic Terms* (1986). Some terms not found in the Princeton volume are explained in Jack Myers and Michael Simms, *Longman Dictionary and Handbook of Poetry* (1985).

Drama

A helpful guide to dramatic terms is Terry Hodgson, The *Batsford Dictionary of Drama* (1988). Some terms are also explained in Phyllis Hartnoll (ed.), *The Oxford Companion to the Theatre*.

Rhetoric

A convenient guide is Richard A. Lanham. A Handlist of Rhetorical Terms (1968). Many of the major rhetorical terms sure discussed in more details for every practitioner, for no one discourse or method or critic can reveal the truth about any social production in isolation from other discourses.

Because cultural poetics critics view an aesthetic work as a social production, a text's meaning resides for them in the cultural system composed of the interlocking discourses of the author, text, and reader. To unlock textual meaning, a cultural poetics critic investigates three areas of concern: The life of the author, the social rules and dictates found within a text, and a reflection of a work's historical situation as evidenced in the text. Because an actual person authors a text, his or her actions and beliefs reflect both individual concerns and those of the author's society and are therefore essential elements of the text itself. In addition, the standard of behavior as reflected in a society's rules of decorum must also be investigated because these behavioral codes simultaneously helped shape and were shaped by the text. And the text must also be viewed as an artistic work that reflects on these behavioral social codes. To begin to understand a text's significance and to realize the complex social structure of which it is a part, cultural poetics critics declare that all three areas of concern must be investigated. If one area is, ignored, the risk of returning to the old historicism, with its lack of understanding of a text as a social production, is great. And during this process of textual analysis critics must not forget to question their own assumptions and methods, for they too are products of and influences on their culture.

To avoid the old historicist's "error" of thinking that each historical period evidences a single political worldview, cultural poetics avoids sweeping generalizations and seeks out the seemingly insignificant details and manifestations of culture usually ignored by most historians and literary critics. Because cultural poetics critics view history and literature as social discourses and therefore battlegrounds for conflicting beliefs, actions, and customs, a text becomes culture in action. By highlighting seemingly insignificant happenings such as a note written by Thomas Jefferson to one of his slaves or a sentence etched on a window pane by Hawthorne, these critics hope to reveal the competing social codes and forces that mold a given society. Emphasizing a particular moment or incident rather than an overarching vision of society, a cultural poetics critic will often point out non-conventional connections such as that between Sophia Hawthorne's having a headache after reading *The Scarlet Letter* and the ending of *Nathaniel Hawthorne's next romance, The House of the Seven Gables*, or between the climate and environs of Elmira, New York, and some locations, descriptions, and actions in Mark Twain's *Huckleberry Finn*. Cultural poetics scholars believe that an investigation into these and similar happenings will demonstrate the complex relationship that exists among all discourses and show how narrative discourses such as history, literature, and other social productions interact, define, and are in turn shaped by their culture. By applying these principles and methodologies, say the cultural poetics critics, we will learn that there is not one voice but many to be heard interpreting texts and culture: Our own voices, those of others, and those of the past, the present, and the future.

9.5 QUESTIONS FOR ANALYSIS

Read Tony Harrison's poem *Marked with a D.* and ask yourself what voices you hear in the poem. What is the text saying about its culture? About its readers? About itself?

After reading Hawthorne's *Young Goodman Brown*, see whether you can discover any propaganda in the story. What was Hawthorne's position on the nature of sin? Of Puritan theology? Of the devil?

Does cultural poetics ask us to make any connections between the 1840s and the 1640s? If so, how are these connections?

How does Hawthorne's *Young Goodman Brown* question dominant cultural values of his day? Of the 1640s?

What is a working definition of the word sin as used in our present culture? In Hawthorne's day? In the 1640s? Why would cultural poetics be interested in this definition?

How is our reading of *Marked with a D.* and *Young Goodman Brown* shaped by our history? Our understanding of our history?

Identify four discourses operating in *Young Goodman Brown* and *Marked with a D.* Show how these discourses interconnect to enable the reader to arrive at an interpretation of each of the works.

Examine the student essay, written at the end of Chapter 9. Describe the student's hegemony on the basis of this essay. Provide evidence to support your answer.

9.6   SAMPLE ESSAYS

In the professional essay, "Is Literary History Still Possible?" what is Arthur Kinney's definition of a text? And what makes a text literary? Explain Kinney's four working premises or axioms for examining texts. How do these axioms support cultural poetics' principles?

Is Literary History Still Possible?

III

But is literary history still possible? My title is taken from a recent study, published in 1992, by David Perkins. He is writing against a simplified "old" history in which events are linked to causes, and works to sources — as *The Winter's Tale* by Shakespeare is discovered in Robert Green's *Pandosto*. The shortcomings of this kind of literary history have been set forth succinctly by Jean E. Howard:

How a literary text relates to a context, whether verbal or social, is one of the many issues rethought in the last several decades of literary study. In the past, contextualizing a literary work often meant turning it into an illustration of something assumed to be prior to the text, whether that something were an idea, a political event, or a phenomenon such as social mobility. This reading strategy had several problematic consequences. First, it seemed to suggest that texts had one primary determining context and that textual meaning could be stabilized by aligning a text with its "proper" context. Second, it seemed suggest that literary texts were always responses to, reflections of, something prior to and more privileged than themselves by which they could be explained. This denied literature an initiatory role in cultural transformations or social struggles, and it seemed to foreclose the possibility that literature could have an effect on other aspects of the social formation, as well as being altered by them. Third, using literature as illustration of a context invited a flattening of that text, a denial of its plurality and contradictions in favour of a univocal reading of its relations to a particular contextual ground.[1]

A new literary history would free itself of such charges by seeing literary texts as the convergence of a number of ideas and forces at the given moment of writing the text, not all of them conscious. Moreover, the ruptures and discontinuities that we now know characterize a series (but not necessarily a sequence) of past events in turn disrupts any attempt at forging an overriding thesis or organicism. Literary history, then, begins as the late E. H. Carr, Wilson Professor of International Politics at the University College of Wales at Aberystwyth, says history itself does — "when men begin to think of the passage of time in terms not of natural processes — the cycle of the seasons, the human life-span — but of a series of specific events in which men are consciously involved and which they can consciously influence."[2] Such a history is dynamic and discontinuous. Yet both the old and the new history — more or less recording,

① HOWARD J. The Stage and Social Struggle in Early Modern England [M].London and New York: Routledge,1994:47.
② CARR E. What is History? [M]. London: Macmillan,1986:134.

more or less creating — are interventions into the flow of time governed by conceptualization and reflection of events from which the historian, as the literary historian, stands apart. Such reflection for Fredric Jameson leads in short order to historicism, however, if the historian himself is not passively witnessing but actively engaged in the project of history; for Jameson, historicism is "our relationship to the past, and of our possibility of understanding the latter's monuments, artifacts, and traces."[1] This is a postmodernist sense of history that is not only disjunctive but, by being fruitfully partial, attempts to be all-encompassing. This is a postmodernist sense of history that, for John Kronik, can mean a cobbler's stew.

In the past few years, Gertrude Himmelfarb has been the most trenchant critic of such postmodern historicism. She locates the beginnings of such a postmodernist history — and by extension postmodernist literary history — in a man like Theodore Zeldin:

Traditional, or narrative, history, he argued, is dependent upon such "tyrannical" concepts as causality, chronology, and collectivity (the latter including such categories as nationality and class). To liberate it from these constraints, he proposed a history on the model of a pointillist painting, composed entirely of unconnected dots. This would have the double advantage of emancipating the historian from the tyrannies of the discipline, and emancipating the reader from the tyranny of the historian, since the reader would be free to make "what lines he thinks fit for himself".[2]

Himmelfarb's Zeldin thus comes close to the practice that Stephen Greenblatt and his followers have made a trademark of New Historicist readings and criticism. Their storytelling, both in a recovered incident and its filiations to other recovered incidents, to which they draw lines, however disjunctive or remote, is often composed by or into a narration or implied narration: this is a postmodernist possibility for literary history that is once historical and (through its close readings of texts especially) literary.

For Himmelfarb, one historian who practices a similar connection between data and narrative is Hayden White:

For White, as for post-modernism generally, there is no distinction between history and philosophy or between history and literature. All of history, in this view, is aesthetic

---

① JAMESON F. Marxism and Historicism, New Literary History II [M]. Washington D.C: The Johns Hopkins University Press,1979: 43.

② HIMMELFARB G. Telling it As You Like it: Postmodernist History and the Flight from Fact[J]. Times Literary Supplement, 1942(42):16.

and philosophic, and its only meaning or "reality" (in the created narrative) is that which the historian chooses to give it in accord with his own sensibility and disposition. What the traditional historian sees as an event that actually occurred in the past, the post-modernist sees as a "text" that exists only in the present — a text to be parsed, glossed, construed, interpreted by the historian, such as a poem or novel is by the critic. And, like any literary text, the historical text is indeterminate and contradictory paradoxical and ironic, so that it can be "textualized" "contextualized" "recontextualized" and inter textualized" at will — the "text" being title more than "pretext" for the creative historian. At the greatest reaches, then, there would be as many histories as historians — something Himmelfarb finds both absurd and intolerable.

From this perspective of history, Brook Thomas identifies two fundamental "strains of the new historicism" that follow naturally. "One tries to offer new narrative structures to present the past. The other retains traditional narrative structures but offers new voices from which to tell the past,"[1] voices often marginalized or silenced until now. In Louis A. Montrose's famous chiasmus of "the textuality of history and the historicity of texts," Greenblatt elides and erases any boundary between them in order to reopen texts to a dynamic field of discursive play, according to Thomas. Indeed, according to Howard Felperin, a distinguishing characteristic of the practice of New Historicists writing literary history is "the extent that traditional opposition between the 'literary' and the 'historical' has been shown... to be reconstructible, as *constructed intertextuality*".[2]

Such an understanding, says Felperin, permits us to separate the older literary history from the new, "for their 'conventionists' understanding of culture as an intertextual construction supersedes an older 'empiricist' or 'realist' identification of the meaning of an historical text with the biographical author's intention or his contemporary audience's understanding of it, as if such things were once monolithically present or linguistically transparent — even for the historical culture concerned — and retain an integrity untouched by the terms and methods of our enquiry

① BROOKS T. The New Historicism and Other Old-Fashioned Topics[M] Princeton: Princeton University Press, 1991: 24-25.

② FELPERIN H. " 'Cultural Poetics' verses 'Cultural Materialism': The Two New Historicisms in Renaissance Studies in Uses of History: Marxism, Postmodernism and the Renaissance" in The Essex Symposia[A]. Ed. FRANCIS B, PETER H, MARGARET I. Manchester: Manchester University Press, 1991:77.

into them"[1]. He goes on:

The very term "representation" at once recuperates and sublates this older historical and naively realist objective of "making present again" a past culture conceived not only as chronologically but onto-logically prior to any construction of it. In so doing, it partly rehabilitates a residually referential aspiration, if not to "commune," at least to correspond with the past…Indeed, such problems have already been confronted and effectively transcended by the post-structuralist move by which the "traces" of history and constructs of culture have been re-framed on the linguistic model of "texts" and "discourses" requiring an ever fresh and renewable "construction" rather than the pseudo-empiricist model of "documents" and "facts" to be "read off" in the effort of definitive reconstruction[2]. Like Pierre Bourdieu, who influenced him, Greenblatt finds formal and historical concerns inseparable while, unlike Bourdieu, deemphasizing or dismissing the importance of extra-textual social and historical concerns, a material culture, in his acts of mediating recovery. But if Greenblatt's particular view ignores the material artifacts of a culture, Felperin writes, he seems at odds metaphorically when, disjoining himself from the cultural materialists in Great Britain, he returns with a Marxist lexicon. As Felperin puts it, the latest terminology of 'circulation,' 'negotiation,' 'social energy' and 'exchange'-basically mercantile, even strangely monetarist, as it is — not effectively render Elizabethan England in terms of a generative grammar of economic exchange common to all societies. But if old history is too narrow in its focus on principal events chronologically or causally arranged, and if new history is flawed by incompleteness and dispersal, how can we write a literary history in our age that is foreshadowed in the seventeenth-century work of Ralegh, for example? And if we could write such a history — seemingly organic; actually just a positional — what makes it "literary"?

IV

These issues are as interrelated as they may seem to be separate. J. R. De J. Jackson provides a means for addressing the first of them in *Historical Criticism and the Meaning of Texts* when

---

[1] FELPERIN H. " 'Cultural Poetics' verses 'Cultural Materialism': The Two New Historicisms in Renaissance Studies in Uses of History: Marxism, Postmodernism and the Renaissance" in The Essex Symposia[A]. Ed. FRANCIS B, PETER H, and MARGARET I. Manchester: Manchester University Press, 1991:37.

[2] FELPERIN H. " 'Cultural Poetics' verses 'Cultural Materialism': The Two New Historicisms in Renaissance Studies in Uses of History: Marxism, Postmodernism and the Renaissance" in The Essex Symposia[A]. Ed. FRANCIS B, PETER H, and MARGARET I. Manchester: Manchester University Press, 1991:80-82.

he defines historical criticism as "criticism that tries to read past works of literature in the way in which they were read when they were new."[1] Jackson also sketches a methodology for this:

> If the aim of the recovery is to know a past literary environment as it was known in its own time so that reference to it in particular works will be comprehensible, three aspects will need to be considered: The range of works that existed: The portion of that range that was well enough known for authors to be able to take it for granted;[2] and the way in which that portion was understood, in so far as it differs from the way in which a modern reader might be expected to understand it.

It is, I think, in just such a semiotic practice as this — of reading texts, customs, and actions as similar and related cultural documents, all constitutive signs of a cultural moment that will impinge on a literary text — that our best and brightest hope for a literary history now rests. One method toward this end is described in the work of Marc Bloch, who argues that history must extend beyond conventional archival resources to include all kinds of evidence — verbal, nonverbal, extraverbal. "Everything that man says or writes, everything that he makes, everything he touches can and ought to teach us about him," Bloch writes in *The Historian's Craft* (posthumously translated and published in 1954). "It would be sheer fantasy," he continues,

> to imagine that for each historical problem there is a unique type of document with a specific sort of use. On the contrary, the deeper the research, the more the light of the evidence must converge from sources of many different kinds. What religious historian would be satisfied by examining a few theological tracts or hymnals? He knows full well that the painting and sculpture of sanctuary walls and the arrangement and furnishing of tombs have at least as much to tell him about dead beliefs and feelings as a thousand contemporary manuscripts.[3]

Bloch's own studies of feudalism or of the royal touch, like his disciple Fernand Braudel's massive study of the Mediterranean, while not themselves poststructuralist, invite the use of other and all disciplines for the self-correcting synchronic presentation of culture that can also provide a fuller, if disjunctive and so postmodernist, foundation for writing (or rewriting) literary history.

---

[1] JACKSON J. Historical Criticism and the Meaning of Texts[M].London: Routledge, 1989: 77.
[2] JACKSON J. Historical Criticism and the Meaning of Texts[M].London: Routledge, 1989: 40.
[3] BLOCK M. The Historian's Craft[M.] Peter P, trans. Manchester: Manchester University Press, 1954: 66-67.

The other question is equally important, if apparently in the different and perhaps somewhat distant field of aesthetics. The distance is more apparent than real. Leah Marcus puts her finger on the issue of literary history in early modern England when in *Puzzling Shakespeare* she asks about "the place of art" in the Renaissance: "Authors were caught between the need for currency, the need to attract an immediate public" by topicality as well as by popular convention "and a newly emerging desire for permanence and monumentality." As one of my students in a seminar at New York University put it a few weeks ago, "When does a performance become a poem?" when does a performative text become a literary one? When does *Volpone* become a candidate for folio *Works of Benjamin Jonson*, and is it thereby transformed by the very fixing of it in print? For Marcus the answer must be both diachronic and synchronic. For her the useful "localization of Shakespeare is based on the assumption that a similar cross-fertilization between the mapping of 'cross-cultural' analysis favored by anthropologists and the longitudinal sequential analysis characteristically practiced by historians will create a range of new vantage points from which to consider how the plays create meaning" (Gandamer, 2000:37). The literary linkage, then, is the representational image, or to paraphrase Jason, what is for all time in the ways it captures and thus represents the moment. A text is literary in, through, and by its metaphoric functioning.

Such a concept is also found in Gandamer's *Truth and Method*, in which he argues that in making an image, verbal or nonverbal, the literary artist makes that image both immediately present and more lastingly representative. Consciously or not, Hans Robert Jauss elaborates on this in his very helpful concern with what he calls the "horizon of expectations".

The reconstruction of the horizon of expectations, in the face of which a work was created and received in the past, enables one…to pose questions that the text initially gave answer to, and thereby (permits us) to discover how (our) contemporary reader who reads the work "as if it were new" could have viewed and understood the work. This approach corrects the most unrecognized norms of a classicist and modernizing understanding of art, and avoids a circular recourse to a general "spirit of the age." It raises to view the hermeneutic difference between the former and the current understanding of a work the "cultural moment" instead of "for all time"; it raises to consciousness the history of its reception, which mediates both positions; and it thereby calls into question as a platonizing dogma of philological metaphysics the apparently self-evident claims that in the literary text, literature is eternally present, and that its objective meaning, determined once and for all, is at all times immediately accessible.

Such an attempt to forge a postmodernist literary history appears in *Puzzling Shakespeare* when Marcus speaks for a "new topicality," which, as Richard Wilson elsewhere defines it, by different and careful local interpreting under discursive contexts, the reader will restore history to the plays, and arouse an awareness that the reader can coordinate with the play. Felperin also helps us to this larger vision that can contain both the wider society and its wider and more varied linguistic constructions by introducing something of the semiotics we have already associated with Saussure. In his opinion, from postmodernism perspective, Elizabethan literature and society are viewed simply as a textual system operating on its own terms — arbitrary, autonomous and autochthonic, he proposes, as a cultural moment, laden with the traces of historical subsequent moments, there can be any number of anthropological descriptions, more or less, but no historical interpretation. It is just such a semiotic practice of reading texts, customs, and actions as similar cultural documents, all constitutive signs of a cultural moment, that can be the basis for a significant (and significantly different) postmodernist literary history. Such moments are, composed of change and continuity — of factors demarcating development and the relatively stable conditions and ideas that sequential moments share. Both are part of a representational, metaphor-oriented text that attempts to mediate or negotiate them. Shakespeare's *Macbeth*, for instance, openly mediates the continuing theory of monarchial rule with the more particularized example of an absolutist Scottish ruler that negotiates tenth-century Scotland with its own Jacobean England.[1]

V

In practice, then, we should acknowledge that signifying texts — verbal and nonverbal texts — both register and interrogate the ideas and values of a culture at the same time presentational imaging and metaphorizing of such ideas and values are a literary means of intervening in that culture and so helping to constitute — and to reconstitute — it. We call "literary" those texts that have great imagining and metaphoric power, and we choose cultural moments that surround or are embedded in those specially striking texts. In this sense, the signs that matter are the signs that inform and illuminate the literary text, being the cultural signs that help constitute it. Some complexly representative texts, operating with metaphoric power within their cultural oments, will show what I have in mind.

---

[1] BLOCK M. The Historian's Craft[M.] Peter P, trans. Manchester: Manchester University Press, 1954: 66-67.

When Sir Philip Sidney's Euarchus, at the close of the comprehensive fiction of *Arcadia*, finds himself unable to accommodate the guilt of his son because the laws of justice do not admit exceptions, the author makes a forceful comment favoring the newer courts of equity and an equally forceful questioning of the courts of common law, dependent wholly on precedent, under Elizabeth I. The fiction does not stop being a fiction, nor the romance a romance, but at the same time the imaging text interrogates the Tudor legal system and interrupts the smugness with which other writers were praising it in London and in the provinces. When Iago in *Othello* is able to challenge the self-confident judgment of his general by showing in the person of the drunken Cassio that Othello chose an inferior man as his lieutenant, that Othello's autocratic wisdom can be called to account and found wanting, Shakespeare not only draws directly for literary representation on military manuals of his day, he also demonstrates the inherent limitations of a military conditioning and mind-set given to absolute commands and irrevocable decisions that can be fallible and opposed to each other — and in his Jacobean reception toward the clear and present danger of James I, who also displays a stubborn self-confidence in writing and publishing his political doctrine of enlightened absolutism. When, in "The Collar", the poet George Herbert, self-exiled Io the small village parish of Bemerton in distant Wales, writes: "I struck board, and cry'd, No more./ I will abroad," he is not merely announcing a frustration with the Christian faith or exemplifying the Christian state of near despair. He is also demonstrating through his textual register of meditative poetry a representational image of how the Christian in this cultural moment who is neither Genevan not papist can yearn for more than the Erastian provisos of the Church of England. He is talking about the plight of the religious in a nation that charts contradictory and unsettled religious paths. In Will Power, Richard Wilson has recently shown how James's presence interrupts the text of *Measure for Measure*; how Brian Annesley's will, recognizing Kentish *gavelkind*, divides his property at his death equally among his children, including the youngest, Cordelia, some four or five years before King Lear; how actual riots inform *2 Henry VI, Julius Caesar, and Coriolanus*; and how Tudor enclosures inform and are informed by *As You Like It*. Elsewhere I have argued how Thomas Deloney's *Jack of Neuburie* is a fictional rewriting of a petition he wrote with William Muggins and one Willington in support of the London weavers of his own day, the eleventh-century history of Francis Thynne for Holinshed's *Chronicles*, to seventeenth-century Jacobean England, much as Bacon rewrites biblical history making it too contemporary and charged with political freight. Such matters as these are surely the concern of any literary history (if appropriate and natural for a postmodern literary history), because they lead us, by showing us something about what that work meant when it was new, to the greater representative and metaphorical range inherent in — and at times dynamic to — the literary text. They are constitutive of both literature and history.

VI

Signs may also come in much more subtle ways, first introduced into contemporary critical study by Derrida in his essay on Jusserl as "le trace". According to Derrida, "The trace is not a presence but is rather the simulacrum of a presence that dislocates, displaces, and refers, beyond itself"; according to his follower Emmanuel Levinas,[1]

> The trace is not a typical sign, but it may play the role of a sign. It may be taken for a sign. The detective examines everything that marks the scene of the crime as a revealing sign, the intentional or unintentional work of the criminal; the hunter follows the trace of the game, which reflects the activity and the tread of the animal he seeks; the historian discovers ancient civilizations,beginning with the vestiges left by their existence, as horizons toour world.[2]

Sheldon P. Zitner, for instance, has seen the intense controversy over Elizabethan Court of Wards in traces in *All's Well That Ends Well*, a play written and first performed when the controversy was at its height. The practice then established, which enabled the crown to profit from the persons and inherited property of minors by selling — or, for a fee, allowing its nobility to sell — the guardianship of orphans, informs the situation of both Helena and Bertram.Helena is clearly such a ward, in effect surrendered by the Countess of Rossillion to the king as a chattel whose perquisite it is to assign control of her for profit; Bertram, on the other hand, is equally without control of property because his father had the bad fortune to die before his son came of age. *All'sWell*, then starts with two recently orphaned youth of different genders whose actions display a hierarchical and relatively closed society. The play is about what they *do*. it is also, from this perspective, about what they *can do*, court and military service for him; nursing and the convent for her. From another perspective, the play conducts a rigorous examination of rank and

---

[1] HEPBURN A. Derrida and Psychology: Deconstruction and its Ab/uses in Critical and Discursive sychologies[EB/OL]. [2018-03-18].http://www.academia.edu/11317172/.

[2] HUSSERL E. Cartesian Meditations: An Introduction to Pure Phenomenology[M]. , Dorion trans. Boston: Martinus Nijhoff Publishers, 1960:50-139.

gender in late Tudor England (as well as France, where the action putatively takes place).

In a different way, *The Merry Wives of Windsor* intervenes in its cultural moment. I think it is no accident that this play is set uniquely in Shakespeare's contemporary England; it means to question the economic conditions of that time and place. Windsor, the play's sole location, was then a royal borough, but it was also a village devastated (as were other parts of the country) by four years of bad harvests between 1593 and 1597, by unusual dearth, poverty, starvation, and death. In this context the gluttonous Falstaff serves as the perfect ironic sign. As in the history plays, he is "out at heels"(fol. 1, sig. D3), while the merchants of the play, the Pages and the Fords, stuff themselves at feast after feast. *The Merry Wives* is a play about the haves and the have-nots, about the deepening economic divide in the late "golden years" of Elizabeth I. This play, too, functions as commentary, entering into the culture for its material, returning that material to the culture as farce. But why farce? Perhaps in analogy to the invention of screwball comedies in Hollywood, musical comedies on Broadway, and the game of Monopoly based on Atlantic City during our Great Depression — to relieve economic distress by making light of it. That, too, is part of its constituent, representational, metaphoric meaning.

Such simultaneity alerts us to redolent dimensions of a cultural moment. Karen Newman's examination of Shakespeare's Taming of the Shrew functions somewhat differently. Newman likens the play, which we customarily date around 1593~1594, to an event in Wetherden, Suffolk:

A drunken tanner, Nicholas Rosyer, staggers home from alehouse. On arriving at his door, he is greeted by his wife with "dronken dogg, pisspott and other seemingly names." When Rosyer tried to come to bed to her, she "still raged against him and badd him out dronken dog dronken pisspot". She struck him several times, clawed his face and arms, spit at him, and beat him out of bed. Rosyer retreated, returned to the alehouse, and drank until he could hardly stand up. Shortly thereafter, Thomas Quarry and others met and "agreed amongst themselves that the said Thomas Quarry who dwelt at the next town … should … ride about the town upon a cowl staff whereby not only the woman which had offended might be shunned for her misdemeanors towards her husband but other women also by her shame might be admonished to offence in like sort."

Newman dates this event "Plough Monday, 1604," well beyond our accepted date of Shakespeare's play, but before the first instance of the play being entered in the Stationer's Register (to one J. Smethwick on 19 November 1607). Perhaps the revival of public punishing of shrews — or the continuation of such punishment — prompted a revival of Shakespeare's play or suggested to the commercially minded Smethsick a new financial possibility. I was myself puzzled by the number of distinct verbal echoes in *Macbeth* of Marlowe's *Tamberline*, first published in 1590, a full fifteen years before Shakespeare's play, until I learned by consulting the Short Title Catalog that *Tamberline* was reprinted (and restaged?)in 1604. The cultural moment thus includes the possibilities of renewing past events and anticipating future ones; the literary cultural moment has no fixed period or lines of demarcation.

VII

Such instances, which help to constitute a literary history in terms of cultural moments, have led me to formulate four working premises or axioms — starting places for examining texts and signs that may be subject to change, addition, or suspension but which nevertheless function as heuristic points of departure:

(1) No text is ever entirely unmarked by its time and place — and its fullest range of meaning depends to a greater or lesser degree on such knowledge.

(2) Every text always has some intention; even when the intention is misconceived, unrealized, or misunderstood, no text is innocent of purpose or reception.

(3) Every text potentially contains multiple readings through multiple interpreters and multiple occasions on which it is interpreted, or conveyed.

(4) No text is completely unequivocal or conclusive: All texts are contingent on further understanding of their cultural moment, when they are new.

The limitation when working with a past period such as the early modern period is that the only cultural signs that are preserved are those in written or pictorial records or in material remains: even our knowledge of Essex's rebellion relies on extant verbal documents that relate or interpret it. Such documents may be as formal as court proceedings or statutes or as informal as gossip recorded in letters or diaries, but they survive as potential objects of our knowledge because they are in written or printed form. In the absence of other means of knowledge, they have privileged writing, and this in turn has often historically privileged literature. But the uniqueness of written transmission does not make literature autonomous nor the only evidence to which it can be made to relate. The *Annales* school forcefully reminds us that other matters — such as Brian Annesley's will or Nicholas Rosyer's punishment — are part of a literary text's meaning at its original moment or time and may be some of the meaning of that text even now. Shakespeare's *Tempest*, written and presented in 1611, for instance, may recall contemporary voyage pamphlets, but it may also recall a much earlier one, in 1606, which tells of five American Indians — potential originals for Caliban in the mind of Shakespeare and in the minds of his audience, for they were still on display in London in 1611, and could be viewed on the way to the theater. Similarly, Henry Smith's 1591 sermon on Jonah finds its echoes in the play and potentially in its significant relationship to Prospero and to Alonso likely it was still being preached, as it was still being printed, in 1611, in later editions of Smith's works.

Finally, crucial cultural signs at a later moment of a literary text's origination may not be evident signs at a later moment of reading. But that likelihood should not prevent us from searching out the signs in force at the cultural moment when the literary text under examination was first conceived and produced, and both are part of a literary history we can now write, or rewrite. The traces and latencies of subsequent moments in such texts have always made reading them richer and more difficult, but we shall never register the fullest possible readings, based on such traces and latencies as well as on the texts, until we first attend closely to all we can recover of the originary moment itself. Just such acts, however, will continue to make literary history — even postmodernist literary history — possible.

Essay by Arthur F. Kinney. Ben Jonson Journal 2: 199-221.

Professor Essay

New Historicism on Ames & Rosement's Translation of *Lunyu*

Two assumptions of Veeser's summary on cultural poetics, or rather New Historicism, are pertinent to the present chapter, the first being that "every expressive act is embedded in a network of material experience", and the second being that "literary and non-literary 'texts' circulate inseparably".[①]

Therefore, it is essential to interpret Ames and Rosement's English Version by starting with the "material experience" of their texts and taking other "literary and non-literary 'texts'" into consideration. The "texts" herein not only refer to texts on paper but also includes political agenda, social institution, educational propaganda and the like. So the present chapter not only goes deeper into *The Analects* but also probes into Ames's experiences for a new historical reading.

---

① MILLER A. Concept of Culture art, Politics [EB/OL].[2018-03-18].https://vdocuments.mx/adam-muller-concepts-of-culture-art-politics-bookosorg.html.

Concerning Ames's Identities

Ames has multiple identities, which are more or less linked with his translation creation. As new historicist, personal identity shapes and is shaped by the culture and society where it Ames takes process philosophy, according to it, text is historical text, it is created by history and culture, to some degree, the text can shape history as its spokesman. Just like what texts and artifacts do. Ames's identities inevitably have something to do with historical context and his literary creation, and the following are analysed about the connections between their identities and literary creation.

Ames is philosopher, sinologist as well as a translator. He reshaped one which is subversive and does whatever he wants out of her free will. Besides, Ames stance is also represented in almost all the other translated versions, such as *Xiao Jing, Yuan Dao and Dao De Jing*. Ames has many other identities, and the three identities mentioned above have more evident influences on his creation, so they are analyzed in detail in the present section.

Concerning *The Analects* from Cultural Poetics viewpoint, it records the historical transformation of Confucius's days and shows that the inner calling of Confucius to the kings of small vessels by his self-sacrificing practices. Therefore, the new historicist will equally detect physical practices in the world and make sense of the interaction between them. In other words, they are aimed at detecting the interaction of cultural and other social practices. New historicists try to reveal that people aims to grasp the desired profits, including fame, power or economic benefits as the text-production's background, and that there are discourses and powers circulating in literary works.

In *The Analects*, a great number of texts are subversive against the dominant powers, yet they get published and disseminated, which is an indication of "containment" of both the literary circle and those in power. Therefore, such a dichotomy assuredly applies to the interpretation of *The Analects*.

A new historist actually connected Ames's literary activities with his life experiences and the times when he created his literary works. Besides, he also proposed therein that the approach of such connection should be applied to literary criticism in general. Therefore, it is feasible to connect the translation of *The Analects* with his life experience so as to conduct the new historical interpretation of his translation, to explain why he more often than not writes Chinese classic about life with philosophical insight. Ames comments on Confucius "Following the proper way, I do notforge new paths, allowing that he was a transmitter rather than an innovator, a classicist rather than a philosopher." With a sense of philosophy, Ames probes into the dichotomy between physical world and psychological world, and that between body and mind. In this way, to probe into Confucius's world and consider him as a philosopher, Ames takes a philosophical perspective. His translation version of *Lunyu* is more interpretation and appreciation of Confucianism rather than translation between source language and target language.[①] Confucius indicates that in his days the physical world imposes restrictions on people living in it, and people try to get away from them psychologically. Thus the title "*Lunyu*" is by no means a free dialogue between teacher and student on life.

Ames's literary experiences also have influences on his translation creation. Ames was so gifted that he had his first translation at university and took on the position as creative director of Writing School of that university. Such experiences could obviously provide him with the access to experimenting on text composing and theory constructing. Besides, he had experiences of writing plays, which may help cultivate is proficiency in dramatic monologue. Thus the widely-utilized philosophical monologue in his translation may result from the experience. *The Analects: a Philosophical Interpretation*, his English selected as materials for the present research, namely, all contains "Dao" of life with philosophical monologue.

"History in this discourse is restored and reproduced, which insinuates that history is tampered and distorted by people. Such a vision is similar to a new historical assumption that history is not an accurate presentation but a construction of past events interpreted by people with subjectivity.

Elimination of the Prejudice from Western Philosophy

Chinese philosophy has been made familiar to Western readers by first "Christianizing" it, and then more recently by locating it within a poetical-mystical-occult worldview. To the extent that Chinese philosophy has become the subject of Western philosophical interest at all, it has usually been analyzed within the framework of categories and philosophical problems of its own.

Before Ames's effort to translate Chinese classics, most previous translators seldom paid attention to the basic differences between Chinese and Western cultures, especially in philosophy.

---

① AMES R, ROSEMENT H. The Analects of Confucius: A Philosophical Translation[M]. New York: Balattine Publishing Group.1999:2.

There is a fatal defect in the way to get insight into Chinese philosophy in the Western academic worlds. For the major concepts in Confucius, in most cases, English equivalents are pursued for nondiscrimination. Afterwards, these equivalents loaded heavily with western connotations are used for the analysis of Confucian thoughts.

Lunyu is a "philosophical" text indeed. However, it has not been engaged properly as such. Initially in the late sixteenth century, it was translated by missionaries, later since the nineteen century by sinologists. That is, up to now, *Lunyu* has merely sporadically been treated philosophically and throughout the nineteenth century, translations of Chinese philosophical literature exerted little effect on European and American philosophy. With a good intention though, most of these missionaries failed to interpret the meaning of Chinese classics well, and their translation works could hardly present the significance of Chinese culture. When the earliest Jesuit missionaries encountered the Chinese intellectuals, their communication was almost a failure, for the Western tradition assumes an externally imposed order, while the Chinese one maintains an immanent order that is inseverable from a spontaneously changing world. The case was the same to those sinologists, whose literary, cultural, historical, profound philological sensibilities and sophisticated language skills, however should not be undervalued in their understanding.

A number of Western assumptions were unconsciously transplanted into such texts, coloring the vocabulary employed to articulate their own understanding. When those unique Chinese philosophical terms were replaced in their translation by familiar terms in Western philosophy; consequently, most Western philosophers did not identify Chinese tradition as real "philosophy", thinking it was merely the footnotes of what had been done in the West in the past centuries. So communication between such opposite cultures should foremost respect and reserve the differences, which are always put at risk of being neglected in translation process.

The greatest obstacles to interpret and translate Chinese texts and to use such "translated" materials lie mostly in lexicons, with little hurdle from phonetic and syntactic limitations. In the previous practice, the semantic implications of key philosophical terms were undervalued, and what was worse, the indiscriminate use of terms permeated with Western implication led to a familiar terrain which should have been a totally alien world. In a word, the received translations of the core Chinese philosophic glossary convey metaphysics without Chinese tradition. This is the harmful consequence of cultural reductionism. Just take a quick look at translations of the following coreterms: Dao 道 — the Way; Tian 天 — Heaven; Ming 命 — fate or Fate; yi 一 — unity, the One; taiji 太极 — Supreme Ultimate; You/Wu 有无 — Being/Nonbeing; Ren 仁 — benevolence/moral character; Li 礼 — ritual; Yi 义 — righteousness; Shan 善 — good; Zhi 知 — knowledge; Wuwei 无为 — doing nothing and so forth. For instance, when Tian 天 is translated into "Heaven" with the letter "H" capitalized, this rendering will bring the image of an omnipotent Creator into readers' mind, invoking a number of Christian associations like sin, soul and afterlife. The same is with "Ming" rendered into "fate/Fate" which reminds readers of predicament and tragedy, notions hardly found in Chinese thought.

Take Ku Hungming as an extreme example. Exposed to the critical period of late Qing Dynasty, with great patriotism, Ku set upon the translation of *Lunyu* to spread Chinese culture. He adapted strategies of domestication to render a version with typical Western styles. Take a look at his treatment of Chinese major concepts. Take Ren 仁 for instance.

Example 1:

子曰："人而不仁，如礼何？人而不仁，如乐何？"(Chapter 3)

Confucius remarked, "If a man is without moral character, what good can the use of the fine arts do him? If a man is without moral character, what good can the use of music do him?"

Throughout the whole text, Ku uses "moral character or moral life" as the English equivalent to this Chinese character Ren 仁, meaning "humanity". Besides, Ku regards *Lunyu* as a book of morality teachings. So for him, "moral character" is the best diction for Ren 仁 from the perspective of Western philosophy. But "moral character" is such a familiar term for Western readers that the peculiarity of Chinese philosophy is covered and neglected. Of course, there is no intention to make any criticism on Ku. His translation is just the product of times, and serves his times well as what he intends for:

I just want to express a will that learned and well-cultivated English people could reflect upon their prejudices toward Chinese after reading my English version and accordingly correct their misunderstandings and shift their attitudes towards the relationships not only between English and the Chinese but between Great Britain and China.

However, this epoch calls for cultural pluralism and cultural integration. Ames recognizes that when an alternative philosophical tradition is made familiar and, at the same time, is adjudicated on the basis of Western standards of evidence that are foreign to it, it can only be an inferior variation of a Western theme. (Thus once again: Chinese writings aren't "truly philosophical".) Therefore, the different readers in different historical periods will encounter different texts in which social situation it is produced by different translators.

Only by discarding ethnocentrism and accepting authentic Confucianism can we hope to erase these misunderstandings to reconstruct Confucian ideology for a new and harmonious world order.

Interaction of *The Analects* and Other Social Texts

One of the new historicist assumptions is that literature is not separable from the political, religious, social and economic conditions at a certain time and place. Instead, a literary text is merely one of such social texts as scientific, philosophical, legal, religious ones and the like, and all these texts are equal because they are all generated and structured by the same historical conditions. Therefore, the new historicist regards a literary text not as an organic whole with fixed meanings but as one of social products which interact and interchange with each other. In other words, a literary text is not an autonomous body but a interpretation by cultural poetics. Social products are open to interpretation and interaction with other social products, or rather social texts.

We have attempted to describe that world, its human inhabitants, and their language, in the hope that the signposts for the Confucian way will come into sharper relief for the contemporary Western readers. Perhaps, Confucianism is the most influential and enduring in Chinese culture. Over the time, it has survived many challenges. Initially, it competed with the "Hundred Schools" like Daoists, Legalists; later for several centuries, it was cast into the shade by Buddhism; then it was overshadowed by Christianity: the Jesuits, Franciscans in the 16th and 17th century and the Protestant and Catholic missionaries in the 19th and 20th century. The earliest missionaries held firm belief in the rationality of traditional Western culture, while the later missionaries resorted to the gunboat diplomacy exerted on China by the Western imperialistic powers. Faced with such severe challenges, the indomitable Confucianism, instead of surrendering, has survived and evolved wonderfully with ever-increasing strength and essence from those adverse forces. Now, Confucianism has shown its influence on the economic development in many nations, such as Japan, and Singapore. Besides its economic significance, to those who are seeking solutions to some urgent problems today, the spirit of *Lunyu* means the hope for a more humane and harmonious future.

New archaeological findings on *Lunyu* provide textual materials that improve the existing knowledge about the text and about the processes of its transmission. Such findings overrule the previous speculation about the date of the compilation of *Lunyu* and cast new light on the meaning and structure of this canonical document in Confucius philosophy. In addition, great challenge has risen to the reliability of current translations. In his *The Analects of Confucius*, Ames focuses the attention on the philosophical significance, and as a result, the philosophical interpretation of *Lunyu* has a strong influence on its translation, which reveals classical Chinese thought as eventful, relational and dynamic. See his translation of major concepts, Xin（心）and Zhi（知）for examples.

Example 2:

子曰："吾十有五志于学，……七十从心所欲，不逾矩。"(Book 2: Chapter 4)

The Master said:"From fifteen, my heart-and-mind was set upon learning; from seventy I could give my heart-and-mind free rein without overstepping the boundaries."

The character Xin 心 is most commonly translated as "heart" or "mind". But Ames combines the two together as "heart-and-mind", a term not elegant but aptly worded, for in Chinese context, the Xin can think. That is, mind and body are not divorced from each other, but entail each other wherever Xin appears. If the mind is departed from the heart, or the cognitive is away from the affective, the interpretation will fail to reveal an authentic Confucius but embrace a pure Western metaphysical rationality. Such rendering of "heart-and-mind", as Ames puts it, will call the reader's attention to the fact that "there are no altogether disembodied thoughts for Confucius, nor any raw feelings altogether lacking 'cognitive content'" .

Example 3:

子曰："回也，其心三月不违仁；其余则日月至焉而已矣。"(Book 6: Chapter 7)

The Master said: "With my disciple, Yan Hui, he could go for several months without departing from authoritative (Ren 仁) thoughts and feelings (Xin 心); as for others, only every once in a long while, might authoritative thoughts and feelings make an appearance."

Ames goes even further to follow the "function" of Xin rather than its "anatomic" nature and renders Xin as "thoughts and feelings" which metaphorically means the organ which such experiences of human beings are related to. Xin can not be interpret as "heart" only from seeming understanding, it should be synthesizes from the functional meaning such as 'knowing', 'acting' and 'feeling'". This rendering of "thoughts and feelings" can remind Western readers of ancient Chinese worldview: the change and process outmatch the stasis and form. Respecting the human body, function prevails over site and physiology excels anatomy.

Example 4:

子曰：" 由，知德者鲜矣。"(Book 15: Chapter 4)

The Master said, "Zilu, those who realize (Zhi 知) excellence (De 德) are rare indeed."

Zhi (知)or Zhi (智) is always translated as "knowledge" "wisdom" or "to know". But Ames adheres to the rendering "to realize", which for him shares the same epistemic implication with "knowledge" and "to know" in English. For one thing, "to realize" weighs heavily the performative connotation of Zhi; for the other thing, with Zhi as "to realize", Ames emphasizes one of Confucian precepts: The unity between knowledge and action (Zhi Xing He Yi知行合一).

Example 5:

子曰：" 知及之，仁不能守之；虽得之，必失之。"(Book 15: Chapter 4)

The Master said, "When persons come to a realization (Zhi, 知)but are not authoritative (Ren, 仁) enough to sustain its implementation, even though they had it, they are sure to lose."

Ames rues in his *The Analects*: "This paragraph with its highly literacy, somewhat empty elaboration, and its placing ritual on a pinnacle far above Goodness, is certainly one of the later additions to the book." "To realize" means "to make real" which invokes no such philosophical associations as implied in the expressions "knowledge". According to the notion of "Nexus" in Process Philosophy, there exists togetherness among actual entities. That is, individual facts are not isolated from but correlated to one another; the world is thus integrity as a whole. Process Philosophy provides an appropriate perspective and terminologies for Ames to interpret Confucianism and establish Chinese philosophy. Confucian thinking is process thinking and *Lunyu* describes a world in motion: Everything is associated with one another.

Besides the discussion about Xin and Zhi above, Confucius' holistic and dynamic thinking process is well presented in the codependency of his ideas about reflecting (Si, 思) and learning (Xue, 学), as shown in "Learning without reflecting leads to perplexity; reflecting without learning leads to perilous circumstances". The same to "Xin", "si" or "reflecting" has both a psychical and physiological implication. To discuss a thinking person with reference only to the psyche without the physical is inevitably misleading. This being the case, Ames is cautions about these key terms.

C. Communication of Western and Chinese Philosophy

A first step in comparative philosophy must be to identify and excavate those shared yet usually unconscious presuppositions or premises that are implicit in the philosophical reflections of all members of a particular cultural tradition. To compare the Chinese and Western culture, a proper context is pursued in Ames's *Anticipating China: Two Cultural Problematics in Practice of Cross-cultural Translation*. Classical Chinese philosophy belongs to the first problematics represented by the mode of analogical thinking, and the mainstream in Western culture belongs to the second one characterized by the mode of causal thinking, the contrast of which is the initial step to bridge Chinese and Western cultures.

Specifically, Ames terms the first problematics as a cosmological — not presuming a single — ordered cosmos, while the second presumes a single-ordered world. Thus, traditional Chinese culture accords great importance to process, particularity, correlative thinking and prefers change to stillness, all of which entail an aesthetic order. In contrast, the Western culture emphasizes fact, substance, causal inference and values of "being" rather than "becoming", affirming that stillness is better than change, the combination of which represent an order of logic. Gernet once makes similar assertion: since the beginning of the 20th century, traditional Western philosophy has encountered subversive challenges from pragmatism, hermeneutics, neo-Marxism, neo-pragmatism, deconstructionism in post-modernism and so on.

History and literature are mutual constructed, and literature is influenced by its historical background in which it is produced. Besides, the practice of a new historical criticism should be a must for a time to criticize the present as well as the past, because the past has shaped the present, and the present construct the future.

New historicists believe that history and literature are in a relationship of mutual construction, and literature is influenced by the contemporary historical background in which it is produced. Besides, in "The Poetics and Politics of Culture", Montrose argues that "the practice of a new historical criticism... necessitates efforts to criticize the present as well as the past", and that "the past has shaped the present".

The "past" herein refers to the past history, while the "present" refers to the present culture, society, ethos, individual activities and the like. Therefore, it is feasible to analyze how past and present historical elements have shaped Ames's subject matters.

Therefore, what culture can reveal is that it shapes the personal identity and is shaped by the people.

According to Tyson, one of the five key concepts of New Historicism is that "personal identity (. . .) is shaped by and shapes the culture in which it emerges". Therefore it is feasible to say that a certain individual has the capacity of influencing the culture and society in which he or she lives. Besides, in the last paragraph of "The Poetics and Politics of Culture", Montrose writes that "it is by constructing literature as an unstable and agnostic field of verbal and social practices... that literary criticism rearticulates itself as a site of intellectually and socially significant work in the historical present". Herein he means that a literary text is not a stable, fixed and closed "organic whole" but an unstable, agnostic and open discourse interacting and negotiating with other discourses, and circulating in both contemporary and future history. Therefore, Ames and his translation are sure to have influences on contemporary and future society, history and culture.

Ames's introduction to *Lunyu* stands out for two points: As to the contents, it is more comprehensive with a length of 66 pages, covering philosophic and linguistic background as well as historical and textual background; as to the methodology, Ames does not only interpret Confucius from the perspective of history and culture but also from that of philosophy whereby Confucius is more a philosopher than a theoretical philosopher and *Lunyu* is a classical work of philosophy. More importantly, this philosopher and philosophical works are no longer the ones familiar to the Westerners, but unfamiliar ones — counterparts of Western philosopher and philosophy.

Historical and Textual Background

To say Confucius is a philosopher rather than a theoretical philosopher is based on the fact that Confucius does not put down his vision of the world in purely descriptive language and *Lunyu* about his thought is the collective work by his disciples for generations through their own experiences. Formed at different times by many hands, *Lunyu* is usually charged with a lack of logic and coherence. But Ames concludes that an intensive and deliberate reading will guarantee a more coherent text, for many sections are in fact gathered according to specific subjects and themes. In addition, Ames includes in this part other canonical texts and later commentaries which convince him that Confucianism after having been tried out and survived in the river of history has shown and will show more significance in modern economic and social life.

Ames classifies them into Process Philosophy in a broader sense for their shared objectives against absolutism and logocentrism. These efforts direct the West to the vitality of a diverse, correlative and processing world. Process Philosophy is a new issue in the West, and its advocator Whitehead argues in his speculative philosophy that there is an urgent need to find a new language for philosophy that can accommodate aesthetic understanding. Naturally, for Whitehead as well as many other scholars in the West, Chinese culture becomes the top choice to meet the need. In this sense, it is true that the so-called "opposite" cultures are indeed "complementary" to each other.

As a comparative philosopher, Ames concentrates on those uncommon assumptions distinguishing cultures — assumptions both as big barriers and big opportunities for intercultural translation. Ames considered Oriental philosophy as a becoming way. It is only in the process of becoming state can we observe the innate elements as the foundation to nature law that Chinese people passed it on generations by generations, including ways of living and thinking. It is the failure to notice such distinctive cultural presuppositions in interpretation and translation that leads to the misunderstanding of Confucius and his thought. In *Thinking through Confucius*, Ames expounds three assumptions to provide a proper interpretive context for the study and translation of Confucius, namely, an immanent cosmos, conceptual polarity and tradition as interpretive context.

An immanent cosmos is the most influential and coherent assumption of the thought of Confucius — assumption of radical immanence, precluding the existence of any transcendent

principle or being. This assumption can be accessed from three implications. The most important is ontology of events instead of substances. Confucius cares more about what the specific person does in particular contexts than what essence the abstract virtues have. The second implication is "order". An aesthetic order as mentioned above is disclosed not closed, related to the realist context not transcendent. The third is "creativity", creative actions practiced by mundane people in particular social contexts not by any extra-mundane force.

Conceptual polarity, the epistemological equivalent of the notion of an immanent cosmos, entails an interdependent relationship between events. Contrary to dualism which requires an essentialistic explanation for the world around, such polarity in ancient Chinese thought calls for contextualist and correlative terms to explain dynamic and processing existence. More specifically, Western philosophy is characterized by dualism — opposition between reality and appearance, God and world, form and body, being and becoming, mind and body, and so on; in contrast, the correlativity featuring Chinese world outlook is reflected in such complementary and correlative vocabulary: yin（阴）/yang（阳）, pattern（理）/energy（气）, heaven（天）/earth（地）, ruler（君）/subject（臣）, husband（夫）/wife（妻）, inner（内）/outer（外）, waxing（盈）/waning（亏）, personal cultivation（修身）/political administration（治国）and so on.

Tradition, instead of history, as interpretive context, is helpful to understand Confucius. Traditional culture emphasizes the aesthetic order of rituals while historical culture resorts to laws and sanctions, the former of which is more powerful for personal cultivation. Individualism in the West is a sign of originality, while the concept of person for Confucius is the attainment of interdependence through creative actions. From the traditional perspective, Confucius is not only a transmitter of the tradition but an originator based on the tradition.

The Western cosmogonic tradition concerns the agency that gives rise to the origins of things, whereas the a osmotic tradition is to conjure a persuasive model for human beings to follow in the society. A basic denotation of a osmotic way of thinking is that it dose not resort to notions like "being" or "not-being". Thinkers in classical Chinese focus their attention on particular or individual things rather than the nature or essence of things, so any effort to find a principle or a concept in *Lunyu* is sure to get nowhere. A better choice is to interpret the moral models according to their particular experiences. An intensive record of Confucius's words and deeds given in *Lunyu* conjures a particular portrait of such exemplary image. For the historical fact that such image gradually attracts more and more adherents and serves as a model for proper conduct, it functions equally as a theory or concept in Western philosophical tradition. So the world of Confucius should be interpreted not by its essence but by correlation: different time, different relations. A human being can at once be a benefactor and beneficiary of his or her friends, relatives, even strangers and so on (See the discussion in Ames's manipulation of key terms: De 德). In this sense, persons are not individuals independent of their actions but are ongoing "events" identified by relationships within specific context.

Through the comparison of distinctive cultural assumptions between Chinese and Western cultures, how literary text functions itself, as a historical discourse interacting with other historical discourses and that all those discourses circulate at one time , one particular space in which are set subjectively so as to represent the power's subversion.

According to New Historicism, the theory is not concerned with historical events as events, but, with historical discourses; that New Historicism focuses on "how literary text functions, itself, as a historical discourse interacting with other historical discourses"; and that all those discourses circulate "at the time and place in which the text is set, at the time the text was published, or at later points in the history of the text's reception.". Besides, Stephen Greenblatt, believes that new historical criticism "has been (...) open to such (literary) works as fields of force, places of dissension and shifting interests, occasions for the jostling of orthodox and subversive impulses" In other words, there are conflicting discourses in literary works, which are what new historical critics should reveal.

Thus it is necessary to take conflicting discourses into consideration when interpreting Ames's texts from the perspectives of new historicism, or rather cultural poetics.

It was Louis A. Montrose who put forward the assumptions of textuality of history and historicity of texts, and the present chapter interprets Ames's texts through the two assumptions respectively. In the present chapter, the "history" refers to the history represented in *The Analects*. In other words, histories are narratives based on historians' own interpretations of other textual forms. On the other hand, Tyson argues that "the writing of history is a matter of interpretations"[①]; and that "there is no history, (...) there are only representations of history"; and that "a literary text (...) is aninterpretation of history", which we can interpret to get to know something about the history.

Therefore, Ames's interpretation of *The Analects*is a collection of interpretations and representations of history, and the present section aims at revealing such interpretations and representations in the translation text. Ames's interpretations of the assumptions of New Historicism, historical accounts are the interpretations of the people who write them at the given time or place, and they are unavoidably subjectively constructed. New historicists are concerned less about historical accounts themselves but more about how such accounts are interpreted and received over time.

Historicity of *The Analects* Montrose argues that all forms of writing, either texts that literary

---

① LOIS TYSON. "New Historicism" in Selective Reading in 20th Century Western Critical Theory. Ed. ZHANG ZHONGZAI. Beijing: Foreign Language Teaching and Research Press, 2002.

critics study or texts in which they study them, are embedded in a social and cultural context at that specific historical moment. In other words, texts are embedded in a certain historical context, and therefore they can tell us something about the history at that time and place in which the texts were produced.

Besides, Tyson argues that a new historical reading normally examines the history of the literary work and how it "shaped and was shaped by discourses circulating at its point of origin and over the passage of time, including speculations about its relationship to possible future audiences".[1] With the same token, *The Analects*, as one of the social discourses, interacts with other discourses in contemporary history and influences current and future history. Thus Ames and Rosement and their translation definitely shape and are shaped by the respective historical contexts, and interpreting the contexts is conducive to revealing historical influences.

Ames has tremendous influences on modern society, such as education, culture, politics and the like. One's culture permeates texts and critics. Just as all of society is intricately interwoven, so are critics and texts, both with each other and with the culture in which the critics live and the texts are produced. Because all critics are influenced by the culture in which they live, New Historicists believe that they cannot escape public and private cultural influences. Each critic therefore arrives at a unique interpretation of a text. Less overtly political than its British counterpart, New Historicism continues to be refined and redefined by its many practitioners.

In addition, Ames's version also has influences on the historical progression of America sinology, and such translation is especially exerting great influences on the world of Sinology.

REFERENCES

[1]ALAN S. Michel Foucault[M]. New York: Horwood and Tavistock, 1985.

[2]BARRY C. Michel Foucault: An Introduction to the Study of His Thought[M]. New York: Edwin Mellen, 1982.

[3]BROOK T. The Historical Necessity for---and Difficulties with---New Historical Analysis in Introductory Literature Courses[J]. College English 49 (September 1987): 509-522.

[4]CLEANTH B, ROBERT P W. Understanding Poetry[M]. New York: H. Holt and Company, 1939.

---

① LOIS TYSON. "New Historicism" in Selective Reading in 20th Century Western Critical Theory. Ed. ZHANG ZHONGZAI. Beijing: Foreign Language Teaching and Research Press, 2002.

[5]CLIFFORD G. The Interpretation of Cultures: Selected Essays[M]. New York: Basic Books, 1973.

[6]CLIFFORD G. Negara: The Theatre State of Nineteenth-Century Bali[M]. Princeton: Princeton University Press, 1980.

[7]D W ROBERTSON JR. "Historical Criticism" in English Institute Essays: 1950[M]. New York: Columbia University Press, 1951, 3-31.

[8]ELIZABETH FOX-GENOVESE. "Literary Criticism and the Politics of the New Historicism" in The New Historicism[M]. New York: Routledge, 1989:213-224.

[9]GERALD G, REGINALD G, eds. Criticism in the University[M]. Evanston: Northwestern University Press, 1985.

[10]ARAM VESSER H, ed. The New Historicism[M]. New York: Routledge, 1989.

[11]HERBERT L. "Toward a New History in Literary Study" in Profession: Selected Articles from the Bulletins of the Association of Departments of English and the Association of Departments of Foreign Languages[M]. New York: MLA, 1984, 16-23.

[12]JEAN E H. The New Historicism in Renaissance Studies[J]. English Literary Renaissance 16 (Winter 1986): 13-43.

[13]JEFFREY N C, LARRY J R, eds. New Historical Literary Study: Essays on Reproducing Texts, Representing History[M]. Princeton: Princeton UNIVERSITY PRESS , 1993.

[14]JENNIFER A W. Advertising Fictions: Literature, Advertisement, and Social Reading[M]. New York: Columbia UNIVERSITY PRESS , 1988.

[15]JEROME MAGANN. The Beauty of Inflections: Literary Investigations in Historical Method and Theory[M]. Oxford: Oxford UNIVERSITY PRESS , 1985.

[16]JEROME MAGANN. Historical Studies and Literary Criticism[M]. Madison: University of Wisconsin Press, 1985.

[17]JEROME MAGANN. Social values and Poetic Act: The Historical Judgment of Literary Work[M]. Cambridge: Harvard UNIVERSITY PRESS , 1988.

[18]JONATHAN D. Radical Tragedy: Religion, Ideology, and Power in the Drama of Shakespeare and His Contemporaries[M]. Chicago: University of Chicago Press, 1984.

[19]JONATHAN D, ALAN S, eds. Political Shakespeare: New Essays in Cultural Materialism[M]. Manchester: Manchester UNIVERSITY PRESS , 1985.

[20]JONATHAN G. James I and the Politics of Literature: Jonson, Shakespeare, Donne, and Their Contemporaries[M]. Baltimore: Johns Hopkins UNIVERSITY PRESS , 1983.

[21]LOUIS M. Renaissance Literary Studies and the Subject of History[J]. English Literary Renaissance 16 (Winter 1986): 5-12.

[22]LOUIS M. "Professing the Renaissance: The Poetics and Politics of Culture" in The New Historicism[M]. Ed. H A VEESER. New York: Routledge, 1989, 15-36.

[23]LOUIS M. "New Historicisms" in Redrawing the Boundaries: The Transformation of English and American Literary Studies[M]. Eds. STEPHEN G and GILES G. New York: Modem Language Association, 1992, 392-418.

[24]LYNN H, ed. The New Cultural History[M]. Berkeley: University of California Press, 1989.

[25]MARK C, ATHAR H. Michel Foucault [M]. New York: St. Martin's, 1984.

[26]MICHEL FOUCAULT. Madness and Civilization[M]. Trans. RICHARD H. New York: Pantheon, 1965.

[27]MICHEL FOUCAULT. The Order of Things[M]. New York: Pantheon, 1972.

[28]MICHEL FOUCAULT. Discipline and Punishment: The Birth of the Prison[M]. Trans. ALAN S. New York: Vintage, 1979.

[29]MICHEL FOUCAULT. The Foucault Reader[M]. Ed. PAUL R. New York: Pantheon, 1984.

[30]MIKE G, ed. Towards a Critique of Foucault[M]. London: Routledge & Kegan Paul, 1987.

[31]PAUL R, ed. The Foucault Reader[M]. New York: Pantheon, 1984.

[32]PETER C, HELGA GEYER-RYAN, eds. Literary Theory Today[M]. Ithaca: Cornell UNIVERSITY PRESS , 1990.

[33]RAYMOND W. Marxism and Literature[M]. Oxford: Oxford University Press, 1977.RENÉ W, AUSTIN W. Theory of Literature[M]. 3rd ed. New York: Harcourt, Brace, & Co., 1964.

[34]ROSS C M, ed. Heart of Darkness: A Case Study in Contemporary Criticism[M]. New York: St. Martin's, 1989.

[35]AMES R, HALL DL. Fousing the Familiar: A Translation and Philosophical Interpretation of the Zhongyong[M]. Honolulu: University of Hawaii Press, 2001.

[36]AMES R, HALL DL. *The Analects* of Confuicus: A Philosophyical Interpretation[M]. New York: Ballantine Books The Ballantine Publishing Group, 2001.

[37]SIMON D. New Historicism[J]. Text and Performance Quarterly 11 (July 1991): 171-189.

[38]STEPHEN G. Renaissance Self-Fashioning: From More to Shakespeare[M]. Chicago: University of Chicago Press, 1980.

[39]STEPHEN G. Introduction. The Forms of Power and the Power of Forms in Renaissance[J]. Genre 15 (Summer 1982): 3-6.

[40]STEPHEN G. Shakespearean Negotiations: The Circulation of Social Energy in Renaissance England[M]. Berkeley: University of California Press, 1988.

[41]STEPHEN G. "Towards a Poetics of Culture" in The New Historicism[M]. Ed. H A VEESER. New York: Routledge, 1989, 1-14.

[42]STEPHEN G. Learning to Curse: Essays in Early Modern Culture[M]. New York: Routledg, 1991.

[43]STEPHEN O. The Illusion of Power, Political Theater in the English Renaissance[M]. Berkeley: University of California Press, 1975.

[44]VICTOR T. Celebration: Studies in Festivity and Ritual[M]. Washington: Smithsonian Institution, 1982.

[45]WALTER B M. The Gold Standard and the Logic of Naturalism: American Literature at the Turn of the Century[M]. Berkeley: University of California Press, 1987.

[46]WESLEY M. Toward a New Historicism[M]. Princeton: Princeton UNIVERSITY PRESS , 1972.

CHAPTER X   CULTURAL STUDIES

The West essentializes these societies as static and undeveloped — thereby fabricating
a view of Oriental culture that can be studied, depicted, and reproduced. Implicit in this
fabrication, is the idea that Western society is developed, rational, flexible, and superior.

— E. Said, 2004

10.1   INTRODUCTION

The 1960s saw a revolution in literary theory. Until this decade, New Criticism dominated
literary theory and practice with its insistence that one ultimately correct interpretation of a
text could be discovered if the critical reader followed the methodology prescribed by the New
Critics. Believing that a text contained its meaning within itself, New Critics paid little attention
to a text's historical context or to the feelings, beliefs, and ideas of a text's reader. For the New
Critics, a text's meaning was inextricably bound to ambiguity, irony, and paradox found within
the structure of the text. By analyzing the text alone, New Critics believed that an astute critic
would be able to identity a text's central paradox and be able to explain how the text ultimately
resolved that paradox while at the same time supporting the text's overarching theme.

Into this seemingly self-assured system of hermeneutics marched Jacques Derrida and his
friends in the 1960s. Unlike the New Critics, Derrida, the founding father of deconstruction,
denied the objective existence of a text. Disavowing this basic assumption of New Criticism,
Derrida and other post-structural critics also challenged the definitions and assumptions of both
reading and writing and from a philosophical perspective asked what it actually means to read
and to write. Joined by reader-response critics, these postmodern thinkers insisted on questioning
what part not only the text but also the reader and the author play in the interpretive process.

Joined by a host of authors and scholars — Stanley Fish, J. Hillis Miller, Michel Foucault,
and many others — these philosopher-critics also questioned the language of texts and of literary
analysis. Unlike the New Critics, who believed that the language of literature was somehow
different from the language of science and everyday conversation, these postmodernists insisted

that the language of texts is not distinct from the language used to analyze such writings. For these critics, all language is discourse. In other words, the discourse or language used in literary analysis helps shape and form the text being analyzed. We cannot separate the text and the language used to critique it. Language, then, helps create what we call objective reality.

Believing that objective reality can be created by language, many postmodernists posit that all reality is a social construct. From this point of view, there is no objective reality, but many subjective understandings of that reality — as many realities as there are people. How, then, do we come to agree on public and social concerns such as values, ethics, and the common good? According to many postmodern thinkers, each society or culture contains within itself a dominant cultural group who determines that culture's ideology or its hegemony — its dominant values, its sense of right and wrong, and its sense of personal self-worth. All people in a given culture are consciously and unconsciously asked to conform to the prescribed hegemony.

What happens when one's ideas, one's thinking, and one's personal background do not conform? For example, what happens when the dominant culture consists of white, Anglo-Saxon males and you are a black female? Or how does one respond to a culture dominated by these same white males when you are a Native American? For People of color living in Africa or the Americas, for Native American, for females, and for a host of others, the traditional answer has been silence. Live quietly, work quietly, think quietly. The message sent to them by the dominant culture has been clear: Conform and be quiet; deny yourself and all will be well.

But many have not been quiet. Writers and thinkers such as Toni Morrison, Alice Walker, Gabriel García Márquez, Carlos Fuentes, Gayatri Spivak, Edward Said, and Frantz Fanon have dared and continued to challenge the dominant cultures and the dictates such culture decree. They have not been silenced. Defying the dominant culture, they believe that an individual's view of life, values, and ethics does matter. Not one culture, but many; not one cultural perspective, but a lot; not one interpretation of life, but countless numbers are their cries.

Joined by postmodern literary theorists and philosophers, Africans, Australians, Native Americans, women, and many other writers are finding their voices among the cacophony of dominant and overpowering cultural voices. Believing that they can effect cultural change, these new voices refuse to conform and be shaped by their culture's hegemony. There newly heard but long-existent voices can now be overheard at the discussions taking place at the literary table, where they present their understandings of reality, society, and personal self-worth.

Known as cultural studies, an analysis and an understandings of these voices can be grouped into three approaches to literary theory and practice: Post-colonialism, African-American criticism, and gender studies. Although each group has its personal concerns, all seek after the same thing: To be heard and understood as valuable and contributing members of society. Their individual and public histories, they assert, do matter. They believe that their past and their present are intricately interwoven. By denying and suppressing their past, they declare that they will be denying themselves. Their desire is to be able to articulate their feelings, concerns, and assumptions about the nature of reality in their particular cultures without becoming marginalized. Often called **subaltern writers** — a term used by Marxist critic Antonio Gramsci to refer to the classes who are not in control of a culture's ideology or its hegemony — these writers provide new ways to see and understand cultural forces at work in literature and in ourselves. Although each approach's literary theory and accompanying methodology are still developing, a brief overview of the central tenets of each of the three approaches will enable us to catch a glimpse of their diverse visions of literature's purposes and functions in today's world. Although no sample student essay is provided, following the synopsis of each of the three approaches is a professional essay that demonstrates the concerns and theoretical interests of postcolonialism.

10.2   POSTCOLONIALISM: THE EMPIRE WRITES BACK

Postcolonialism or post-colonialism (either spelling is acceptable, but each represents slightly different theoretical assumptions) can be defined as an approach to literary analysis that concerns itself particularly with literature written in English in formerly colonized countries. It usually excludes literature that represents either British or American viewpoints, and concentrates on writings from colonized cultures in Australia, New Zealand, Africa, South America, and other places and societies that were once dominated by but outside of the white, male European cultural, political, and philosophical tradition. Often called third-world literature by Marxist critics — a term many other critics think pejorative — postcolonial literature and theory investigate what happens when two cultures clash and when one of them with its accompanying ideology empowers and deems itself superior to the other.

The beginnings of such literature and theoretical concerns date back to the 1950s. During this decade, France ended its long involvement in Indochina, Jean-Paul Sartre and Albert Camus parted ways on their differing views about Algeria, Fidel Castro delivered his now-famous speech

"History Shall Absolve Me", and Alfred Sauvy coined the term *Third World* to represent countries that philosophically, politically, and culturally were not defined by Western metaphysics. During the 1960s, Frantz Fanon, Albert Memmi, George, Lamming, and other authors, philosophers, and critics began publishing texts that would become the cornerstone of postcolonial writings.

The terms *post-colonial* and *postcolonialism* first appear in the late 1980s in many scholarly journal articles and as a subtitle in Bill Ashcroft, Gareth Griffiths, and Helen Tiffin's text *The Empire Writes Back: Theory and Practice in Post-Colonial Literatures* (1989) and again in 1990 in Ian Adam and Helen Tiffin's *Past the Last Post: Theorizing Post-Colonialism and Post-Modernism*. By the mid-1990s, the terms had become firmly established in scholarly writing, and now postcolonialism usually refers to literature of cultures colonized by the British Empire.

Like deconstruction and other postmodern approaches to textual analysis, postcolonialism is a heterogeneous field of study where even its spelling provides several alternatives. Some argue that it should be spelled postcolonialism with no hyphen between post and colonialism, whereas others insist on using the hyphen as in post-colonialism. Many of its adherents suggest there are two branches: Those who view postcolonialism as a set of diverse methodologies that possess no unitary quality, as suggested by Homi Bhabha and Arun P. Murkerjee, and those who see postcolonialism as a set of cultural strategies centered in history. Even this latter group however, can be subdivided into two branches: Those who believe postcolonialism refers to the period after the colonized societies or countries have become independent and those who regard postcolonialism as referring to all the characteristics of a society or culture from the time of colonization to the present.

However post-colonialism is defined, that it concerns itself with diverse and numerous issues becomes evident when we examine the various topics discussed in one of its most prominent texts, Ashcroft, Griffiths, and Tinin's *The Post-Colonial Studies Reader* (1995). Such subjects include universality, difference, nationalism, postmodernism, representation and resistance, ethnicity, feminism, language, education, history, place and production. As diverse as these topics appear, all of them draw attention to one of post-colonialism's major concerns: Highlighting the struggle that occurs when one culture is dominated by another. As postcolonial critics are ever ready to point out, to be colonized is to be removed from history. In its interaction with the conquering culture, the colonized or indigenous culture is forced to go underground or to be obliterated .

Only after colonization occurs and the colonized people have had time to think and then to write about their oppression and loss of cultural identity does postcolonial theory come into existence. Born out of the colonized peoples' frustrations, their direct and personal cultural clashes with the conquering culture, and their fears, hopes, and dreams about the future and their own identities, postcolonial theory slowly emerges. How the colonized respond to changes in language, curricular matters in education, race differences, and a host of her discourses, including the act of writing, become the context and the theories of post colonialism.

Because different cultures that have been subverted, conquered, and often removed from history will necessarily respond to the conquering culture in a variety of ways, no one approach to postcolonial theory, practice, or concerns is possible or even preferable. What all postcolonialist critics emphatically state, however, is that European colonialism did occur, that the British Empire was at the center of this colonialism, that the conquerors not only dominated the physical land but also the hegemony or ideology of the colonized people, and that the effects of these colonizations are many and are still being felt today.

An inherent tension exists at the center of post-colonial theory, for those who practice this theory and provide and develop its discourse are themselves a heterogeneous group of critics. On one hand, critics such as Fredric Jameson and George Gugelberger come from a European and American cultural, literary , scholarly background. Another group that includes Gayatri Spivak, Edward Said, Homi K. Bhabha, and many others were raised in Third world cultures but now reside study, and write in the West. And still another group that includes writers such as Aijaz Ahmad live and work in the Third World. A theoretical and a practical gap occurs between the theory and practice of those trained and living in the West and the Third World, subaltern writers living and writing in non-Western cultures. Out of such tension postcolonial theorists have will continue to discover problematic topics for exploration and debate.

Although a number of postcolonial theorists and critics such as Frantz Fanon, Homi K. Bhabha, and Gayatri Chakravorty Spivak have contributed to postcolonialism's ever-growing body of theory and its practical methodology, the key text in the establishment of postcolonial theory is Edward W. Said *Orientalism* (1978). In this text, Said chastises the literary world for not investigating and taking seriously the study of colonization or imperialism. According to Said, nineteenth-century Europeans tried to justify their territorial conquests by propagating a manufactured belief called Orientalism — the creation of non-European stereotypes that suggested "Orientals" were indolent, thoughtless, sexually immoral, unreliable and demented. the European conquerors, Said notes, believed that they were accurately describing the inhabitants of their newly conquered land. What they failed to realize, maintains Said, is that all human knowledge can be viewed only through one's political, cultural, and ideological framework. No theory either political or literary, can be totally objective.

That no political, social, or literary theory can be objective also holds true for a person living and writing in a colonized culture. Such an author must ask of himself or herself three question: Who am I? how did I develop into the person that I am? To What country or countries or to what cultures am I forever linked? In asking the first question, the colonized author is connecting himself or herself to historical roots. By asking the second question, the author is admitting a tension between these historical roots and the new culture or hegemony imposed on the writer by the conquerors. And by asking the third question, the writer confronts the fact that he or she is both an individual and a social construct created and shaped by the dominant culture. And the writing penned by these authors will necessarily be personal and always political and ideological. Furthermore, its creation and its reading may also be painful, disturbing, and enlightening. Whatever the result, the story will certainly be a message sent back to the Empire, telling the Imperialists what they did wrong and how their Western hegemony damaged and suppressed the ideologies of those who were conquered.

10.3   POST COLONIALISM AND AFRICAN –AMERICAN CRITICISM

The growing interest in post colonialism in American literary theory during the late 1970s to the present provided a renewed interest in African-American writers and their works. To say that postcolonialism or other postmodern theories initiated African-American criticism and theory, however, would be incorrect. For the first seven decades of the twentieth century, African-American criticism was alive and well, its chief concern being the relationship between the arts (writing, music, theater, poetry, etc.) and a developing understanding of the nature of African-American culture. During this time, writers such as Langston Hughes (*Not Without Laughter, The Weary Blues*), Richard Wright (*Black Boy, Native Son*), Zora Neale Hurston (*Their Eyes Were Watching God, Dust Tracks on a Road*), James Baldwin (*Go Tell It on the mountain, The First Next Time*), and Ralph Ellison (*The Invisible Man*), wrote texts depicting African-Americans interacting with their culture. In this body of literature, these subaltern writers concerned themselves mainly with issues of nationalism and helped to expose the treatment of African Americans — a suppressed, repressed, and colonized subculture — at the hands of their white conquerors. Presenting a variety of themes in their fiction, essays, and autobiographical writings, such, as the African American's search for personal identity; the bitterness of the struggle of black men and women in America to achieve political, economic, and social success, and both mild and militant pictures of racial protest and hatred, these authors gave to America personal portraits of what it meant to be a black writer struggling with personal, cultural, and national identity.

Although literature authored by black writers was gaining in popularity, more often than not it was interpreted through the lens of the dominant culture, a lens that, for the most part, could see only one color: white. A black aesthetic had not yet been established, and critics and theorists alike applied the principles of Western metaphysics and Western hermeneutics to this ever-evolving and steadily increasing body of literature. Although theoretical and critical essays by W. E. B. DuBois, Langston Hughes, Richard Wright, and Ralph Ellison had begun to announce to America and the literary world that black literature was a distinctive literary practice with its own aesthetics and should not be dubbed a subcategory or a footnote of American literature, it was not until the late 1970s and 1980s that black theorists began to articulate the distinctiveness of African-American literature.

In this ever-increasing group of literary critics, two stand out: Abdul R. JanMohamed and Henry Louis Gates, Jr. The founding editor of *Cultural Critique*, JanMohamed is one of the most influential postcolonial theorists. A professor of English at the University of California at Berkeley, JanMohamed has authored a variety of scholarly articles and texts that stress the interdisciplinary nature of literary criticism. Raised in Kenya (and therefore not considered by some to be an African American), JanMohamed witnessed first hand the British Imperialists' attempt to dominate and eliminate the colonized culture. He has thus spent his life studying the effects of colonization with its accompanying economic and social dynamics, concerning both the conqueror and the conquered. Of particular importance is his text *Manichean Aesthetics: The Politics of Literature in Colonial Africa* (1983). In this work, JanMohamed argues that literature authored by the colonized (Africans in Kenya and African-Americans in America, for example) is more interesting for its **noematic** value — the complexities of the world it reveals — than its noetic or subjective approach to what it perceives. Consequently, Jan Mohamed delineates the antagonistic relationship that develops between a hegemonic and a non-hegemonic literature.

In African-American literature, for example, he notes that black writers such as Richard Wright and Frederick Douglass were shaped by their personal socioeconomic conditions. At some point in their development as writers and as people who were on the archetypal journal of self-realization, these writers became "agents of resistance" and were no longer willing to "consent" to the hegemonic culture. According to JanMohamed, subaltern writers, at some time, resist being shaped by their oppressors and become literary agents of change. It is this process of change from passive observers to resistors that forms the basis of JanMohamed's aesthetics.

Perhaps the most important and leading African-American theorist, however, is Henry Louis Gates Jr. Unlike many African-American writers and critics, Gates directs much of his attention to other African-American critics, Gales attempts to provide a theoretical framework for developing a specifically African-American literary canon. In this new framework, he insists that African-American literature be viewed as a form of language, not a representation of social practices or culture. For black literary criticism to develop, he contends that its principles must be derived from the black tradition itself and must include what he calls "the language of blackness, the signifying difference which makes the black tradition our very own." In his texts *The Signifying Monkey* (1988) and Figures in Black: Words, Signs, and the "Racial" Self (1987), Gates develops these ideas and announces the "double-voicedness" of African-American literature — that is, African-American literature draws on two voices and cultures, the white and the black. It is the joining of these two discourses, Gates declares, that produces the uniqueness of African-American literature.

Along with other theorists such as Houston Baker and a host of African-American feminist critics, present-day African-American critics believe that they must develop a culturally specific theory of African-American literature. Theirs, they believe, is a significant discourse that has for too long been neglected. The study of this body of literature, they insist, must be reformed. The beginnings of this reformation have brought to the foreground another body of literature that has also been ignored or at least relegated to second-class citizenship: The writings of females with its accompanying literary theory, gender studies.

10.4 GENDER STUDIES: NEW DIRECTIONS IN FEMINISM

What do Toni Morrison, Alice Walker, and Gloria Naylor have in common? All are African-American women writers who have successfully bridged the gap between subaltern authors and the dominant culture. Each has achieved a place of prominence in American culture, with Toni Morrison winning the Nobel Prize for Literature in 1993: Thanks, at least in part, to an increasing interest in postcolonial literature, these female authors have bridged not only the cultural but also the gender gap. As models for other women, these writers have found their voices in a society dominated by males and Western metaphysics, and their works have become seminal texts in feminist and gender studies.

Concerned primarily with feminist theories of literature and criticism and sometimes used synonymously with feminism or feminist theories (see Chapter 8 for an explanation of feminist theories and practice), gender studies broaden traditional feminist criticism to include an investigation not only of femaleness but also maleness. What does it mean it asks, to be a woman or a man? Like traditional feminist theory, gender studies continue to investigate women and men view such terms as *ethics*, definition of truth, personal identity, and society. Is it possible, gender specialists question, that women view each of these differently than men?

Into the multivoiced feminist theories, gender studies add the ever-growing and ever-diverse voices of black feminists, the ongoing concerns of French feminism, and the impact of poststructural theories on customary feminist issues. Its authors include the almost canonical status of writers such as Adrienne Rich, Bonnie Zimmerman, and Barbara Smith, along with those of Elaine Showalter, Sandra Gilbert, Susan Gubar, Gayatri Chakravorty Spivak, and Toril Moi. But new authors and critics such as Yyvonne Vera, Anne McClintlock, Sara Suleri, Dorothea Drummond Mbalia, and Sara Mills also appear, asking and adding their own unique questions to feminist theory.

Striving to develop a philosophical basis of feminist literary theory, gender studies re-examines the canon and questions traditional definitions of the family, sexuality, and female reproduction. In addition, it continues to articulate and investigate the nature of feminine writing itself. And it joins feminist scholarship with postcolonial discourse, noting that postcolonial literature and feminist writings share many characteristics, the chief being that both are examples of oppressed peoples.

As with feminist theory, the goal of gender studies is to analyze and challenge the established literary canon. Women themselves, gender specialists assert, must challenge the hegemony and free themselves from the false assumptions and the long-held prejudices that have prevented them from defining themselves. By involving themselves in literary theory and its accompanying practices, gender specialists believe women and men alike can redefine who they are, what they want to be, and where they want to go.

In the professional essay that follows, note how uses the principles and theories of post-colonialism to arrive at his conclusions. After carefully reading this article, be able to cite the post-colonial terms, interests, and theories that Hulme uses. Do you agree or disagree with analysis? Be able to defend your position.

10.5 SAMPLE ESSAY

On *Zhongyong* Translated by Roger T. Ames and Ku Hungming in Light of Post-colonialism

As one of the most influential Confucian classics, *Zhongyong* is the highlight of Chinese sages' fruitful thoughts. But the Chinese philosophy that is embedded in the book has ever been neglected or misunderstood in the West over a long period of time. In Westerner's eyes there is no Chinese philosophy.

Thus the translation of *Zhongyong* not only plays an important role in spreading Chinese philosophy and culture, but also in correcting the misunderstanding of Chinese philosophy, so the research on its translation is very necessary. *Zhongyong* has achieved its prominence through constant retranslations diachronically or synchronically both in China and in the West. Scholars have made every effort to explore its translations, hoping to account for the effective factors that exert effects on each version of *Zhongyong*.

Postcolonial translation theory provides a new perspective for its translation studies. Postcolonial translation theory is a kind of cultural and political translation theory, which breaks the assumption that language is equal in traditional translation theories, and makes us start to focus on power differentials behind translation activity. Due to their different times and nationalities, Roger T. Ames's and Ku's English Versions of *Zhongyong* are full of their own features. On one hand, the two translators are different from other translators in their cultural identities and cultural visions.

Postcolonial Translation Studies Abroad

In the late 1990s, post-colonial theory was initially involved in translation studies. Politics, military, culture, economic research and colonial translation interact with each other. The binary opposition of power and discourse not only reflects the will of the imperial conqueror, but also reflects the fact that translation is not pure activities of language and text. As a cross-disciplinary theory covering translation studies, anthropology, psychology, political science and other fields, post-colonial translation theory examines translation act under different historical conditions, and concerns the operating mechanism of power struggle hidden in translation and deformation of two cultures.

Theoretically speaking, post-colonial translation theory holds that there are power differentials between different cultures which have never had an equal dialogue, and thus denies the Utopian assumptions of language equality in traditional translation theory. Wang Dongfeng said post-colonial theory studied translators' conscious or unconscious values, behavior and translation strategies in the context of power differentials. (Wang Dongfeng, 2003:4) Niranjana, Venuti, Robinson and Maria Tymoczko are representatives of post-colonial translation theory.

In1992, Niranjana published a book *Siting Translation: History, Post-structuralism, and the Colonial Context* in which she discussed Indian translation in post-colonial context and attempted to open the door for translation studies from the viewpoint of culture and politics. Through borrowing Said's and Foucault's view into translation studies, Niranjana held that translation act was a kind of political behavior, and translation was a place where unequal power relations among different ethnic groups, language and country extended. Colonial power rebuilt rewritten Oriental images by translation. In the process of translation and rewriting, the colonizers imposed their ideology on the other. If the colonized wanted to reproduce their own values, they could only shape themselves in accordance with the needs of colonial control. Influenced by Said's Orientalism, Niranjana further criticized western discourse, especially the practice of translation that marginalized "the other", and thus called for translators to assume "intervention" strategy to resist colonial discourse. In 1995, Lawrence Venuti investigated translation strategy from the aspect of power relations between the sovereign state and the colonial state. A large amount of data showed the unequal translation history and the "surplus" between Britain and other European languages (Venuti,1995: 6-12) form the backbone of post-colonial translation theory (Robinson, 1997:33). He believed that in Anglo-American culture, dominant fluent translation covered the intervention of translators; domestication was actually aimed to preserve Anglo-American values. The translators' invisibility revealed the hegemony of translation, so he borrowed Lewis's "abusive fidelity" as resistance strategy. Venuti believed that only "abusive fidelity" would respect and reflect the poetic value and cultural identity of the original. Only in this way could we input difference into target culture, reconstruct the false cultural archetype which was shaped by "normal fidelity" with domestication trend, and subvert American mainstream value which was protected by "normal fidelity". Douglas Robinson's book *Translationand Empire* (1997) was the integration of post-colonial theory. In this book, the author summarized various sides of post-colonial theory, put imperial politics, culture and social factors into the scope of translation studies, and gave prominence to translation's function in development of colonization and decolonization. Robinson pointed out that post-colonial translation embodied "power relations". Translation was a tool of colonization, but it was also a means of decolonization. In the post-colonial context, translation maintained not only language inequality and translation non-equivalence, but also binary opposition of "self and other". Translation could maintain differences and cultural diversity by closely following the original, but domestication and foreignization may sustain the colonial mind to some extent. Maria Tymoczko has a high international reputation in post-colonial translation studies. Her representative works like *Translation in a Post-colonial Context* (1999), *Translation and Power* (2002), *Translation as Resistance* (2006) and *Enlarging Translation, Empowering Translators* (2007) are important research results of post-colonial translation. Maria Tymoczko advocated studying translation from a cultural perspective, especially, from the perspective of description. In *Translation in a Post-colonial Context*, Maria Tymoczko investigated Irish translation practice in their struggle for independence, demonstrated translators' and writers' resistance to British colonial culture when they translated Irish National Literature and reproduced the Irish patriotic theme. In addition, Maria Tymoczko made a detailed discussion on post-colonial translation and writing, and she put great emphasis on relations between translation and power in the post-colonial context. In her view, translation research must involve changes in the operation of power in society; power operation meant cultural production, while the translation was part of cultural production. Translators in the other place ardently responded to post-colonial translation studies. Brazilian Cannibalism took on a place in post-colonial translation studies. The Campos brothers thought that the Brazilian not only ate colonists and their language, from which they gained spiritual power, but also purified themselves from their ritual ceremonies. Specifically, the Campos Cannibalism included the following points: (1) Empowering act: swallowing the original symbolized their respect and love for the object swallowed, and gained energy from the body; (2) Nourishing act: the source of life lied in swallowing the original, and the translator gained nutrition from the original language and culture which is embodied in version after transformation; (3) Act of affirmative play: translation is a life-giving act, only through translation can the original be passed and reborn.

Post—colonial Translation Studies in China

Ever since 1990s, domestic scholars have also launched a systematic studyon post-colonialism and post-colonial translation theory.Although having started later in China, post-colonial translation studies have gained fruitful achievements in China. In 2001, Xu Baoqiang and Yuan Wei introduced translation thoughts of post-colonial scholars such as Niranjana, Spivak and Venuti in their collection *The Politics of Languages and Translation*. In 2005, Fei Xiaoping's doctoral thesis *The Politics of Translation: Translation Studies and Cultural Studies* gave a clear elaboration of post-colonial translation. In the same year, Dr. Sun Huijun verified post-colonial theory from the macro aspects in his thesis *Universality and Difference: a Post-colonial Approach to Translation Studies*. In 2008, Dr. Wu Wen'an traced back to the origin of post-colonial theory, and analyzed the relations between post-colonial translation and post-colonialism, deconstruction, post-colonial writing, translation strategies in his paper *Post-colonial Translation Studies — Translation and Power Relations*. In addition to these monographs, there are many papers about post-colonial translation theory. These articles studied post-colonial translation theory from different aspects, which expanded the scope of post-colonial study. In 2003, Wang Dongfeng discussed several key words of post-colonial translation studies such as post-colonialism, decolonization, Orientalism and hybridity. Li Hongman put translation within the framework of broad international politics, analyzed the effect that power differential had on translation activity in terms of the flow rate, selection, strategy and discourse respectively. Viewing from the post-colonial perspectives, Chen Liming compared two versions of *The Dream of Red Mansions*, analyzed "colonial gazing" embodied in Hawk's version and pointed out post-colonial dialogue should not premise on the lack of cultural identity. Pan Xuequan & XiaoFuping (2005) thought that colonial literature was affected by colonial ideology, reinforcing inequalities between the colonizer and the colonized. Su Qi (2007) held that "the Orient", which was created by the west, stood for the primitive, mysterious, backward "other". Western translators were not aimed at learning, but at finding weaknesses of oriental culture to show the west was better than the east. In post-colonial context, we should break away from western shackles, completely get rid of long-existing "oriental image", and promote national culture. Ruan Hongfang focused on religious and traditional elements of translation, and analyzed different strategies to deal with cultural differences between strong and weak culture and the underlying power relations. In short, post-colonial translation study inspects translation activity from the post-colonial perspective. It tries to reveal the power relationship behind translation activity. And due to many scholars' effort, it has achieved great development.

As one of the most influential Confucian works, *Zhongyong* is not confined in China, but disseminated to the west. As early as 300 years ago, *Zhongyong* has been introduced into the west through translation. At that time it was mainly interpreted by western missionaries. The first one who translated *Zhongyong* into foreign language was an Italian missionary, named Matteo Ricci(1552-1610). In 1593, he translated the four books including *Zhongyong* into Latin but the version had never been published. The existent complete Latin version of the *Zhongyong* was published in 1687 in Paris. Since then, *Zhongyong* has been continuously introduced to the west with the effort of many scholars. In 1828, David Collie also produced an English version of the four books, but it didn't evoked strong repercussions.

In the later half of 19th century, James Legge translated *The Four Books and Five Classics* with the help of Chinese scholar Wang Tao. At that time, Legge was viewed as one of the most important and influential sinologists of Confucian classics.

His version of *Zhongyong* entitled *The Doctrine of the Mean was incorporated* in *The Chinese Classics* which has been regarded as the most authoritative English version ever produced by western scholars.

In 1906, Ku Hungming published his English version of *Zhongyong*, named The Universal *Order or Conduct of Life*. This was the first version translated by Chinese scholar. Later the title was changed to *The Conduct of Life or the Universal Order of Confucius* and had been quite popular among western readers. Later Roger T. Ames and David Hall translated *Zhongyong* together. Their version, entitled *Focusing the Familiar: A Translation and Philosophical Interpretation of Zhongyong*, was published by Press of Hawaii University in 2001.

Ku Hungming in *his In modern China*, he was considered as an eccentric figure. Speaking of him, most people have the impression that Ku was an old fogy with long braid of the Qing Dynasty. Though receiving western education, he was in favor of taking a concubine and foot-binding. Ku Hungming had a legendary life experience. He was born into an overseas Chinese family at Malaya on July 19, 1857. When he was a child, Ku Hungming was so bright that the

Browns (his father's employer) liked him very much and adopted him. In 1867, the Browns left for Scotland and took Ku Hungming to study in Europe. There he received western education systematically and master so many languages like English, Germany, Italian, Latin and etc. In 1883, he encountered Ma Jianzhong who persuaded Ku into appreciating Chinese traditional culture. Influenced by Ma Jianzhong, Ku began to study Chinese culture. After his back to China, he worked with Chang Chih-tung (张之洞), an important statesman at the end of the Qing Dynasty. From then on, Ku Hungming devoted himself to Confucian culture and became more and more conservative. At that time, Confucian works were translated by western missionaries. Ku thought their translation had a lot of misunderstandings of Chinese Confucianism. In order to make western people know real Confucianism, change their prejudice and arrogant attitude to China, and alter their policy to China, Ku decided to retranslate Chinese Confucian classics.

He devoted most of his lifetime to spreading Chinese culture (especially Confucianism) to the western world. In the preface to *Lunyu*, he wrote, "we hope the cultivated English people find time to read our translation. After reading it, they can realize their prejudice to China, alter it and change their attitude to Chinese and China, and later improve relationship between two countries." He had translated *Lunyu*, *Zhongyong* and Daxue into English, and only *Zhongyong* and *Lunyu* had been published. His translation, including *Lunyu* and *Zhongyong*, played a significant role in disseminating traditional Chinese culture to the western world. Among them, English version of *Zhongyong* is the most popular, which had ever been compiled into Eastern Wisdom Books, Lin Yutang's Wisdom of Confucius and The Wisdom of China and Indian successively. In London, this version had been reprinted four times from 1908 to 1928. The prevalence of *Zhongyong* made Ku Hungming become "the greatest Confucian authority" in the westerner's eyes. Many scholars made comments on his English version of *Zhongyong*. Wang Guowei wrote a very influential article entitled *Words after Reading Ku's English Version of Zhongyong* in 1907. In his article, Wang Guowei criticized Ku's translation of *Zhongyong*. He pointed out that Ku's translation principles were inappropriate because Ku put too much emphasis on expounding the thoughts of the ancients on one hand and interpreting the book with the western philosophy on the other, thus Wang arrived at the conclusion that it was not a faithful translation. Chen Fukang agreed with Wang's statement. He thought Wang's opinion was "harsh but wonderful" in that it conformed to "dynamic equivalence" in the present translation studies. However, Kong Qingmao believed that Ku's strategy of interpreting Chinese philosophy with the

Western philosophy is not unacceptable if taking Ku's intention into consideration." Both Huang Xintao and Ma Zuyi held that Wang's criticism was important but ignored Ku's contribution in the history of spreading Confucian works to the Western world.

Roger T. Ames and His Version

Contemporary American sinologist Roger T. Ames is now an important person among overseas sinologists. He is a professor in the department of philosophy at the University of Hawaii, a principal of Asian Studies Development Program, editor in chief of *Eastern and Western philosophy* and *The International China Review* and has served as the director of the center of Chinese Studies at the University of Hawaii for eight years. He has begun to study Chinese philosophy and culture since his boyhood.

In 1966, he was sent to study in Hong Kong as an exchange student. Under the influence of Tang Junyi and Mu Zongshan, he started to contact Confucian philosophy and was absorbed in its ideology. From then on, Ames has dedicated himself to Chinese philosophy. But it took him thirteen years to gain his Doctor's degree because he could not find a place to learn Chinese philosophy in the West. Western philosophers still insist that Anglo-European philosophy is the only philosophy. That means Anglo-European philosophy has no interest in the wisdom of other countries. After learning and living in Hong Kong for a time, Ames found that this viewpoint is narrow. In his later academic career, he dedicates himself to challenging this narrow ethnocentrism in the whole western philosophical system. Ames wrote a lot of books concerning with Confucianism, Taoism in a paradigm of comparative philosophy between West and China. Those books are *Thinking through Confucius, Thinking from the Han: Self, Truth, and Transcendence in Chinese and Western Culture, Anticipating China: Thinking through the Narratives of Chinese and Western Culture, The Democracy of the Dead: Dewey, Confucius, and the Hope for Democracy in China*, etc. He improves Confucian research to the level of social ideology. He holds that Chinese Confucianism contains rich democratic ideology. China should find source from himself, and this source can be absorbed by the world democracy. More importantly, he thinks that Confucianism and Dewey pragmatism has much in common. If the two are combined together, the result from the combination will stand for the direction of future democracy. His statement is affirmation and expectation to Chinese culture.

He also translated many Chinese classics, including *Dao De Hing, Lunyu, Zhongyong,*

Huainanzi, Sunzibingfa, Sunbinbingfa etc. Among them, *Lunyu* and *Zhongyong* are the most famous. The moment when Ames's translation of *Zhongyong* was published, it aroused scholars' great interest. Ames and Hall themselves reinterpreted several key words such as Cheng, Xing, Qing, Li, Jiao by comparing western culture with Chinese culture and exposed the coherent structure and unique religion *Zhongyong* contains. Ni Peimin held that the Ames and Hall's version of *Zhongyong* replaced substance language with dynamic language, revealing the holistic and dynamic *Zhongyong* contained. But his emphasis on metaphysics shades the important Confucian level of *Zhongyong*. In Ni's words, "the fundamental aim of *Zhongyong* is not to describe what or how the world is; it is rather to instruct people how to live their lives. Ames and Hall come close to this point in numerous places, but fall short of making it clear." But at last Ni continued that though their translation did not reveal Confucian level, it established foundation for it. Li Chenyang stated at the outset, "*Zhongyong's* central theme is the ideal of grand harmony in the universe and how humans can promote such an ideal; Ames and Hall have missed this central theme in their interpretation of *Zhongyong*…failure to identity this central concept and ideal in *Zhongyong* is a major oversight of the text's central message." Ronnie Little John argued that Ames and Hall "worried over their appeal to the language of transcendence and immanence in making a distinction between classical Chinese process cosmology and classical western ontology. He maintained that "their persistence in the use of transcendent/immanent distinction leads Ames and Hall into inconsistencies and interpretive difficulties they could avoid by relying on the underlying physics of *Zhongyong*". He concludes with a few suggestive remarks with regard to how the correlative physics of *Zhongyong* holds the promise of contributing significant insights to western philosophy.

Nathan Sivin mainly criticized their emphasis upon novelty and creativity in their interpretation of *Zhongyong*. He worried that with "creativity" being such a contemporary western value, Ames and Hall might be looking for their own importance in this ancient Chinese text. He said, "The explorations of Ames and Hall, like much other contemporary history of philosophy, can become more productive if they fully engage what we are now coming to understand about society, politics, and means of livelihood. However, the work of Ames and Hall challenges us to set aside the old habits that made ancient Chinese philosophy a series of exotic, diverse but not very successful attempts to foreshadow the philosophic fashions of the modern west Wen Haiming argues that "Ames and Hall's studies on Confucianism, particularly in the recent version

Focusing the Familiar: A Translation and Philosophical Interpretation of Zhongyong, have provided an opportunity to reflect and improve the understanding and interpretation of Chinese philosophy." He compared the key terms in Ames and Hall's new translation with those of James Legge's translation of *Zhongyong, The Doctrine of the Mean*, to show how Ames and Hall try to overcome the "Christianization" of Chinese texts and avoid theologically-laden terms such as "Heaven" (Tian, 天), "righteousness" (Yi, 義), "rites" (Li, 禮) and "virtue" (De, 德). He comes to a conclusion that Ames and Hall's reexamination of such key terms is a search for a more appropriate understanding of the Chinese way of thinking.

Traditionally, translation studies have paid more attention to the division like "word-for-word" and "sense-for-sense" translation, "overt" and "covert" translation, "foreignizing" and "domesticating" translation. Actually, it isn't that simple. Though linguistic and literary approaches to translation have grown complex, the old dualism for the study of translation is proving inadequate for discussions of an important new approach to translation, born in the mid-to-late 1980s out of neither linguistics nor literary studies but anthropology, ethnography and colonial history: Post-colonial translation studies. With the rise of post-colonial translation theory, contemporary studies on translation are increasingly aware of the need to examine in depth the relationship between the production of knowledge in a given culture and its transmission, relocation, and interpretation in the target culture. This obviously has to do with the production and ostentation of power and with the strategies used by this power in order to present the other culture.

Translation as a Cultural and Political Practice

After the cultural turn of translation in the 1990s, post-colonialism has rapid development. Post-colonial translation study focuses on politics, nation, imperialism and other issues with strong political color, and explores the nature of translation from the political perspective. Traditional translation theory believes that translation is a neutral and innocent act; the cultural misunderstanding occurred in which is just an academic question; and translation should be transparent, equivalent and faithful. However, this view becomes the main target post-colonial translation theory scholars attack.

Post-colonial translation theory reveals the power issue inherent in translation, rediscovers political relations between translation and the reality of the time. As a cross-language and cross-cultural communication behavior, translation is inevitably marked with the brand of ideology, more or less influenced by political factors from the start. Translation, fundamentally speaking, is to input the exotic culture and ideology into the local one; translation is a purposeful act, so the translation is a cultural and political act. Althusser noted that any kind of reading can not be innocent, let alone translation? To realize the equal exchange of two different cultures via right or good translation is bound to be a universal illusion. In fact, the issue of "faithfulness, expressiveness and elegance" in translation behavior is a political issue. Translation is the main way to impose an additional meaning, and hide power relations behind it when imposing meaning. Translation is always in the network of power relations constituted by the original and the translation context. As a matter of fact, translation is not neutral and pure conversion activities, staying away from political, ideological struggle and interest conflict, but a cultural, philosophical and ideological transformation, deformation and re-creation one culture exerts on another. Spivak stressed that translation from the original to the third world language was often political activities. Translation activities contained cultural and political conflicts. Translation became the weapon of post-colonial discourse. Chen Yongguo pointed out that translation itself contains difference.

The important factors that lead to these differences are society, economy, history, religion and politics. In this sense, any translation is a political act. Translation is a process in which the chain of signifiers that constitutes the source-language text is replaced by a chain of signifiers in the target language which the translator provides for the strength of their subjective interpretation. While the viability of a translation is established by its relationship to the cultural and social conditions under which it is produced and read. This relationship points to the violence that resides in the very purpose and activity of translation: The reconstruction of the foreign text in accordance with values, beliefs and representation that preexist it in the target language, always configured in hierarchies of dominance and marginality, and always determining the production, circulation, and reception of text. The violent effects of translation are universal. On one hand, translation wields enormous power in the construction of national identities for foreign cultures, and hence it potentially figures in ethnic discrimination, geopolitical confrontations, colonialism, terrorism, and war.

In conclusion, translation always implies an unstable balance between the power one culture can exert over another. Translation is not the production of one text equivalent to another text, but rather a complex process of rewriting that run parallel both to the overall view of language and of the "other" people have throughout history; and to the influences and balance of power that exist between one culture and another. As Javier Franco states in his article, when translating we are confronted with four basic types of problems: Linguistics, interpretive (those who have denied the possibility that translation could become a science), pragmatic or inter-textual (based on conventions of expression for each type of discourse, which are different for each society), and cultural (with its vibrance of historical distance). Every linguistic community also has its own set of values, norms, and classification systems which at times will differ from those of the target culture, and coincide with them at other times. According to Franco, this creates a factor of variability which the translator must somehow resolve, from the conservation and acceptance of the difference to naturalization depending on the degree of tolerance. Therefore, the translator's conduct will never be innocent.

Translation as a Means of Resistance

Traditionally translation is considered as a channel of colonization. Many post-colonial translation scholars have done this research. Eric Cheyfitz, Tejaswini Nirannjana, Vicente Rafael and Lawrence Venuti all wrote a number of articles on this argument. But they are not confined to it. They also explore the ways translation has been used, and should be used, to resist or redirect colonial or post-colonial power. Douglas Robinson stresses that translation also serves as a channel of decolonization.

Translation has been or can be used to fight against oppression, to liberate minds and bodies. Niranjana argues for a transformative practice of "retranslation", the radically new translation of Indian and other colonized peoples' text in ways that seek to further the ongoing process of decolonization. Jean-MarcGouanvic stresses that there are resistant spirit in the process of translation. Ramakrishna put forward the concept of "counter-translation". For his part, "counter-translation" means translation in which the choice of translation object and translation models not influenced by colonial power. He deemed that it is a channel against hegemony. The Egyptian scholar Samia Mehrez explores the way in which recent writers in North Africa have drawn on hybridized versions of French and Arabic, in order to break down the colonial power hierarchies among French, Arabic and various local vernaculars. Cronin believes that translation has the function of resistance to colonial power. He concludes two forms of resistance.

One is resistance at the level of positionality. Translators are defined by their class, race, gender — their general position in networks of power and influence. However, depending on the configurations of power, translators can shift their allegiances. They are therefore not to be trusted. Another is resistance at the level of text. Cronin mentioned two forms of textual resistance. The first is macaronic subversion. An example taken from Irish literary history is the tradition of political macaronic verse in eighteen-century Ireland, where the lines of the poem in English appeared blameless or conciliatory, while the lines in Irish carried a very different political message — a message that was considerably more hostile to the authority. The second is attributive subversion. In this case, translation is a form of insubordination that exploits the deferred responsibility of translation. Cannibalism is also a form of resistance. Cannibalism devours the original and translates it creatively. It changes the silent state of the third world. It has great significance in fighting against cultural hegemony.

Concerns about the Cultural Identity

From the beginning of human life, cultural identity has been in existence. What is cultural identity? Scholars define it from different perspective. According to Hamers and Blanc, cultural identity is part of social identity. The integration of the complex configuration of culture into the individual's personality constitutes his cultural identity. Stuart Hall holds that, "cultural identity refers to 'those aspects of identities' which arise from our 'belonging' to distinctive ethnic, racial, linguistic, religious and above all, national cultures."[1]

Zhang Yuhe regards that cultural identity is a self-image that one individual, one group or one nation achieves in comparison with other individuals, groups, or nations. The most important elements constitute cultural identity are values, language, family, system, life mode and spirit world. Kramsch points out that, cultural identity is bureaucratically self-ascribed membership in a specific culture". Cultural identity refers to "the link between subjective experience of the world and historical setting that constitutes this subjectivity."[2] From the macro dimension, cultural identity includes national identity, personal identity, language identity and regional identity. From the micro dimension, cultural identity is the rules shaped by the same mainstream culture group

---

① Language and Culture Identity[EB/OL].[2018-05-10].http://www.lib.csu.ru/ER/ER_LINGKUL/fulltexts/KramschC65-78.

② KAFRAUNI R. The role of subjectivity category in understanding the community context and the transforming intervention. [EB/OL].(2012-6-22)[2018-05-10].http://www.scielo.br/scielo.php?script=sci_arttext&pid=S0103-166X2013000100013

according to different regions, occupations, genders, ages and classes.

As far as post-colonial context is concerned, cultural identity means that imperialism's cultural colonization on internal and external culture makes marginal body have to make identity choice between the colonized and sovereign. Therefore, the issue of cultural identity comes out strongly in this context, which arouses high value. As long as conflicts and asymmetries exist in the collision of different cultures, the issue of cultural identity occurs Said once pointed out, the construction of cultural identity is closely related to power relationships of each society. The construction of cultural identity depends on the kind of "otherness". "Self" can only be defined by the comparison, interaction and consultation with "the other". Strong mainstream culture makes the weak culture be "the other" to locate their own identity and obtain a "positional superiority".

Post-colonial translation theory's attention to cultural identity is reflected in two aspects: The first is the translation effect on the shaping of cultural identity; the second is the positioning of the translator's cultural identity and its effect on translation. Translation wields enormous power in constructing representations of foreign cultures, but there also hides domestic culture and politics under this construction. The selection of foreign texts and the development of translation strategies can establish peculiarly domestic canons for foreign literature, canons that conform to domestic aesthetic values and therefore reveal exclusions and admissions, centers and peripheries that deviate from those current in the foreign language. Foreign literature tends to be de-historicized by the selection of texts for translation, and removed from the foreign literary traditions where they draw their significance. And foreign texts are often rewritten to conform to styles and themes that currently prevail in domestic literature. Translation can establish fixed stereotypes for foreign cultures, excluding values, debates, and conflicts that don't serve domestic agenda. In creating stereotypes, translation may attach esteem or stigma to specific ethnic, racial, and national groupings, signifying respect for cultural difference or hatred based on ethnocentrism, racism, or patriotism. In the long run, translation figures in geopolitical relations by establishing the cultural grounds of diplomacy, reinforcing alliances, antagonism, and hegemonies between nations. In the late of 18th century, British colonizer formed Indian the squalid and fatuous image via translation, thus to show the nobility of European civilization and found excuse for its colonial expansion. Spivak pointed out in his work *Outside in the Teaching Machine* that "translation was a simple mimic performance", exhibiting the trace of "other" in "self" vividly.

Another case in point is the translation of modern Japanese fiction into English. Venuti found, the translation shaped Japan as "an aestheticized realm" when Japan was being transformed from a mortal enemy during the Pacific War to an indispensable ally during the Cold War era. The English-language canon of Japanese fiction functioned as a domestic cultural support for American diplomatic relations with Japan. Yet since translations are usually designed for specific cultural constituencies, they set going a process of identity formation that is double-edged. As translation constructs a domestic representation for a foreign text and culture, it simultaneously constructs a domestic subject, a position of intelligibility. When John Jones's existentialist-informed translations of Aristotle displaced the dominant academic reading, they acquired such institutional authority as to become a professional qualification for classical scholars. Specialists in Aristotle and Greek tragedy are expected to demonstrate familiarity with Jone's study in teaching and research publications. Accordingly, Jones rates a mention in introductory surveys of criticism, whether they are devoted to the tragic genre or to specific tragedian. Because translation can contribute to the invention of domestic literary discourse, it has inevitably been enlisted in ambitious cultural projects, notably the development of a domestic language and literature. And such projects have always resulted in the formation of cultural identity aligned with specific social groups, classes and nations.

In *Translation Strategies of the Post-colonial Translation Theory*, Translation strategy usually refers to the whole target which guides specific translation method when translating. It is one of the hot topics in translation circle in 1990s. Generally speaking, there are two kinds of translation strategies: Foreignizing translation and domesticating translation. In 1813, German philosopher and translator Frieddirch Schleiermacher stated in his lecture "On the Different Methods of Translating" "there were only two methods of translation: Either the translator leaves the writer alone as much as possible and moves the reader toward the writer, or he leaves the reader alone as much as possible and moves the writer toward the reader. In 1995, Lawrence Venuti summed up these methods in his book *The Translator's Invisibility* with two terms: Foreignizing translation and domesticating translation. Before 1995, most disputes about foreignizing translation and domesticating translation were confined to linguistic and literary level. After Lawrence Venuti put forward the two terms and with the development of post-colonial translation theory, the dispute of foreignizing translation and domesticating translation came into a new stage. This guide many scholars to rethink foreignizing translation and domesticating translation from a new perspective. From post-colonial perspective, the choice between the two strategies tends to be effected by power differentials between the two cultures involved and always reflects the translator's attitude towards the two cultures. The most famous representatives who discuss a lot in terms of the two strategies are LawrenceVenuti and Douglas Robinson. According to LawrenceVenuti, domesticating translation is "a term used to describe the translation strategy in which a transparent, fluent style is adopted in order to minimize the strangeness of the foreign text for TL reader." Robinson agrees mostly with his statement, whereas he also put forward his oppugn. Nowadays, with the development of globalization, more and more scholars realize that the simple dualism of foreignizing translation and domesticating translation is not enough; there must have some ways better.

LawrenceVenuti's *Comments on Domestication and Foreignization* makes him one of the major figures in contemporary U.S. translation theory. Not only has his publication broken new ground theoretically, building powerful historical and ideological cases against what he calls "invisibility" or "transparency" of "fluent" or "domesticating" translation and in favor of what he calls the resistant dissidence of "foreignizing" translation, he also worked institutionally to win translation studies a more prominent place in the academy. In 1995, based on Schleiermacher's lecture on the different methods of translation, Lawrence Venuti concluded that translator could choose between a domesticating method (an ethnocentric reduction of the foreign text to target-language cultural values, bringing the author back home) and a foreignizing method (an ethno-deviant pressure on those values to register the linguistic and cultural difference of the foreign text, sending the reader abroad). By studying western translation history, Lawrence Venuti criticized that traditional translation shaped foreign texts on the value of ethnocentrism and imperialism, the translation it advocated was domesticating translation. Venuti put forward his opposition to it and set forth a new strategy to fight against this fluent translation. The reason why he was against domestication and for foreignizing translation was that he wanted to develop a translation theory and practice which was aimed to express discrepancy of foreign texts in their language and culture. He said, "Foreignizing translation is a dissident cultural practice, maintaining a refusal of the dominant by developing affiliations with marginal linguistic and literary values at home, including foreign cultures that have been excluded because of their own resistance to dominant values. On one hand, foreignizing translation enacts an ethnocentric appropriation of the foreign text by enlisting it in a domestic cultural political agenda, like dissidence; on the other hand, it is precisely this dissident stance that enables foreignizing translation to signal the linguistic and cultural difference of the foreign text and perform a work of cultural restoration, admitting the ethno-deviant and potentially revising domestic literary canons."[1] The "foreign" in foreignizing translation is not a transparent representation of an essence that resides in the foreign text and is valuable in itself, but a strategic construction whose value is contingent in the current target-language situation. Foreignizing translation translation signifies the difference of the foreign text, yet only by disrupting the cultural codes that prevail in the target language. Consequently, in its effort to meet the demand of target readers, this method unavoidably disrupts the code of source language, deviating enough from native norms to stage an alien reading experience-choosing to translate a foreign text excluded by domestic literary canons, for instance, or using a marginal discourse to translate Venuti continuously suggested that insofar as foreignizing translationsought to restrain the ethnocentric violence of translation it was highly desirable today, a strategic cultural intervention in the current state of world affairs, pitched against the hegemonic English-language nations and the unequal cultural exchanges in which they engaged their global others. Foreignizing translation in English can be a form of resistance against ethnocentrism and racism, cultural narcissism and imperialism, in the interest of democratic geopolitical relations. On the contrary, domestication is "an ethnocentric reduction of the foreign text to target-language cultural values" in which a transparent, fluent style is adopted in order to minimize the strangeness of the foreign text for target language readers. This kind of translation distorts foreign texts. It is the conspirator of the sovereign to control the colonies. He emphasized translation's challenge to Anglo-American cultural hegemony and exaggerated the binary opposition of foreignizing and domesticating translation.

Later, his translation thought changed a little. He accentuated self-criticism to Anglo-American postmodern culture and cleared up the opposition of foreignizing and domesticating translation. On one hand, he held on to foreignizing translation; on the other hand, he deconstructed himself in some of his arguments. For example, in his book *The scandals of Translation*, he believed that Yan Fu's translation criterion was the extension of ethnocentrism. His translation strengthened the dominant value of Chinese. But instead of expressing his denial attitude to it, he said, "The practice of late Qing translators like Lin Shu and Yan Fu demonstrate

---

[1]   VENITI L. The Translator's Invisibility: A History of Translation[M]. Routledge, London & New York, 1995:148.

that domesticating strategies, especially when used in situation of cultural and political subordination, can still result in a powerful, hybridity that initiated unanticipated changes." So he believed that even ethnocentric translation could signal the foreign, depending on the nature of the foreign text and the receiving culture situation.

Comments on Domestication and Foreignization

For Venuti's part, domesticating translation is a primary tool of empire insofar as it encourages colonial powers (or more generally the "stronger" or "hegemonic" cultures) to translate foreign texts into their own terms, thus eradicating cultural differences and creating a buffer zone of assimilated "sameness" around them. Members of hegemonic cultures are therefore never exposed to true differences, for they are strategically protected from the disturbing experience of the foreign. Members of peripheralized cultures in turn are forced to "write for translation", to pre-shape their cultural expressions to meet hegemonic expectations. In this way diversity is gradually leached out of the world. And we are all immeasurably impoverished. For the post-colonial foreignizes, the remedy to this situation is a mode of translation designed to retain and assert difference and diversity by sticking closely to the contours of the source text. However, Douglas Robinson put forward his critique of this solution as follows:

(1) It is not clear that foreignizing and domesticating translations are all that different in their impact on a target culture. All translations are based on interpretations, and interpretations will vary from translator to translator; foreignizing translations do not necessarily add to the existing diversity of this situation.

(2) The impact of domesticating and foreignizing translations on the target-language readers is neither as monolithic nor as predictably harmful or salutary as the foreigners' claims. There is an implicit reader-response assumption behind foreign theories, that domesticating translation will colonize the reader, to enforce colonial hegemony in that reader's thinking, while foreignizing translation will help to decolonize the reader, undermine colonial hegemony and thus conduce to effective political and cultural action in the service of increased freedom from the colonial past...Foreignize theories of translation are inherently elitist. Venuti and Niranjana have struggled valiantly to undo this elitism, to harness foreignism for dissident or counter-hegemonic politics, but the imaginative leap that would make this shift possible remains extremely difficult to make.

(3) The domesticating and foreignizing translation presumes a stable separation of source and target languages. A domesticating translation is one that makes all translational decisions in terms of a stabilized or objectified target language or culture; a foreignizing translation is one that owes a stronger loyalty to a stabilized or objectified source languageor culture. Butin fact, post-colonial texts, originals and translations begin to inhabit a middle or hybridized ground between "source" and "target"; it is no longer clear which part of a text is original and which is translated from another language when the distinction between original and translation itself begins to break down.[①]

In this sense, domesticating and foreignizing translation cannot be separated distinctly. Whether domesticating translation is a tool of colonization or decolonization; whether foreignizing translation is a tool of resistance or not, they both cannot be defined arbitrarily. It needs to consider cultural identity, historical background, and translation motivation of the translator.

Hybridity as the Means and Result of Post−colonial Translation

As mentioned above, foreignizing translation and domesticating translation can not be separated distinctively. In his book *The Translator's Invisibility*, Venuti has begun to move toward a position that would appropriate these hybridized middle ground for foreignism. Samia Mehrez, an Egyptian translation scholar, explores the ways in which recent writers in francophone North Africa have drawn on hybridized versions of French and Arabic, in order to break down the colonial power hierarchies among French and various local vernaculars. The term "hybridity" is first employed in the field of biology. Later it became a key term in nineteenth-century positivist discourse, hybridity moves the multiple thinking modes and help breaking the the established formulation and rational thinking. Today, "the use of hybridity prompts questions about the ways in which contemporary thinking has broken absolutely with the rationalized of formulations of the past". Bakhtin introduced the concept of hybridity in postmodern literature. For Bakhtin, hybridity defines the way in which language, even a single sentence, can be double voiced. It is a mixture of two social languages within the limits of a single utterance, an encounter, and within the arena of an utterance, between two different linguistic consciousness which were separated from one another by an epoch, by social differentiation or by some other factors. It is through

---

① ROBINSON, D, Translation and Empire: Post-colonial Empire.

hybrid construction that one voice is able to unmask the other within a single discourse. It is at this point that authoritative discourse becomes undone. Authoritative discourse is univocal. In post-colonial theory, standing in the history interweaves with culture, said believed that "every culture is hybrid. All kinds of cultural factors entangle together to constitute overlapped terrain and interlaced history". He employed cultural "hybridity" strategy to fight against cultural hegemony. In the hybrid and equal dialogue between western and oriental cultures, cultural hegemony has no place to exist. Cultural hegemony is cleared up in the process of hybridity. Hybridization as a subversion of authority in a dialogical situation of colonialism is examined by Homi Bhabha who introduced "hybridity" into postcolonial theory and made it prevalent. He analyzes different types of hybridizations produced by various postcolonial societies. In a colonial context, cultural hybridity is produced at the moment of the colonial encounter, when self and other are inseparable from mutual contamination with each other. The colonial encounter is therefore embedded a priority in power relations, and requires constant awareness of the limitations and possibilities of representation. Bhabha transforms Bakhtin's definition of the hybridity into an active moment of challenge and resistance to the dominant cultural power. He sees hybridity as a "sign of the productivity of colonial power, its shifting forces and fixity" and as a moment in which the discourse of colonial authority loses its univocal claim to meaning. In Bhabha's words: Hybridity is a problematic of colonial representation and individuation that reverse the effects of the colonialist disavowal, so that other "denied" knowledge enter the dominant discourse and estrange the basis of its authority — its rules of recognition. He argued against rigid binary oppositions of translation strategies. He reckoned that there was in-between space between the opposite poles. When the "other" of foreign culture communicates with the 'self' of local culture, if they are not negotiated and translated in the in-between space, they are not intelligible. In the third space, the strong and weak cultures remove the impact from their unequal power status, and dialogue equally on the basis of mutual difference, which makes the weak culture gain their discourse right, thus makes "other" and "self" refuse with each other. The space-in-between is therefore a fertile and, at the same time, disquieting space where the dialectical interaction of at least two cultures take place. It is a place where the dominant culture and language can be subverted, and thus functions as a sort of resistance. Following Bhabha's definition of hybridity, Michaela Wolf stressed that hybridity is a way to challenge and resist dominant culture.

Hybridity is a kind of strategy to subvert colonial cultural hegemony. It is the only way through which the weak culture becomes stronger in the post-colonial context. For one thing, hybridity disintegrates binary opposition between the sovereign and the colonized, between the strong culture and the weak culture, and provides a way for the weak culture to free away from the control of colonial culture or western authority; for another, the weak culture can rewrite dominant colonial culture through hybridity, making the residents from the sovereign feel the strangeness in his culture and lost in his own culture, thus making the western culture localization.

For example, the Indian resident did not accept the doctrine of the Bible completely, and did not give up their own tradition, but chose according to their need. So what they believed in was the hybridity of colonizers' religion and their traditional religion. Their hybridity of Christianism reversed the colonizers' control and clear up the colonizers' authoritative status in the process of spreading Christianism.

Zhongyong is one of the most influential Chinese classics in its depository. As *Zhongyong* is the most philosophical work among the Confucian classics, interpretation of the work is crucial to our appreciation of traditional Chinese philosophical wisdom. How to interpret it correctly is a great and significant issue. As mentioned above, many scholars translated it into different language. Among them, there are two influential English versions of *Zhongyong*, translated by American sinologist and philosopher Roger T. Ames in modern times and by Chinese scholar Ku Hungming in the late Qing Dynasty respectively. Ku's translation is much better than those of missionaries and sinologists with regard to the understanding of Confucianism. Roger T Ames's *Focusing on the Familiar: A Translation and Philosophical Interpretation of Zhongyong* is an interpretation with the emphasis on the cultural and philosophical aspects. Many scholars have made research on them to explore sound reasons to account for these two versions. From the aspect of translator's cultural identity, translation motivation and translation strategy, this essay provide a new interpretation of Chinese culture classics.

Translators' Cultural Identity

Translators' cultural identity is very complicated, which is formed from various aspects, such as his nation, region, class, gender, language, etc. Translator's cultural identity mainly includes national identity, personal identity, foreign identity and language identity. It is generally admitted that the translator's language competence, cultural background and his personality have a great effect on his translation and get involved in constructing his cultural identity. In the translating process, the translator will reveal his cultural identity intentionally or unintentionally, which directly determines the translator's cultural attitude and influences his views on translation. What's more, the translator reveals his cultural identity, cultural position and translation motivation by choosing works to translate and employing specific translation strategies. Therefore, it is necessary to take the translator's cultural identity into account to fully analyze his translation. Ku's cultural identity is very complicated. Having studied in Europe for several decades, Ku Hungming received systematic western education and mastered many languages. However, since he was influenced by European romanticism, Ku Hungming was dissatisfied with the deficiency of the western material civilization. Besides, he deeply tasted defiance from western people. After his return to China, he soon had great admiration for Chinese culture and was absorbed in Confucian culture and later became extremely conservative. Ku once said, "Through a comparative study of Eastern and Western civilizations, it is natural to arrive at a significant conclusion that our oriental civilization is, if not superior to Western civilization, at least not worse than them."

Ku Hungming learned the whole Western culture and digested and absorbed them. He was familiar with Goethe as a German, knew the Bible like a Christian, but he was absorbed in his own ancient culture. This unique cultural combination formed his unique cultural vision and identity, which finally have a significant impact on his translation of *Zhongyong*. In addition to his personal experience, the times he was in also helped to shape his cultural identity. At that time, China was suffering from imperial invasion. Imperialism trampled Chinese politics, economy, and culture. Chinese people including scholars lost their confidence in Chinese traditional cultures so much so that they tried to find a way to strengthen their country from the west. Hence, a new ideology tide sprang up in China, which proposed following the west. Under this circumstance, Chinese history was forced to be written in the light of western style. Chinese self-culture sank under the surface of history. So constructing Chinese cultural identity and removing the anxiety of interpreting Chinese cultural identity had a great importance. Just as Spivak said "can the subaltern voice?" Only by reversing the fate of being written can China make his voice. Ku retranslated Confucian classics to deconstruct Western power discourse in the representation of

Chinese cultural identity. Missionaries had translated Chinese Confucian classics[①]. But Ku was very dissatisfied with their translations. In the preface to *Lunyu*, he said, "Now, anyone, even if he knows nothing about the Chinese language, can't help feeling dissatisfied with James Legge's version, if he reads his version thoroughly."

He thought their versions couldn't reveal the true orient. Missionaries thought their researches on the orient reflected the real orient, but in fact, due to the potential or direct influence from the western value system, the oriental knowledge they showed was full of western ideology and discourse. It didn't reflect the true orient, but only their imagination. Therefore, Ku retranslated Confucian classics to fight against Orientalism, and eventually reconstruct Chinese cultural identity. In brief, Ku's cultural identity is Chinese, Confucian and anti-orientalism.

Roger T. Ames came to Hongkong as an exchange student, where he began to learn Chinese philosophy and was absorbed in its ideology. Since then, he devoted himself to comparative philosophy between western and Chinese culture. He came to realize that western philosophy ignored the existence of Chinese philosophy. He once wrote, "Western academic community had deadly flaw in their research modes of Chinese philosophy. Chinese philosophy system consists of abstruse philosophical works, like *Lunyu, Zhongyong, Dao De Jing, Sun Zi Bingfa*, etc., but what is philosophical about these texts did not still gain their deserved recognition in the West."[②] He thought this is the embodiment of western egotism and cultural chauvinism. Ames put much more attention to the introduction of Chinese philosophy. In *Focusing the Familiar: A Translation and Philosophical Interpretation of Zhongyong*, he employed the language of focus and field to express philosophical ideology contained in *Zhongyong*. Such language presumes a world constituted by an interactive field of process and events in which there are no final elements, only shifting "foci" in the phenomenal field, each of which focuses the entire field from its finite perspective. Besides, Ames thought the ignorance of Chinese philosophy was due to Western egotism and cultural chauvinism. Western philosophical community holds that Anglo-European philosophy is the only philosophy. There is no philosophy existing in China. But in fact, western and Chinese philosophy is compensatory. For instance, *Yijing* contains the world view of process which is now new in western philosophy. So Ames devoted himself to challenging western

---

① HUAN G, XIN TAO , The Discourse and Sayings of Confucius[A]. 辜鸿铭文集 . 海口：海南出版社 ,1996:345.

② R. T. Ames. Seeking Harmony not Sameness: Mutual-communication between Chinese and Western Philosophy[M]. Beijing: Peking University Press, 2009: 5.

ethnocentrism, and let Chinese philosophy make its voice in the western world. In this sense, Ames's cultural identity is philosophical and anti-ethnocentrism.

Translators' Motivation

The translator's cultural identity determines his translation motivation. Imperial powers invaded China in the late Qing Dynasty. China was in a weak state in every field like politics, economy and culture. A tide of following the west sprang up in China, seeking reform in political and economic filed. But at this time, Ku Hungming went against this tide. He devoted himself to the translation of Confucian classics. Actually, he regarded translation as a means to resist western cultural hegemony. He wanted to disseminate real Chinese culture to the west. In 1883, he attacked the sinologist's superficiality and false pride. He maintained that the translation of Chinese classics by the western sinologists distorted the features of Chinese literature and the image of Chinese people, because of their improper research approaches and lack of right understanding of Chinese culture. And their national prejudices and cultural superiority lead to their defiance on Chinese people and literature. The image of China reflected in their translation version and their articles about Chinese culture which mislead western people's attitude to China is not the real China, but their imagination of Orientalism features. Ku Hungming wanted to correct their distortion of Chinese culture, show the real Chinese civilization and its value to the west. In this way, he has the motivation to fight against Orientalism. In addition, he put himself to disseminate civilization to change western people's prejudice. He once stated, "most people think that Chinese old system is dying away, they all greet the arriving new knowledge and advanced civilization. But I personally believe that Chinese old order will not be out of date, because I know the old order, Chinese civilization and social order is the moral civilization and real social order."[1]

In the preface to *The Discourses and Saying of Confucius*, he said, "we only want to express one wish that the educated and wise English men could correct their prejudice against Chinese people, and alter their personal attitudes toward China in international exchange after reading this translation version." When translating *Zhongyong*, he expressed this wish again. He said, "if this book can help to make European people, especially those staying in China, understand 'tao' better, form a moral responsibility so that they can abandon European "gun" and 'violence'

---

① KU HONGMING, The Spirit of the Chinese People[A].1999:346.

civilization when treating China and Chinese. Instead, they will follow moral responsibility in their communication with Chinese either as a person or as a nation. — Then I will feel my effort on understanding and translation this book is not in vain."[1]

As for Ames, the reason why he chose to retranslate Confucius classics was that he believed the philosophical ideology contained in these texts was not interpreted correctly by missionaries and sinologists. In their introduction to *Focusing the Familiar: A Translation and Philosophical Interpretation of Zhongyong*, Roger T. Ames and David L. Hall critique the Christianization of Chinese texts done by early translators, saying that such practices "have not served us well". Under the Christianization translation, the inexhaustible Chinese philosophical resources are reduced to a simple doctrine that had already been clearly stated by a great western thinker. In this sense, Chinese philosophical texts come out as pale imitations of already familiar western ideas. They call attention to the translation of key Chinese concepts that they believed are freighted with connotations from Christian theology: Tian 天 (heaven), Yi 义 (righteousness), Li 礼 (rites), and De 德 (virtue). As a corrective to these past errors, they say, our present circumstance obviously require a fuller inventory of the semantic resources available to us if we are to produce appropriate translations of Chinese texts. Fortunately, recent development in Anglo-European philosophy have foregrounded interpretive vocabulary more relevant to the articulation of Chinese sensibilities. In place of the traditional language, vocabulary of process and change has increasingly become available to those interested in interpreting Chinese thought for western audience. So they employed a language of process in order to illuminate the context and arguments of *Zhongyong*. By doing so, they will reach their aim to disseminate Chinese philosophy and resist western ethnocentrism.

Translators' Translation Strategies

The translator's cultural identity and motivation determine his translation strategies; in turn, his translation strategies embody his cultural identity and motivation. For Ku Hungming's part, he mainly wanted to make the western people change their prejudice against and attitude to Chinese people and China after reading his version of *Zhongyong*, so his strategy is reader-orientation. He used lots of western vocabulary and many annotations. But for Ames, he mainly wanted to maintain Chinese philosophy in his version of *Zhongyong* to change the phenomena that Chinese philosophy had been always ignored by western philosophical community, thus coming to the

---

[1]   KU HONGMING. The Universal Order or Conduct of Life[M].Shanghai: Mereury, Ltd, 1906:13.

aim to resist western ethnocentrism and Chauvinism and make Chinese philosophy has its voice. So his strategy is source-orientation. In this section, the author will compare Ku's translation strategy with Ames's from four aspects: Confucian key terms, holistic interpretation of the text, cultural comparative studies of the text, and hybrid language.

Analysis of the Confucian Key Terms

Speaking of the translation of Confucian key terms, translators cannot find lexical matched as there is not always one-to-one equivalence between Chinese and English. How to translate Confucian key terms successfully is crucial to the whole translation. As D.C. Lau once stated, "the difficulty lies in the different concepts of Chinese and English languages and the corresponding English words cannot be found on many occasions…The difficulty may become even greater when coming across a concept which does not exist in the West." In this section, I will focus on Ku's and Ames's different interpretations of several Confucian key words which show their different cultural identity, different translation purposes and translation strategy.

Zhongyong (中庸)

The two characters in the title " *Zhongyong*" mean respectively "what is central"(Zhong, 中) and "what is universal, common and ordinary" (Yong, 庸). According to Zhu Xi, it means "plain without bias"(2005:19). Ku and Ames have distinct interpretation as follows:

Example1:

仲尼曰：" 君子中庸，小人反中庸。君子之中庸也，君子，而时中；小人之中庸也，小人，而无忌惮也。"(*Zhongyong* Chapter 2)

Ku: Confucius remarked: "The life of the moral man is an exemplification of the universal moral order. The life of the vulgar person, on the other hand, is a contradiction of the universal moral order." The moral man's life is an exemplification of the universal order, because he is a moral person who constantly lives his true self or moral being. The vulgar person's life is a contradiction of the universal order, because he is a vulgar person who in his heart has no regard for, or fear of, the moral order."

Ames: Confucius said: "exemplary persons (Junzi, 君子) focus (Zhong, 中) the familiar affairs of the day; petty persons distort them. Exemplary persons are able to focus the affairs of the day because, being exemplary, they themselves constantly abide in equilibrium (Zhong). Petty persons are a source of distortion in the affairs of the day because, being petty persons, they lack the requisite caution and concern."

Ku chose to translate "*Zhongyong*" as "the universal moral order" in that he wanted to show its connotative fully to the western readers. Ames, on the contrary, thought that the former translation of this expression was unfortunate rendering. A more comprehensive and coherent translation of it is "focusing the familiar affairs of the day. The term "familiar" shares the same root as "family", and thus evokes the notion of "family" that is at the center of the Confucian socio-religious experience.

Cheng (诚)

The idea of Cheng (诚) occupied a key position in *Zhongyong*. According to "Shuowenjiezi" (说文解字), it means Xin 信 (truthfulness, faithfulness). Kong Yingda signified this meaning with another definition, "Cheng means Shi 实 (reality). Zhu Xi argued that "cheng" is "principle of reality"(Shili 实理); it also means "sincerity"(Chengque 诚阕). Cheng Yi changed this trend by interpreting it primarily as "principle of reality". This term is mostly translated in the earlier literature as either "integrity" or "sincerity". Ku and Ames have their different understanding.

Example 2: 诚者，天之道也。诚之者，人之道也。诚者，不勉而中，不思而得，从容中道，圣人也。诚之者，择善而固执之者也。(*Zhongyong* Chapter 1)

Ku: Truth is the law of God. Acquired truth is the law of man. The truth that comes from intuition is the law implanted in man by God. The truth that is acquired is a law arrived at by human effort. He who intuitively apprehends truth, is one who, with effort, hits what is right and without thinking, understands what he wants to know; whose life easily and naturally is in harmony with the moral law. Such a one is what we call a saint or a man of divine nature. He who acquires truth is one who finds out what is good and holds fast to it.

Ames: Creativity (Cheng 诚) is the way of Tian (天之道); creating is the proper way of becoming human (人之道). Creativity is achieving equilibrium and focus (Zhong 中) without coercion; it is succeeding without reflection. Freely and easily traveling the center of the way — this is the sage (Shengren 圣人). Creating is selecting what is efficacious (Shan, 善) and holding on to it firmly.

Ku chose western philosophical term "truth" to express the meaning of Cheng (诚) because he was aimed to remove the strangeness of Chinese culture and make it acceptable to the westerners. Ames, on the contrary, translated Cheng as "creativity". He said "the parsing of cheng as "creativity" brings attention to the centrality of cosmic creativity as the main theme of *Zhongyong*. It suggests that creativity involves a dynamic partnership between the living human world and its natural, social and cultural contexts.

Tian (天)

Zhongyong upholds Tian 天 as the ultimate reality and basis for human morality. Tian is not only transcendental but also immanent, residing within us as human nature. Ku and Ames have different translation of it as follows:

Example 3: 天命之谓性。(*Zhongyong* Chapter 1)

Ku: The ordinance of God is what we call the law of our being.

Ames: What Tian (天) commands (Ming 命) is called natural tendencies (Xing 性).

In order to cater for the Christian tradition of the English world, Ku translated Tian as "God". That made it easy for western readers to understand, but inevitably cannot express the secular mindset of Confucius. Ames chose to leave Tian untranslated. He believed its conventional English rendering as "Heaven" could not but conjure up misleading associations drawn from our Judeo-Christian tradition. These theological associations are largely irrelevant to the Chinese experience but have often overwritten Chinese cultural practices with presuppositions that are alien to them. Tian in classic Chinese is the world. Tian is both what our world is and how it is. The "ten thousand processes and events (Wanwu, 万 物)" are not the creatures of Tian, rather, they are constitutive of it.

Dao (道)

Dao occurs pervasively in *Zhongyong*, and is of central importance for interpreting the thinking of this document.

Example 4: 子曰："道不远人；人之为道而远人，不可以为道。"(*Zhongyong* Chapter 1)

Ku: Confucius remarked: "The moral law is not something away from the actuality of human life. When men take up something away from the actuality of human life as the moral law, that is not the moral law."

Ames: The Master said, "The proper way (Dao, 道) is not at all remote from people. If someone takes as the way that which distances them from others, it should not be considered the proper way."

Ku translated "Dao" into "the moral law". He once argued that the nearest equivalent in the European language for Dao is moral law.

Ames holds on to translate Dao as "the proper way". Dao denotes the active project of "moving ahead in the world" and by extension, to connote a pathway that has been made, and hence can be traveled. It is because of this connotation that Dao is often be translated into "the way". But it is somewhat problematic. To realize Dao is to experience, to interpret, and to influence the world in such a way as to reinforce and extend a way of life inherited from one's cultural precursors. Ames chose to translate Dao as "the proper way".

Junzi (君子)

Junzi appeared many times in *Zhongyong*. The Shuowen lexicon defines Jun (君) as "of high rank", and then derivatively "to honor" or "to hold in high esteem."

Example 5: 子曰："射有似乎君子；失诸正鹄，反求诸其身。"

Ku：Confucius remarked, "In the practice of archery we have something resembling the principle in a moral man's life. When the archer misses the centre of the target he turns around and seeks for the cause of his failure within himself."

Ames: The Master said, "As in archery, so in the conduct of the exemplary person; in failing to hit the bull's-eye, look for the reason within oneself."

Ku rendered Junzi as "the moral man" in that he thought moral is very important in Chinese culture. Ames translated Junzi as "the exemplary person". He believed that the conduct of the Junzi is most often described socially as a model for other persons. Junzi are in fact defined as those who are able to focus the familiar affairs of the day. They know many rituals and much music, and perform all of their communal functions not only with felicity, but also with grace, dignity, and beauty.

"God", "truth" "the universal order" "the moral law", "the moral man" are chosen to translate " 天 " " 诚 " " 中 庸 " " 道 " " 君 子 " etc. This choice depended on his translation purposes. He once said "Chinese wisdom and virtue exhibited in Legge's version made western people feel strangeness, just like Chinese appearance and clothes in their eyes." So he "made his effort to translate Confucian classics in the light of the mode of cultivated western people." He wanted to make most western people accept Confucianism and realize that Chinese culture was excellent by adopting Christian terms in his translation. Therefore, though he adopted domesticating translation, he did not succumb to western hegemony. On the contrary, he resisted western hegemony in this way. Ames does not pretend to reconstruct in modern English exactly what was going on in the mind of an author more than two thousand years ago. Ames has honestly designed his strategy of translation to keep right in front of the reader's eyes the bedrock differences between the way his authors saw, touched, and responded to the world around them, and the common sense ontology of Americans today. From above examples, we find that Ames used foreignizing translation to preserve Chinese philosophical ideology in his version. This also depended on his aim to give Chinese philosophy its deserved status in the world, make the western change their egoism and ethnocentrism and make the whole philosophy progress by mutual learning.

The Holistic Interpretation of the Text

Though lived in different times, Ku and Ames both interpret *Zhongyong* holistically. In the late Qing Dynasty, moral corruption existed in every corner of the society. At the same time, imperial countries invaded China, blazoning forth that western culture was superior to the Chinese culture. This discrimination against Chinese culture hurts Chinese pride. Influenced by European romanticism, Ku animadverted on western substance civilization. Translation helped him to fight against such situation. On one hand, he could wake up Chinese people; on the other hand, to retort western cultural hegemony. Ku thought, there were great differences between oriental civilization and western civilization. Confucian civilization is a kind of ethnic, spirit civilization, while western civilization is a kind of substantial, uncultured civilization. As Arnold stated, "whatever the whole literature — the entire history of human, or a great literary work, only by leaning and understanding it and regarding it as an organic integrity can the real literary force be showed." Influenced by Arnold, Ku Hungming deemed that, western sinology was inadequate for a lack of correct research approaches; it did not master the principle of literature and philosophy, that it, it did not take a national culture as an organic integrity. In 1883, he critiqued that those sinologists were superficial and arrogant, and their sinology research had no the view of integrity. Later he continued, "No matter in his preface or annotation, no any words showed that Legge had holistic and philosophical understanding of Confucianism". So in the translating process, he insisted on the rule of holistic interpretation. In his version of *Zhongyong*, " 性 " is "the law of our being", "moral nature" or "our moral being"; " 道 " is "the moral law"; " 君子 " is "moral man"; " 中 " is "our true selves", or "moral being"; " 和 " is "moral order"; " 中庸 " is "the universal moral order"; " 仁 " is "moral sense". The translation of these Confucian key terms all has the "moral" from the beginning to the end. This holistic interpretation rule showed Ku's intention to exhibit to the western people that Chinese civilization is a moral one. The fatuous, uncultured image of China is the distortion by the Orientalist.

For Ames's part, Chinese philosophy contains a dynamic process. Limitations placed upon the translation of Chinese texts are associated with the employment of the default vocabulary of both demotic and philosophical discourse in the West. "Western languages are substance-oriented and are, therefore most relevant to the descriptions and interpretations of a world defined by discreteness, objectivity, and permanence. Such languages are ill-disposed to describe and interpret a world, such as that of the Chinese, which is primarily characterized by continuity, process, and becoming."

As a philosopher, he regarded the whole text as a dynamic integrity. As a consequence, he employed a language of process in order to illuminate the context and argument of *Zhongyong*. Such a language style presumes a world constituted by an interactive field of processes and events in which there are no final elements, only shifting "foci" in the phenomenal field, each of which focuses the entire field from its finite perspective.

Translation is the dialogue between cultures. In order to make readers understand his translation, the translator first needs to be "an expert in culture". The translator should adapt to the readers in cultural dimension, and help readers to conquer the inimical mood to "the otherness". Ku realized that, to let western readers, especially those common readers, understand Confucian culture fundamentally, he must remove the strangeness of the source text. So he chose domesticating translation, made cultural comparison between western and Chinese culture. He compared some famous persons in Chinese with their counterparts in the West.

For example, in Chapter 6 of *Zhongyong*, " 舜其大知也与 !" Ku translated it as "there was the Emperor Shun. He was perhaps what may be considered a truly great intellect." Following it was his annotation, "what is here said of the Emperor Shun in ancient China may be also said of the two greatest intellects in modern Europe — Shakespeare and Goethe." In addition, he cited ideas from the Bible, Emersion, Arnold, Goethe and Shakespeare to echo some Confucian ideology. For instance,

"子曰：中庸其至矣乎！民鲜能久矣！"

Ku translated it as follows:

"Confucius remarked: — 'to find and get into the true central (中) balance of our moral being, i.e., our true moral ordinary (庸) slves , that indeed is the highest human attainment. People are seldom capable of it for long.' Emersion says: 'from day to day the capital facts of human life are hidden from our eyes. Suddenly the mist rolls up and reveals them, and we think how much good time is gone that might have been saved had any hint of these things been shown.'" He cited Emersion's saying to echo Confucian thought. This is a good way to show Chinese civilization is excellent because "we can find in the writing of modern European great thinker such viewpoint that are similar to those contained in *Zhongyong* written two thousand year ago."

This comparative strategy is so well to resist the orientalist's distorted imagination that Chinese civilization is fatuous.

Ames thought *Zhongyong* is a distinctly philosophical work. But most western philosophers have been notoriously uninterested in any claims on the part of proponents of Chinese thought that there is much of philosophical significance in the text of ancient China. When translating Confucian classics, the earlier missionaries and sinologist have put many western assumptions on these texts intentionally or unintentionally. Translators use so many terms familiar to the western philosophical community that it makes people think that Chinese classics is only the Chinese narrative of western ideology. The connotation of Chinese philosophy was discounted in the process of translation. He stated that "translators cannot realize their Gadamerian prejudice, so they can't help resorting to so-called objective lexicon. But as a matter of fact, lexicon itself contains serious cultural prejudices. This kind of translation does not betray its reader once but twice". (Roger T. Ames, 2009:6) So he tried to subvert and challenge this existent translation. In his version of *Zhongyong*, he set forth three sets of concepts like "things/processes/events", "casuality/power/creativity", and "clarity/linguistic clustering" from comparative philosophy of west and east. He expatiated the central argument of *Zhongyong*, such as Cheng, Xing, Qing, Li. By so doing, his version makes western readers learn philosophical connotation of Chinese key terms, thus makes them understand Chinese texts easily.

Hybrid Language of the Text

Translation obviously no longer means bridging a gap between two different cultures but, rather, producing meanings which are created through the encounter of cultures that are already characterized by multiculturality. Recently, most post-colonial theorists regard hybridity as an effective means to resist cultural-hegemony. As far as translation process and strategy are concerned, hybridity is a means; from the aspect of the text, hybridity is a result. Ku Hungming and Ames both use hybridity strategy and their versions both appear as a hybrid text. Ku Hungming cited quotations from western religion, literature and philosophy. What's more he directly used many quotations by great thinkers, like Emersion, Wordsworth, Arnold, to echo Chinese philosophical thoughts. The hybridity of western philosophy and Chinese Confucianism makes his version acceptable by western readers and broadens the range of Confucianism.

Example 6:

"喜怒哀乐之未发谓之中。发而皆中节谓之和。中也者，天下之大本。和也者，天下之达道。"

Ku: When the passions, such as joy, anger, grief and pleasure, have not awakened, that is our true selves（中）or moral being. When these passions awaken and each and all attain due measure and degree, that is the moral order（和）. Our true selves or moral being is the great reality（大本, lit great root）of existence, and moral order is the universal law（达道）in the world. "our true selves" — literally our central（中）inner selves, or as Mr. Matthew

Arnold calls it, "the central clue in our moral being which unite us with the universal order". Mr. Arnold also calls it our "permanent self". Hence the text above says, it is the root of our being. Mr. Arnold says, "All the forces and tendencies in us are like our proper central moral tendency, in themselves beneficent, but they require to be harmonized with this central tendency." — St. Paul and Protestantism. The translation emphasized the concept of "zhong（中）and he（和）". But Ku cited a lot of words from Emersion to echo the content of this part. The western culture was combined with Chinese culture, so the whole passage takes on hybrid features.

Example 7:

《诗》曰：" 嘉乐君子，宪宪令德，宜民宜人，受禄于天。保佑命之，自天申之。"

Ku: The book of Songs says:

"He is our good and noble King.

And oh! How charming in all his way!

> The land and people all do sing.
>
> The praise of his impartial sway.
>
> Heaven to his sires the Kingdom gave.
>
> And him with equal favour views;
>
> Heaven's strength and aid will ever save.
>
> The throne whose grant it oft renews."[①]

Besides cultural hybridity, the style of Ku's version also takes on hybrid features. In the above example, Ku employed English poetic style to translate Chinese poem. Ames's version also takes on hybrid feature. When translating Confucian key words, he often adds it with pinyin and Chinese character in the bracket.

Example 8:

率性之谓道。

Ames: Drawing out these natural tendencies is called the proper way (Dao, 道)

From example mentioned above, we come to a conclusion that Ku and Ames use hybridity in their versions. Though their aims are different, and their hybrid forms are different, they all enhance Chinese status and serve as a resistance to cultural hegemony.

Translation as a social activity always takes place in a specific historical and political context that voluntarily or involuntarily involves the asymmetrical power relations. In the long run of communication between the western and eastern cultures, especially in the history of introducing Chinese culture in the western world, the translators have always been influenced by this kind of power relationship and embodying this relationship in their practices. Thus translation is a political act in essence.

The author mainly takes a post-colonial parameter to reexamine the two English versions of *Zhongyong*. After the explanation of post-colonial translation studies, this thesis compares the two versions from post-colonial perspective. Based on the discussion and analysis in the previous chapters, we can come to conclusions as follows.

First, in the post-colonial context, translation wields enormous power in constructing representations of foreign cultures, but is simultaneously engaged in the formation of domesticated identities. As a Chinese Confucian scholar, Ku disseminated Chinese culture to

---

① HUANGXINTAO. The Discourse and Sayings of Confucius[A]. 辜鸿铭文集 . 海口：海南出版社，1996:527.

the west, dedicated himself to reform the cultural identity of China, while Ames chiefly wants to introduce Chinese philosophy into the west, and to change western philosophical ethnocentrism.

Second, domesticating and foreignizing translation cannot be defined as a tool of colonization or decolonization arbitrarily. Whether it is a tool of colonization or decolonization depends on the social background of translation and the translator's motivation. Ku mainly employed domesticating translation to translate *Zhongyong*. Many former scholars used to believe that Ku's version was a betrayal to Chinese identity, and means his subjugation to western imperial power. But after this analysis, we conclude that though he employed domesticating translation, he wanted to disseminate Chinese civilization to the west, to change their prejudices against Chinese people and China, to alter orientalists' distorted image of China. Hence, the domesticating translation he used is not to colonize China, but to resist colonial power, to reveal Chinese own voice in the world. Ames mainly used foreignizing translation to translate *Zhongyong*. Though he is a foreigner, he canonizes Chinese philosophy. He was dissatisfied with the westerner's ignorance of Chinese philosophy. He was discontent with western ethnocentrism. In his view, only through mutual learning can the western and Chinese philosophy improve themselves. So he maintains a lot of "otherness" in his version of *Zhongyong* to make the western readers know the authentic philosophical thought of China. Hence his translation strategy plays a role in resisting western ethnocentrism in modern world.

Third, from the analysis of the former chapters, we know their cultural identities and cultural position are different. As a conservative Chinese, Ku, via translation, aimed to spread Chinese Confucianism, to show Chinese moral civilization to the westerners and make the westerners change their attitudes to China. Ames, as a philosopher and sinologist, aimed to give Chinese philosophy its deserved status in the world and break up ethnocentrism of westerners. Their translation motivations are not identical, but the result they achieved is similar consciously or unconsciously. Their versions of *Zhongyong* both play a role in disseminating Chinese culture and anti-hegemony. And there are similarities and differences in their translation strategies. The sameness is they all use holistic rule, comparative rule and hybrid language. The difference is their interpretation of Chinese Confucian key terms.

This research reveals power relations behind two translators' translation activity. They can provide a proper and objective way to understand Chinese cultural classics in the world.

REFERENCES

[1]ABDUL R JANMOHAMED. Manichean Aesthetics: The Politics of Literature in Colonial Africa[M]. Amherst: University of Massachusetts Press, 1983.

[2]ALEXANDER S. Rev. A Source Book in Chinese Philosophy[J]. By WING-TSIT CHAN. Artibus Asiae 3/4(1963): 361-362.

[3]AMES,R. & HALL,D.A Translation and Philosophical Interpretation of the Zhongyong[M]. United States of America: University of Hawaii Press, 2001.

[4]ANGELA Y D. Women, Race, and Class[M]. New York: Vintage, 1983.

[5]ANNE M. Imperial Leather: Race, Gender, and Sexuality in the Colonial Context[M]. London: Routledge, 1995.

[6]ARIF D. The Postcolonial Aura: Third World Criticism in the Age of Global Capitalism. Boulder: Westview, 1997.

[7]BILL A, GARETH G, HELEN T. The Empire Whites Back: Theory and Practice in Post-Colonial Literatures[M]. London: Routledge, 1989.

[8]CHINUA A. An Image of Africa: Racism in Conrad's Heart of Darkness[J]. Massachusetts Review.1977: 782-794.

[9]EDWARD L S. Rewriting Early Chinese Texts[M]. Albany: State University of New York Press, 2006.

[10]EDWARD SAID. Orientalism[M]. New York: Vintage, 1979.

[11]EDWARD SAID. The World, the Text, and the Critic[M]. Cambridge: Harvard University Press , 1983.

[12]EDWARD SAID. Figures, Configurations, Transfigurations[J]. Race & Class 1.1990.

[13]EDWARD SAID. Culture and Imperalism[M]. New York: Knopf, 1993.

[14]ERIC R W. Europe and the People Without History[M]. Berkeley: University of California Press, 1982. GAURI V. Masks of Conquest: Literary Study and British Rule in India[M]. New York: Columbia University Press, 1989.

[15]FRANTZ F. A Dying Colonialism[M]. Trans. HAAKON C. New York: Grove, 1965.

[16]FRANTZ F. Black Skin, White Masks[M]. Trans. CHARLES L M. New York: Grove, 1967.

[17]FRANTZ F. Toward the African Revolution: Political Essays[M]. Trans. HAAKON C. New York: Grove, 1967.

[18]FRANTZ F. The Wretched of the Earth. Trans. Constance Farrington[M]. New York: Grove, 1968.

[19]FREDRIC J. Third-World Literature in the Era of Multinational Capitalism[J]. Social Text.1986: 65-88.

[20]GAYATRI C S. "Subaltern Studies: Deconstructing Historiography" in Subaltern Studies: Writings on South Asian History and Society, Vol. 4[M]. Ed. RANAJIT G. Delhi: Oxford University Press, 1985, 330-363.

[21]GAYATRI C S. "Can the Subaltern Speak?" in Marxism and the Interpretation of Culture[M]. Eds. CARY N and LAWRENCE G. Urbana: University of Illinois Press, 1988, 271-313.

[22]GAYATRI C S. In Other Worlds: Essays in Cultural Politics[M]. New York: Routledge, 1988.

[23]GAYATRI C S. The Post-Colonial Critic: Iinterviews, Strategies, Dialogues[M]. Ed. SARAH H. New York: Routledge, 1990.

[24]GAYATRI C S. The Making of Americans, the Teaching of English, and the Future of Culture Studies[J]. New Literary History .1990: 781-798.

[25]GEORGE L. The Pleasure of Exile[M]. London: Michael Joseph, 1960.

[26]HAZEL V C. Reconstruction Womanhood: The Emergence of the Afro-American Woman Novelist[M]. New York: Oxford University Press, 1987.

[27]HENRY L G JR, ed. Black Literature and Literary Theory[M]. New York: Methuen, 1984.

[28]HENRY L G JR. "Race," Writing, and Difference[M]. Chicago: University of Chicago Press, 1986.

[29]HENRY L G JR. Figures in Black: Words, Signs, and the "Racial" Self[M]. New York: Oxford University Press , 1987.

[30]HENRY L G JR. The Signifying Monkey: A Theory of African-American Literary Criticism[M]. New York: Oxford University Press , 1988.

[31]HENRY L G JR. "Authority, (White) Power, and the (Black) Critic; or, It's All Greek to Me" in The Future of Literary Theory[M]. Ed. RALPH C. New York: Routledge, 1989, 324-346.

[32]HENRY L G JR. Critical Fanonism[J]. Critical Inquiry 17.3 (1991): 457-470.

[33]HENRY L G JR. Loose Canons: Notes on the Culture Wars[M]. New York: Oxford University Press , 1992.

[34]HOMI K B, ed. Nation and Narration[M]. New York: Routledge & Kegan Paul, 1990.

[35]HOMI K B, ed. "Postcolonial Criticism" in Redrawing the Boundaries: The Transformation of English and American Literary Studies[M]. Eds. STEPHEN G, GILES G. New York: Modern Language Association, 1992, 437-465.

[36]HOMI K B, ed. The Location of Culture[M]. London: Routledge, 1994.

[37]HUAN GXINTAO. The Discourse and Sayings of Confucius[A]. 辜鸿铭文集．海口：海南出版社，1996.

[38]KU HONGMING.The Universal Order or Conduct of Life[M].Shanghai: Mereury, Ltd, 1906.

[39]IAN A, HELEN T, eds. Past the Long Post: Theorizing Post-Colonialism and Post-Modernism[M]. Hemel Hempstead: Harvester Wheatsheaf, 1991.

[40]JOSEPH T, TILLY W, eds. Understanding Others[M]. Urbana: National Council of Teachers of English, 1992.

[41]KWAME A A. In My Father's House: Africa in the Philosophy of Culture[M]. New York: Oxford University Press, 1992.

[42]LINDA H. "Introduction: Complexities Abounding" in Colonialism and the Postcolonial Condition[J]. Special issue of PMLA 110.1 (1995): 7-16.

[43]MALCOLM E. Signifying Nothing: Truth's True Contents in Shakespeare's Text[M]. Athens: University of Georgia Press, 1986.

[44]MARIO V L. The Storyteller[M]. Trans. HELEN L. New York: Penguin, 1989.

[45]MAY S. Remastering Morals with Aristotle and Confucius[M]. Cambridge: Cambridge University Press, 2007.

[46]NEIL L. Resistance in Postcolonial African Fiction[M]. New Haven: Yale University Press, 1990.

[47]NGUGI W T. Decolonising the Mind: The Politics of Language in African Literature[M]. London: James Currey, 1986.

[48]ONWUCHEKWA J C, IHECHUKWU M. Toward the Decolonization of African Literature. Vol. 1, African Fiction and Poetry and Their Critics[M]. Washington: Howard University Press, 1983.

[49]OYEKAN O, ed. A History of Twentieth-Century African Literatures[M]. Lincoln: University of Nebraska Press, 1993.

[50]PATRICK B. History and Empire[J]. Journal of Victorian Literature and Culture, 1992 (19): 317-327.

[51]PARTHA C. "More on Modes of Power and the Peasantry" in Selected Subaltern Studies[M]. Eds. Ranajit Guha and Gayatri Chakravorty Spivak. New York: Oxford University Press, 1988, 351-390.

[52]RANAJIT G, GAYATRI C S, eds. Selected Subaltern Studies[M]. New York: Oxford University Press, 1988.

[53]RAYMOND W. Keywords: A Vocabulary of Culture and Society[M]. Oxford: Oxford University Press 1983.

[54]RENATE Z. Frantz Fanon: Colonialism and Alienation[M]. New York: Monthly Review,1974.

[55]RICHARD C. Imagining India[M]. London: Macmillan, 1990.

[56]ROBERT W S. Methodologies of Comparative Philosophy: The Pragmatist and Process Traditions[M].

Albany: State University of New York Press, 2009.

[57]SALMAN R. Imaginary Homelands: Essays and Criticism, 1981-91[M]. London: Penguin, 1991.

[58]SARAH S. The Rhetoric of English India[M]. Chicago: University of Chicago Press, 1992.

[59]ROBERT W S. Woman Skin Deep: Feminism and the Postcolonial Condition[J]. Critical Inquiry 18.4 (Summer 1992).

[60]SIMA QIAN. Selections from Records of the Historia[M]. Beijing: Foreign Languages Press, 2008.

[61]SIMON D. Postmodernism or Post-Colonialism Today[J]. Textual Practice 1.1 (1987): 32-47.

[62]STEINER G. After Babel: Aspects of Language and Translation[M]. Shanghai: Shanghai Foreign Language Education Press, 2001.

[63]SUSSAN B, PETER B, eds. The Translator as Writer[M]. London: Continuum, 2006.

[64]TEJASWINE N. Sitting Translation: History, Post-Structuralism, and the Colonial Context[M]. Berkeley: University of California Press, 1990.

[65]THOMAS R. The Imperial Archive: Knowledge and the Fantasy of Empire[M]. London: Verso, 1993.

[66]WALTER B. The Origin of German Tragic Drama[M]. Trans. JOHN O. London: New Left Books, 1997.

[67]WALTER R. How Europe Underdeveloped Africa[M]. Dar es Salaam: Tanzania Publishing House, 1972.

[68]W J T MITCHELL. Postcolonial Culture, Postimperial Criticism[J]. Transition 56 (1992): 11-19.